BLUE PERIOD

TSUBASA YAMAGUCHI

2

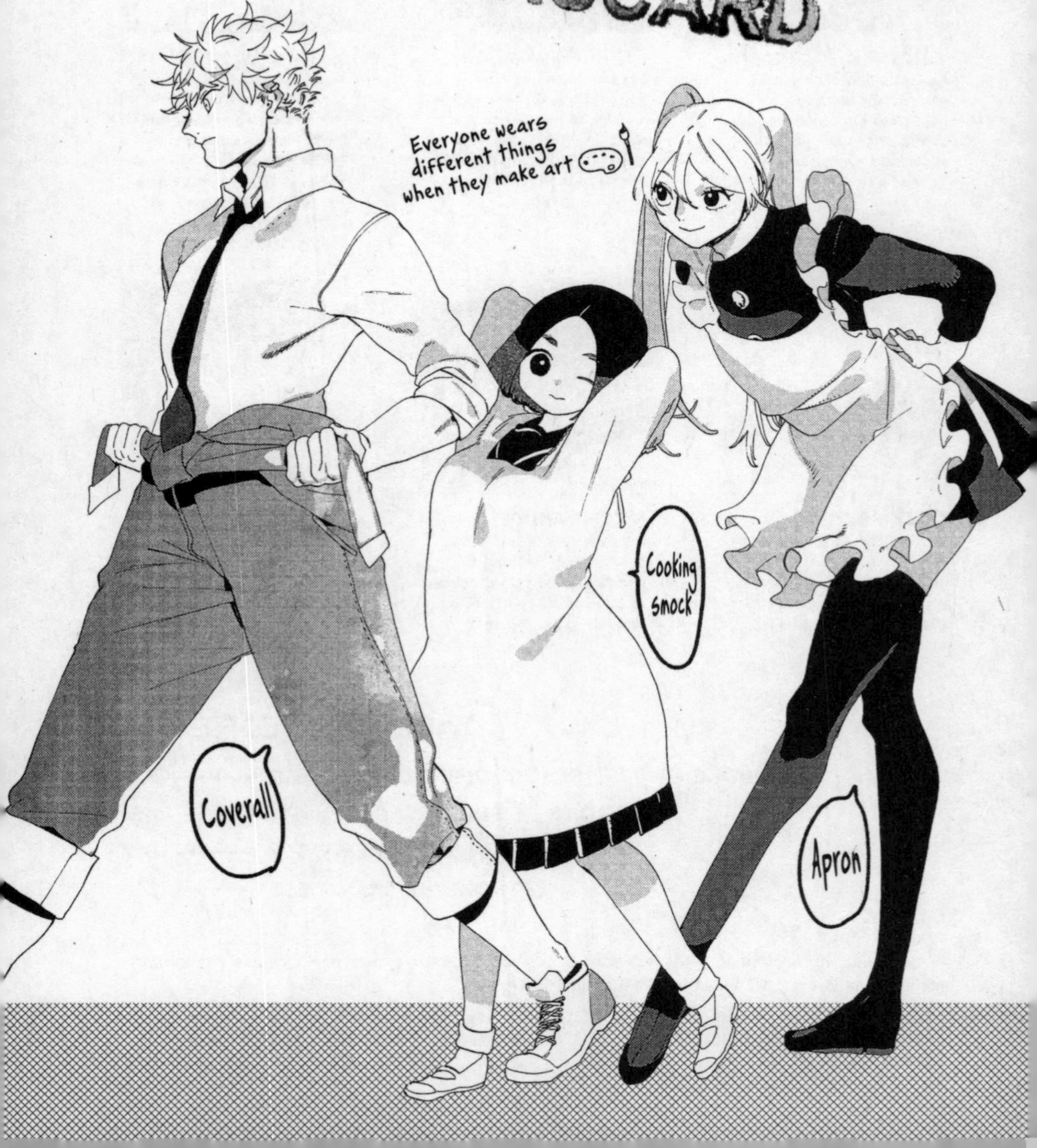
Everyone wears different things when they make art
Cooking smock
Coverall
Apron

CHARACTERS

Yotasuke Takahashi
A second-year high school student who attends the same prep school as Yatora. His talent, skill, and unsociable character inspire Yatora to be a better artist.

Ryuji Ayukawa
Goes by the name Yuka. A boy who dresses in women's clothing. A member of the Art Club who's in the same class as Yatora. Yuka invited Yatora to the Art Club.

Yatora Yaguchi
A second year in high school. After seeing Mori-senpai's painting, he discovered the joy of making art and was hooked. He sets his sights on Tokyo University of the Arts, the most competitive of all Japanese art colleges.

Saeki-sensei
The advisor for the Art Club. She uses her skills, insight, and resourcefulness to give solid guidance to motivated students. She also lets less motivated students enjoy themselves in their own way.

Mori-senpai
A third-year student in the Art Club. Her painting of angels opened Yatora's eyes to art. She will be attending Musashino Art University.

Haruka Hashida
A student who's in the same year and school as Yotasuke. He attends the same prep school as Yatora.

TABLE OF CONTENTS

WARNING: This volume contains mentions of suicide. If you are experiencing suicidal thoughts or feelings, you are not alone, and there is free, 24/7 help.

National Suicide Prevention Lifeline offers specific resources for kids, LGBTQ+ people, survivors, and more. You can call 1-800-273-TALK (8255) or go to SuicidePreventionLifeline.org

The Trevor Project offers call, text, and online chat for LGBTQ+ youth. You can call 1-866-488-7386, or go to TheTrevorProject.org

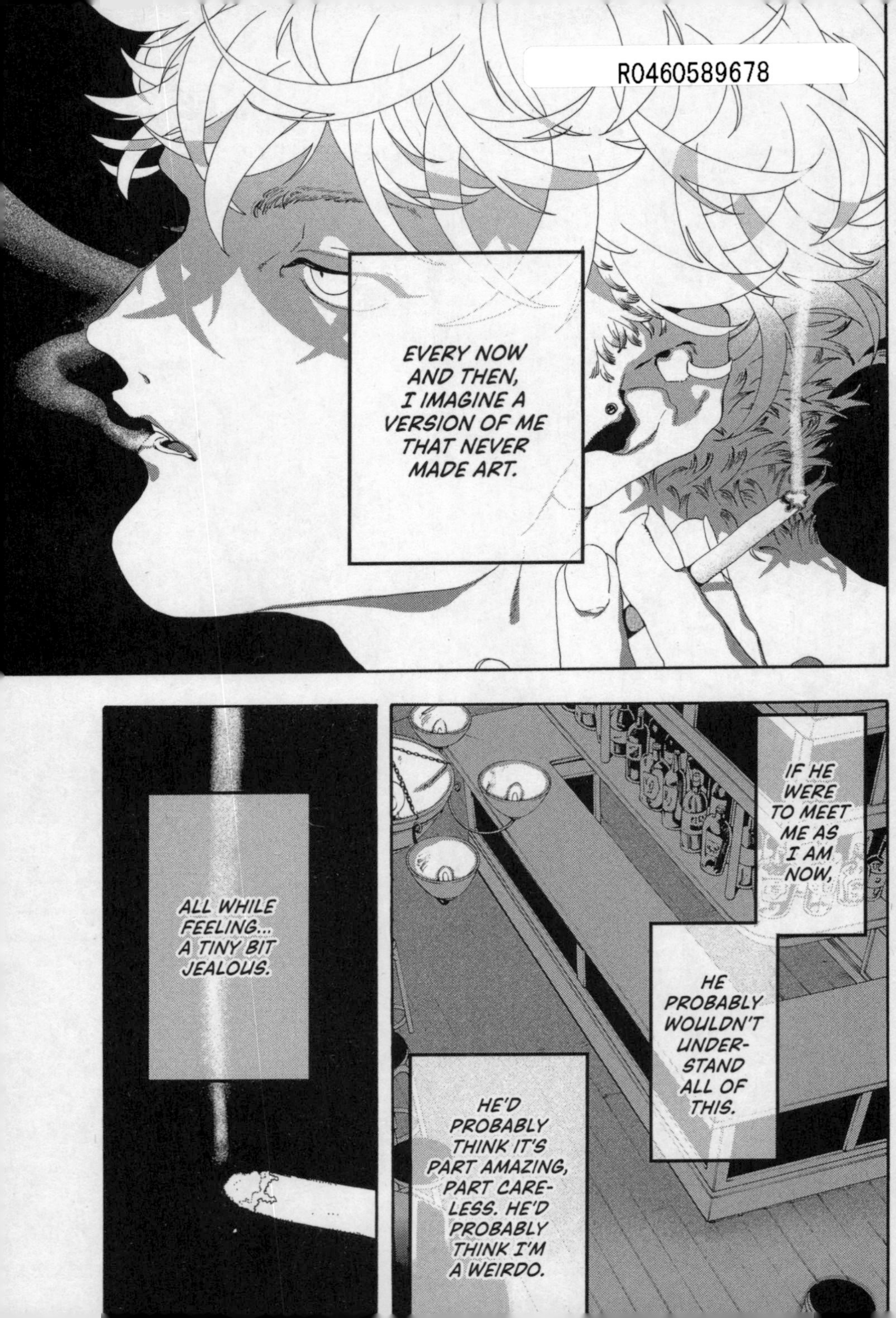
EVERY NOW AND THEN, I IMAGINE A VERSION OF ME THAT NEVER MADE ART.
IF HE WERE TO MEET ME AS I AM NOW,
HE PROBABLY WOULDN'T UNDER-STAND ALL OF THIS.
HE'D PROBABLY THINK IT'S PART AMAZING, PART CARE-LESS. HE'D PROBABLY THINK I'M A WEIRDO.
ALL WHILE FEELING... A TINY BIT JEALOUS.

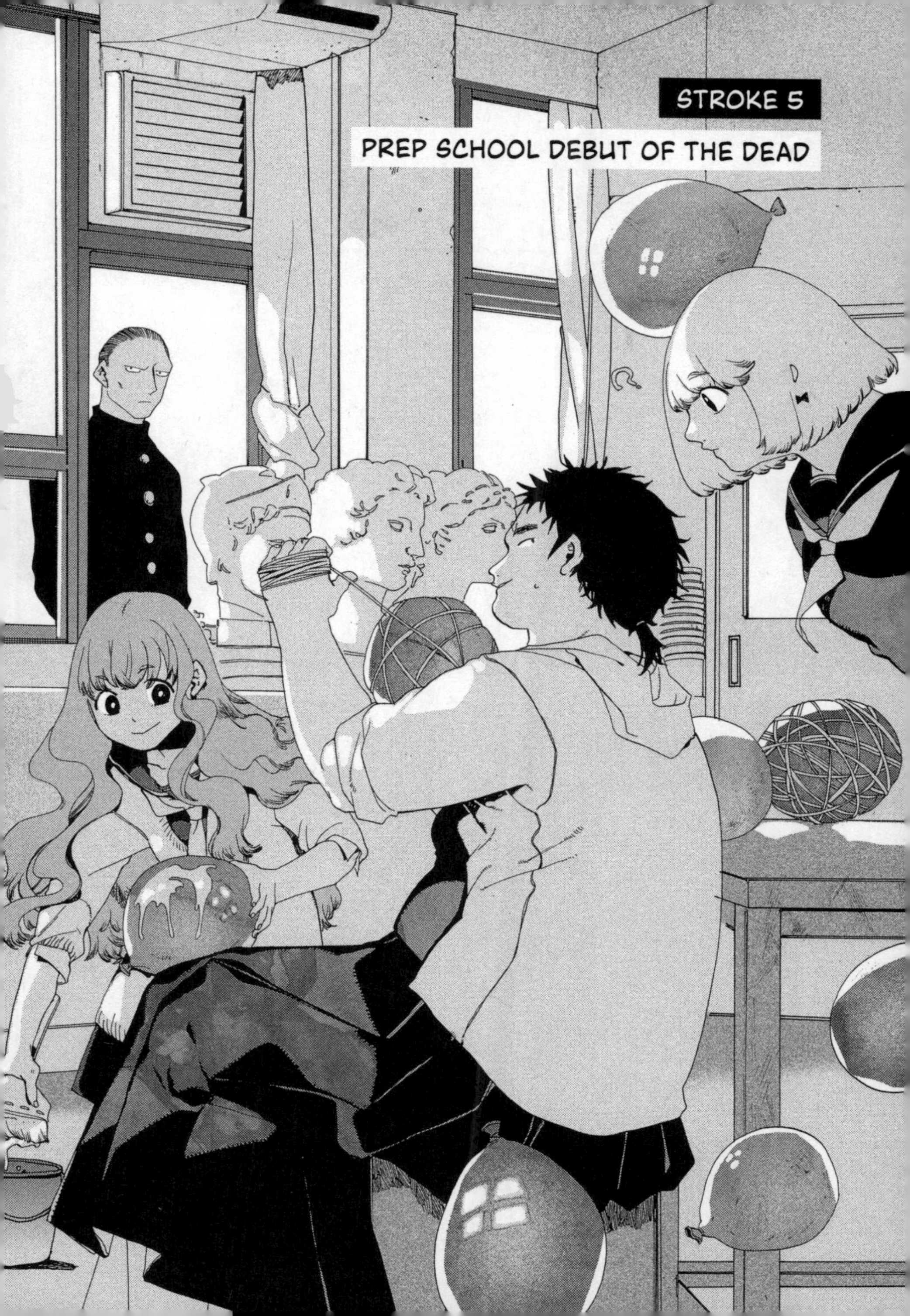
STROKE 5
PREP SCHOOL DEBUT OF THE DEAD

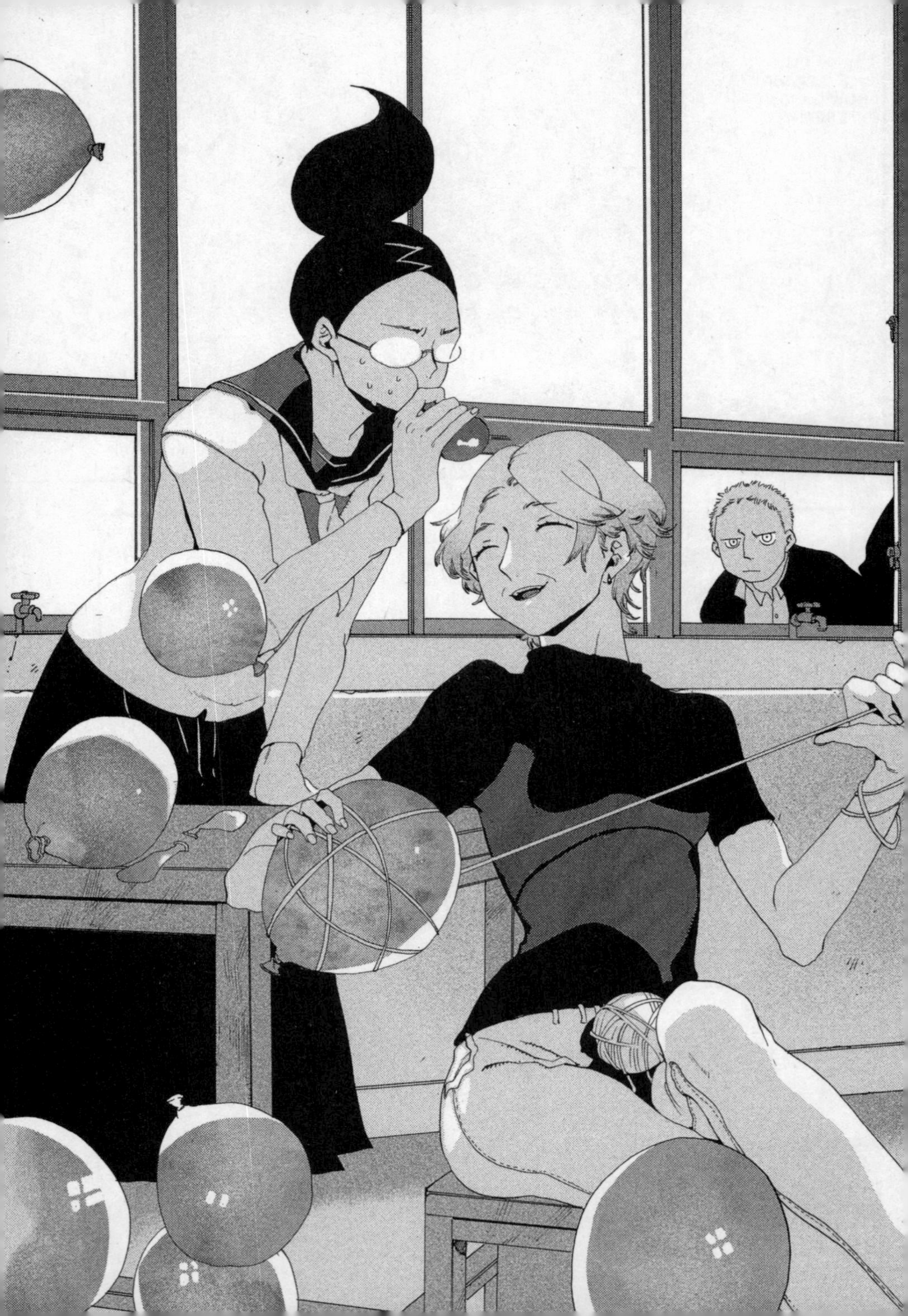

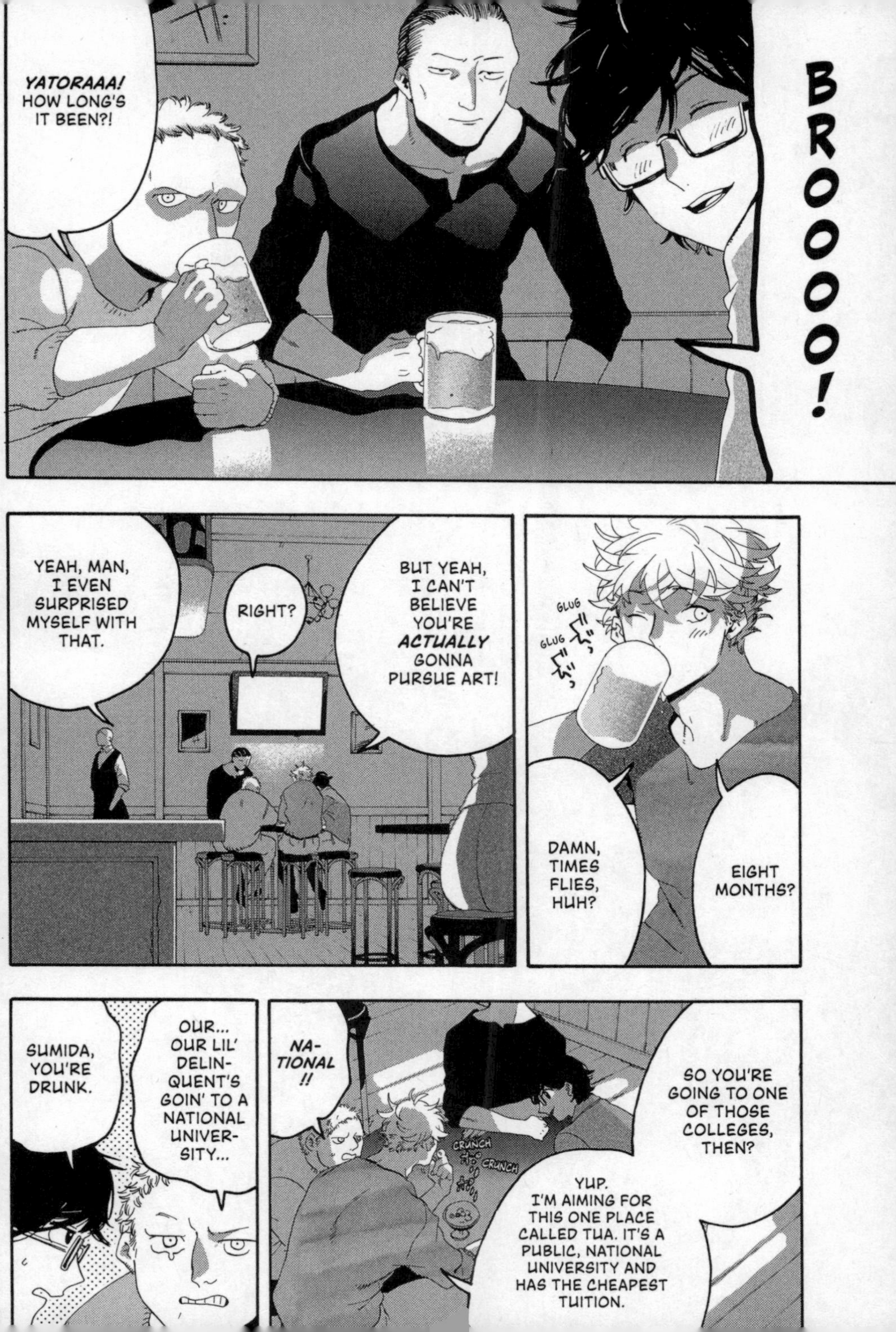
BROOOOO!
YATORAAA! HOW LONG'S IT BEEN?!
GLUG GLUG
EIGHT MONTHS?
DAMN, TIMES FLIES, HUH?
BUT YEAH, I CAN'T BELIEVE YOU'RE ACTUALLY GONNA PURSUE ART!
RIGHT?
YEAH, MAN, I EVEN SURPRISED MYSELF WITH THAT.
SO YOU'RE GOING TO ONE OF THOSE COLLEGES, THEN?
YUP. I'M AIMING FOR THIS ONE PLACE CALLED TUA. IT'S A PUBLIC, NATIONAL UNIVERSITY AND HAS THE CHEAPEST TUITION.
NA-TIONAL!!
CRUNCH CRUNCH
OUR... OUR LIL' DELIN-QUENT'S GOIN' TO A NATIONAL UNIVER-SITY...
SUMIDA, YOU'RE DRUNK.

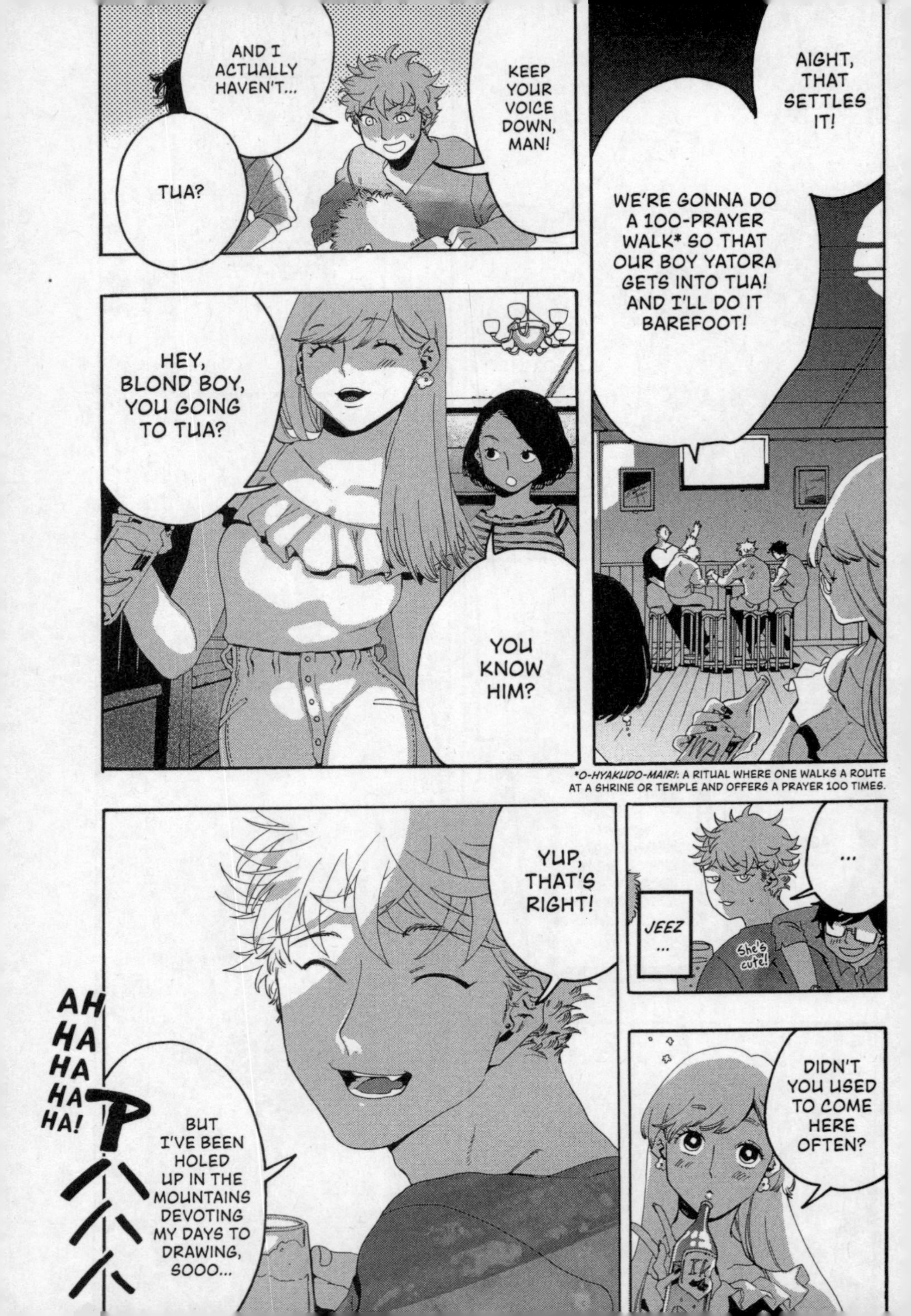
AIGHT, THAT SETTLES IT!
WE'RE GONNA DO A 100-PRAYER WALK* SO THAT OUR BOY YATORA GETS INTO TUA! AND I'LL DO IT BAREFOOT!
KEEP YOUR VOICE DOWN, MAN!
AND I ACTUALLY HAVEN'T...
TUA?
HEY, BLOND BOY, YOU GOING TO TUA?
YOU KNOW HIM?
...
JEEZ...
She's cute!
DIDN'T YOU USED TO COME HERE OFTEN?
YUP, THAT'S RIGHT!
BUT I'VE BEEN HOLED UP IN THE MOUNTAINS DEVOTING MY DAYS TO DRAWING, SOOO...
AH HA HA HA HA!
アハハハ

*O-HYAKUDO-MAIRI: A RITUAL WHERE ONE WALKS A ROUTE AT A SHRINE OR TEMPLE AND OFFERS A PRAYER 100 TIMES.

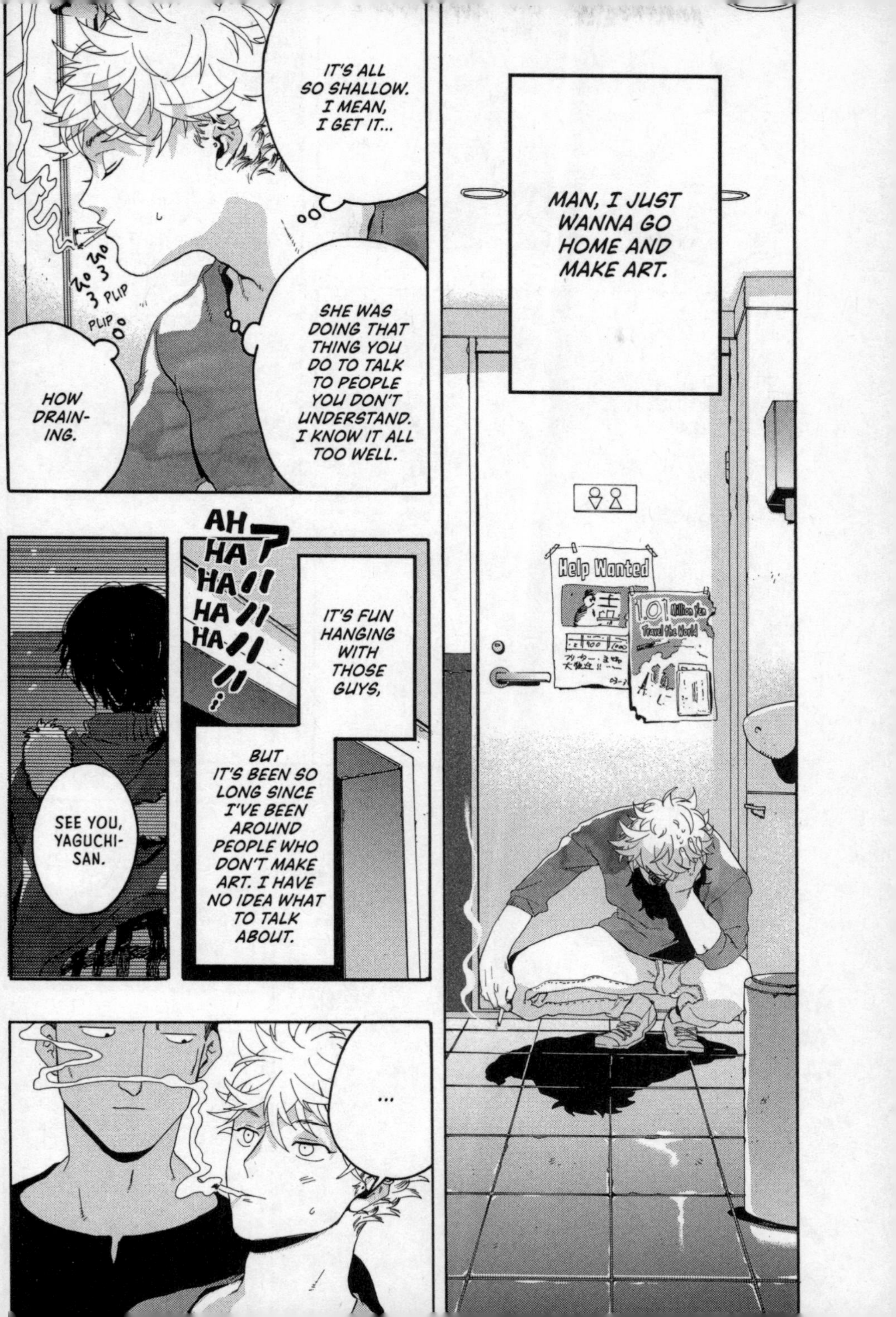
MAN, I JUST WANNA GO HOME AND MAKE ART.
Help Wanted
1.01 Million Yen
Travel the World
IT'S ALL SO SHALLOW. I MEAN, I GET IT...
SHE WAS DOING THAT THING YOU DO TO TALK TO PEOPLE YOU DON'T UNDERSTAND. I KNOW IT ALL TOO WELL.
PLIP
PLIP
HOW DRAINING.
AH HA HA HA HA
IT'S FUN HANGING WITH THOSE GUYS,
BUT IT'S BEEN SO LONG SINCE I'VE BEEN AROUND PEOPLE WHO DON'T MAKE ART. I HAVE NO IDEA WHAT TO TALK ABOUT.
SEE YOU, YAGUCHI-SAN.
...

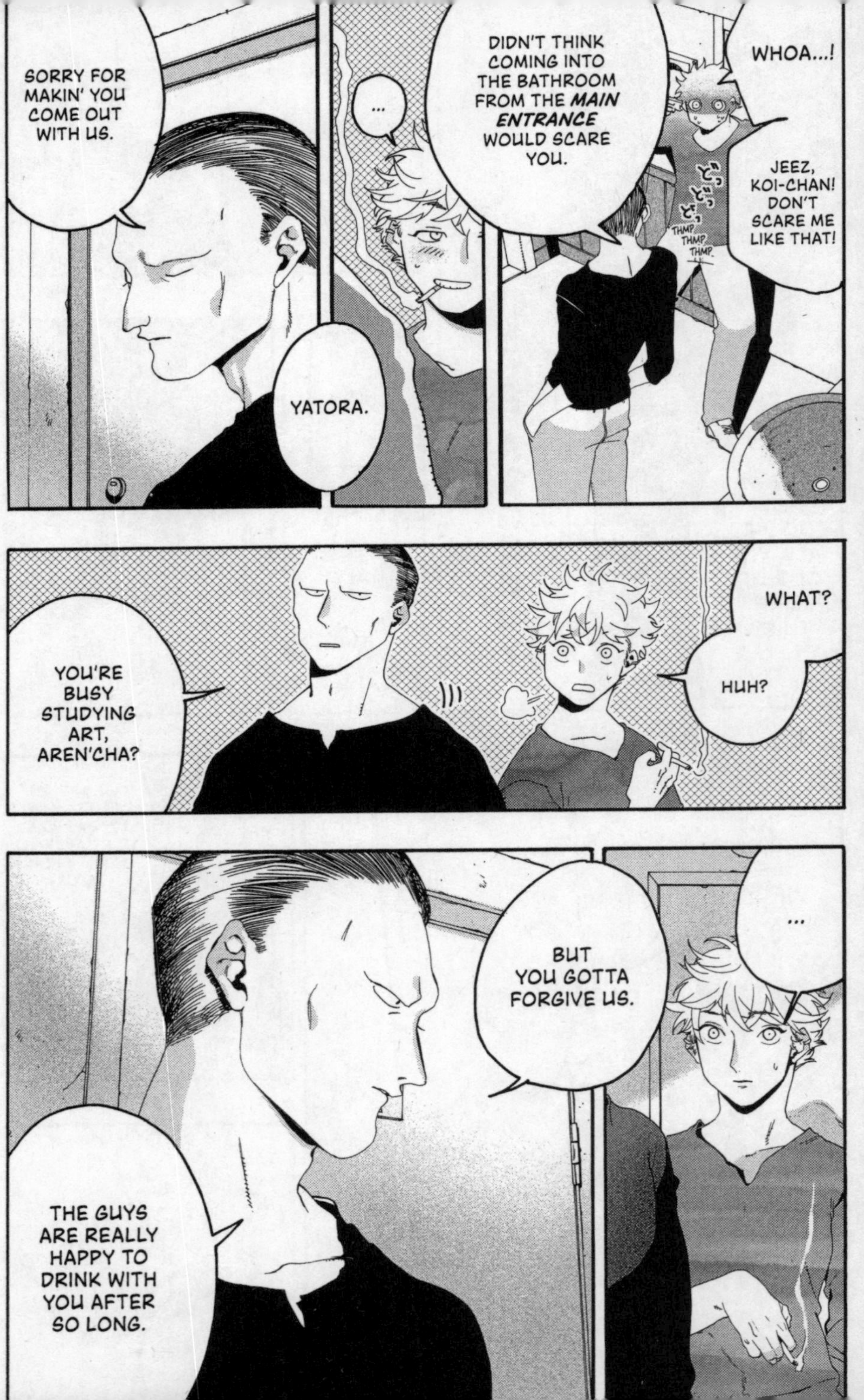
WHOA...!
JEEZ, KOI-CHAN! DON'T SCARE ME LIKE THAT!
どっどっどっ
THMP THMP THMP
DIDN'T THINK COMING INTO THE BATHROOM FROM THE ***MAIN ENTRANCE*** WOULD SCARE YOU.
...
SORRY FOR MAKIN' YOU COME OUT WITH US.
YATORA.
WHAT?
HUH?
YOU'RE BUSY STUDYING ART, AREN'CHA?
...
BUT YOU GOTTA FORGIVE US.
THE GUYS ARE REALLY HAPPY TO DRINK WITH YOU AFTER SO LONG.

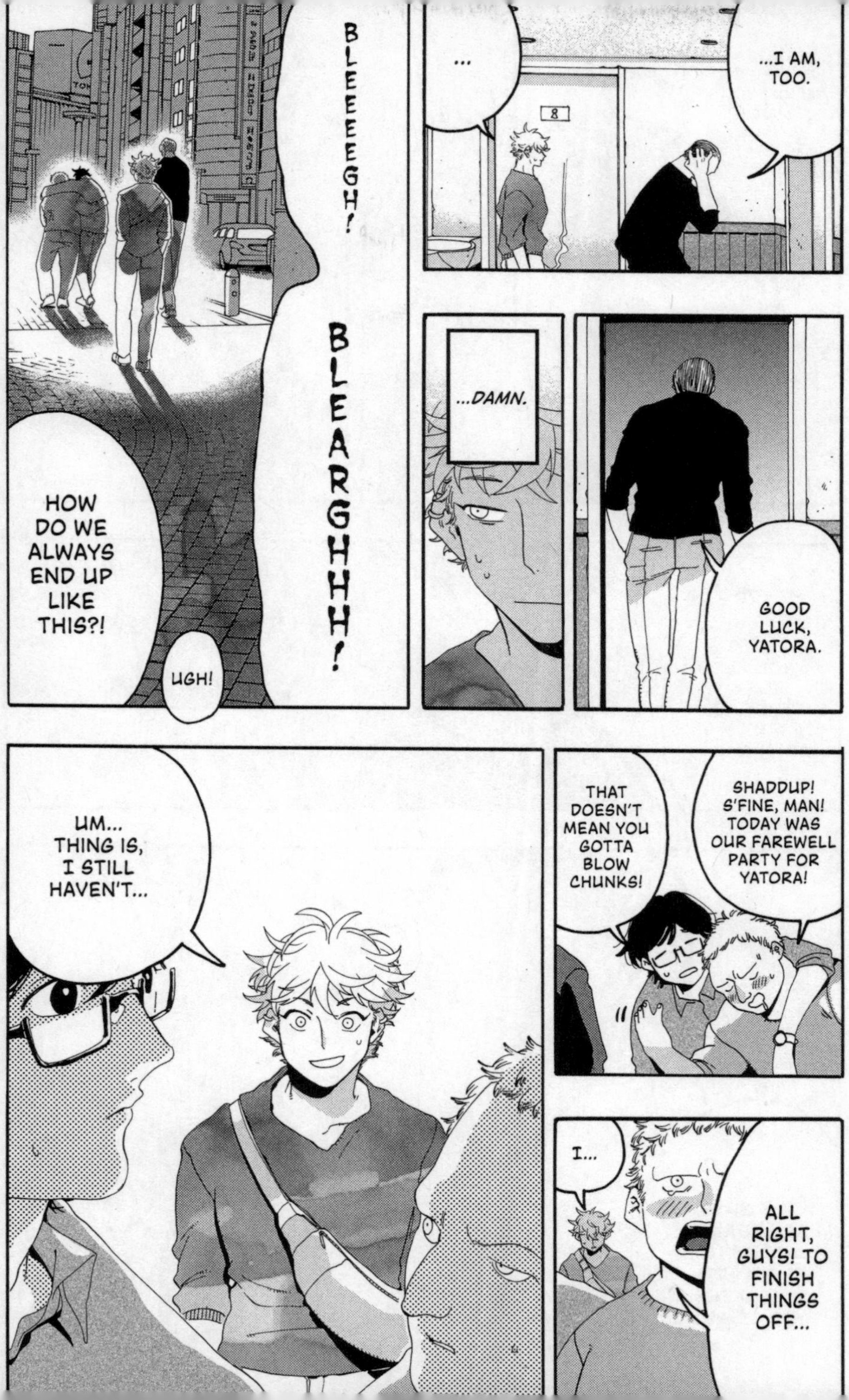
...I AM, TOO.
...
GOOD LUCK, YATORA.
...DAMN.
BLEEEEEGH!
BLEARGHHH!
HOW DO WE ALWAYS END UP LIKE THIS?!
UGH!
SHADDUP! S'FINE, MAN! TODAY WAS OUR FAREWELL PARTY FOR YATORA!
THAT DOESN'T MEAN YOU GOTTA BLOW CHUNKS!
ALL RIGHT, GUYS! TO FINISH THINGS OFF...
I...
UM... THING IS, I STILL HAVEN'T...

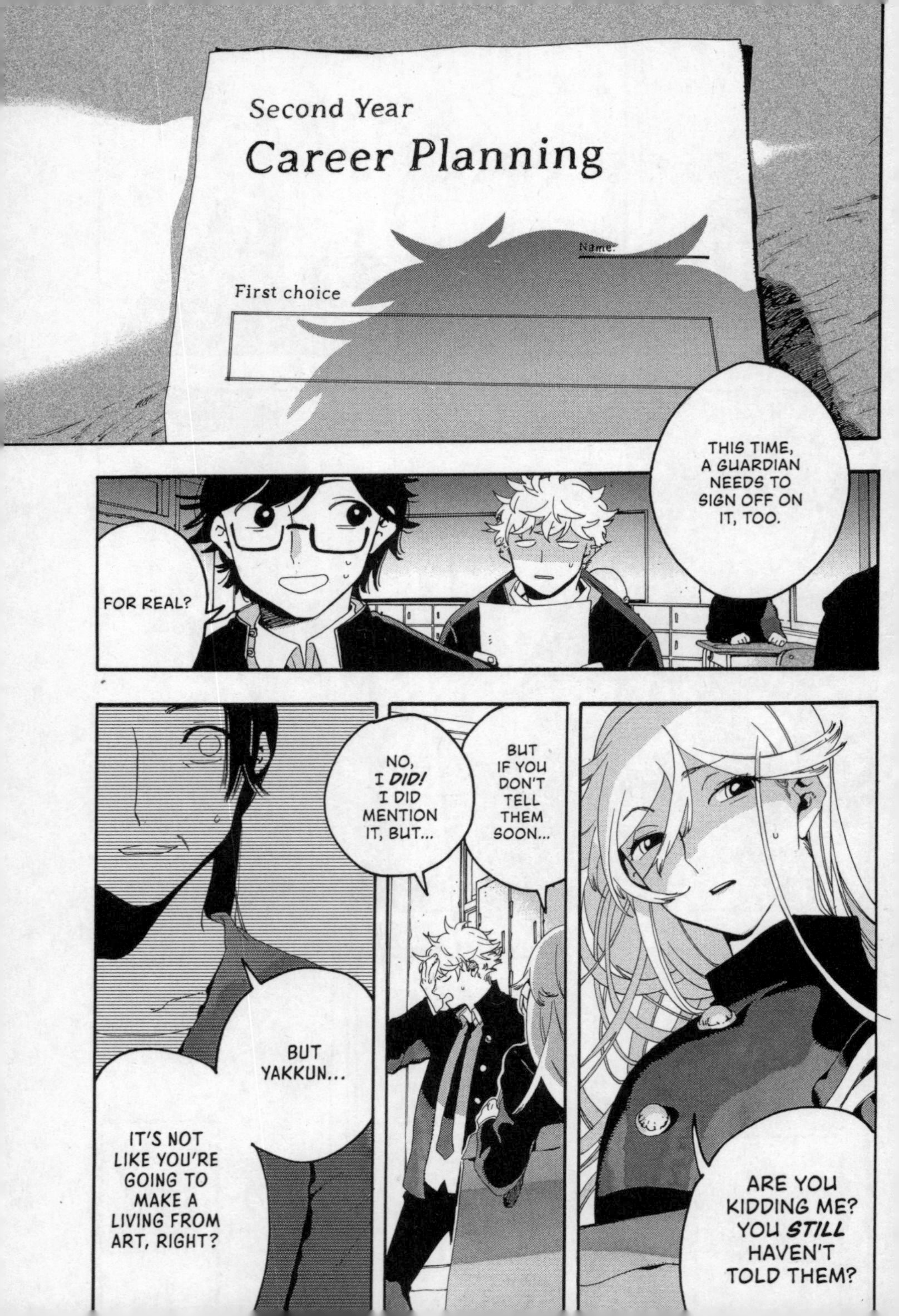
Second Year
Career Planning
Name:
First choice
THIS TIME, A GUARDIAN NEEDS TO SIGN OFF ON IT, TOO.
FOR REAL?
ARE YOU KIDDING ME? YOU *STILL* HAVEN'T TOLD THEM?
BUT IF YOU DON'T TELL THEM SOON...
NO, I *DID!* I DID MENTION IT, BUT...
BUT YAKKUN...
IT'S NOT LIKE YOU'RE GOING TO MAKE A LIVING FROM ART, RIGHT?

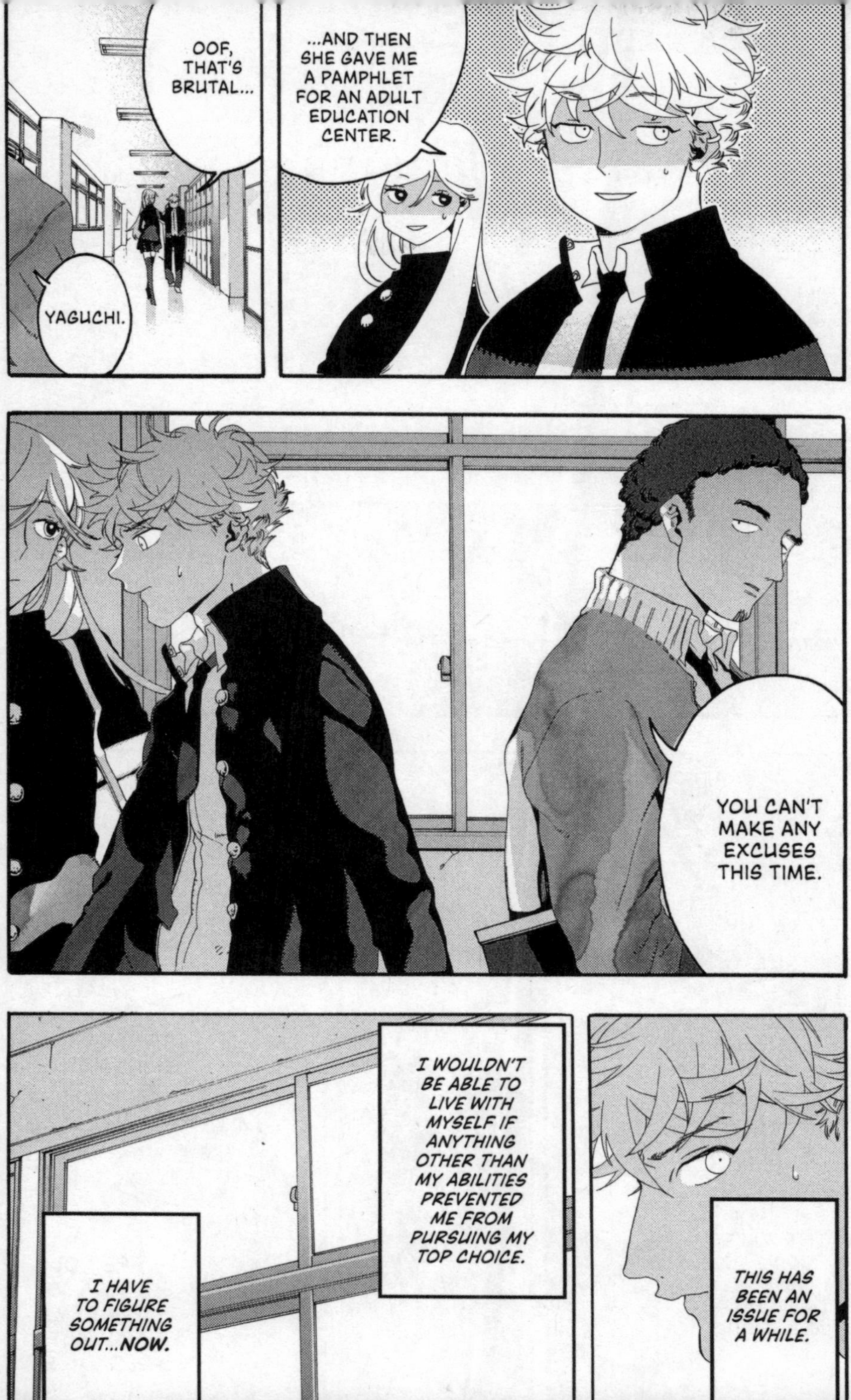
...AND THEN SHE GAVE ME A PAMPHLET FOR AN ADULT EDUCATION CENTER.
OOF, THAT'S BRUTAL...
YAGUCHI.
YOU CAN'T MAKE ANY EXCUSES THIS TIME.
THIS HAS BEEN AN ISSUE FOR A WHILE.
I WOULDN'T BE ABLE TO LIVE WITH MYSELF IF ANYTHING OTHER THAN MY ABILITIES PREVENTED ME FROM PURSUING MY TOP CHOICE.
I HAVE TO FIGURE SOMETHING OUT...NOW.

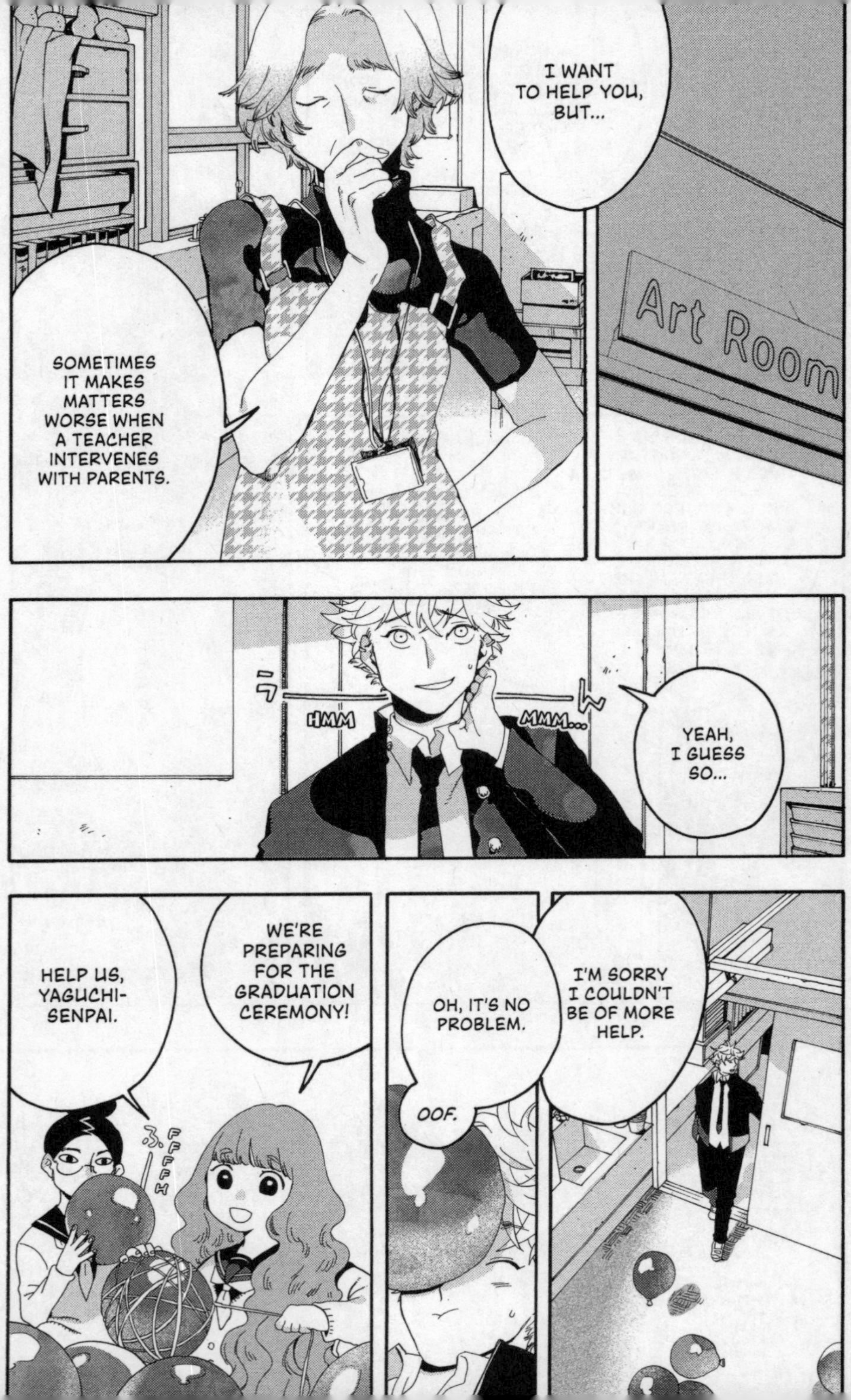
Art Room
I WANT TO HELP YOU, BUT...
SOMETIMES IT MAKES MATTERS WORSE WHEN A TEACHER INTERVENES WITH PARENTS.
YEAH, I GUESS SO...
ん MMM...
ラ HMM
I'M SORRY I COULDN'T BE OF MORE HELP.
OH, IT'S NO PROBLEM.
OOF.
WE'RE PREPARING FOR THE GRADUATION CEREMONY!
HELP US, YAGUCHI-SENPAI.
ふ FFFFH

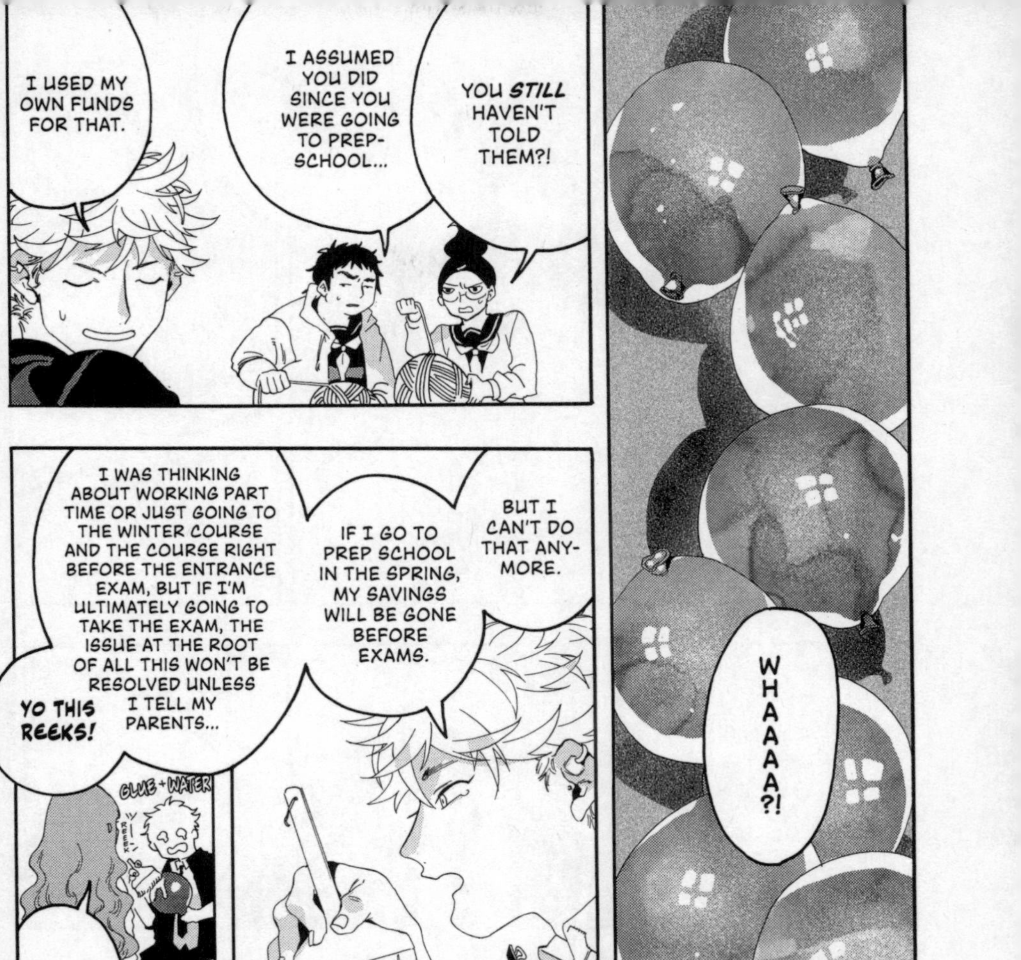
WHAAAAA?!
YOU STILL HAVEN'T TOLD THEM?!
I ASSUMED YOU DID SINCE YOU WERE GOING TO PREP-SCHOOL...
I USED MY OWN FUNDS FOR THAT.
I WAS THINKING ABOUT WORKING PART TIME OR JUST GOING TO THE WINTER COURSE AND THE COURSE RIGHT BEFORE THE ENTRANCE EXAM, BUT IF I'M ULTIMATELY GOING TO TAKE THE EXAM, THE ISSUE AT THE ROOT OF ALL THIS WON'T BE RESOLVED UNLESS I TELL MY PARENTS...
IF I GO TO PREP SCHOOL IN THE SPRING, MY SAVINGS WILL BE GONE BEFORE EXAMS.
BUT I CAN'T DO THAT ANYMORE.
YO THIS REEKS!
GLUE + WATER
REEK
20 MORE TO GO.

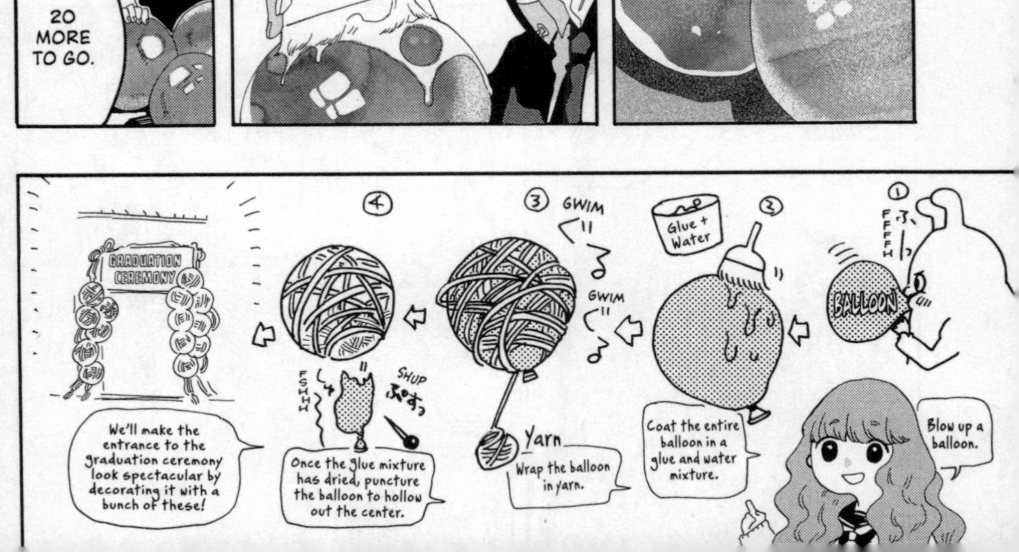
①
FFFFH
BALLOON
Blow up a balloon.
②
Glue + Water
Coat the entire balloon in a glue and water mixture.
③
GWIM
GWIM
Yarn
Wrap the balloon in yarn.
④
FSHHH
SHUP
Once the glue mixture has dried, puncture the balloon to hollow out the center.
GRADUATION CEREMONY
We'll make the entrance to the graduation ceremony look spectacular by decorating it with a bunch of these!

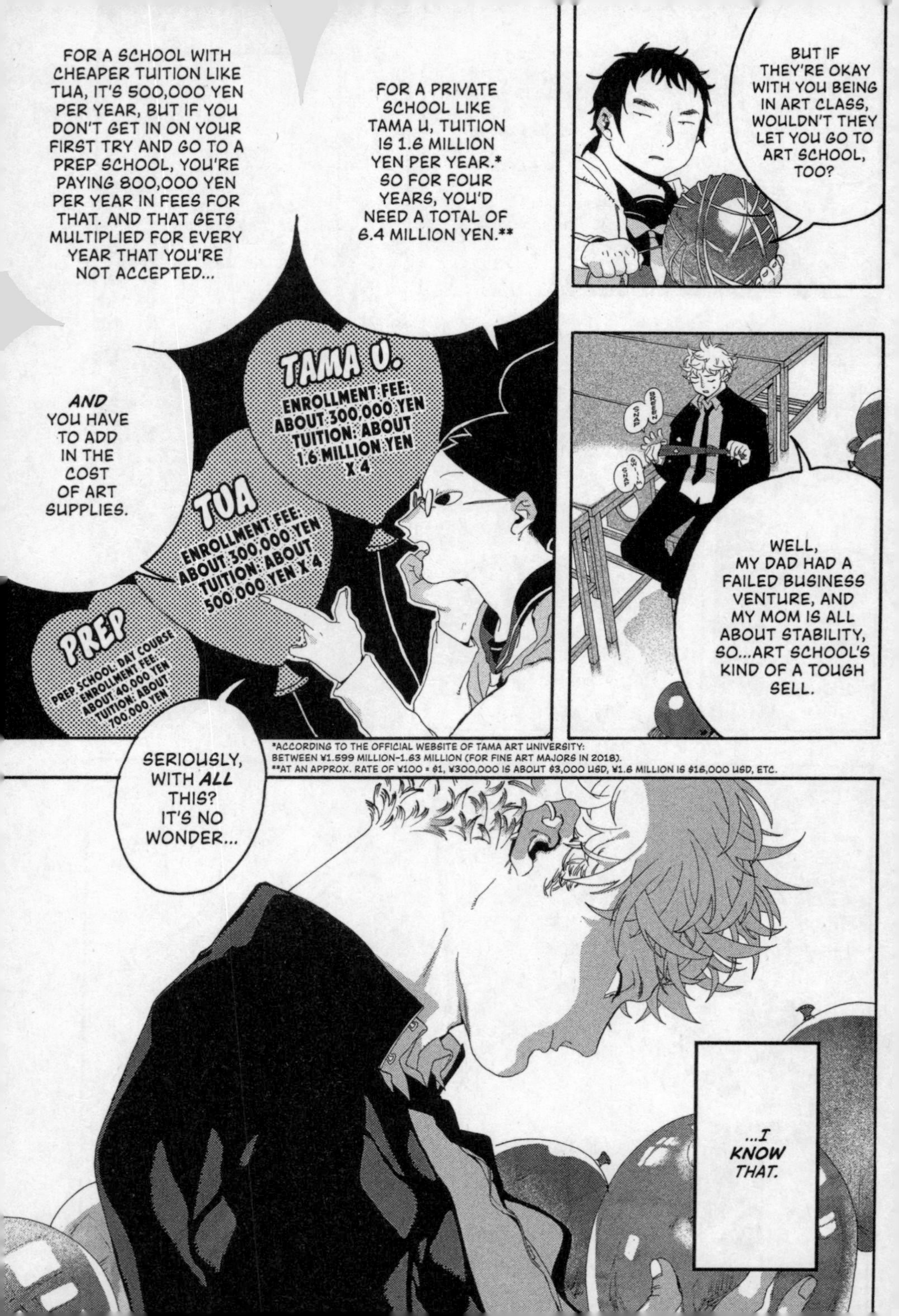
BUT IF THEY'RE OKAY WITH YOU BEING IN ART CLASS, WOULDN'T THEY LET YOU GO TO ART SCHOOL, TOO?
BREEEN
SNAP
SW---M
SNAP
WELL, MY DAD HAD A FAILED BUSINESS VENTURE, AND MY MOM IS ALL ABOUT STABILITY, SO...ART SCHOOL'S KIND OF A TOUGH SELL.
FOR A PRIVATE SCHOOL LIKE TAMA U, TUITION IS 1.6 MILLION YEN PER YEAR.* SO FOR FOUR YEARS, YOU'D NEED A TOTAL OF 6.4 MILLION YEN.**
FOR A SCHOOL WITH CHEAPER TUITION LIKE TUA, IT'S 500,000 YEN PER YEAR, BUT IF YOU DON'T GET IN ON YOUR FIRST TRY AND GO TO A PREP SCHOOL, YOU'RE PAYING 800,000 YEN PER YEAR IN FEES FOR THAT. AND THAT GETS MULTIPLIED FOR EVERY YEAR THAT YOU'RE NOT ACCEPTED...
TAMA U.
ENROLLMENT FEE: ABOUT 300,000 YEN TUITION: ABOUT 1.6 MILLION YEN X 4
TUA
ENROLLMENT FEE: ABOUT 300,000 YEN TUITION: ABOUT 500,000 YEN X 4
PREP
PREP SCHOOL: DAY COURSE ENROLLMENT FEE: ABOUT 40,000 YEN TUITION: ABOUT 700,000 YEN
AND YOU HAVE TO ADD IN THE COST OF ART SUPPLIES.
SERIOUSLY, WITH *ALL* THIS? IT'S NO WONDER...
...I *KNOW* THAT.

*ACCORDING TO THE OFFICIAL WEBSITE OF TAMA ART UNIVERSITY: BETWEEN ¥1.599 MILLION–1.63 MILLION (FOR FINE ART MAJORS IN 2018).
**AT AN APPROX. RATE OF ¥100 = $1, ¥300,000 IS ABOUT $3,000 USD, ¥1.6 MILLION IS $16,000 USD, ETC.

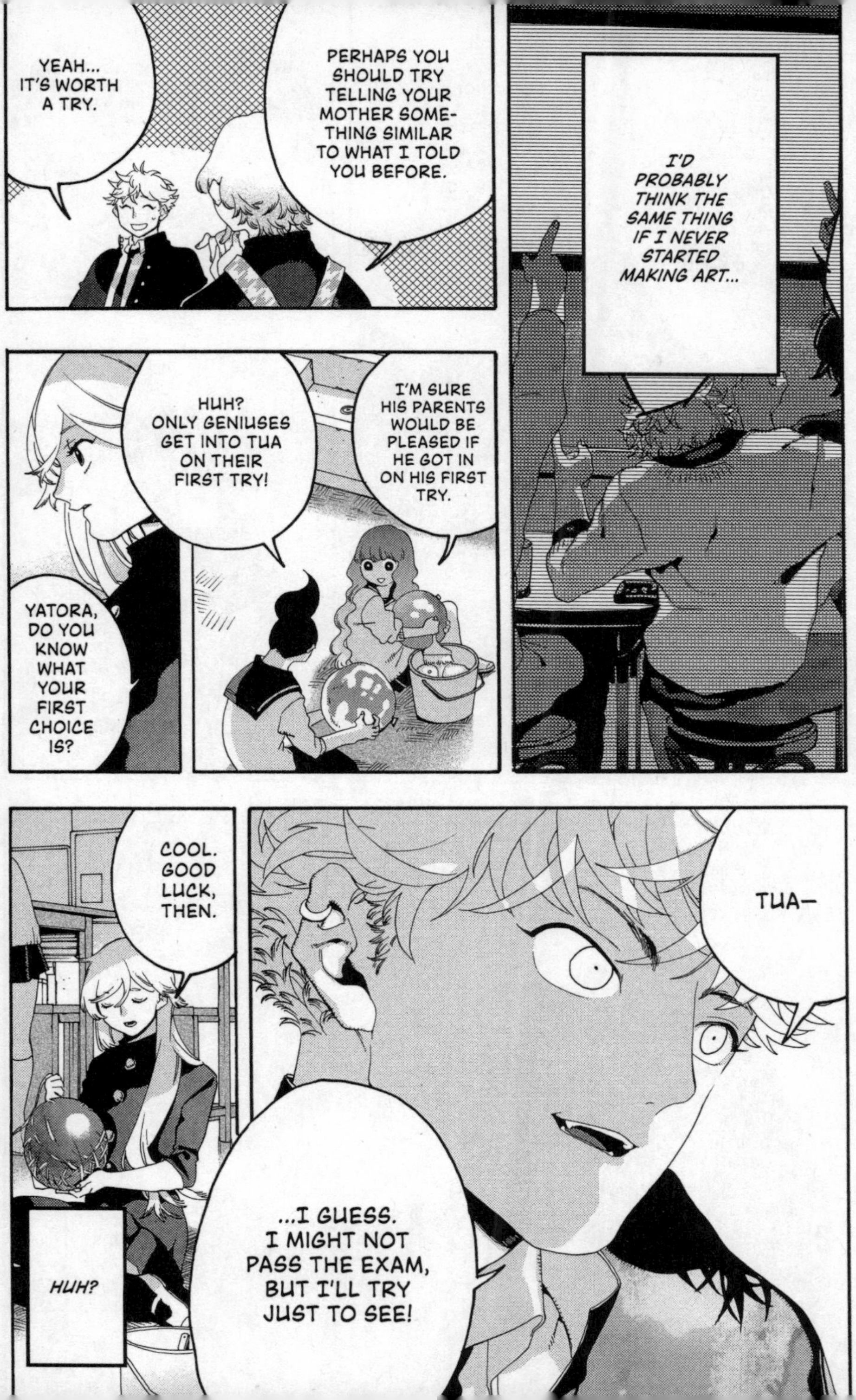
I'D PROBABLY THINK THE SAME THING IF I NEVER STARTED MAKING ART...
PERHAPS YOU SHOULD TRY TELLING YOUR MOTHER SOME-THING SIMILAR TO WHAT I TOLD YOU BEFORE.
YEAH... IT'S WORTH A TRY.
I'M SURE HIS PARENTS WOULD BE PLEASED IF HE GOT IN ON HIS FIRST TRY.
HUH? ONLY GENIUSES GET INTO TUA ON THEIR FIRST TRY!
YATORA, DO YOU KNOW WHAT YOUR FIRST CHOICE IS?
TUA—
...I GUESS. I MIGHT NOT PASS THE EXAM, BUT I'LL TRY JUST TO SEE!
COOL. GOOD LUCK, THEN.
HUH?

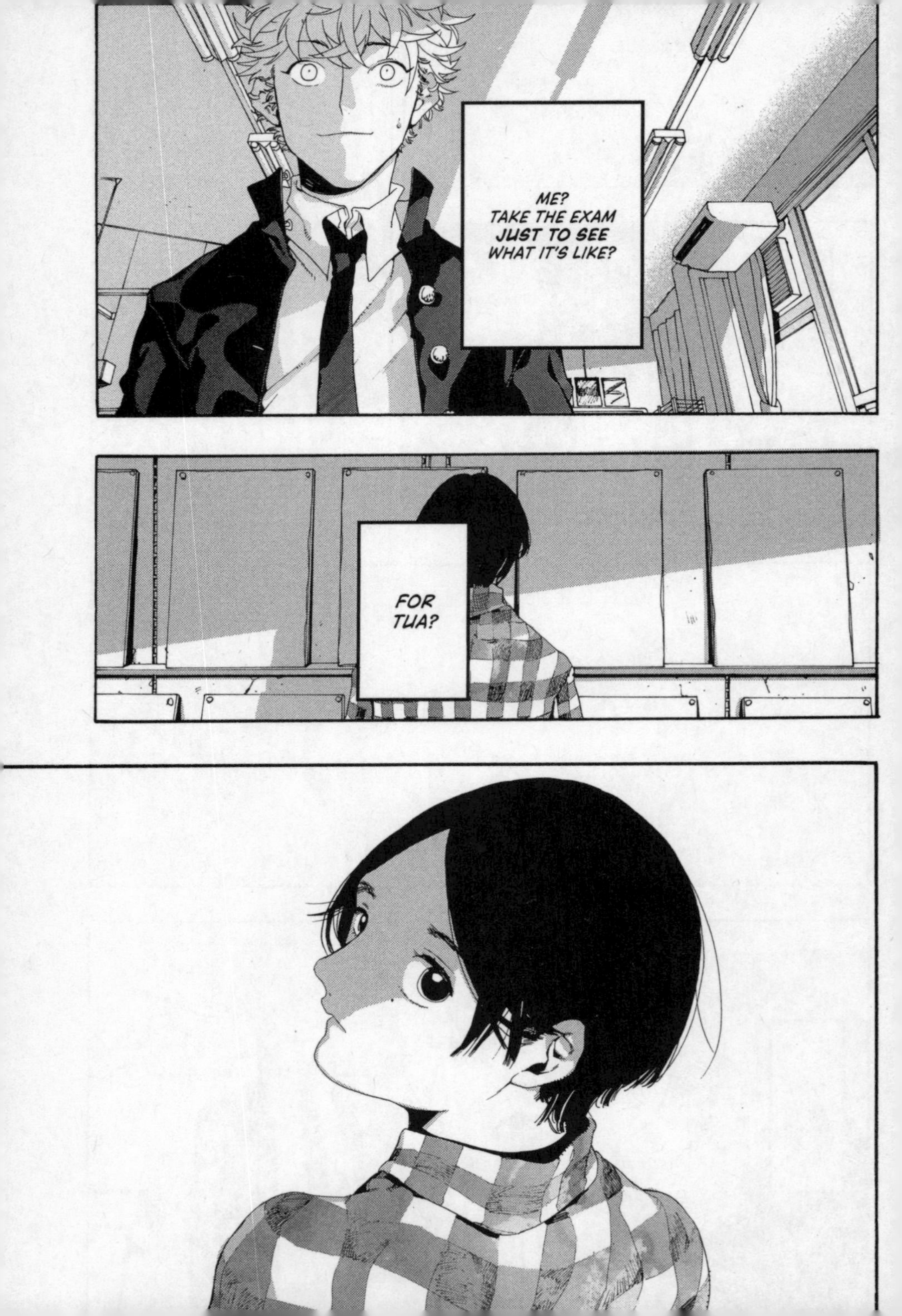
ME?
TAKE THE EXAM
JUST TO SEE
WHAT IT'S LIKE?
FOR
TUA?

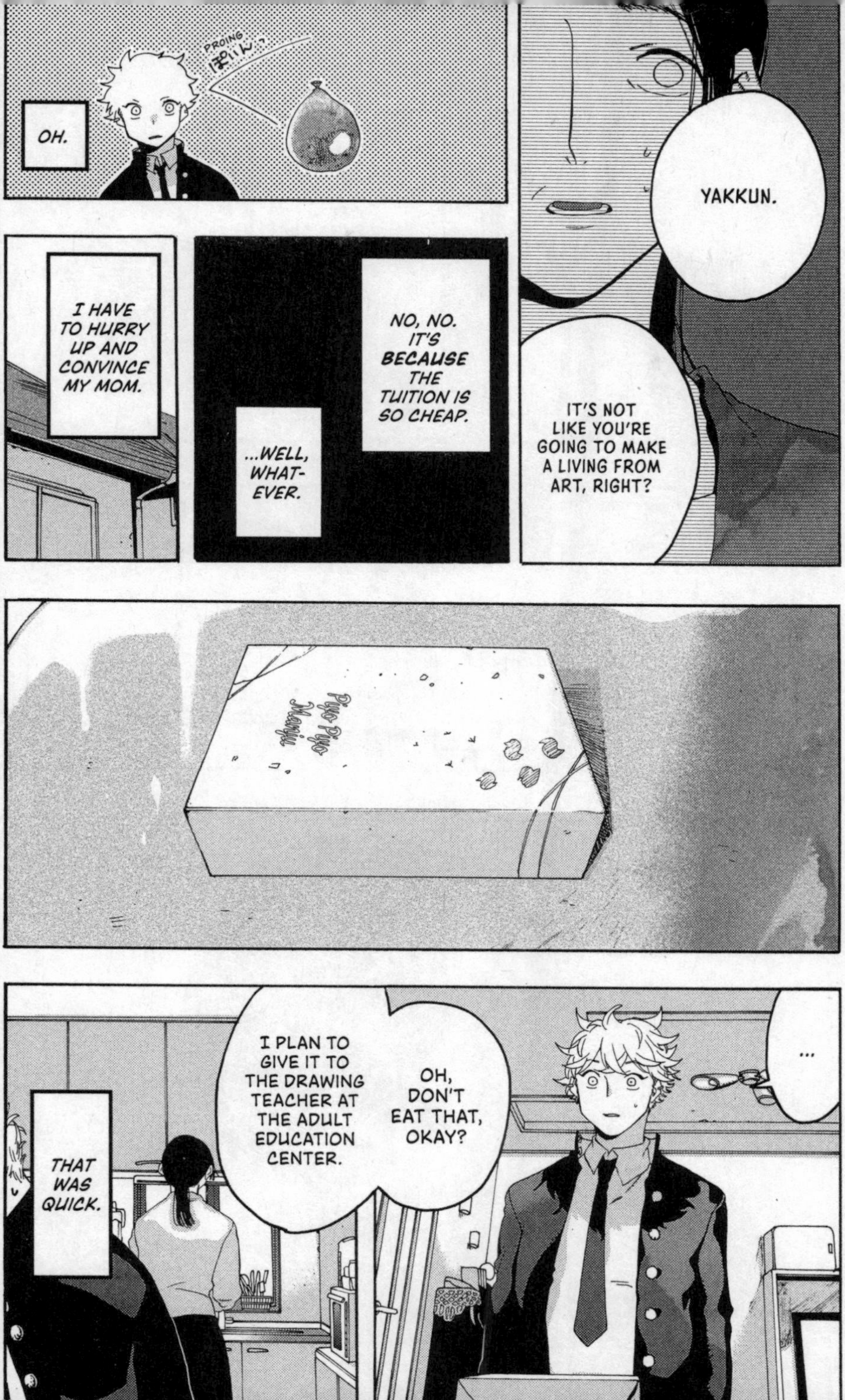
YAKKUN.
IT'S NOT LIKE YOU'RE GOING TO MAKE A LIVING FROM ART, RIGHT?
PROING
ぽいん
OH.
NO, NO. IT'S BECAUSE THE TUITION IS SO CHEAP.
...WELL, WHAT-EVER.
I HAVE TO HURRY UP AND CONVINCE MY MOM.
Piyo Piyo Manju
...
OH, DON'T EAT THAT, OKAY?
I PLAN TO GIVE IT TO THE DRAWING TEACHER AT THE ADULT EDUCATION CENTER.
THAT WAS QUICK.

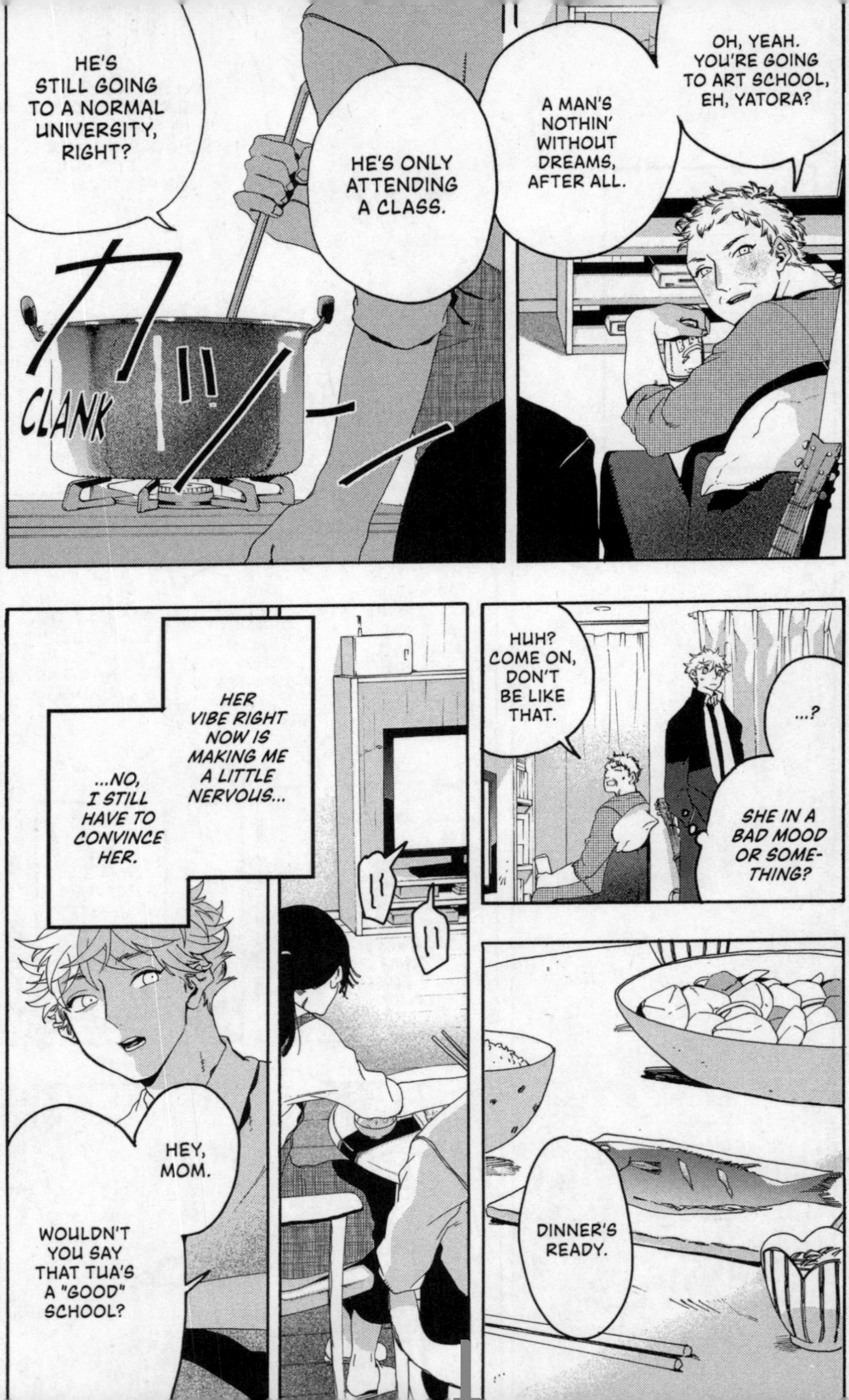
OH, YEAH. YOU'RE GOING TO ART SCHOOL, EH, YATORA?
A MAN'S NOTHIN' WITHOUT DREAMS, AFTER ALL.
HE'S ONLY ATTENDING A CLASS.
HE'S STILL GOING TO A NORMAL UNIVERSITY, RIGHT?
CLANK
HUH? COME ON, DON'T BE LIKE THAT.
...?
SHE IN A BAD MOOD OR SOME-THING?
DINNER'S READY.
HER VIBE RIGHT NOW IS MAKING ME A LITTLE NERVOUS...
...NO, I STILL HAVE TO CONVINCE HER.
HEY, MOM.
WOULDN'T YOU SAY THAT TUA'S A "GOOD" SCHOOL?

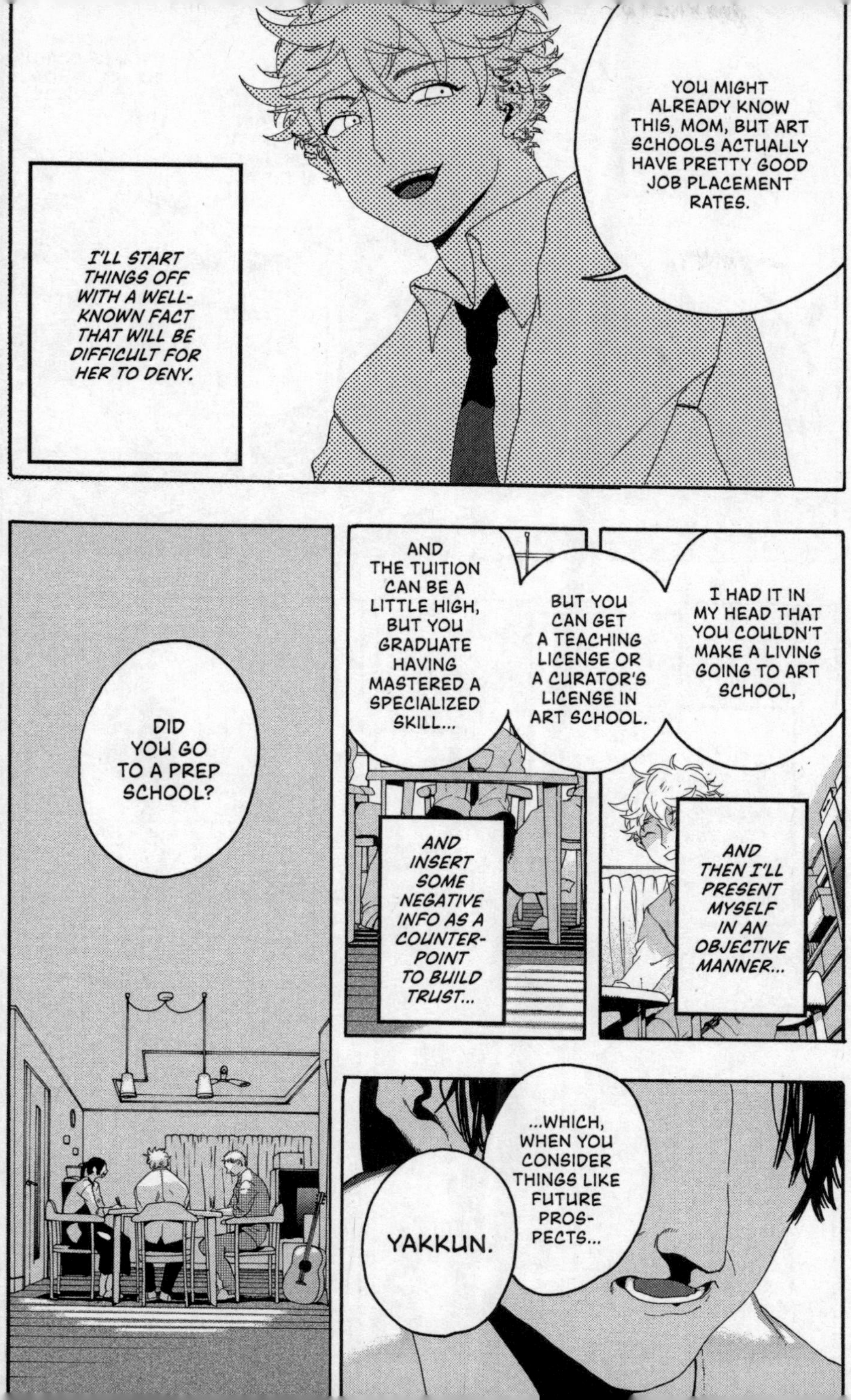
YOU MIGHT ALREADY KNOW THIS, MOM, BUT ART SCHOOLS ACTUALLY HAVE PRETTY GOOD JOB PLACEMENT RATES.
I'LL START THINGS OFF WITH A WELL-KNOWN FACT THAT WILL BE DIFFICULT FOR HER TO DENY.
I HAD IT IN MY HEAD THAT YOU COULDN'T MAKE A LIVING GOING TO ART SCHOOL,
BUT YOU CAN GET A TEACHING LICENSE OR A CURATOR'S LICENSE IN ART SCHOOL.
AND THEN I'LL PRESENT MYSELF IN AN OBJECTIVE MANNER...
AND THE TUITION CAN BE A LITTLE HIGH, BUT YOU GRADUATE HAVING MASTERED A SPECIALIZED SKILL...
AND INSERT SOME NEGATIVE INFO AS A COUNTER-POINT TO BUILD TRUST...
...WHICH, WHEN YOU CONSIDER THINGS LIKE FUTURE PROS-PECTS...
YAKKUN.
DID YOU GO TO A PREP SCHOOL?

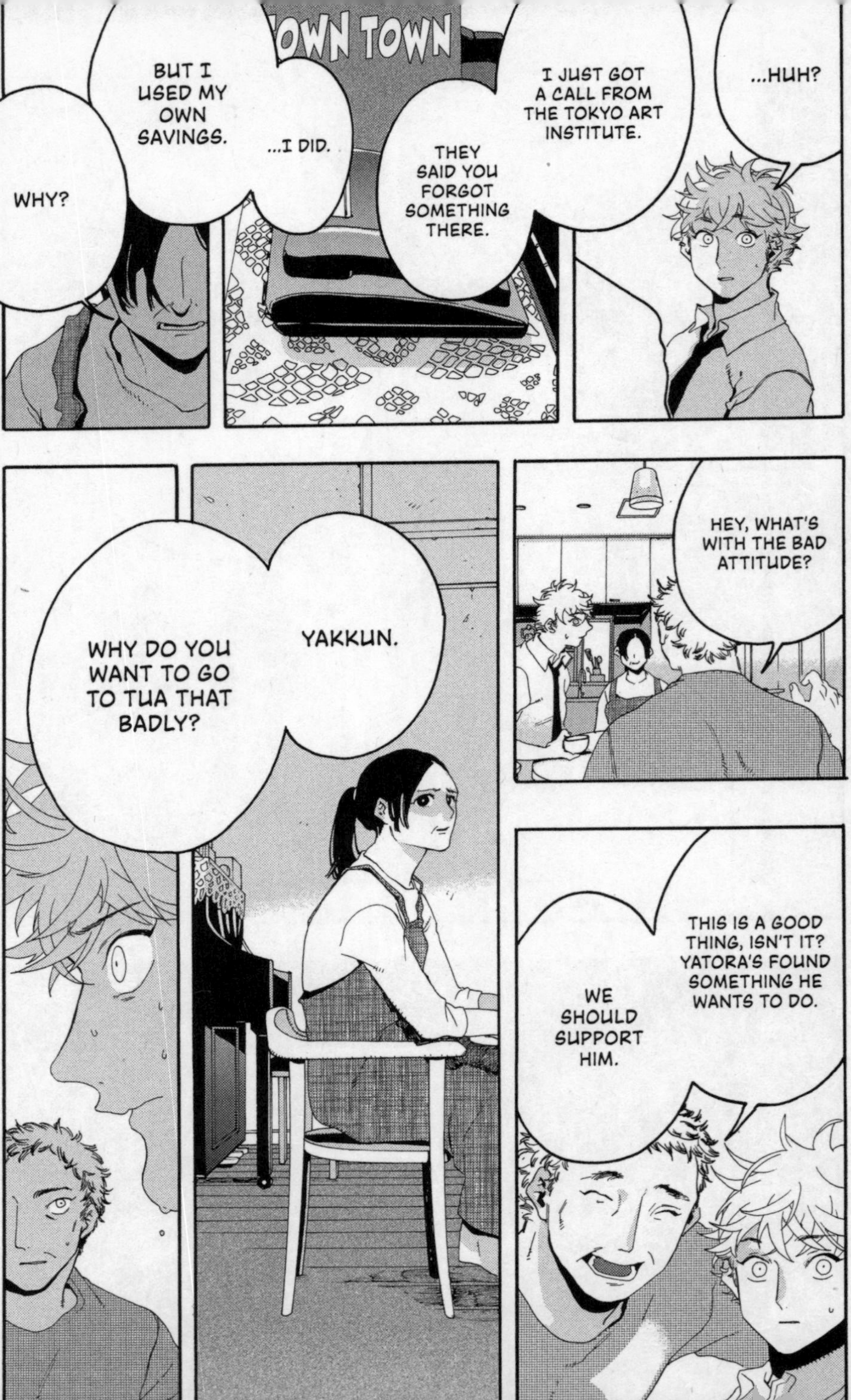
...HUH?
OWN TOWN
I JUST GOT A CALL FROM THE TOKYO ART INSTITUTE.
THEY SAID YOU FORGOT SOMETHING THERE.
...I DID.
BUT I USED MY OWN SAVINGS.
WHY?
HEY, WHAT'S WITH THE BAD ATTITUDE?
THIS IS A GOOD THING, ISN'T IT? YATORA'S FOUND SOMETHING HE WANTS TO DO.
WE SHOULD SUPPORT HIM.
YAKKUN.
WHY DO YOU WANT TO GO TO TUA THAT BADLY?

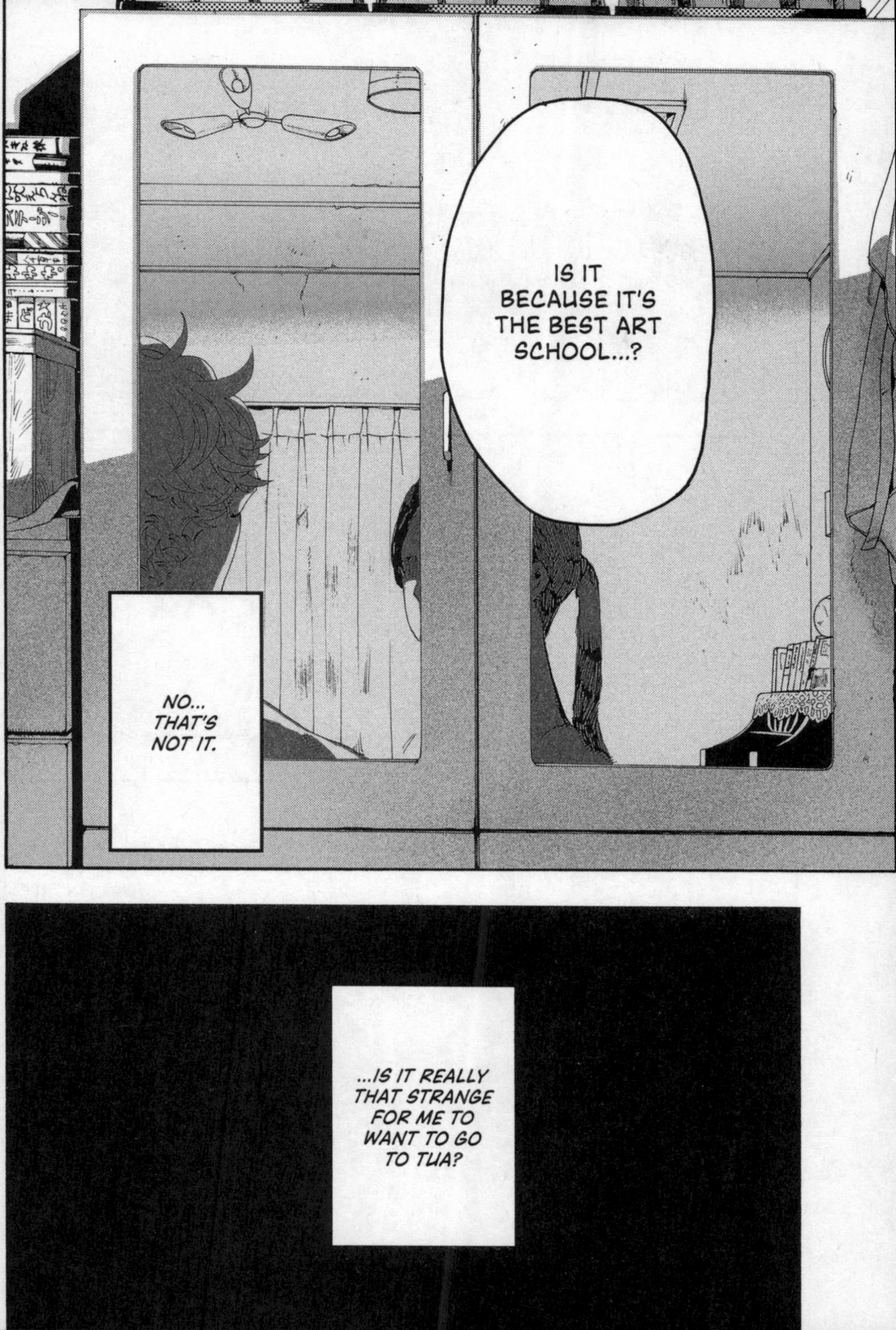
IS IT BECAUSE IT'S THE BEST ART SCHOOL...?
NO... THAT'S NOT IT.
...IS IT REALLY THAT STRANGE FOR ME TO WANT TO GO TO TUA?

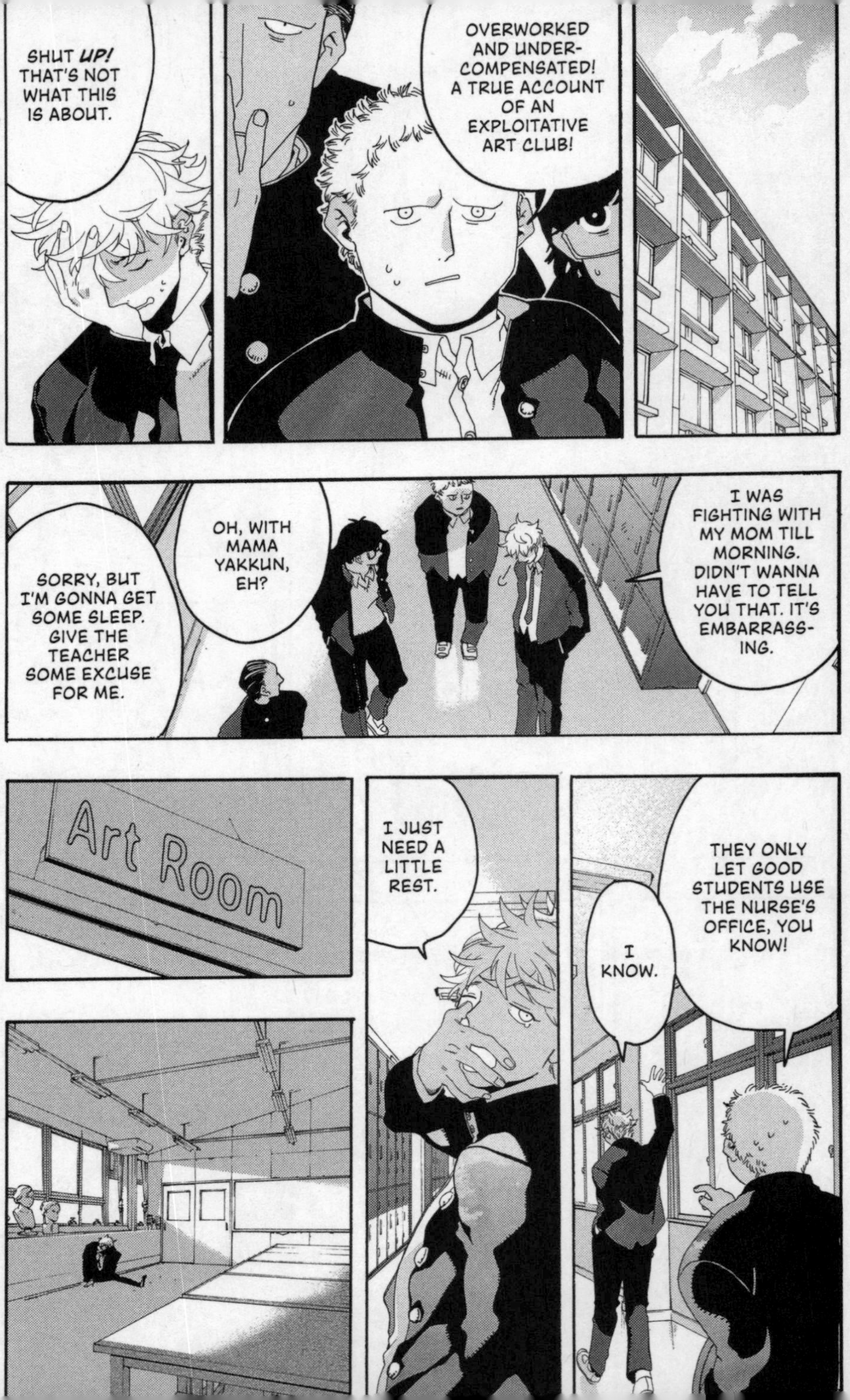
OVERWORKED AND UNDER-COMPENSATED! A TRUE ACCOUNT OF AN EXPLOITATIVE ART CLUB!
SHUT *UP!* THAT'S NOT WHAT THIS IS ABOUT.
I WAS FIGHTING WITH MY MOM TILL MORNING. DIDN'T WANNA HAVE TO TELL YOU THAT. IT'S EMBARRASS-ING.
OH, WITH MAMA YAKKUN, EH?
SORRY, BUT I'M GONNA GET SOME SLEEP. GIVE THE TEACHER SOME EXCUSE FOR ME.
THEY ONLY LET GOOD STUDENTS USE THE NURSE'S OFFICE, YOU KNOW!
I KNOW.
I JUST NEED A LITTLE REST.
Art Room

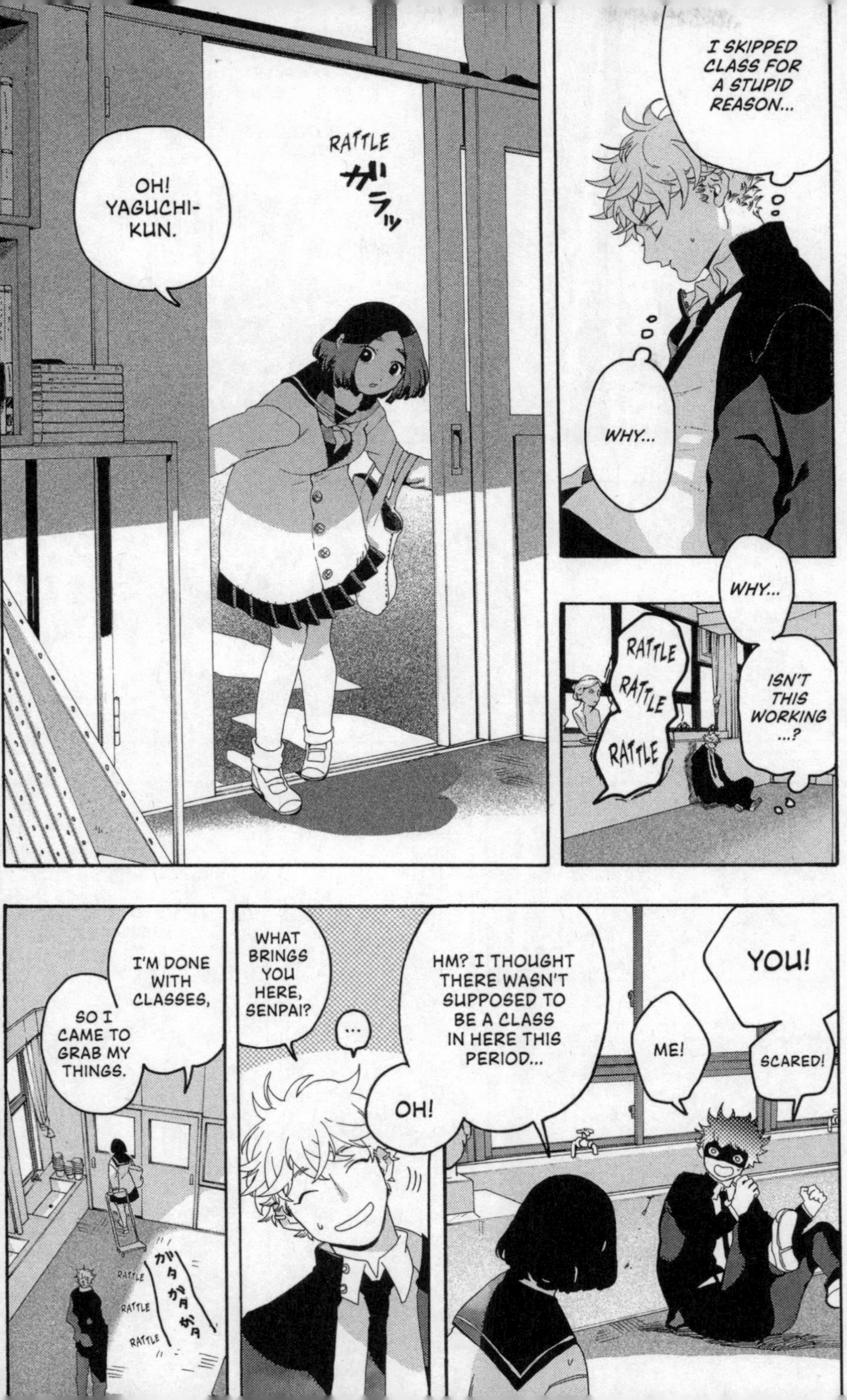
I SKIPPED CLASS FOR A STUPID REASON...
WHY...
WHY...
RATTLE RATTLE RATTLE
ISN'T THIS WORKING ...?
RATTLE
ガラッ
OH! YAGUCHI-KUN.
YOU!
SCARED!
ME!
HM? I THOUGHT THERE WASN'T SUPPOSED TO BE A CLASS IN HERE THIS PERIOD...
OH!
WHAT BRINGS YOU HERE, SENPAI?
...
I'M DONE WITH CLASSES,
SO I CAME TO GRAB MY THINGS.
RATTLE RATTLE RATTLE
ガタガタガタ

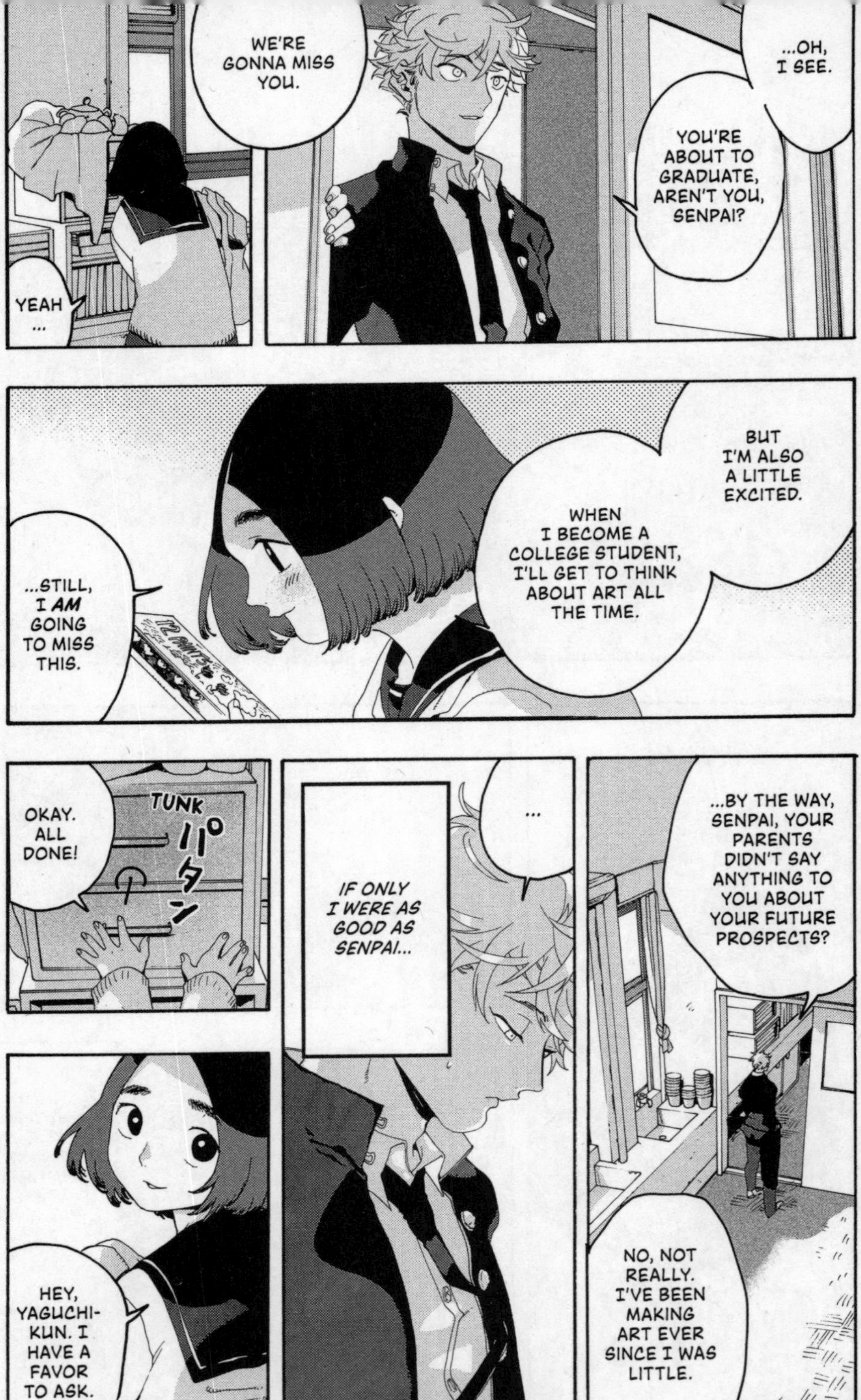
...OH, I SEE.
YOU'RE ABOUT TO GRADUATE, AREN'T YOU, SENPAI?
WE'RE GONNA MISS YOU.
YEAH...
BUT I'M ALSO A LITTLE EXCITED.
WHEN I BECOME A COLLEGE STUDENT, I'LL GET TO THINK ABOUT ART ALL THE TIME.
...STILL, I *AM* GOING TO MISS THIS.
...BY THE WAY, SENPAI, YOUR PARENTS DIDN'T SAY ANYTHING TO YOU ABOUT YOUR FUTURE PROSPECTS?
NO, NOT REALLY. I'VE BEEN MAKING ART EVER SINCE I WAS LITTLE.
...
IF ONLY I WERE AS GOOD AS SENPAI...
TUNK
パタン
OKAY. ALL DONE!
HEY, YAGUCHI-KUN. I HAVE A FAVOR TO ASK.

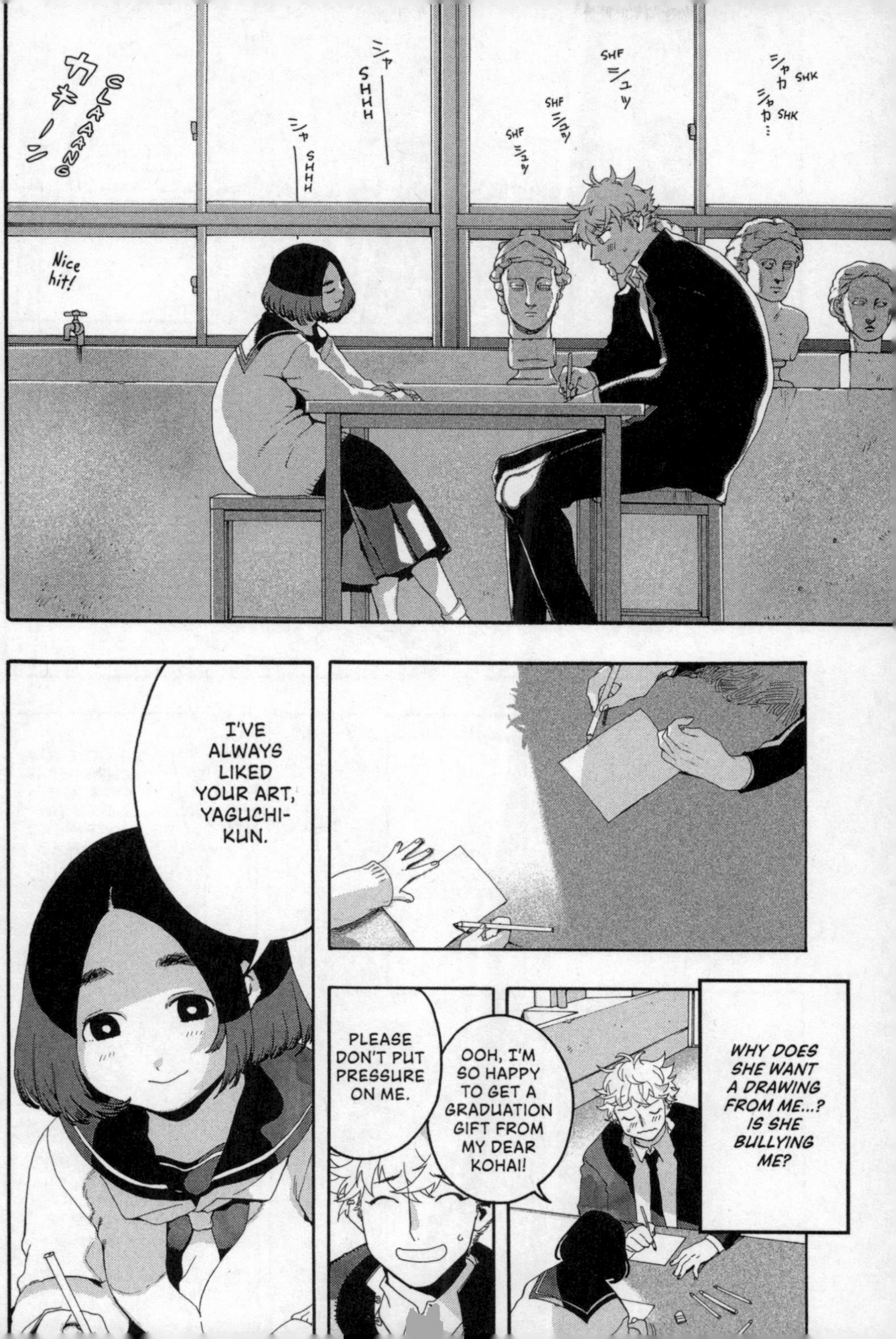
シャカ SHK
シャカ… SHK
シュッ SHF
シュッ SHF
シュッ SHF
シャー SHHH
シャ SHHH
カキーン CLAAANG
Nice hit!
WHY DOES SHE WANT A DRAWING FROM ME...? IS SHE BULLYING ME?
OOH, I'M SO HAPPY TO GET A GRADUATION GIFT FROM MY DEAR KOHAI!
PLEASE DON'T PUT PRESSURE ON ME.
I'VE ALWAYS LIKED YOUR ART, YAGUCHI-KUN.

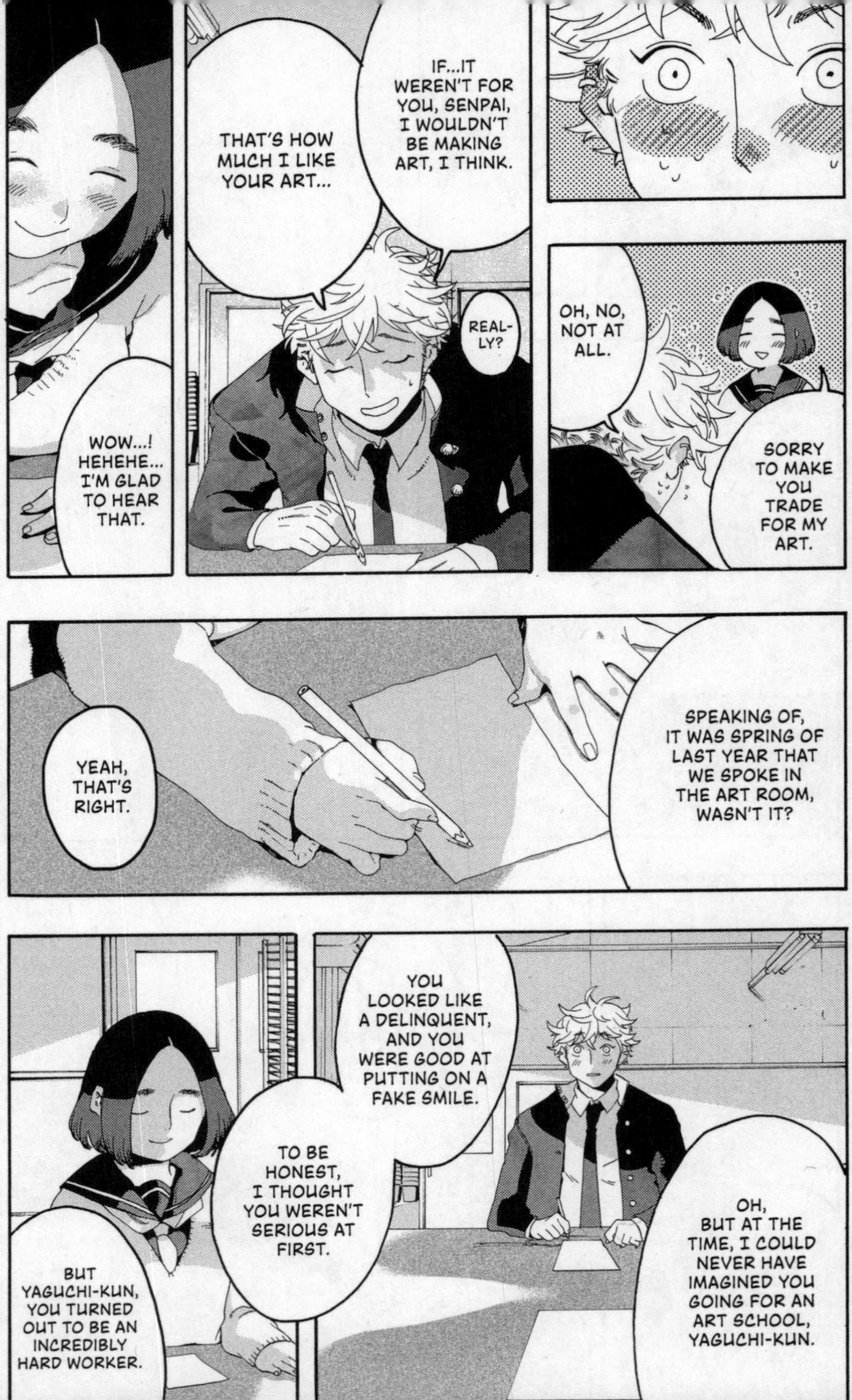
SORRY TO MAKE YOU TRADE FOR MY ART.
OH, NO, NOT AT ALL.
IF...IT WEREN'T FOR YOU, SENPAI, I WOULDN'T BE MAKING ART, I THINK.
THAT'S HOW MUCH I LIKE YOUR ART...
REAL-LY?
WOW...! HEHEHE... I'M GLAD TO HEAR THAT.
SPEAKING OF, IT WAS SPRING OF LAST YEAR THAT WE SPOKE IN THE ART ROOM, WASN'T IT?
YEAH, THAT'S RIGHT.
OH, BUT AT THE TIME, I COULD NEVER HAVE IMAGINED YOU GOING FOR AN ART SCHOOL, YAGUCHI-KUN.
YOU LOOKED LIKE A DELINQUENT, AND YOU WERE GOOD AT PUTTING ON A FAKE SMILE.
TO BE HONEST, I THOUGHT YOU WEREN'T SERIOUS AT FIRST.
BUT YAGUCHI-KUN, YOU TURNED OUT TO BE AN INCREDIBLY HARD WORKER.

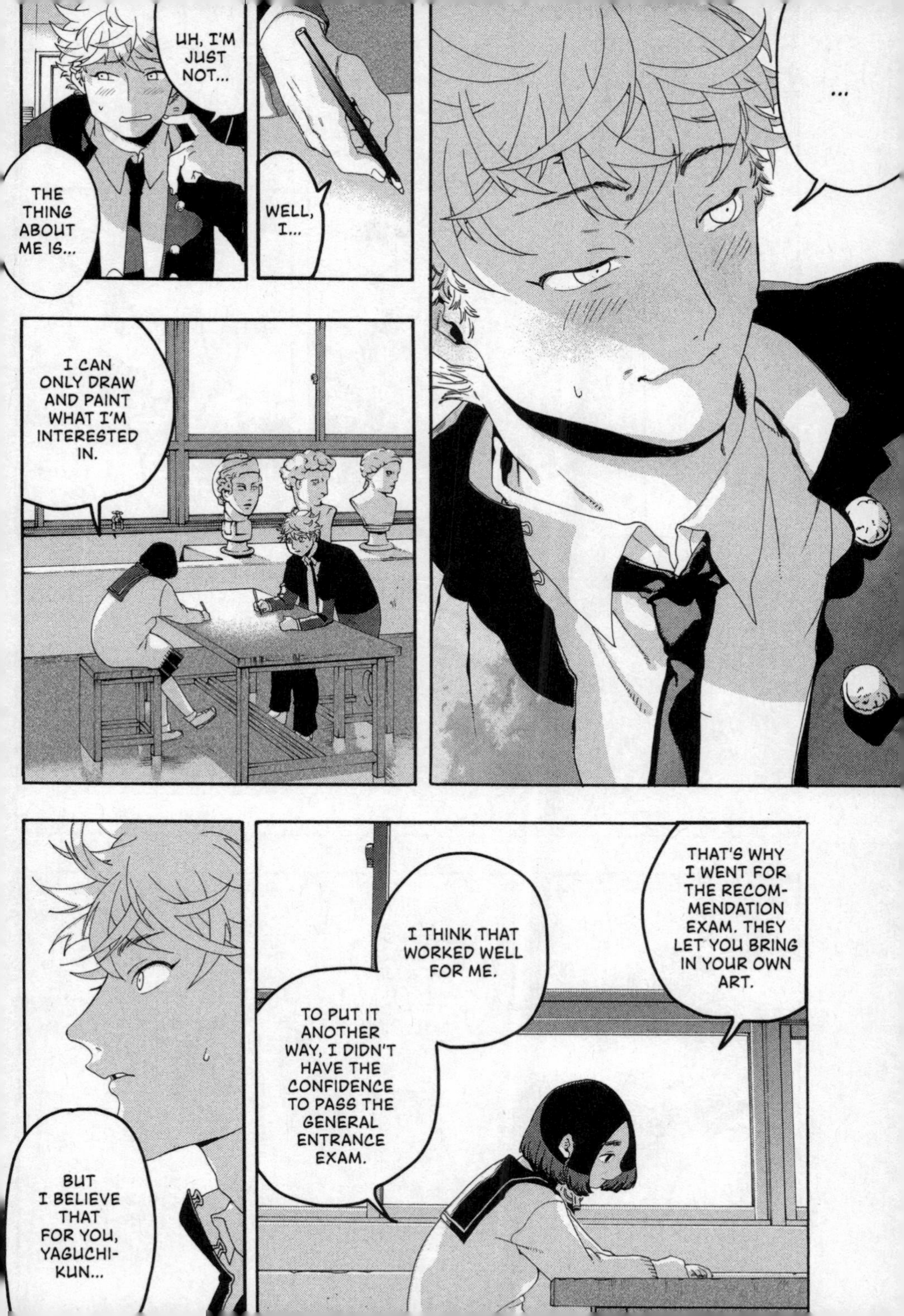
...
WELL, I...
UH, I'M JUST NOT...
THE THING ABOUT ME IS...
I CAN ONLY DRAW AND PAINT WHAT I'M INTERESTED IN.
THAT'S WHY I WENT FOR THE RECOM-MENDATION EXAM. THEY LET YOU BRING IN YOUR OWN ART.
I THINK THAT WORKED WELL FOR ME.
TO PUT IT ANOTHER WAY, I DIDN'T HAVE THE CONFIDENCE TO PASS THE GENERAL ENTRANCE EXAM.
BUT I BELIEVE THAT FOR YOU, YAGUCHI-KUN...

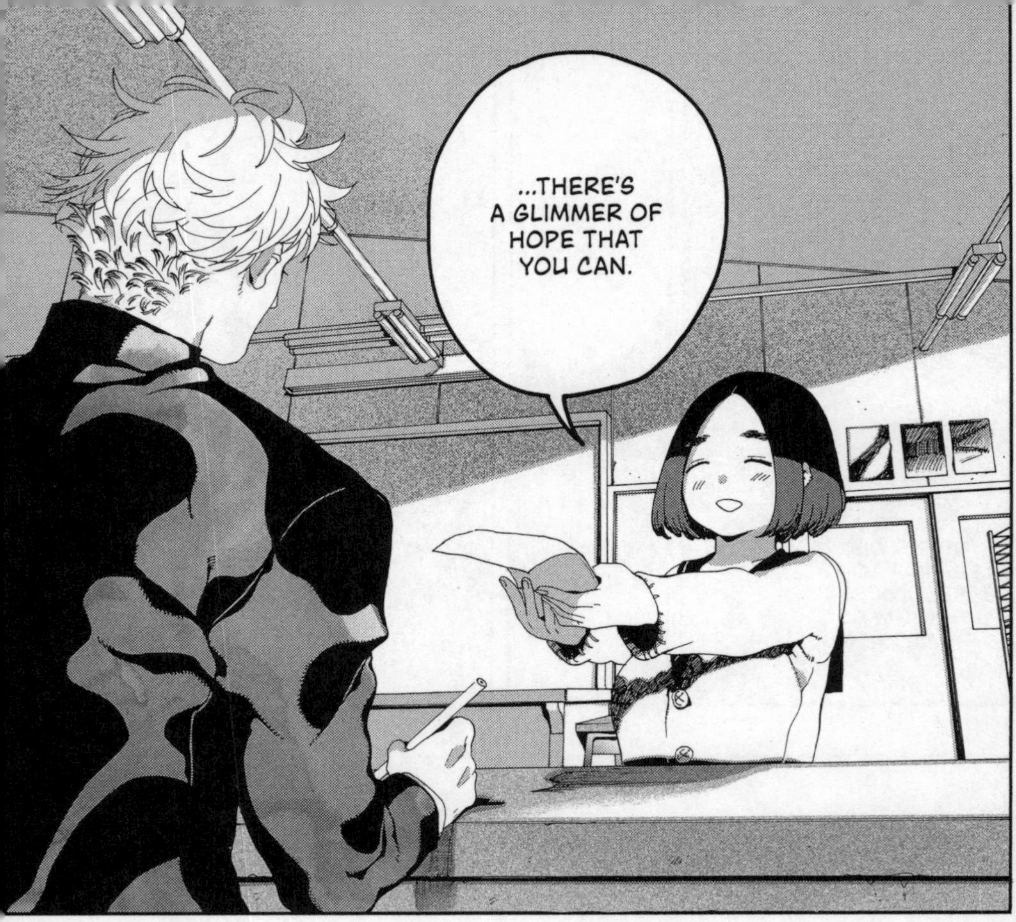
...THERE'S A GLIMMER OF HOPE THAT YOU CAN.

ART: MARIMO TOMORI

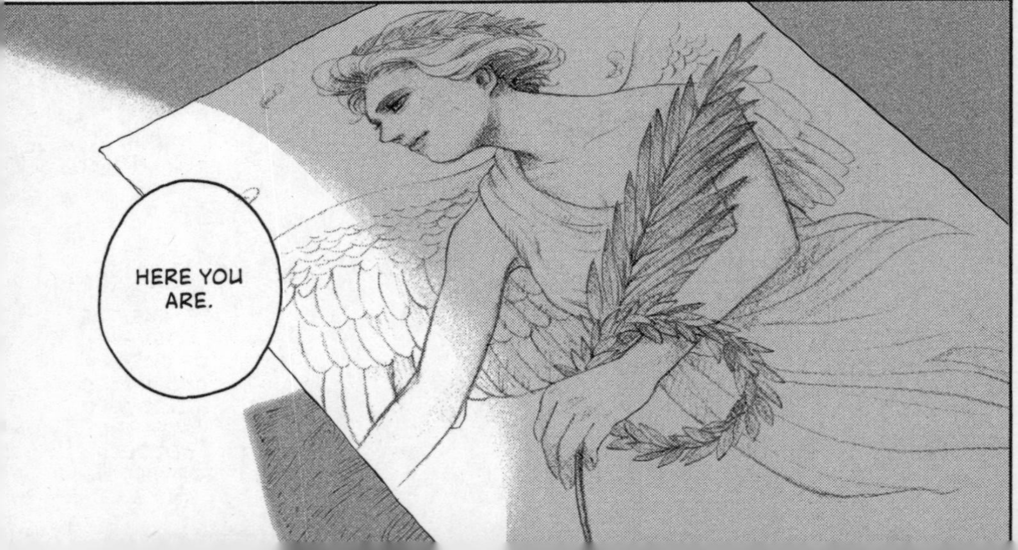
HERE YOU ARE.

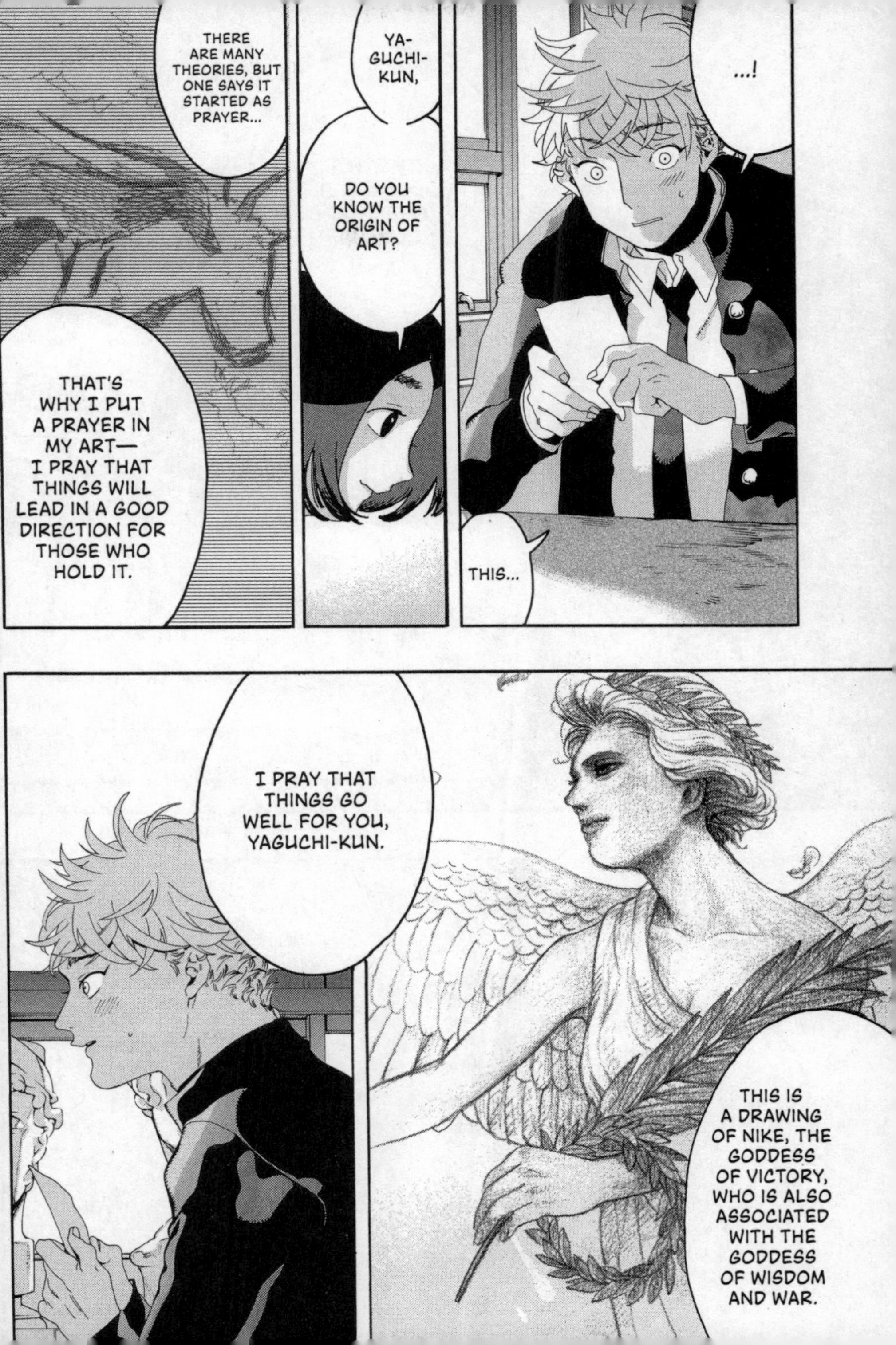
...!
THIS...
YA-GUCHI-KUN,
DO YOU KNOW THE ORIGIN OF ART?
THERE ARE MANY THEORIES, BUT ONE SAYS IT STARTED AS PRAYER...
THAT'S WHY I PUT A PRAYER IN MY ART—I PRAY THAT THINGS WILL LEAD IN A GOOD DIRECTION FOR THOSE WHO HOLD IT.
THIS IS A DRAWING OF NIKE, THE GODDESS OF VICTORY, WHO IS ALSO ASSOCIATED WITH THE GODDESS OF WISDOM AND WAR.
I PRAY THAT THINGS GO WELL FOR YOU, YAGUCHI-KUN.

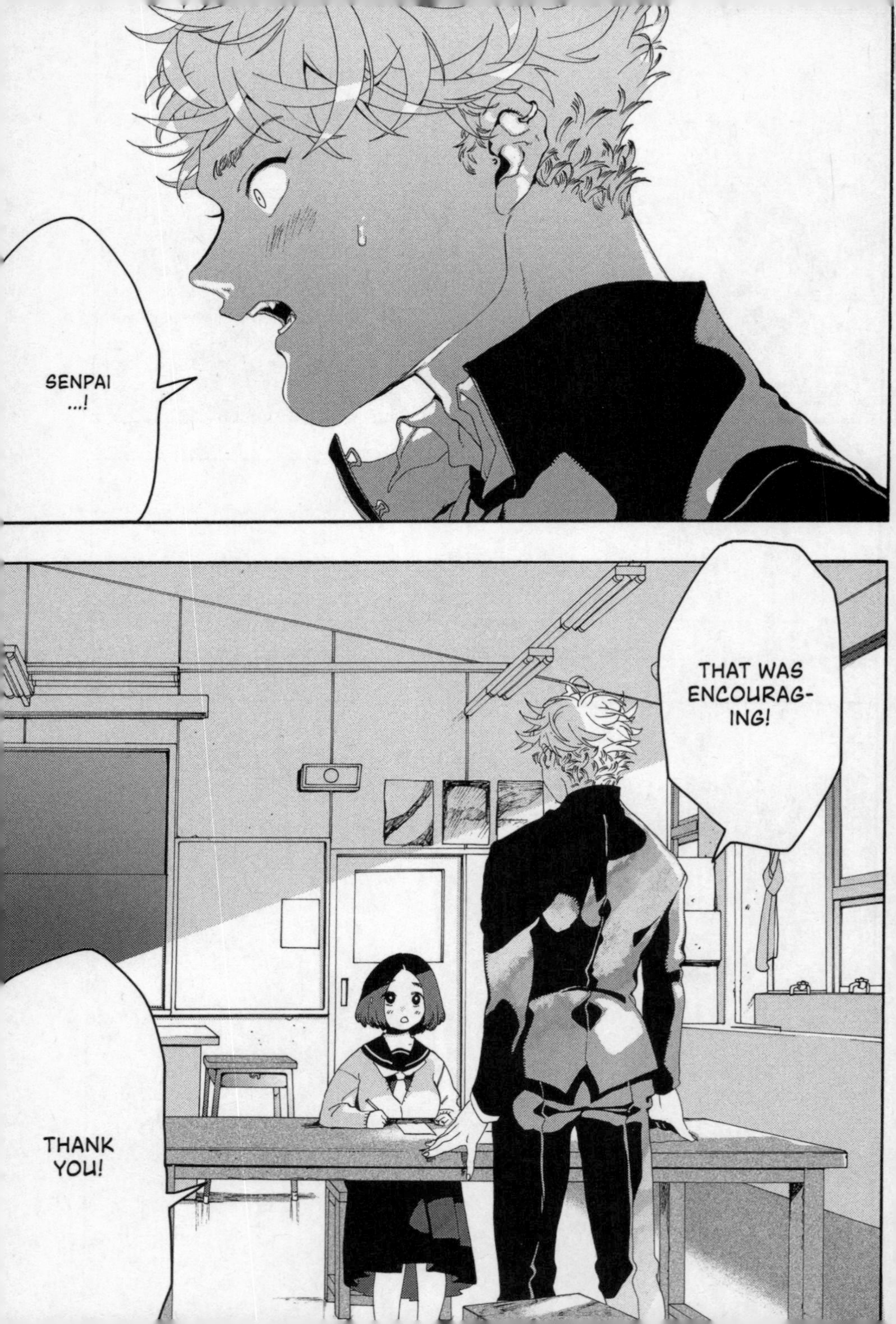
SENPAI ...!
THAT WAS ENCOURAG-ING!
THANK YOU!

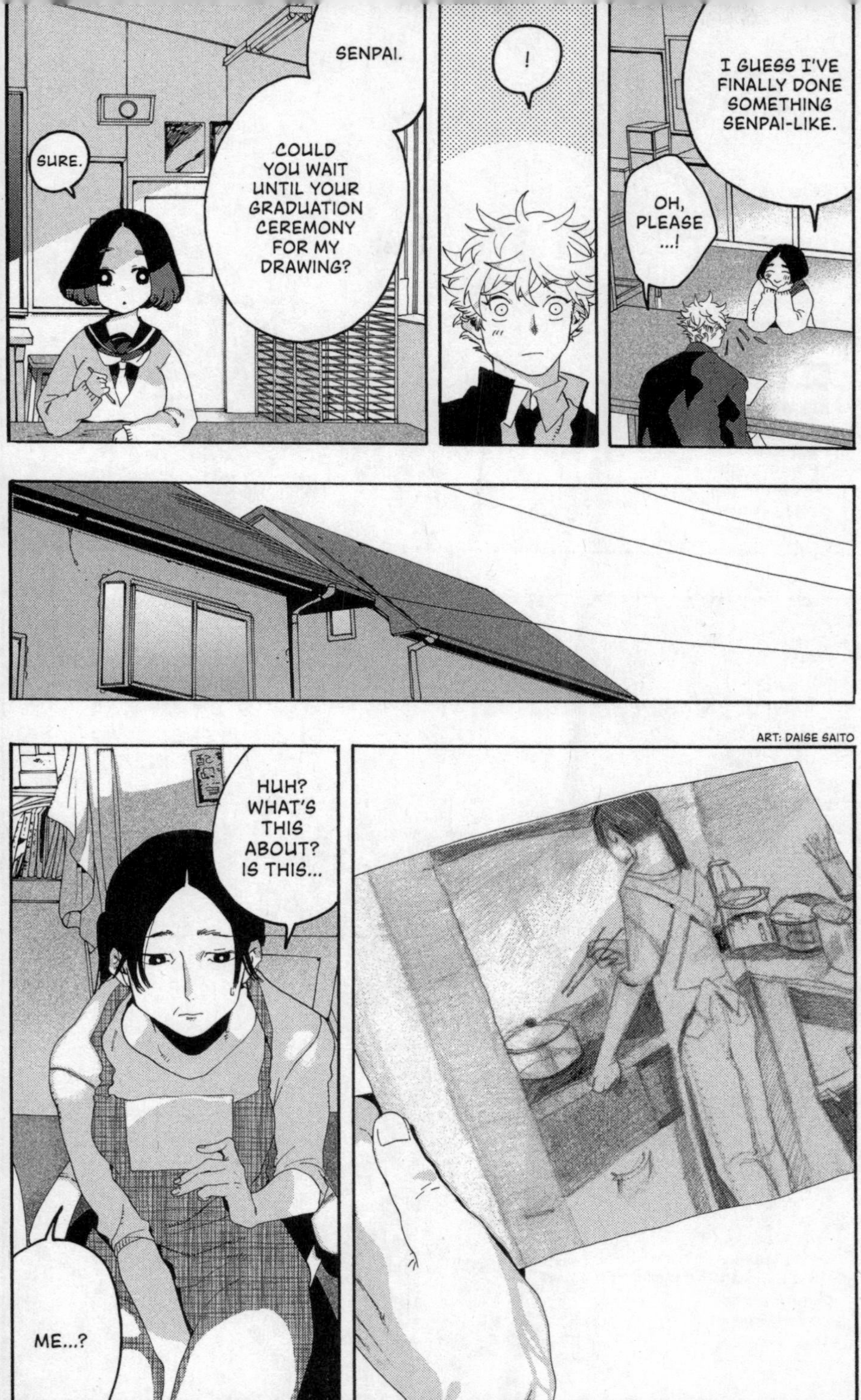
I GUESS I'VE FINALLY DONE SOMETHING SENPAI-LIKE.
OH, PLEASE ...!
!
SENPAI.
COULD YOU WAIT UNTIL YOUR GRADUATION CEREMONY FOR MY DRAWING?
SURE.
ART: DAISE SAITO
HUH? WHAT'S THIS ABOUT? IS THIS...
ME...?

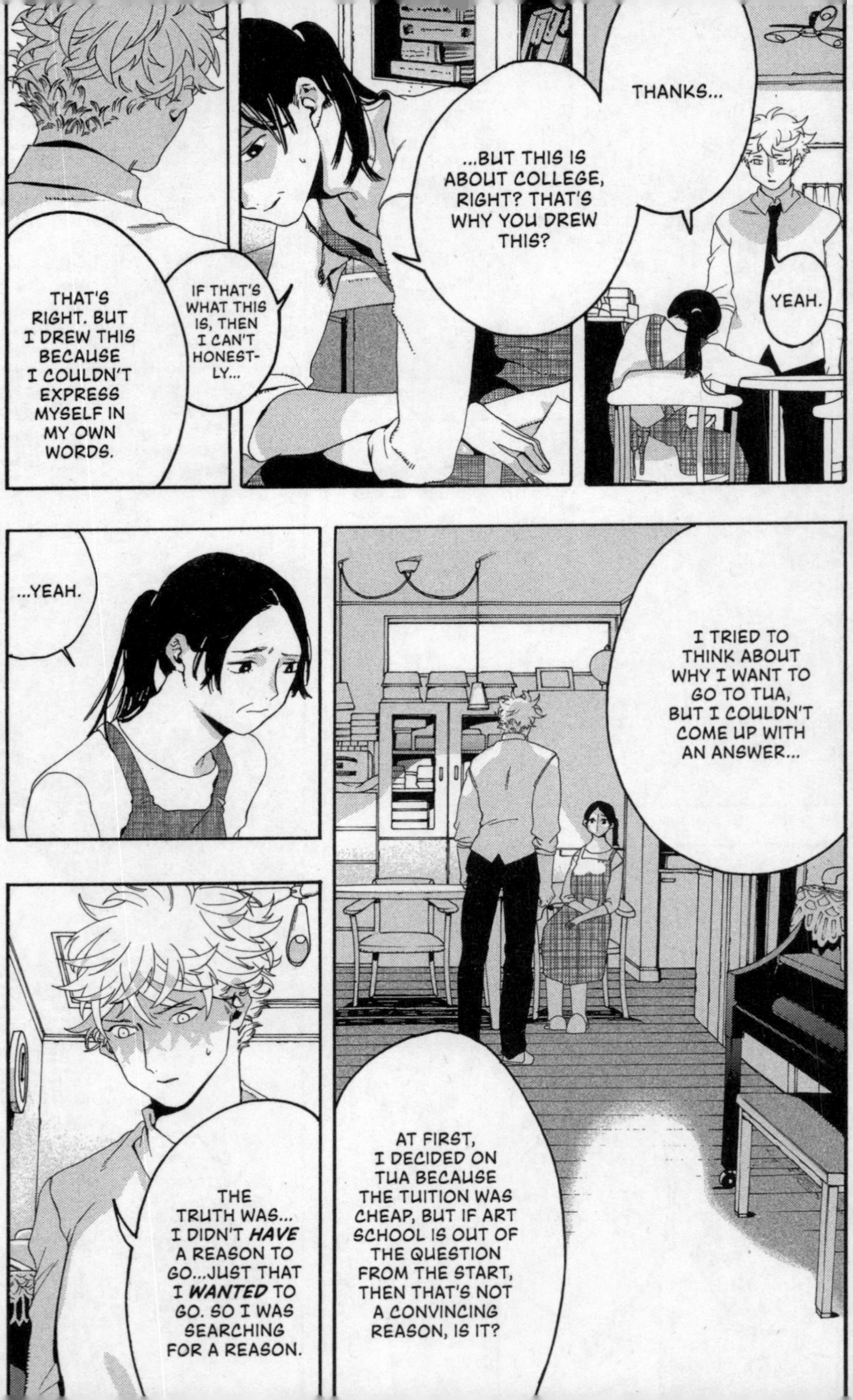
THANKS...
...BUT THIS IS ABOUT COLLEGE, RIGHT? THAT'S WHY YOU DREW THIS?
YEAH.
IF THAT'S WHAT THIS IS, THEN I CAN'T HONESTLY...
THAT'S RIGHT. BUT I DREW THIS BECAUSE I COULDN'T EXPRESS MYSELF IN MY OWN WORDS.
I TRIED TO THINK ABOUT WHY I WANT TO GO TO TUA, BUT I COULDN'T COME UP WITH AN ANSWER...
AT FIRST, I DECIDED ON TUA BECAUSE THE TUITION WAS CHEAP, BUT IF ART SCHOOL IS OUT OF THE QUESTION FROM THE START, THEN THAT'S NOT A CONVINCING REASON, IS IT?
...YEAH.
THE TRUTH WAS... I DIDN'T *HAVE* A REASON TO GO...JUST THAT I *WANTED* TO GO. SO I WAS SEARCHING FOR A REASON.

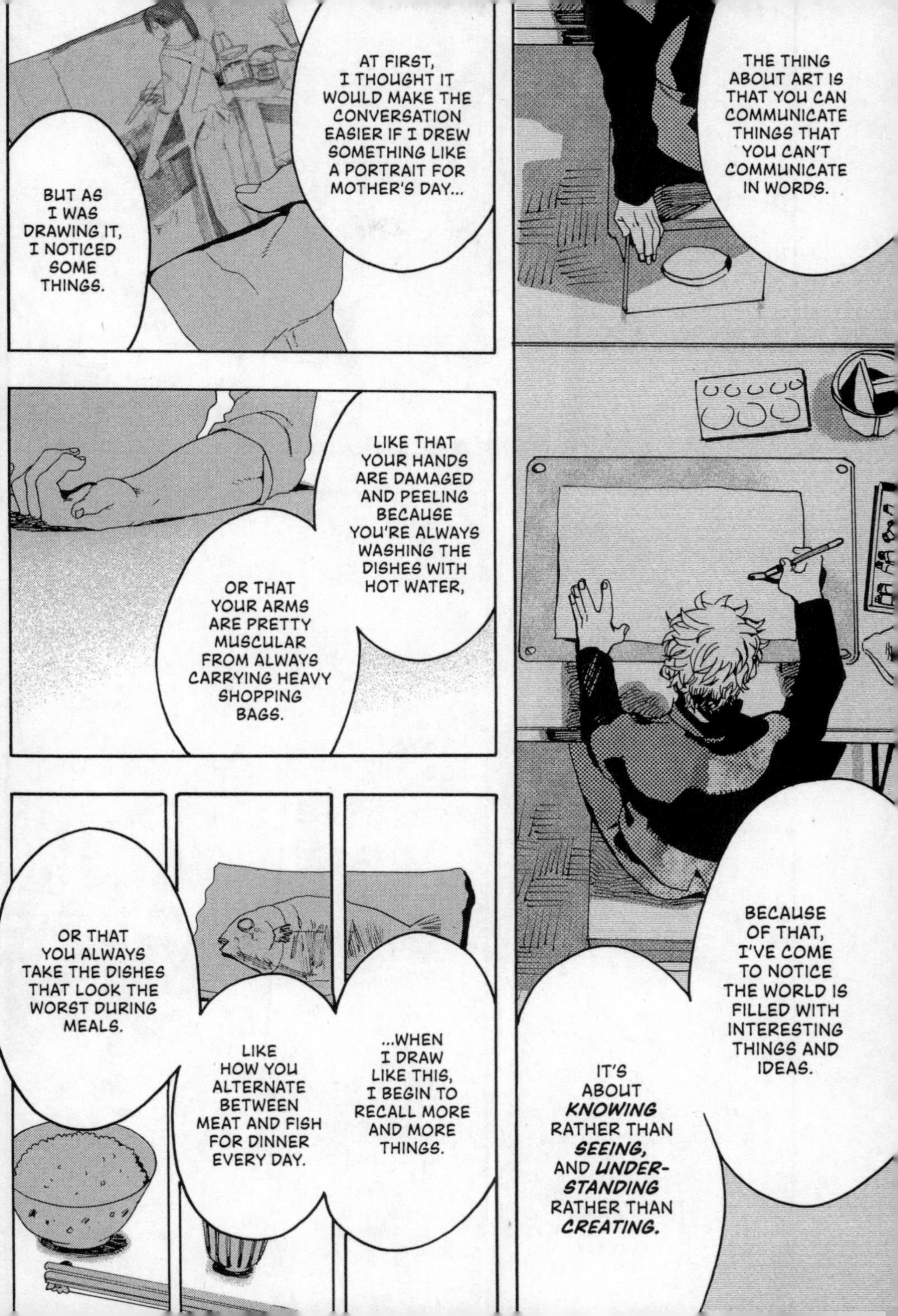
AT FIRST, I THOUGHT IT WOULD MAKE THE CONVERSATION EASIER IF I DREW SOMETHING LIKE A PORTRAIT FOR MOTHER'S DAY...
BUT AS I WAS DRAWING IT, I NOTICED SOME THINGS.
LIKE THAT YOUR HANDS ARE DAMAGED AND PEELING BECAUSE YOU'RE ALWAYS WASHING THE DISHES WITH HOT WATER,
OR THAT YOUR ARMS ARE PRETTY MUSCULAR FROM ALWAYS CARRYING HEAVY SHOPPING BAGS.
...WHEN I DRAW LIKE THIS, I BEGIN TO RECALL MORE AND MORE THINGS.
LIKE HOW YOU ALTERNATE BETWEEN MEAT AND FISH FOR DINNER EVERY DAY.
OR THAT YOU ALWAYS TAKE THE DISHES THAT LOOK THE WORST DURING MEALS.
THE THING ABOUT ART IS THAT YOU CAN COMMUNICATE THINGS THAT YOU CAN'T COMMUNICATE IN WORDS.
BECAUSE OF THAT, I'VE COME TO NOTICE THE WORLD IS FILLED WITH INTERESTING THINGS AND IDEAS.
IT'S ABOUT *KNOWING* RATHER THAN *SEEING*, AND *UNDERSTANDING* RATHER THAN *CREATING*.

UNGH...

...THAT YOU ONLY EVER THINK OF YOUR FAMILY.

IF I NEVER MADE ART, I WOULDN'T HAVE EVEN NOTICED THESE THINGS.

I'M SORRY...

SORRY, MOM...

I'M SORRY FOR NOT BEING A GOOD SON...

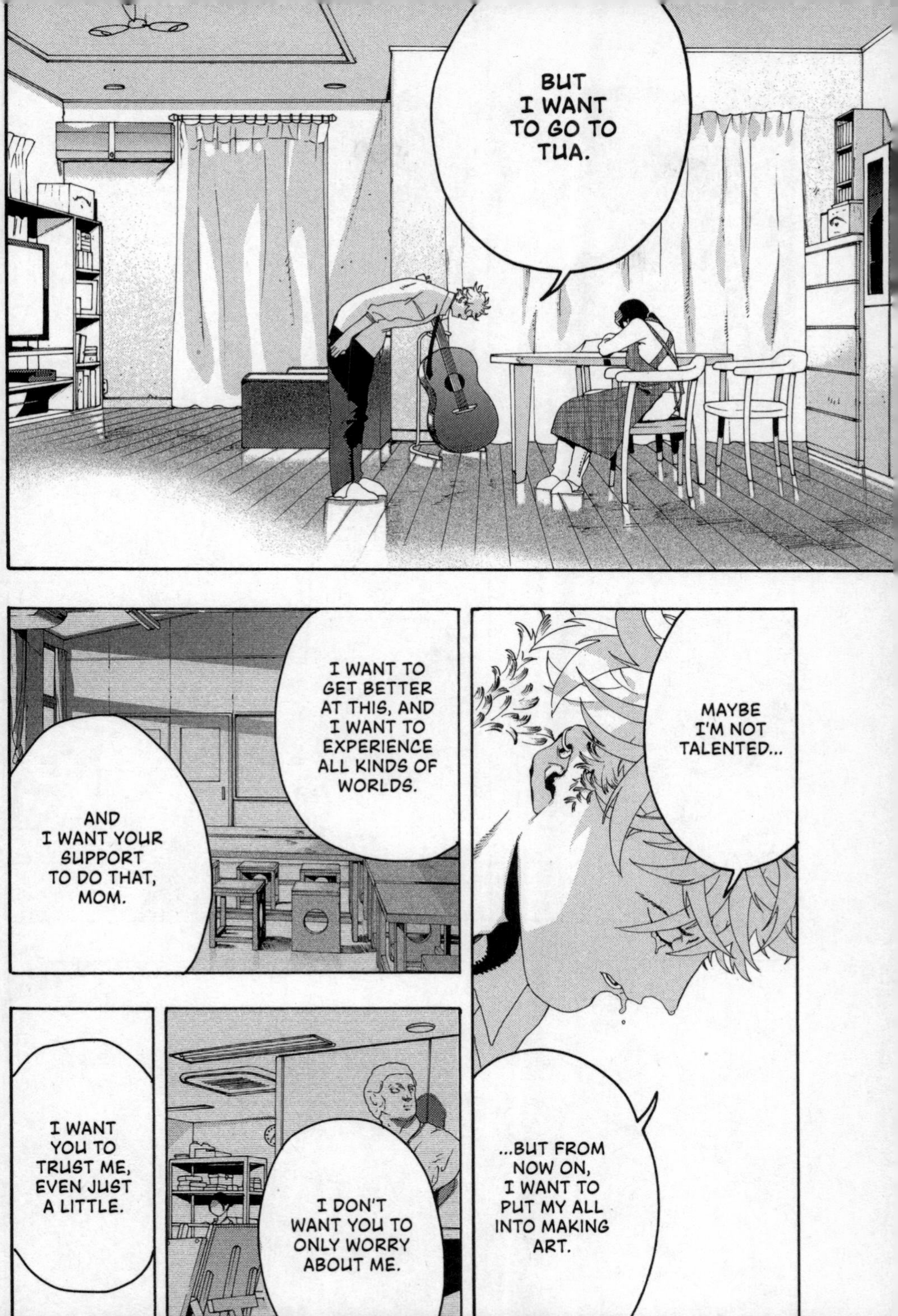
BUT I WANT TO GO TO TUA.
MAYBE I'M NOT TALENTED...
...BUT FROM NOW ON, I WANT TO PUT MY ALL INTO MAKING ART.
I WANT TO GET BETTER AT THIS, AND I WANT TO EXPERIENCE ALL KINDS OF WORLDS.
AND I WANT YOUR SUPPORT TO DO THAT, MOM.
I DON'T WANT YOU TO ONLY WORRY ABOUT ME.
I WANT YOU TO TRUST ME, EVEN JUST A LITTLE.

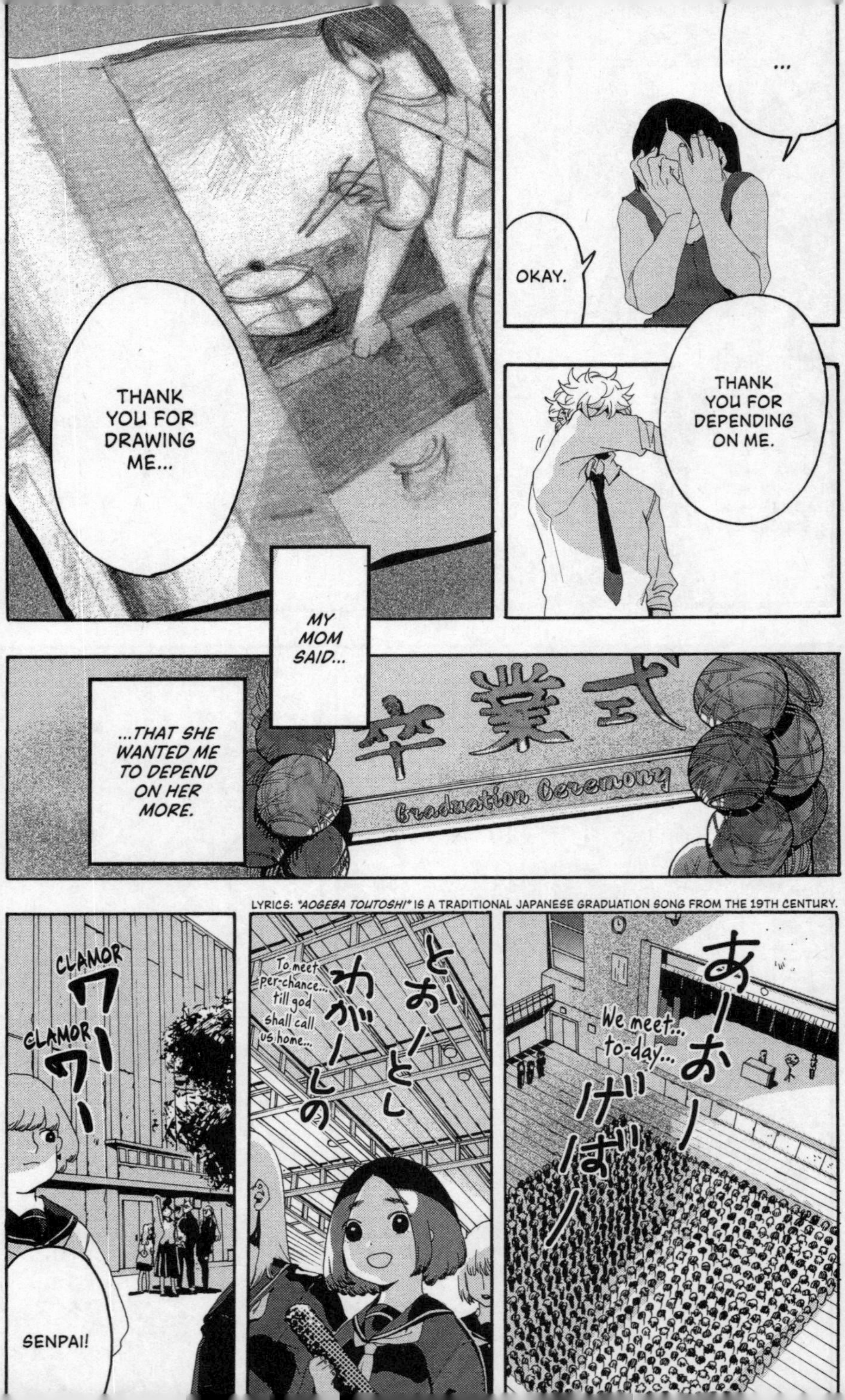
...
OKAY.
THANK YOU FOR DEPENDING ON ME.
THANK YOU FOR DRAWING ME...
MY MOM SAID...
卒業式
Graduation Ceremony
...THAT SHE WANTED ME TO DEPEND ON HER MORE.
LYRICS: "AOGEBA TOUTOSHI" IS A TRADITIONAL JAPANESE GRADUATION SONG FROM THE 19TH CENTURY.
あーおーげーばー
We meet... to-day...
とーおーとし
わがーしの
To meet per-chance... till god shall call us home...
CLAMOR
ワー
CLAMOR
ワー
SENPAI!

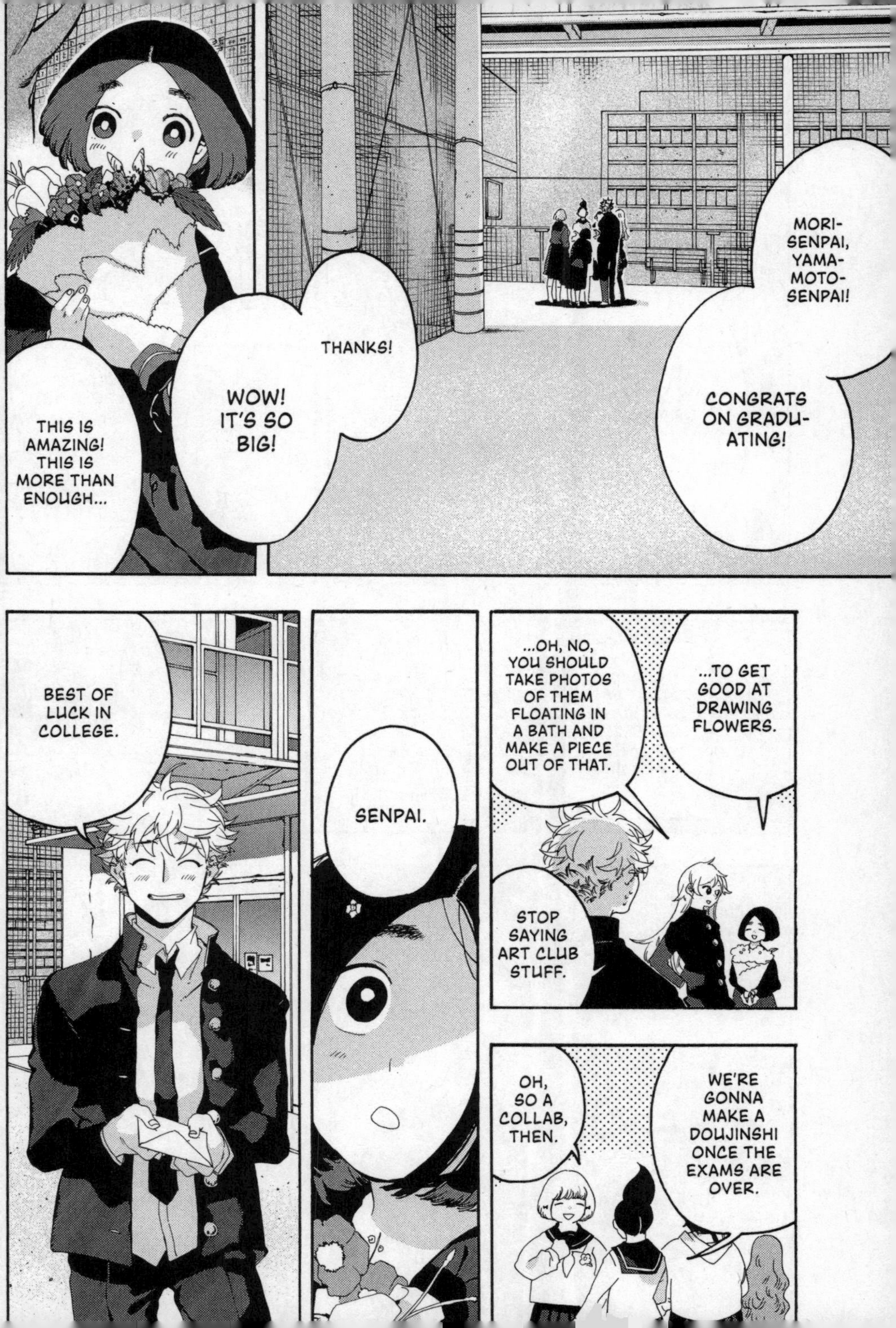
MORI-SENPAI, YAMA-MOTO-SENPAI!
CONGRATS ON GRADU-ATING!
THANKS!
WOW! IT'S SO BIG!
THIS IS AMAZING! THIS IS MORE THAN ENOUGH...
...TO GET GOOD AT DRAWING FLOWERS.
...OH, NO, YOU SHOULD TAKE PHOTOS OF THEM FLOATING IN A BATH AND MAKE A PIECE OUT OF THAT.
STOP SAYING ART CLUB STUFF.
WE'RE GONNA MAKE A DOUJINSHI ONCE THE EXAMS ARE OVER.
OH, SO A COLLAB, THEN.
SENPAI.
BEST OF LUCK IN COLLEGE.

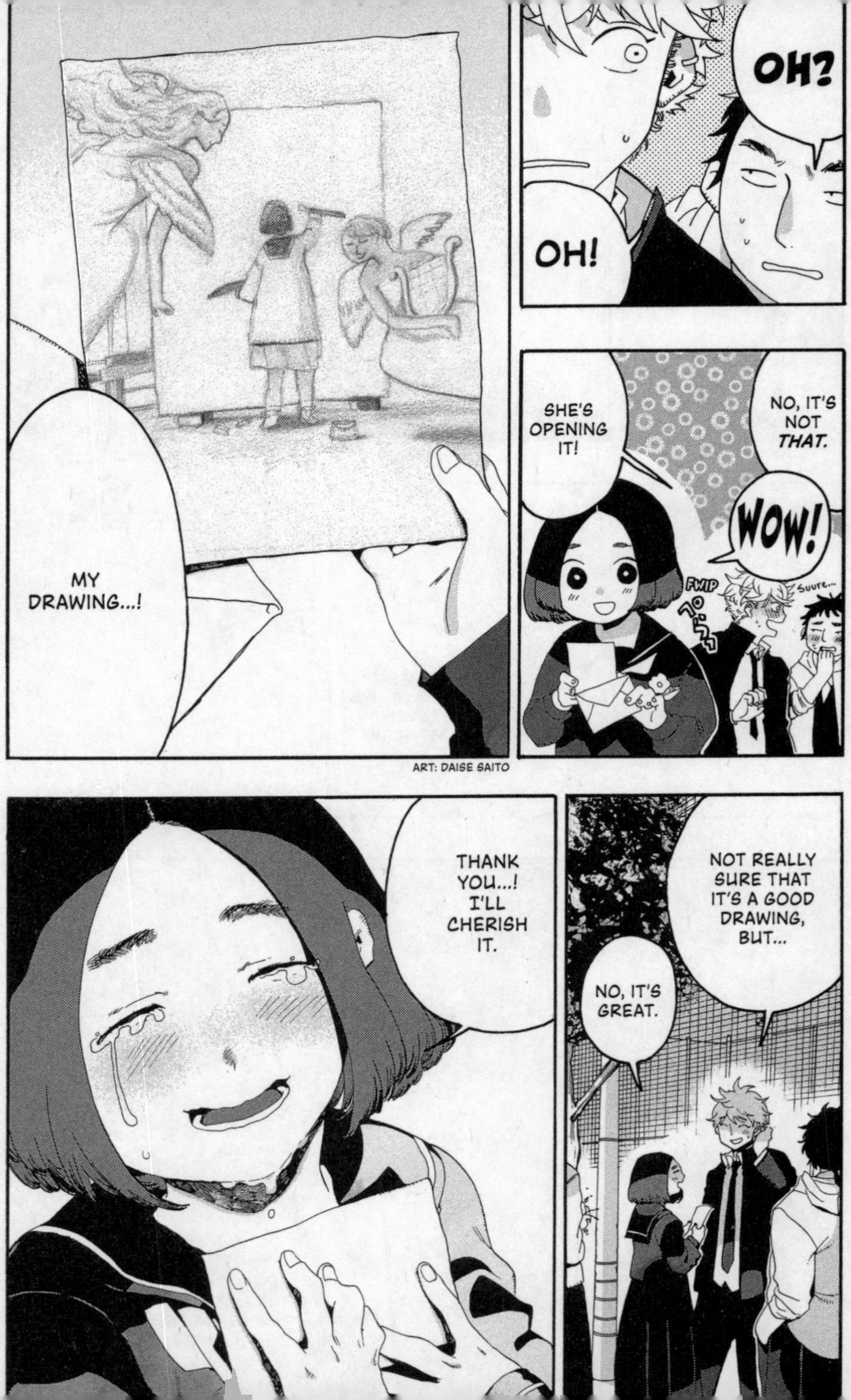
OH?
OH!
NO, IT'S NOT *THAT.*
SHE'S OPENING IT!
WOW!
Suure...
FWIP
MY DRAWING...!
NOT REALLY SURE THAT IT'S A GOOD DRAWING, BUT...
NO, IT'S GREAT.
THANK YOU...! I'LL CHERISH IT.
ART: DAISE SAITO

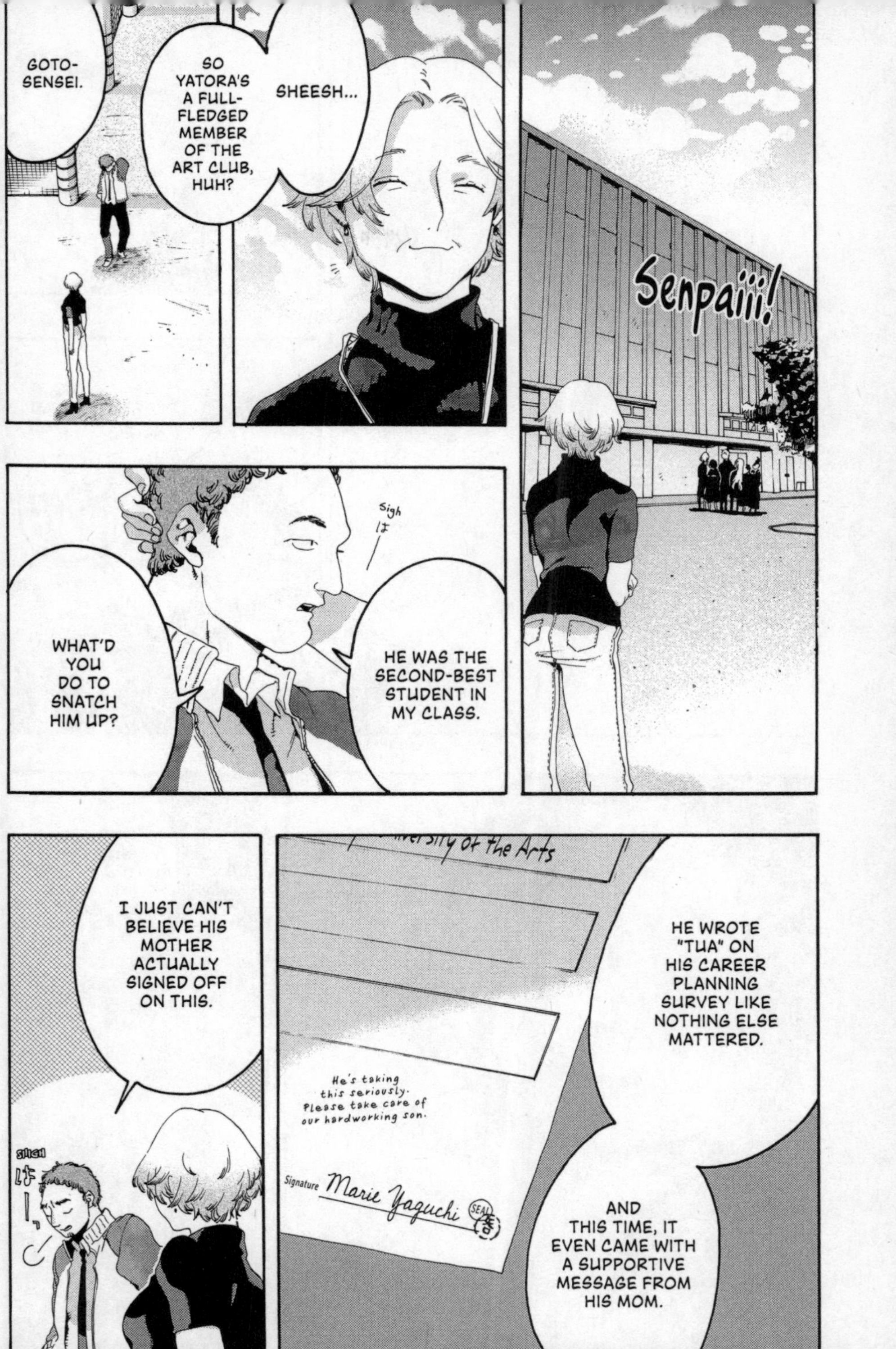
Senpaiii!
SHEESH...
SO YATORA'S A FULL-FLEDGED MEMBER OF THE ART CLUB, HUH?
GOTO-SENSEI.
Sigh
HE WAS THE SECOND-BEST STUDENT IN MY CLASS.
WHAT'D YOU DO TO SNATCH HIM UP?
University of the Arts
HE WROTE "TUA" ON HIS CAREER PLANNING SURVEY LIKE NOTHING ELSE MATTERED.
He's taking this seriously. Please take care of our hardworking son.
Signature Marie Yaguchi SEAL
AND THIS TIME, IT EVEN CAME WITH A SUPPORTIVE MESSAGE FROM HIS MOM.
I JUST CAN'T BELIEVE HIS MOTHER ACTUALLY SIGNED OFF ON THIS.
SIGH

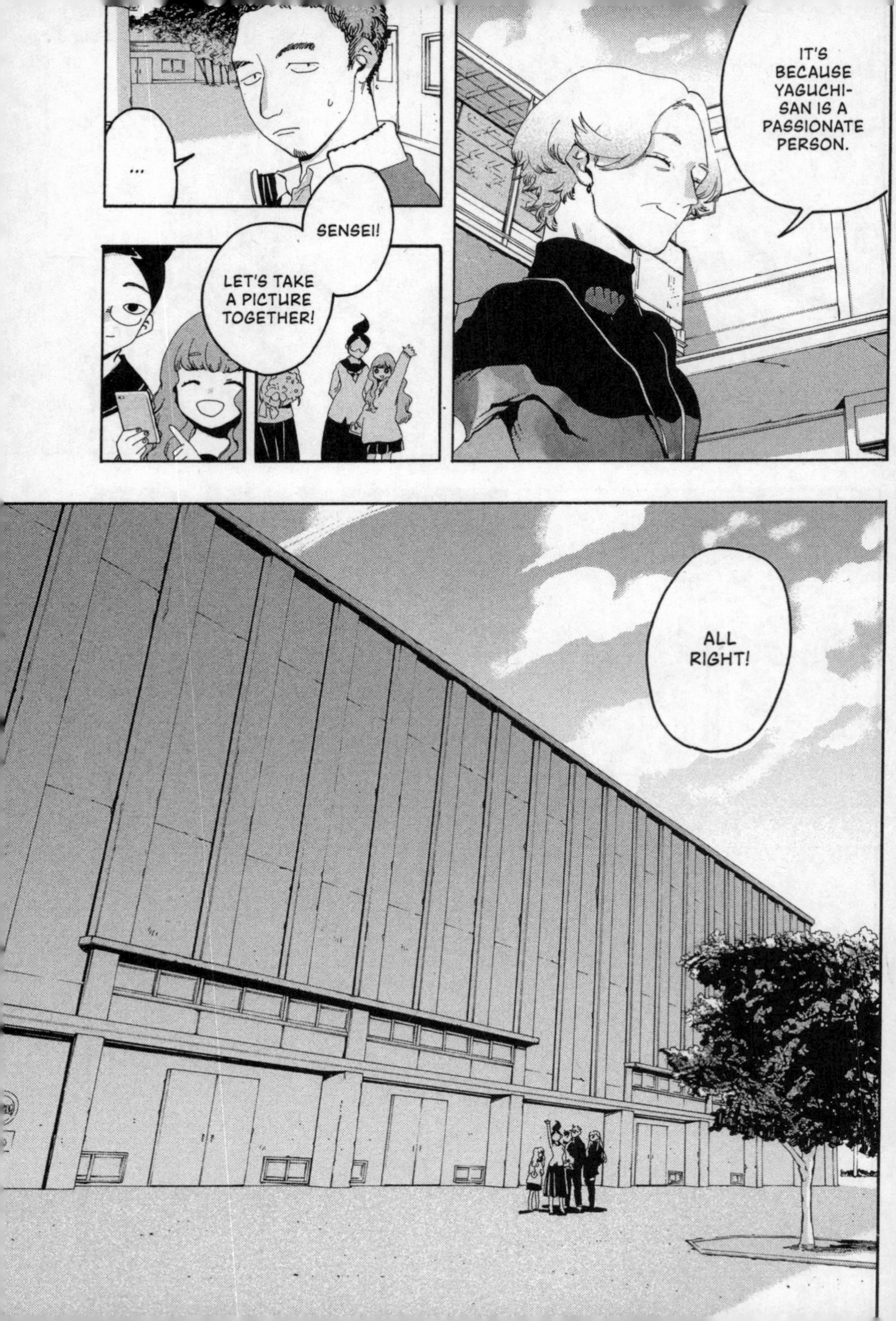
IT'S BECAUSE YAGUCHI-SAN IS A PASSIONATE PERSON.
...
SENSEI!
LET'S TAKE A PICTURE TOGETHER!
ALL RIGHT!

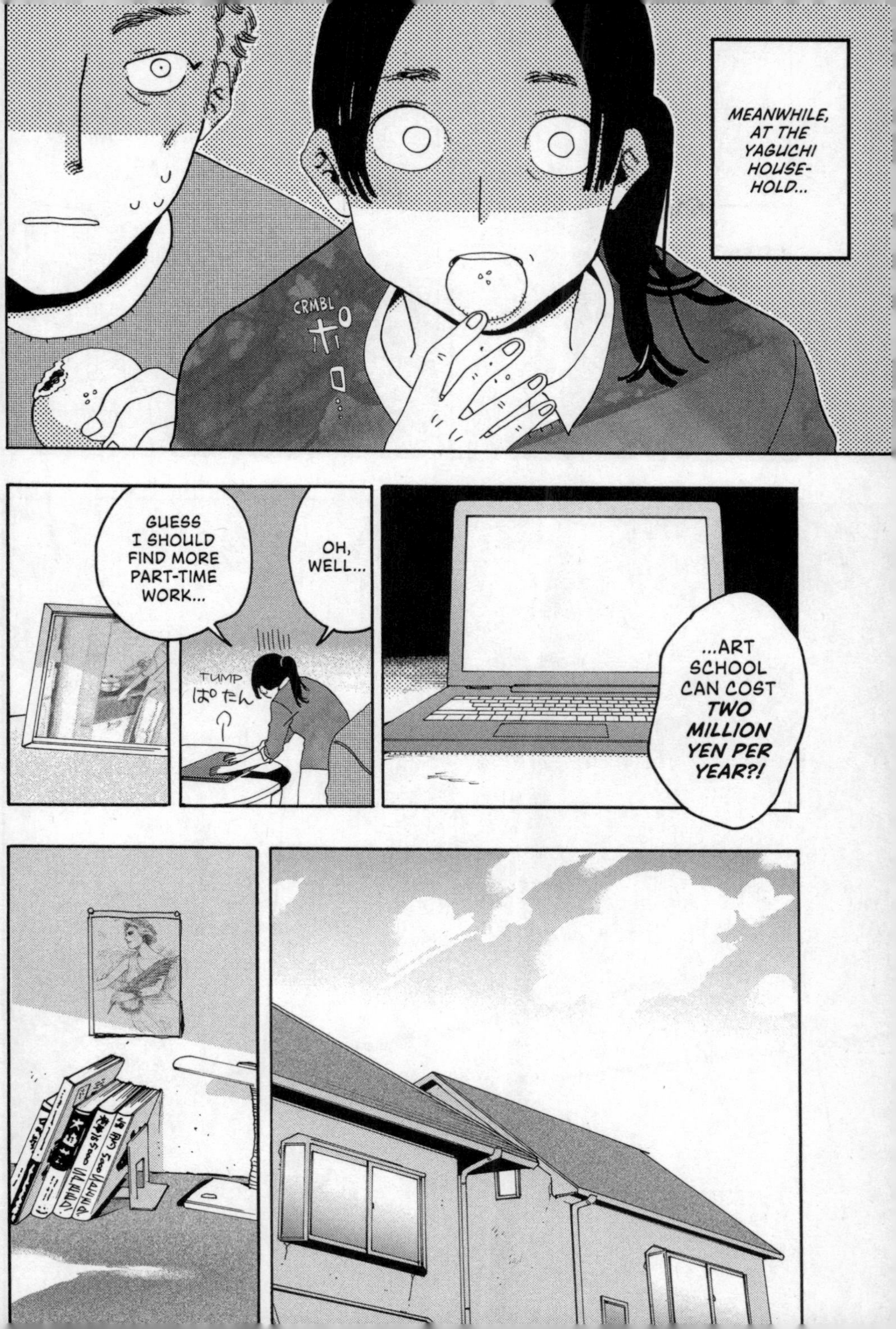
MEANWHILE, AT THE YAGUCHI HOUSEHOLD...
CRMBL
ポロ
...ART SCHOOL CAN COST TWO MILLION YEN PER YEAR?!
OH, WELL...
GUESS I SHOULD FIND MORE PART-TIME WORK...
TUMP
ぱたん

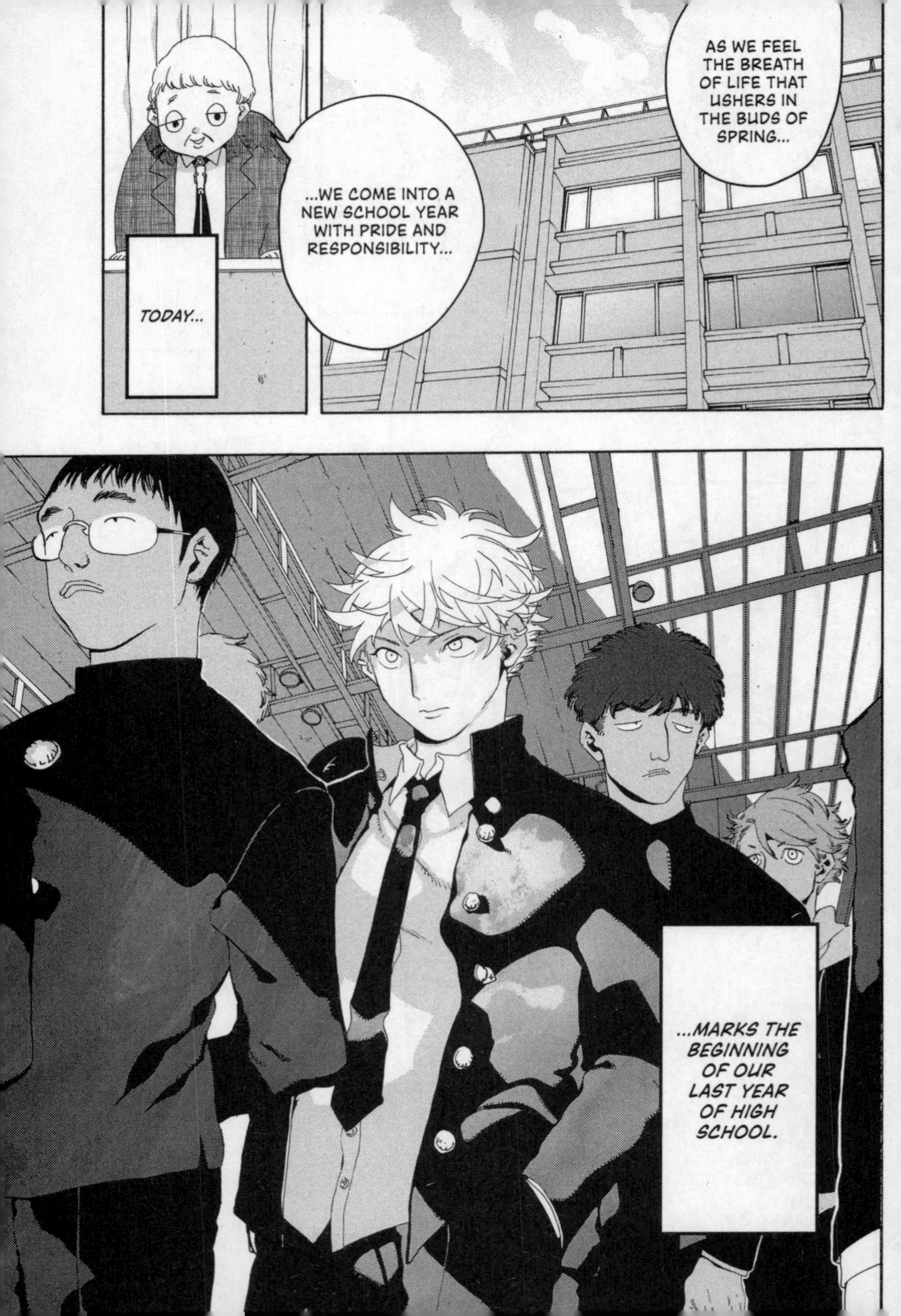
AS WE FEEL THE BREATH OF LIFE THAT USHERS IN THE BUDS OF SPRING...
...WE COME INTO A NEW SCHOOL YEAR WITH PRIDE AND RESPONSIBILITY...
TODAY...
...MARKS THE BEGINNING OF OUR LAST YEAR OF HIGH SCHOOL.

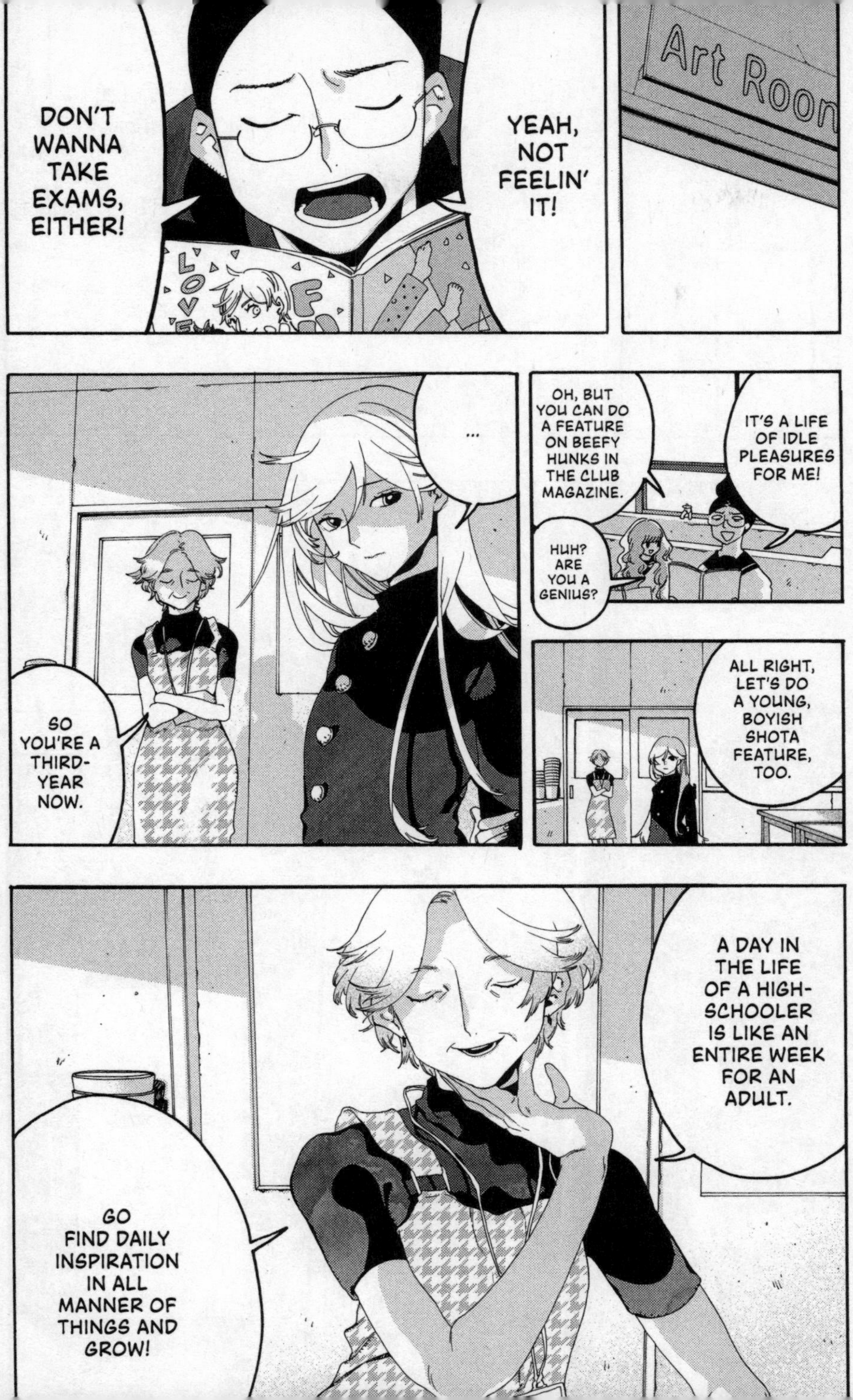
Art Roo
YEAH, NOT FEELIN' IT!
DON'T WANNA TAKE EXAMS, EITHER!
IT'S A LIFE OF IDLE PLEASURES FOR ME!
OH, BUT YOU CAN DO A FEATURE ON BEEFY HUNKS IN THE CLUB MAGAZINE.
HUH? ARE YOU A GENIUS?
ALL RIGHT, LET'S DO A YOUNG, BOYISH SHOTA FEATURE, TOO.
...
SO YOU'RE A THIRD-YEAR NOW.
A DAY IN THE LIFE OF A HIGH-SCHOOLER IS LIKE AN ENTIRE WEEK FOR AN ADULT.
GO FIND DAILY INSPIRATION IN ALL MANNER OF THINGS AND GROW!

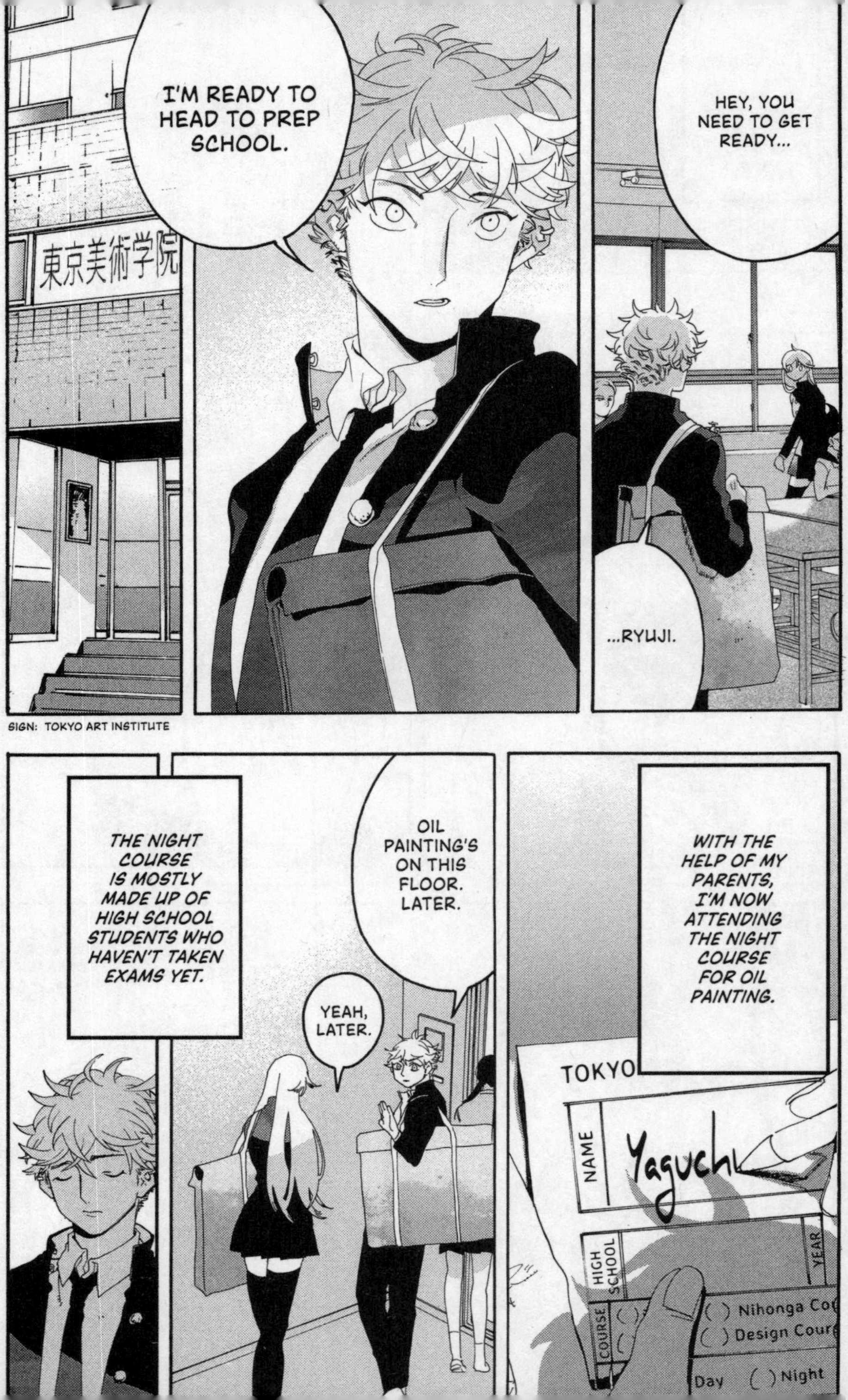
HEY, YOU NEED TO GET READY...
...RYUJI.
I'M READY TO HEAD TO PREP SCHOOL.
東京美術学院
SIGN: TOKYO ART INSTITUTE
WITH THE HELP OF MY PARENTS, I'M NOW ATTENDING THE NIGHT COURSE FOR OIL PAINTING.
TOKYO
NAME
Yaguch
HIGH SCHOOL
YEAR
COURSE
( ) Nihonga Co
( ) Design Cour
Day
( ) Night
OIL PAINTING'S ON THIS FLOOR. LATER.
YEAH, LATER.
THE NIGHT COURSE IS MOSTLY MADE UP OF HIGH SCHOOL STUDENTS WHO HAVEN'T TAKEN EXAMS YET.

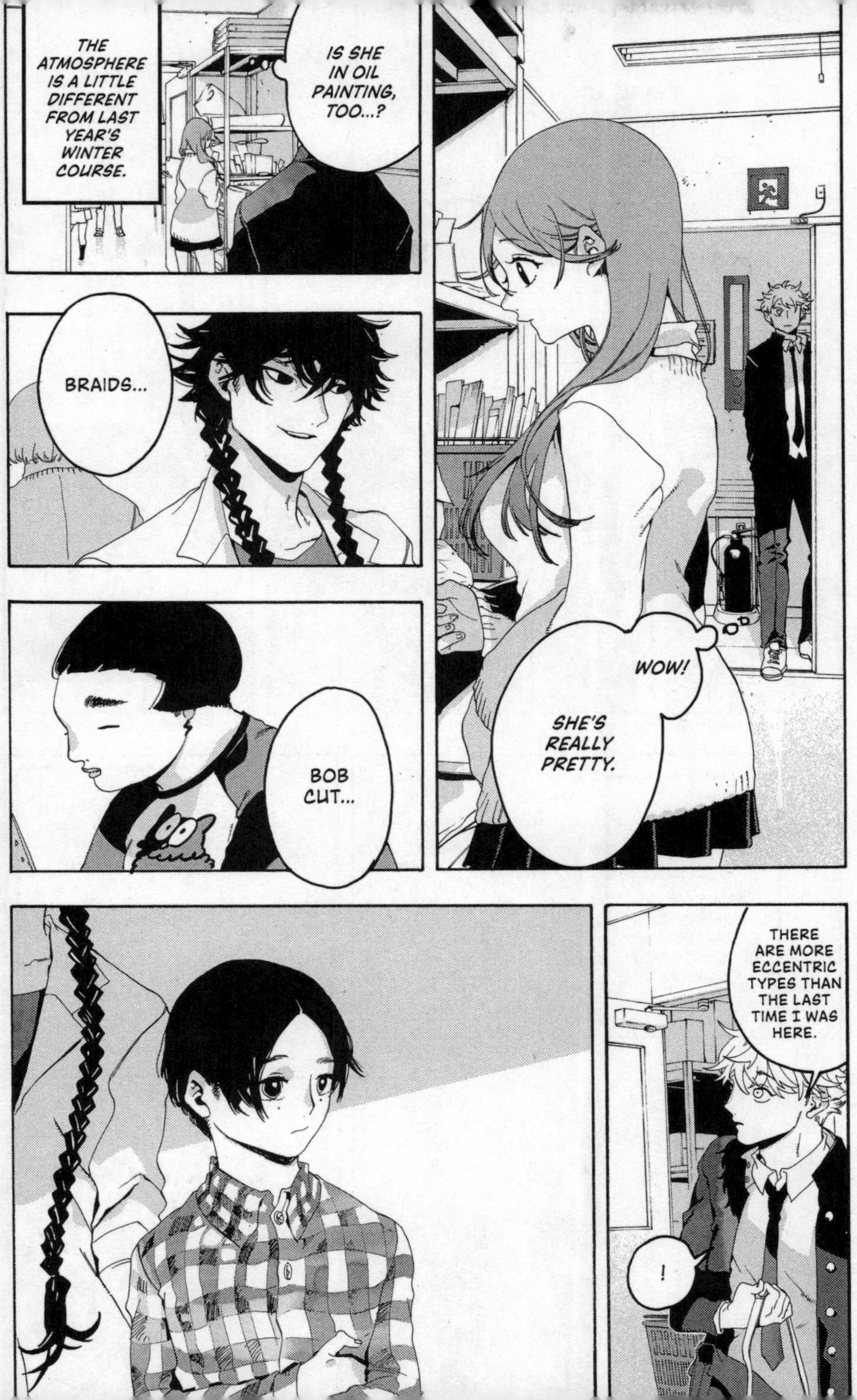
WOW!
SHE'S REALLY PRETTY.
THE ATMOSPHERE IS A LITTLE DIFFERENT FROM LAST YEAR'S WINTER COURSE.
IS SHE IN OIL PAINTING, TOO...?
BRAIDS...
BOB CUT...
THERE ARE MORE ECCENTRIC TYPES THAN THE LAST TIME I WAS HERE.
!

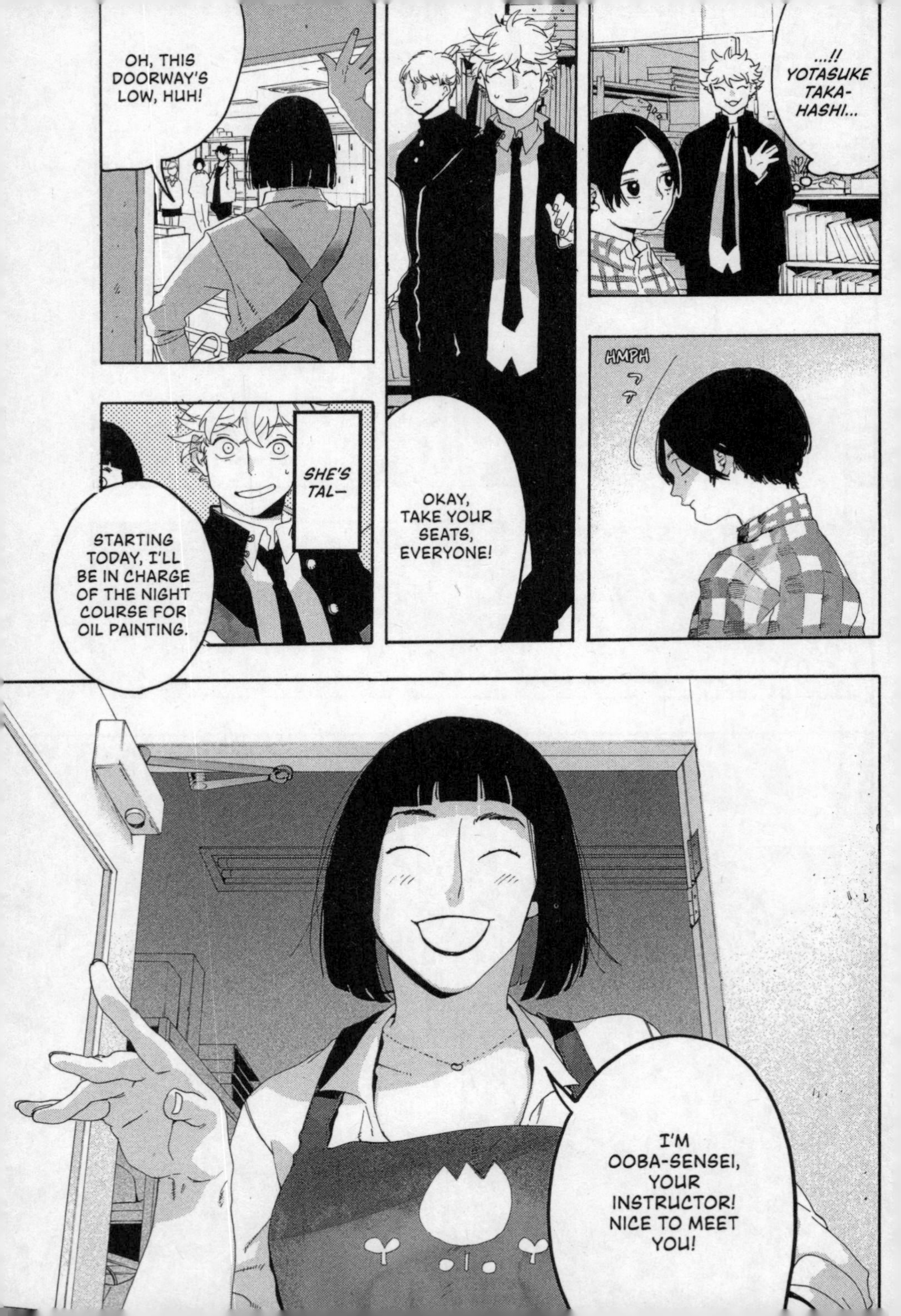
...!! YOTASUKE TAKA-HASHI...
OH, THIS DOORWAY'S LOW, HUH!
HMPH
OKAY, TAKE YOUR SEATS, EVERYONE!
SHE'S TAL—
STARTING TODAY, I'LL BE IN CHARGE OF THE NIGHT COURSE FOR OIL PAINTING.
I'M OOBA-SENSEI, YOUR INSTRUCTOR! NICE TO MEET YOU!

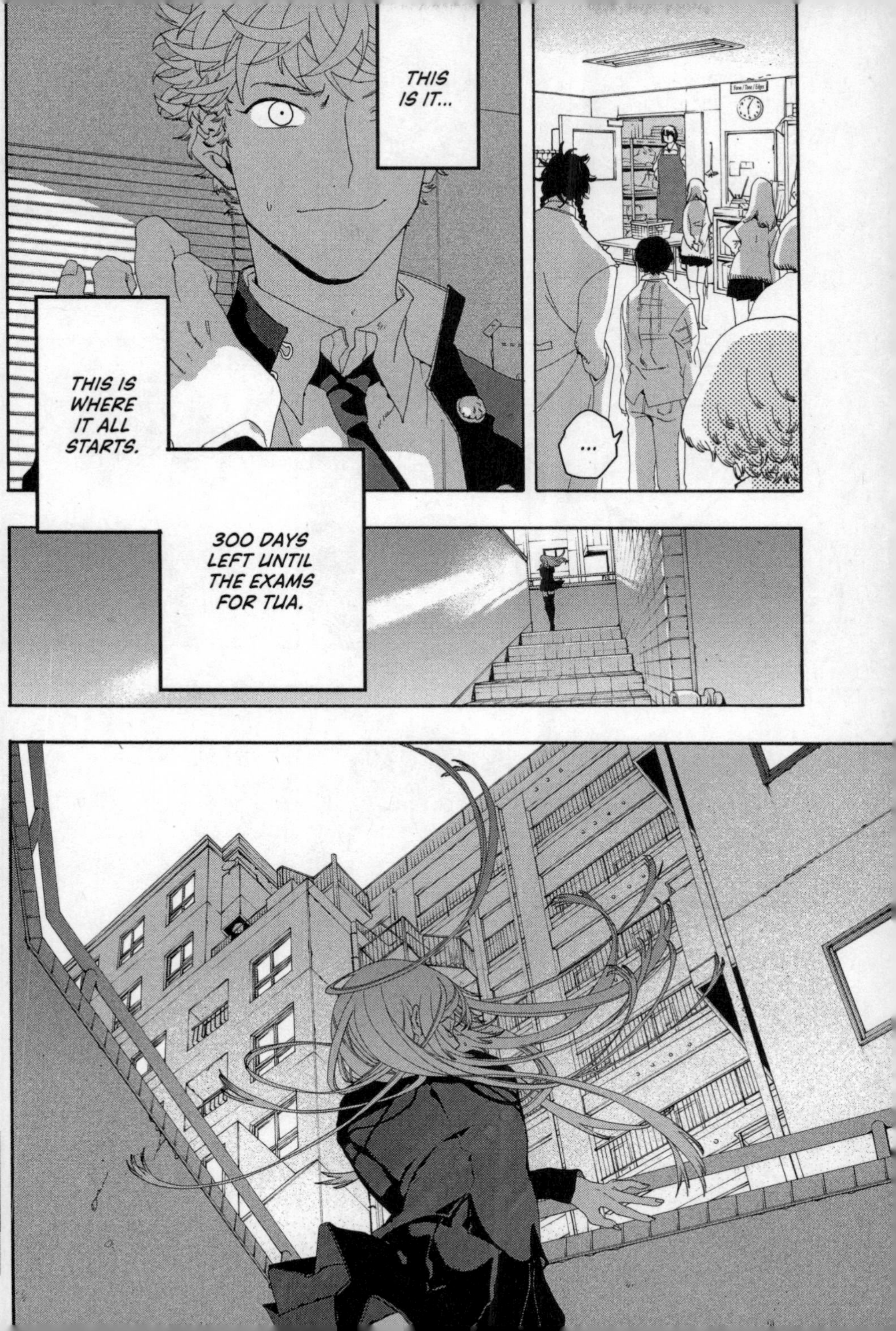
...
THIS IS IT...
THIS IS WHERE IT ALL STARTS.
300 DAYS LEFT UNTIL THE EXAMS FOR TUA.

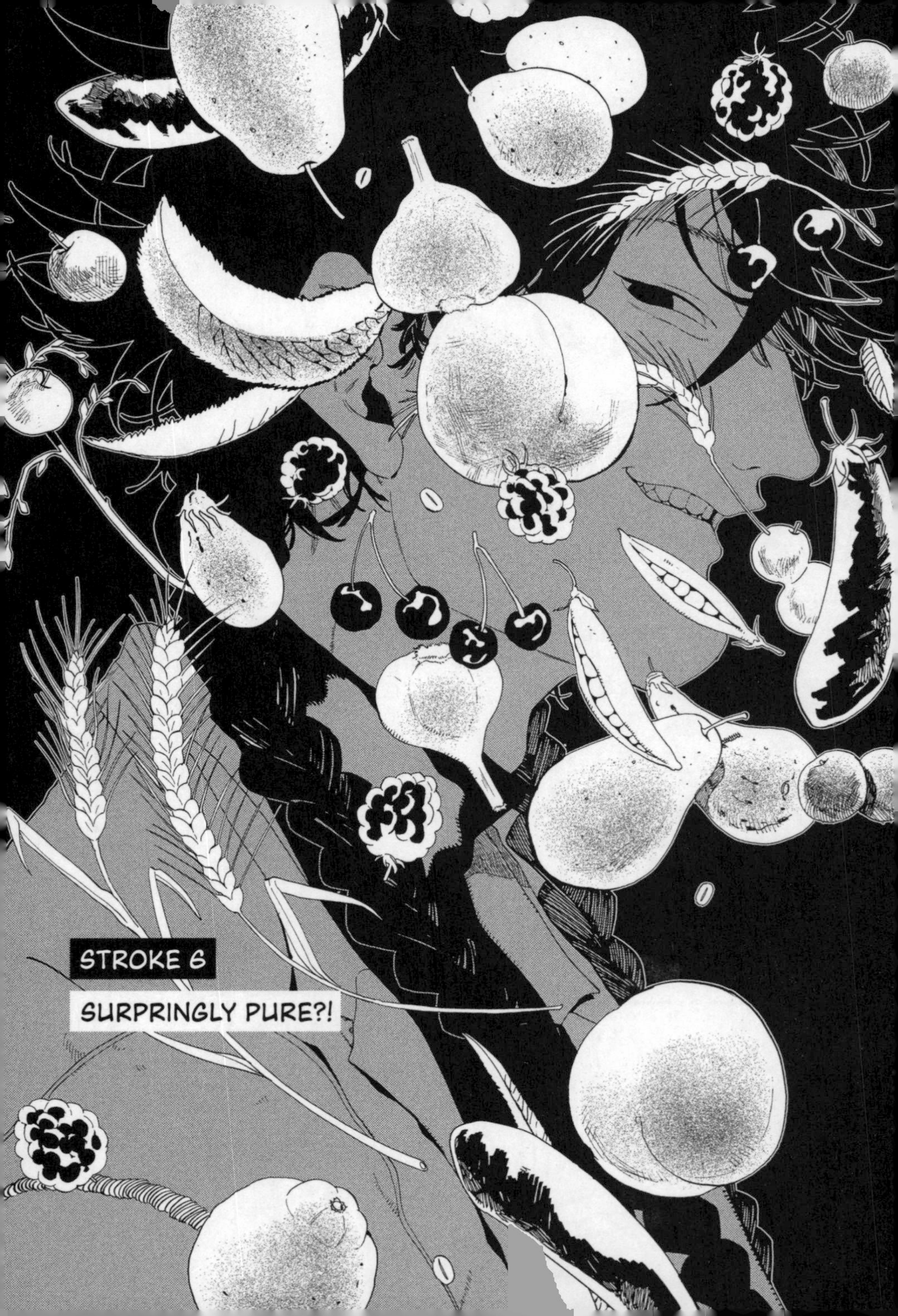
STROKE 6
SURPRINGLY PURE?!

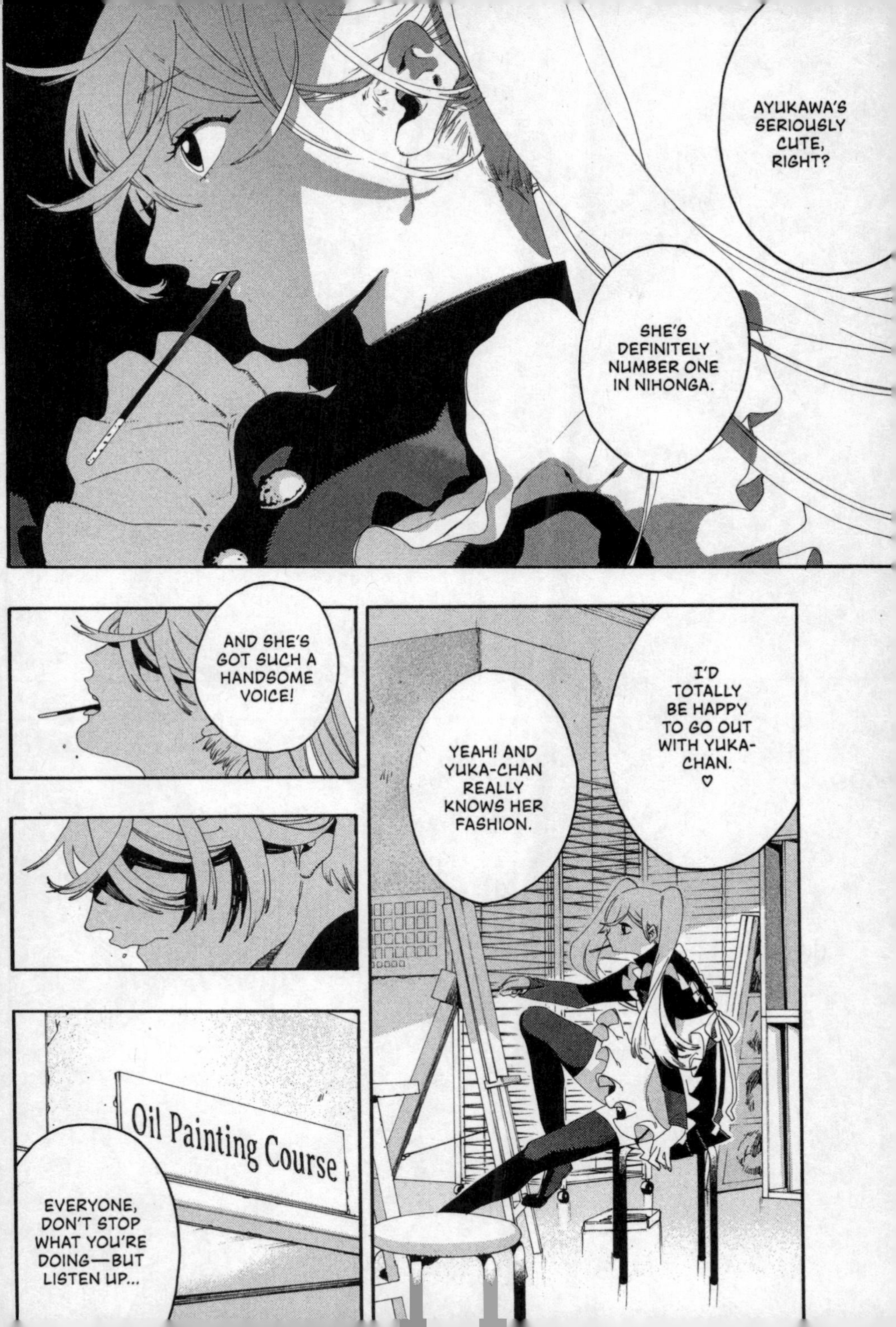
AYUKAWA'S SERIOUSLY CUTE, RIGHT?
SHE'S DEFINITELY NUMBER ONE IN NIHONGA.
I'D TOTALLY BE HAPPY TO GO OUT WITH YUKA-CHAN. ♡
YEAH! AND YUKA-CHAN REALLY KNOWS HER FASHION.
AND SHE'S GOT SUCH A HANDSOME VOICE!
Oil Painting Course
EVERYONE, DON'T STOP WHAT YOU'RE DOING—BUT LISTEN UP...

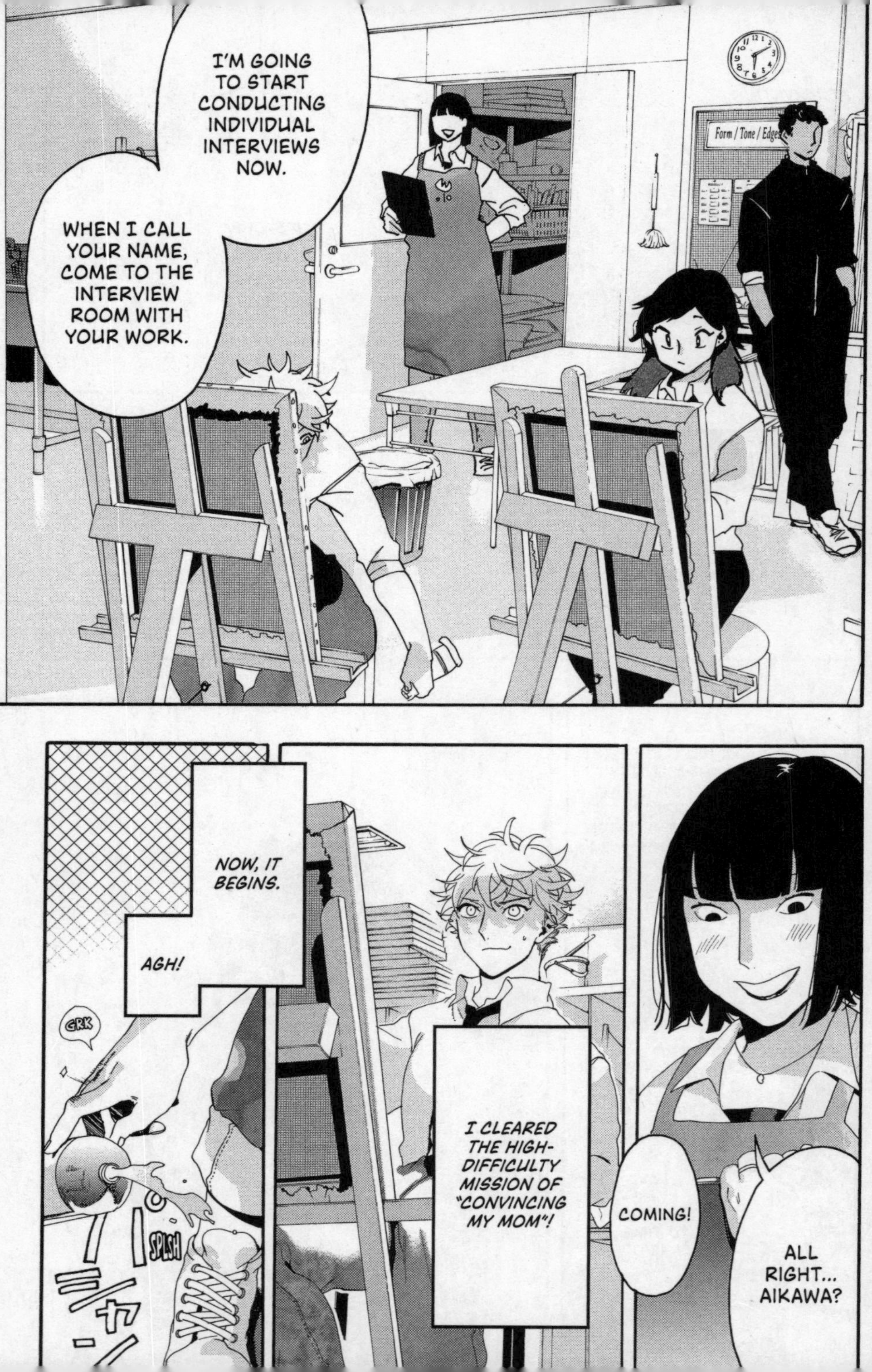
I'M GOING TO START CONDUCTING INDIVIDUAL INTERVIEWS NOW.
WHEN I CALL YOUR NAME, COME TO THE INTERVIEW ROOM WITH YOUR WORK.
Form / Tone / Edge
ALL RIGHT... AIKAWA?
COMING!
I CLEARED THE HIGH-DIFFICULTY MISSION OF "CONVINCING MY MOM"!
NOW, IT BEGINS.
AGH!
GRK
SPLSH

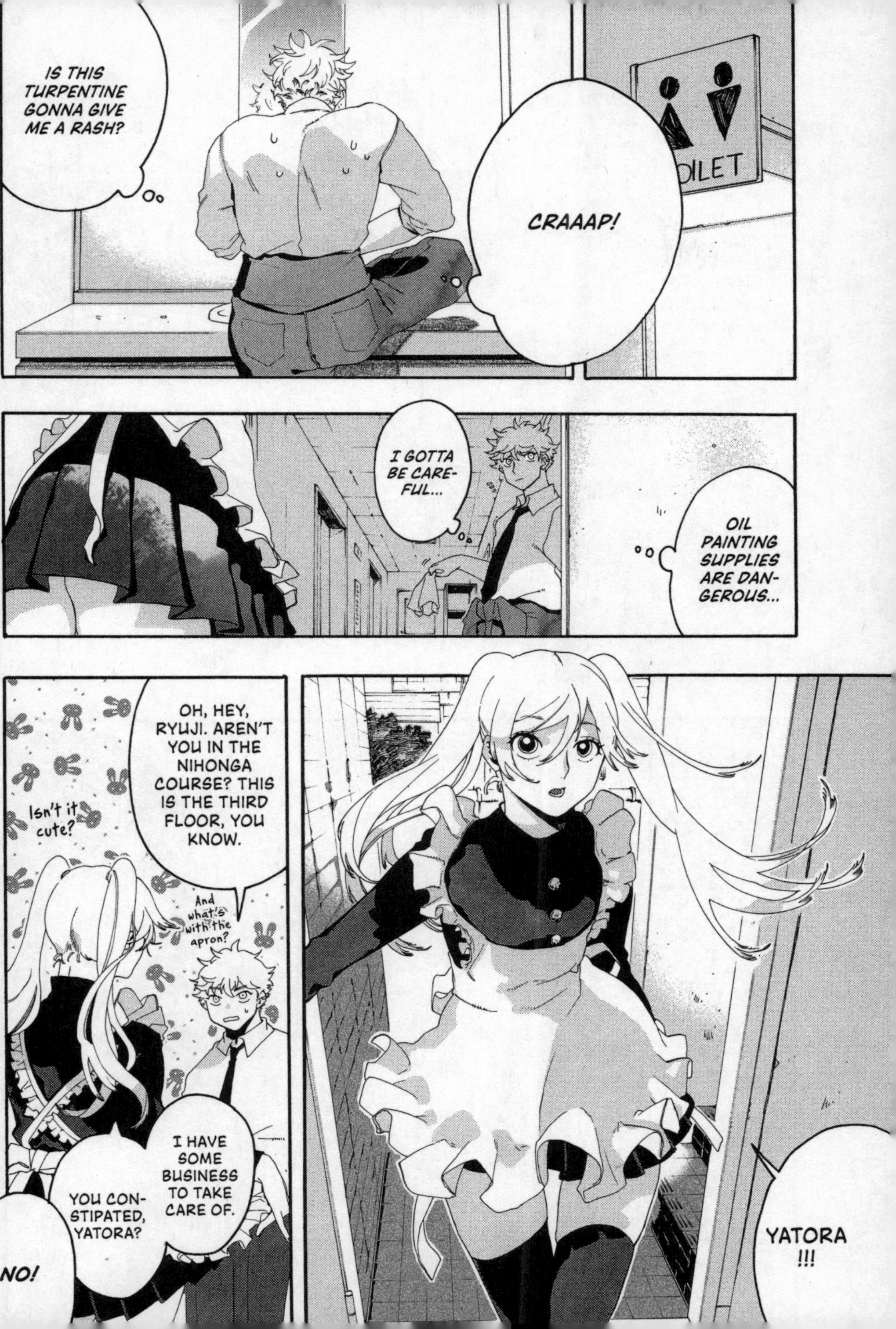
OILET
CRAAAP!
IS THIS TURPENTINE GONNA GIVE ME A RASH?
OIL PAINTING SUPPLIES ARE DANGEROUS...
I GOTTA BE CAREFUL...
YATORA !!!
OH, HEY, RYUJI. AREN'T YOU IN THE NIHONGA COURSE? THIS IS THE THIRD FLOOR, YOU KNOW.
Isn't it cute?
And what's with the apron?
I HAVE SOME BUSINESS TO TAKE CARE OF.
YOU CONSTIPATED, YATORA?
NO!

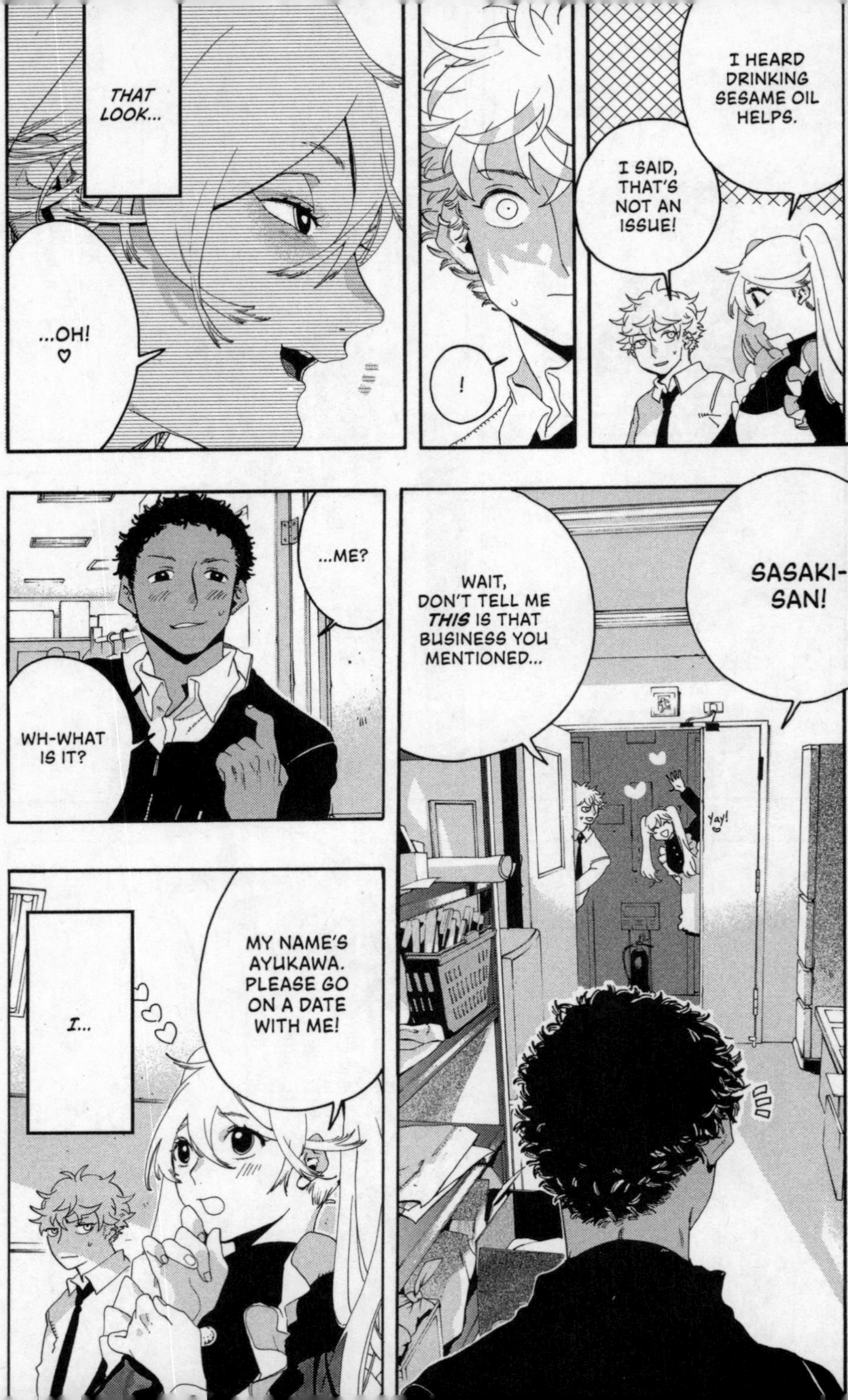
I HEARD DRINKING SESAME OIL HELPS.
I SAID, THAT'S NOT AN ISSUE!
!
THAT LOOK...
...OH! ♡
SASAKI-SAN!
WAIT, DON'T TELL ME *THIS* IS THAT BUSINESS YOU MENTIONED...
Yay!
...ME?
WH-WHAT IS IT?
MY NAME'S AYUKAWA. PLEASE GO ON A DATE WITH ME!
I...

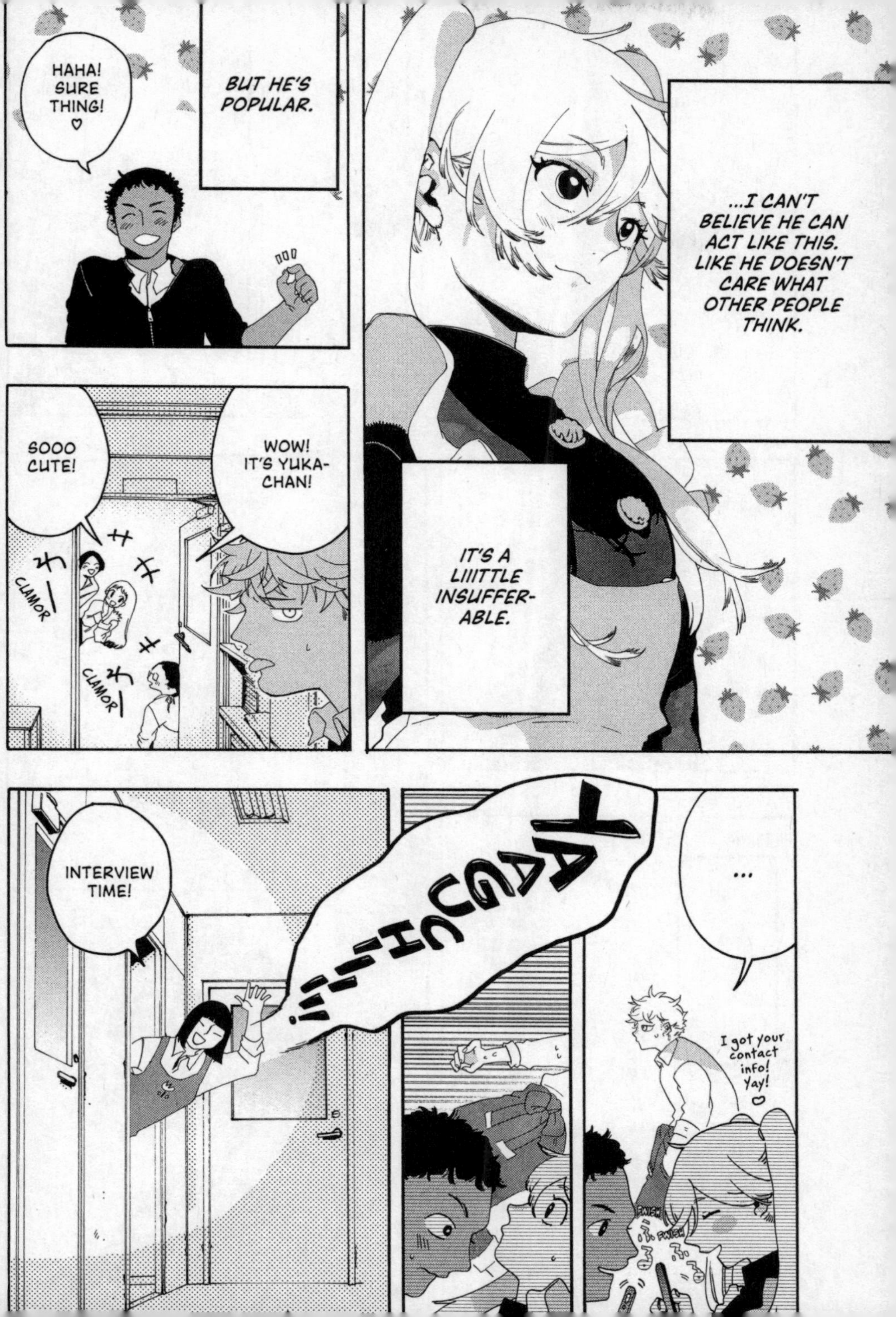
...I CAN'T BELIEVE HE CAN ACT LIKE THIS. LIKE HE DOESN'T CARE WHAT OTHER PEOPLE THINK.
IT'S A LIIITTLE INSUFFER-ABLE.
BUT HE'S POPULAR.
HAHA! SURE THING! ♡
WOW! IT'S YUKA-CHAN!
SOOO CUTE!
CLAMOR
CLAMOR
...
I got your contact info! Yay! ♡
YAGUCHI---!!
INTERVIEW TIME!

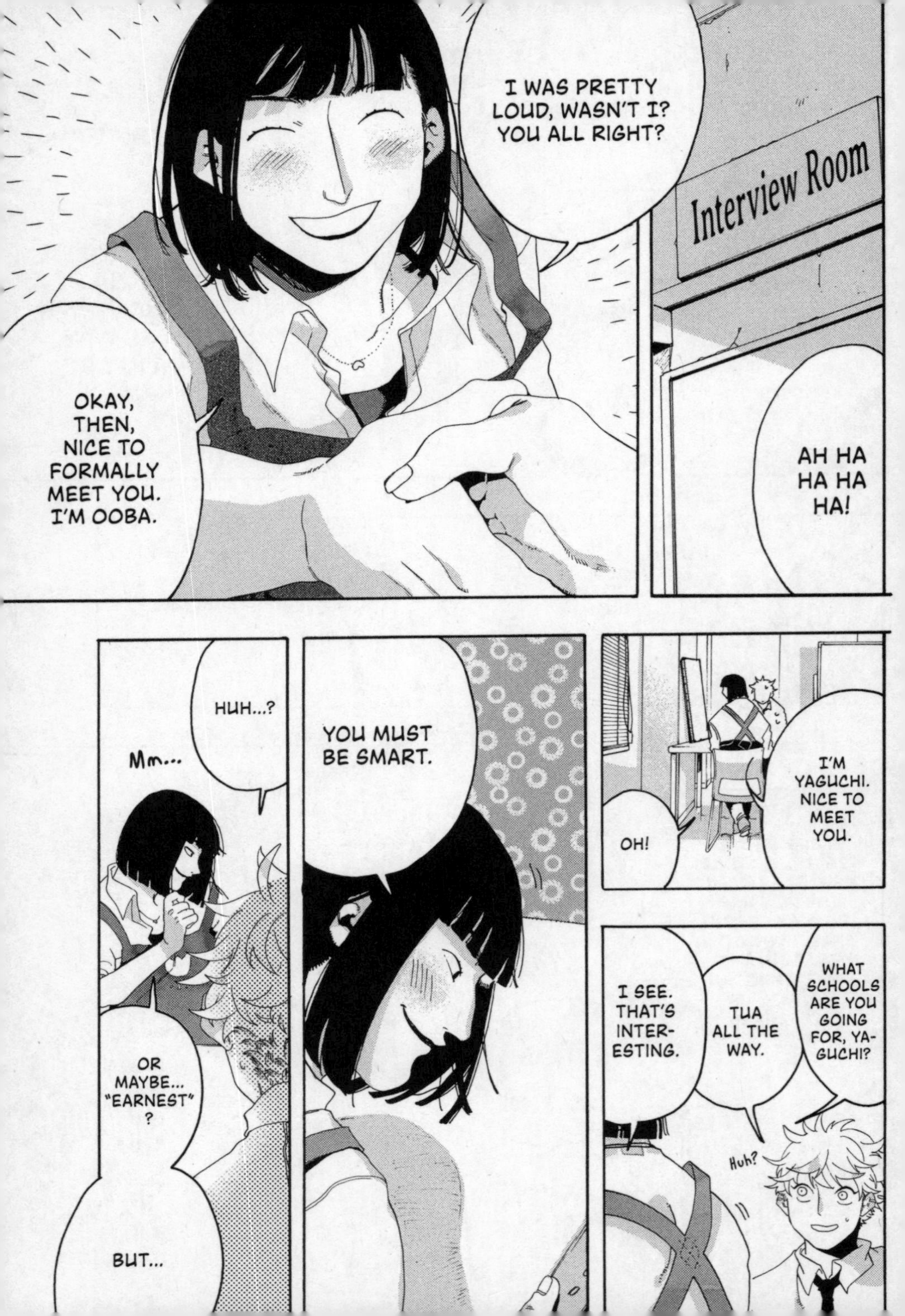
Interview Room
AH HA HA HA HA!
I WAS PRETTY LOUD, WASN'T I? YOU ALL RIGHT?
OKAY, THEN, NICE TO FORMALLY MEET YOU. I'M OOBA.
I'M YAGUCHI. NICE TO MEET YOU.
OH!
WHAT SCHOOLS ARE YOU GOING FOR, YAGUCHI?
TUA ALL THE WAY.
I SEE. THAT'S INTERESTING.
Huh?
YOU MUST BE SMART.
HUH...?
Mm...
OR MAYBE... "EARNEST"?
BUT...

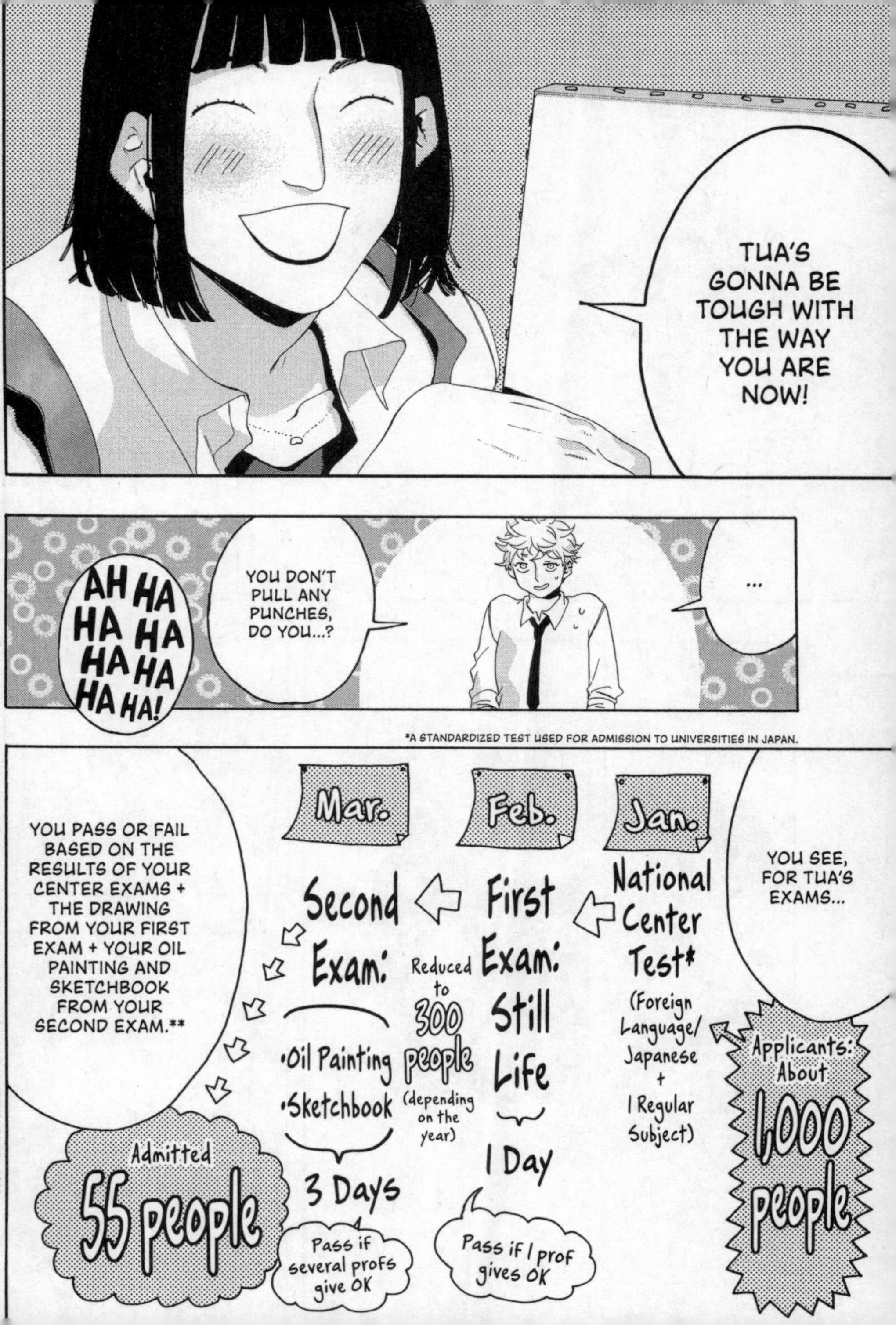
TUA'S GONNA BE TOUGH WITH THE WAY YOU ARE NOW!
...
YOU DON'T PULL ANY PUNCHES, DO YOU...?
AH HA HA HA HA HA HA HA!
YOU SEE, FOR TUA'S EXAMS...
Applicants: About 1,000 people
Jan.
National Center Test* (Foreign Language/Japanese + 1 Regular Subject)
Feb.
First Exam: Still Life
1 Day
Pass if 1 prof gives OK
Reduced to 300 people (depending on the year)
Mar.
Second Exam:
·Oil Painting
·Sketchbook
3 Days
Pass if several profs give OK
Admitted 55 people
YOU PASS OR FAIL BASED ON THE RESULTS OF YOUR CENTER EXAMS + THE DRAWING FROM YOUR FIRST EXAM + YOUR OIL PAINTING AND SKETCHBOOK FROM YOUR SECOND EXAM.**

*A STANDARDIZED TEST USED FOR ADMISSION TO UNIVERSITIES IN JAPAN.

**AS RESEARCHED BY THE AUTHOR IN 2017. THIS INFORMATION DIFFERS YEAR BY YEAR.

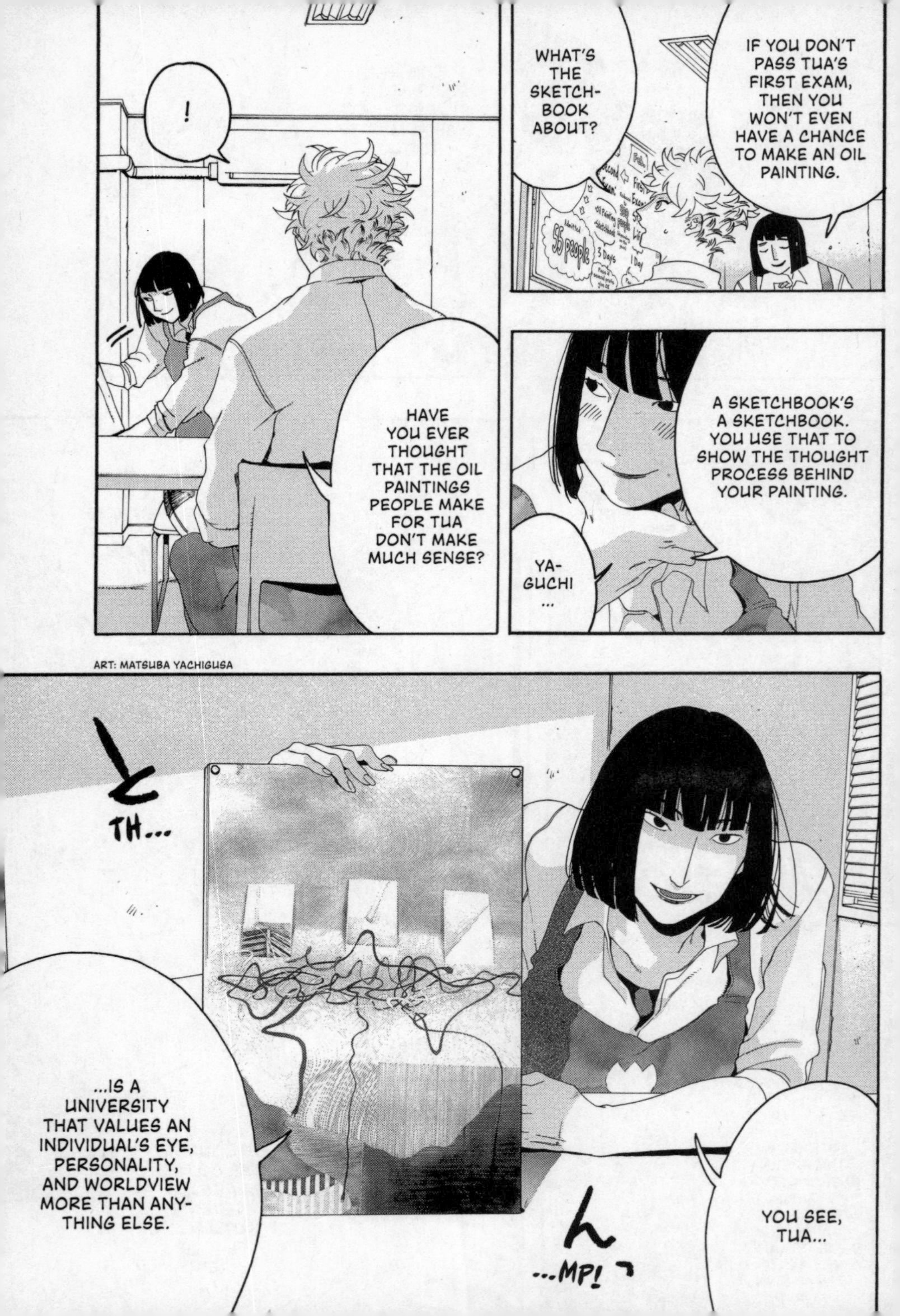
IF YOU DON'T PASS TUA'S FIRST EXAM, THEN YOU WON'T EVEN HAVE A CHANCE TO MAKE AN OIL PAINTING.
WHAT'S THE SKETCH-BOOK ABOUT?
A SKETCHBOOK'S A SKETCHBOOK. YOU USE THAT TO SHOW THE THOUGHT PROCESS BEHIND YOUR PAINTING.
YA-GUCHI ...
!
HAVE YOU EVER THOUGHT THAT THE OIL PAINTINGS PEOPLE MAKE FOR TUA DON'T MAKE MUCH SENSE?
ART: MATSUBA YACHIGUSA
TH...
YOU SEE, TUA...
...IS A UNIVERSITY THAT VALUES AN INDIVIDUAL'S EYE, PERSONALITY, AND WORLDVIEW MORE THAN ANY-THING ELSE.
...MP!

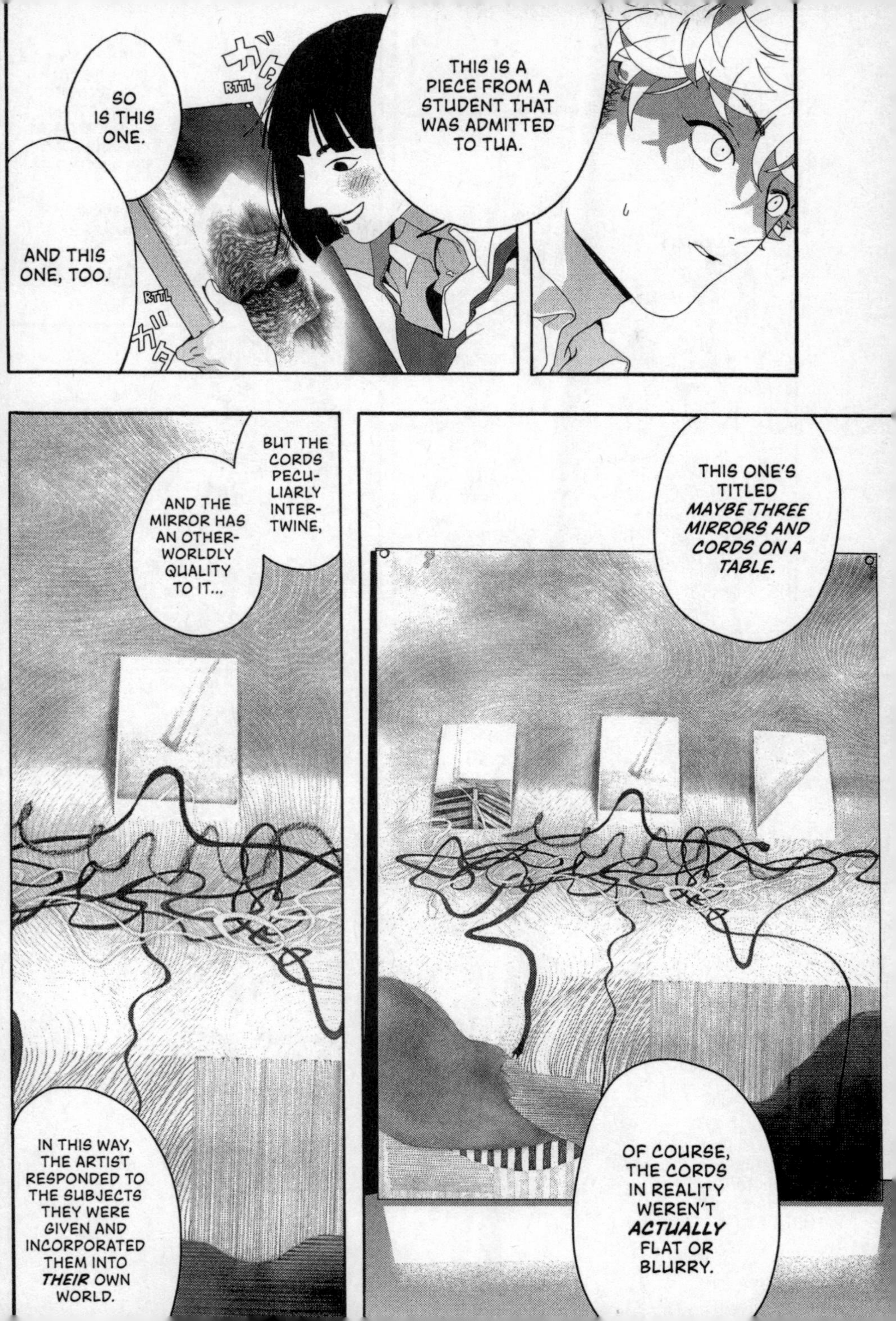
THIS IS A PIECE FROM A STUDENT THAT WAS ADMITTED TO TUA.
SO IS THIS ONE.
RTTL
AND THIS ONE, TOO.
RTTL
THIS ONE'S TITLED *MAYBE THREE MIRRORS AND CORDS ON A TABLE.*
OF COURSE, THE CORDS IN REALITY WEREN'T ***ACTUALLY*** FLAT OR BLURRY.
BUT THE CORDS PECULIARLY INTERTWINE,
AND THE MIRROR HAS AN OTHERWORLDLY QUALITY TO IT...
IN THIS WAY, THE ARTIST RESPONDED TO THE SUBJECTS THEY WERE GIVEN AND INCORPORATED THEM INTO ***THEIR*** OWN WORLD.

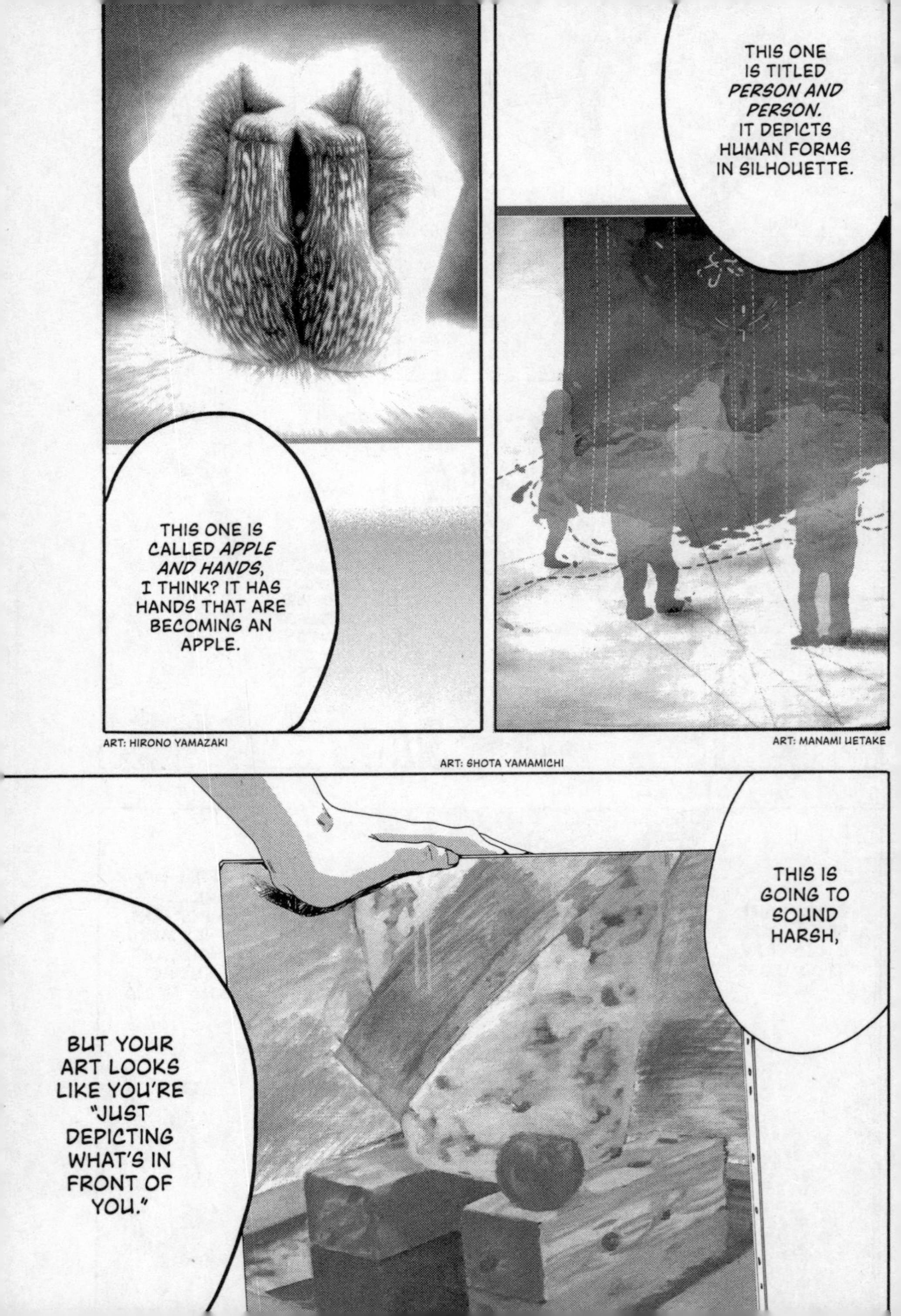
THIS ONE IS TITLED *PERSON AND PERSON.* IT DEPICTS HUMAN FORMS IN SILHOUETTE.
ART: MANAMI UETAKE
THIS ONE IS CALLED *APPLE AND HANDS*, I THINK? IT HAS HANDS THAT ARE BECOMING AN APPLE.
ART: HIRONO YAMAZAKI
ART: SHOTA YAMAMICHI
THIS IS GOING TO SOUND HARSH,
BUT YOUR ART LOOKS LIKE YOU'RE "JUST DEPICTING WHAT'S IN FRONT OF YOU."

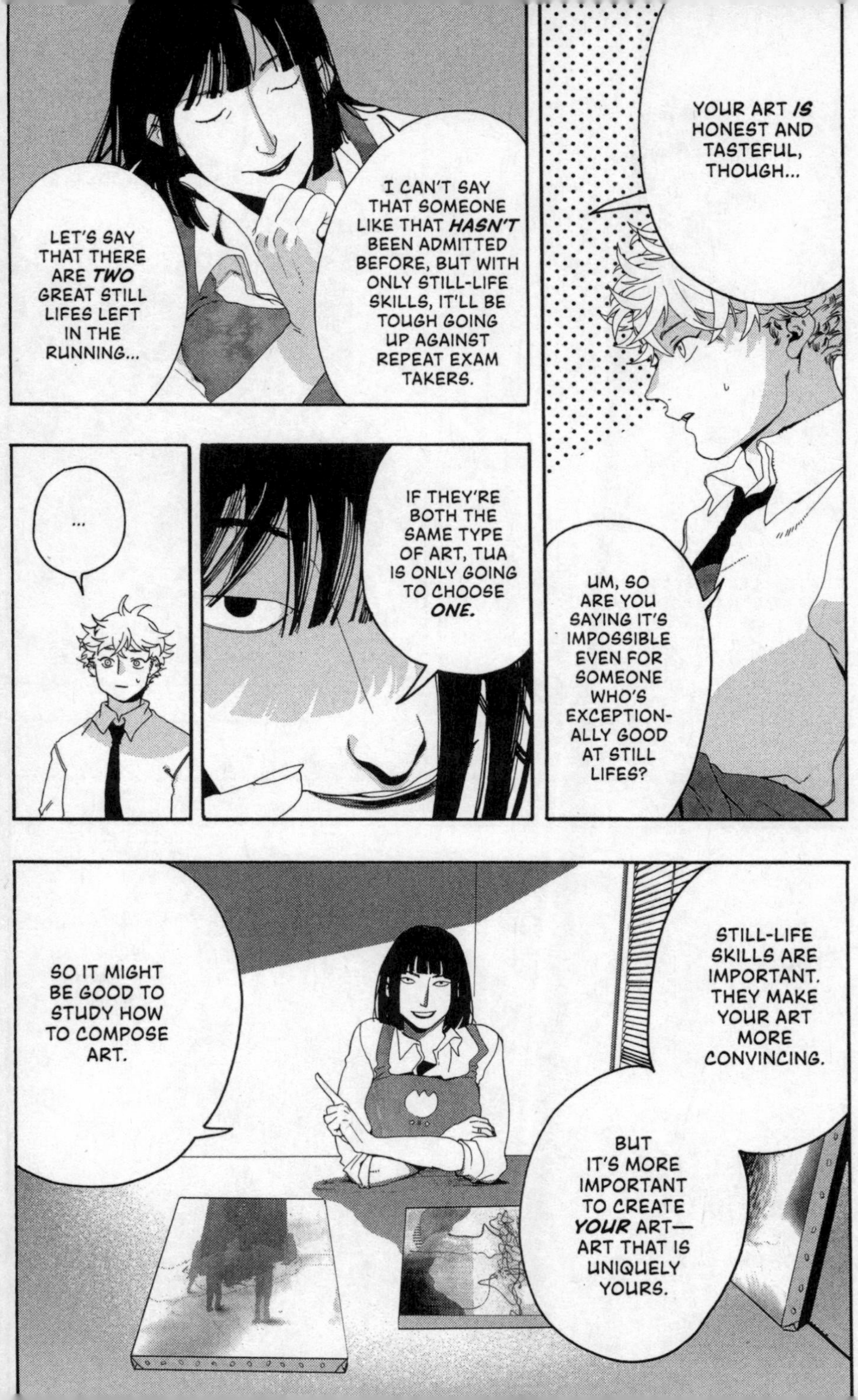
YOUR ART *IS* HONEST AND TASTEFUL, THOUGH...
UM, SO ARE YOU SAYING IT'S IMPOSSIBLE EVEN FOR SOMEONE WHO'S EXCEPTION-ALLY GOOD AT STILL LIFES?
I CAN'T SAY THAT SOMEONE LIKE THAT ***HASN'T*** BEEN ADMITTED BEFORE, BUT WITH ONLY STILL-LIFE SKILLS, IT'LL BE TOUGH GOING UP AGAINST REPEAT EXAM TAKERS.
LET'S SAY THAT THERE ARE ***TWO*** GREAT STILL LIFES LEFT IN THE RUNNING...
IF THEY'RE BOTH THE SAME TYPE OF ART, TUA IS ONLY GOING TO CHOOSE ***ONE.***
...
STILL-LIFE SKILLS ARE IMPORTANT. THEY MAKE YOUR ART MORE CONVINCING.
BUT IT'S MORE IMPORTANT TO CREATE ***YOUR*** ART— ART THAT IS UNIQUELY YOURS.
SO IT MIGHT BE GOOD TO STUDY HOW TO COMPOSE ART.

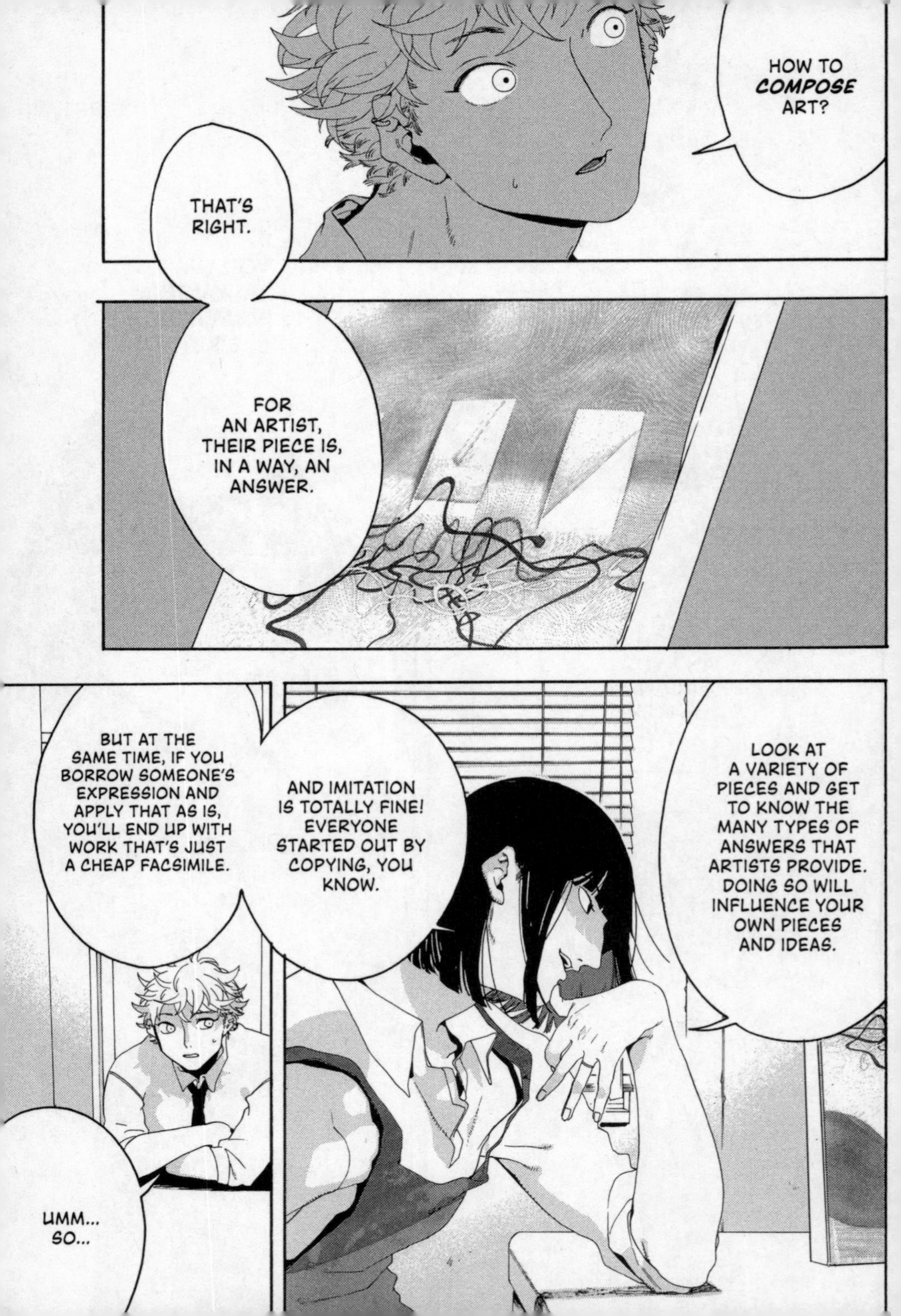
HOW TO *COMPOSE* ART?
THAT'S RIGHT.
FOR AN ARTIST, THEIR PIECE IS, IN A WAY, AN ANSWER.
LOOK AT A VARIETY OF PIECES AND GET TO KNOW THE MANY TYPES OF ANSWERS THAT ARTISTS PROVIDE. DOING SO WILL INFLUENCE YOUR OWN PIECES AND IDEAS.
AND IMITATION IS TOTALLY FINE! EVERYONE STARTED OUT BY COPYING, YOU KNOW.
BUT AT THE SAME TIME, IF YOU BORROW SOMEONE'S EXPRESSION AND APPLY THAT AS IS, YOU'LL END UP WITH WORK THAT'S JUST A CHEAP FACSIMILE.
UMM... SO...

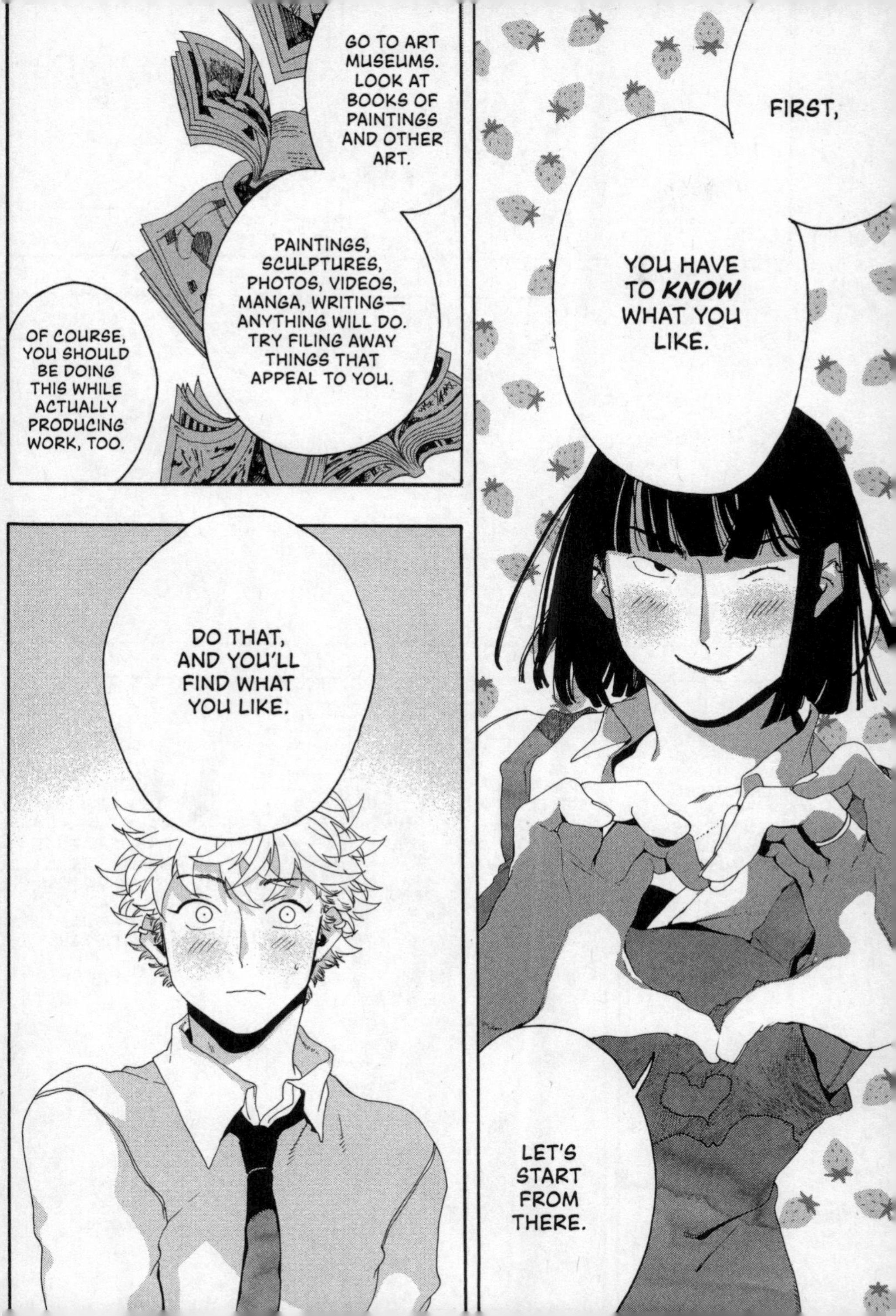
FIRST,
YOU HAVE TO *KNOW* WHAT YOU LIKE.
LET'S START FROM THERE.
GO TO ART MUSEUMS. LOOK AT BOOKS OF PAINTINGS AND OTHER ART.
PAINTINGS, SCULPTURES, PHOTOS, VIDEOS, MANGA, WRITING—ANYTHING WILL DO. TRY FILING AWAY THINGS THAT APPEAL TO YOU.
OF COURSE, YOU SHOULD BE DOING THIS WHILE ACTUALLY PRODUCING WORK, TOO.
DO THAT, AND YOU'LL FIND WHAT YOU LIKE.

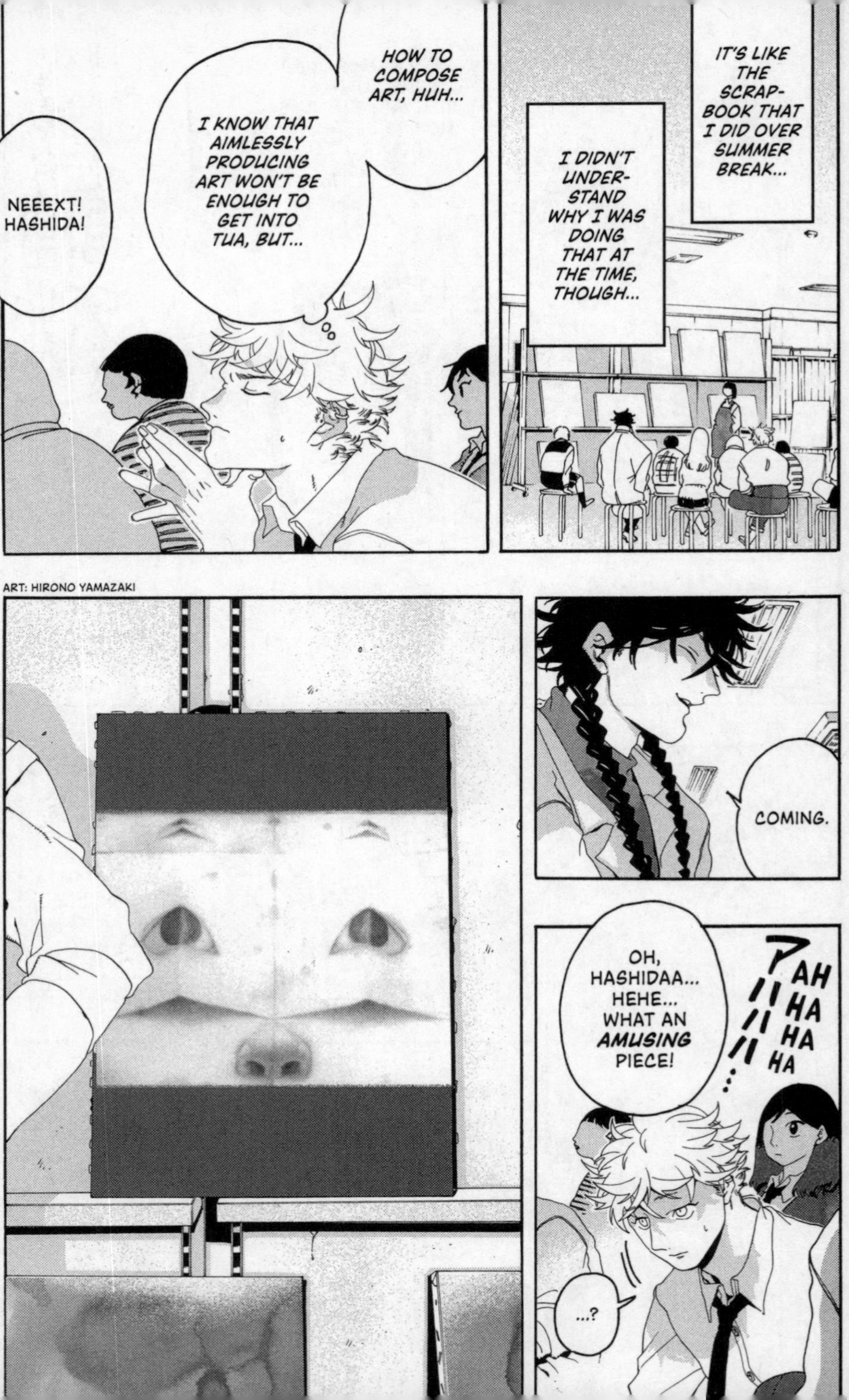
IT'S LIKE THE SCRAPBOOK THAT I DID OVER SUMMER BREAK...
I DIDN'T UNDERSTAND WHY I WAS DOING THAT AT THE TIME, THOUGH...
HOW TO COMPOSE ART, HUH...
I KNOW THAT AIMLESSLY PRODUCING ART WON'T BE ENOUGH TO GET INTO TUA, BUT...
NEEEXT! HASHIDA!
COMING.
OH, HASHIDAA... HEHE... WHAT AN AMUSING PIECE!
PAHAHAHAHA
...?
ART: HIRONO YAMAZAKI

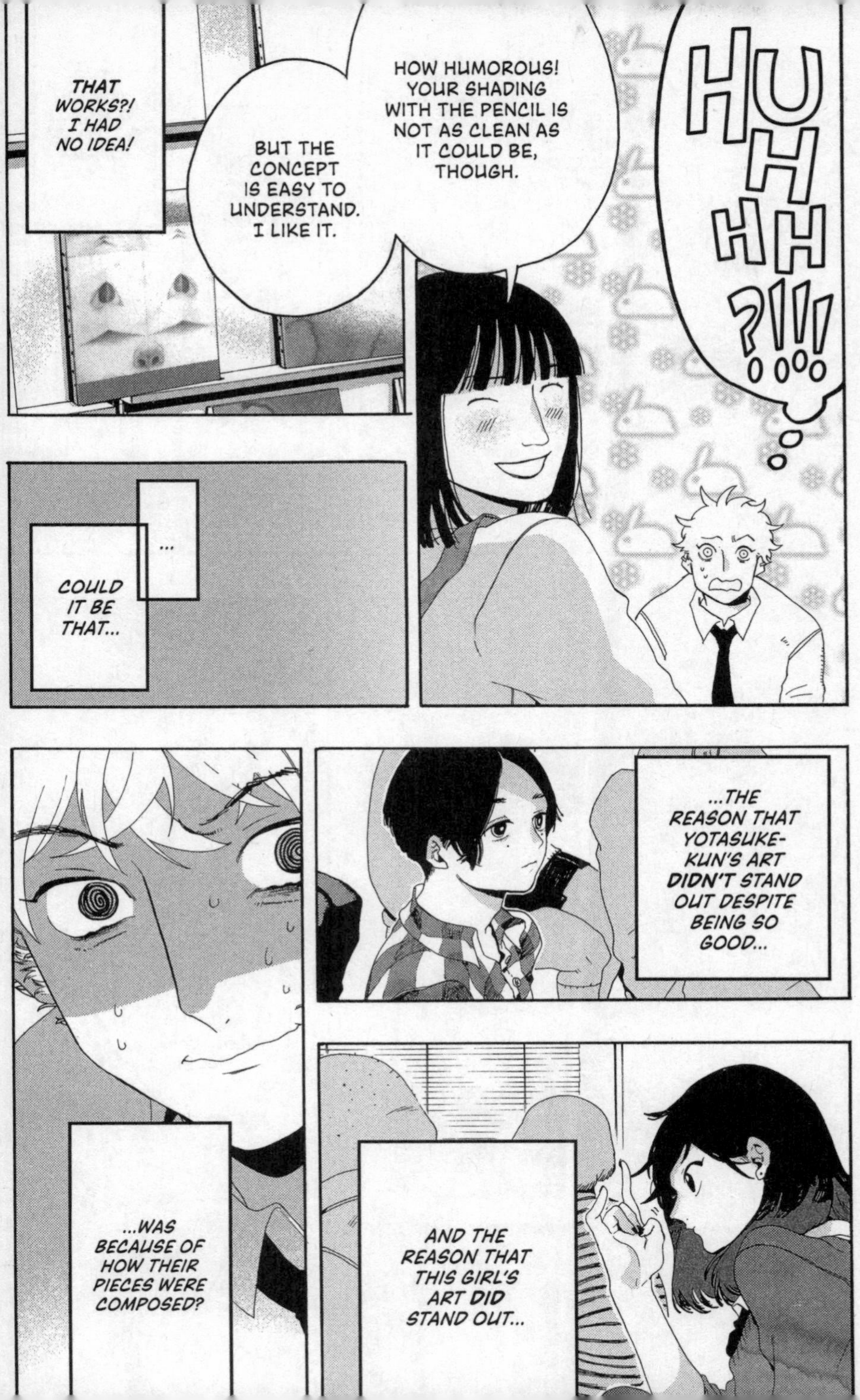
HUHHHHH?!!!
HOW HUMOROUS! YOUR SHADING WITH THE PENCIL IS NOT AS CLEAN AS IT COULD BE, THOUGH.
BUT THE CONCEPT IS EASY TO UNDERSTAND. I LIKE IT.
THAT WORKS?! I HAD NO IDEA!
...
COULD IT BE THAT...
...THE REASON THAT YOTASUKE-KUN'S ART DIDN'T STAND OUT DESPITE BEING SO GOOD...
AND THE REASON THAT THIS GIRL'S ART DID STAND OUT...
...WAS BECAUSE OF HOW THEIR PIECES WERE COMPOSED?

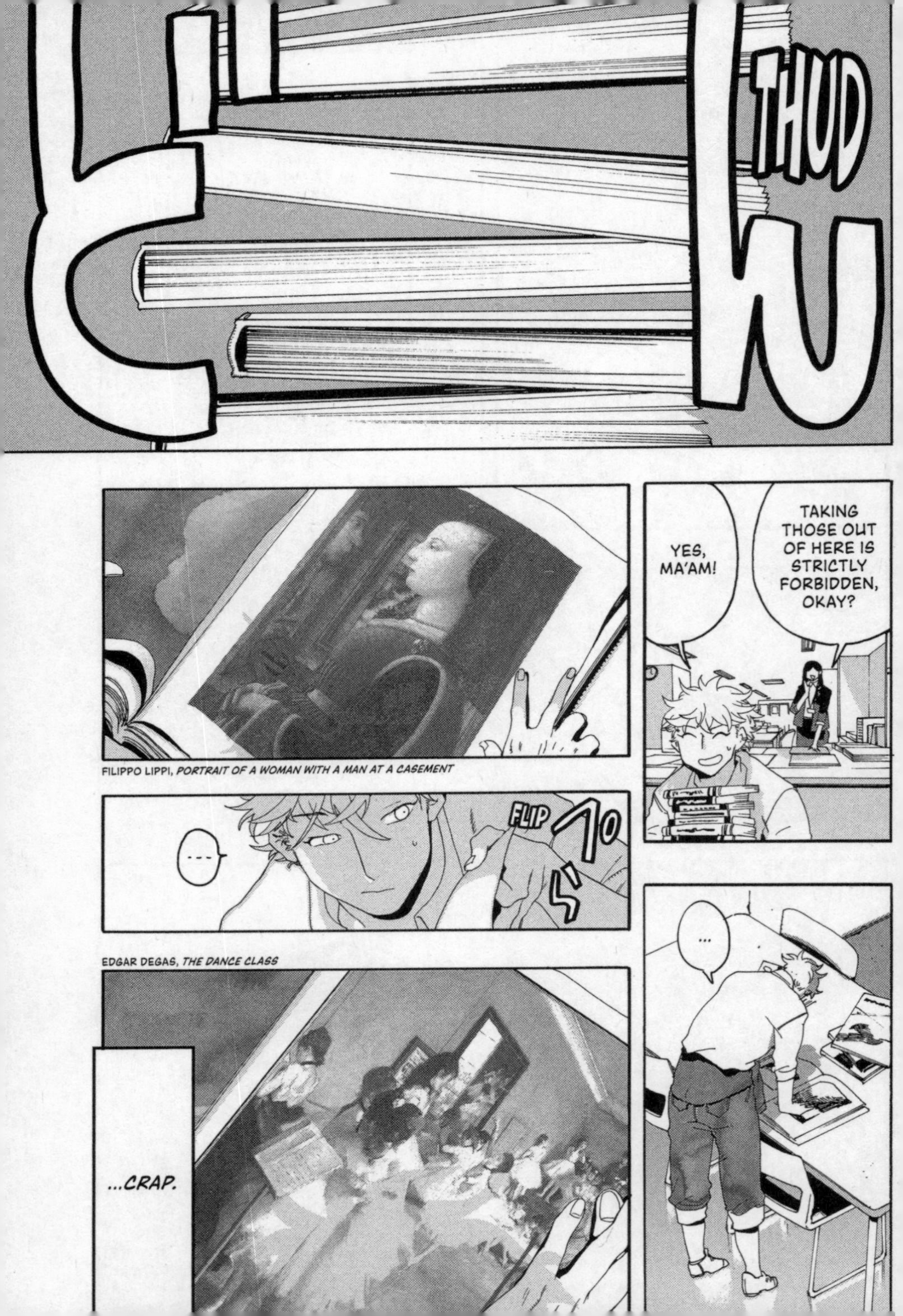
THUD
TAKING THOSE OUT OF HERE IS STRICTLY FORBIDDEN, OKAY?
YES, MA'AM!
...
FILIPPO LIPPI, *PORTRAIT OF A WOMAN WITH A MAN AT A CASEMENT*
- - -
FLIP
EDGAR DEGAS, *THE DANCE CLASS*
...CRAP.

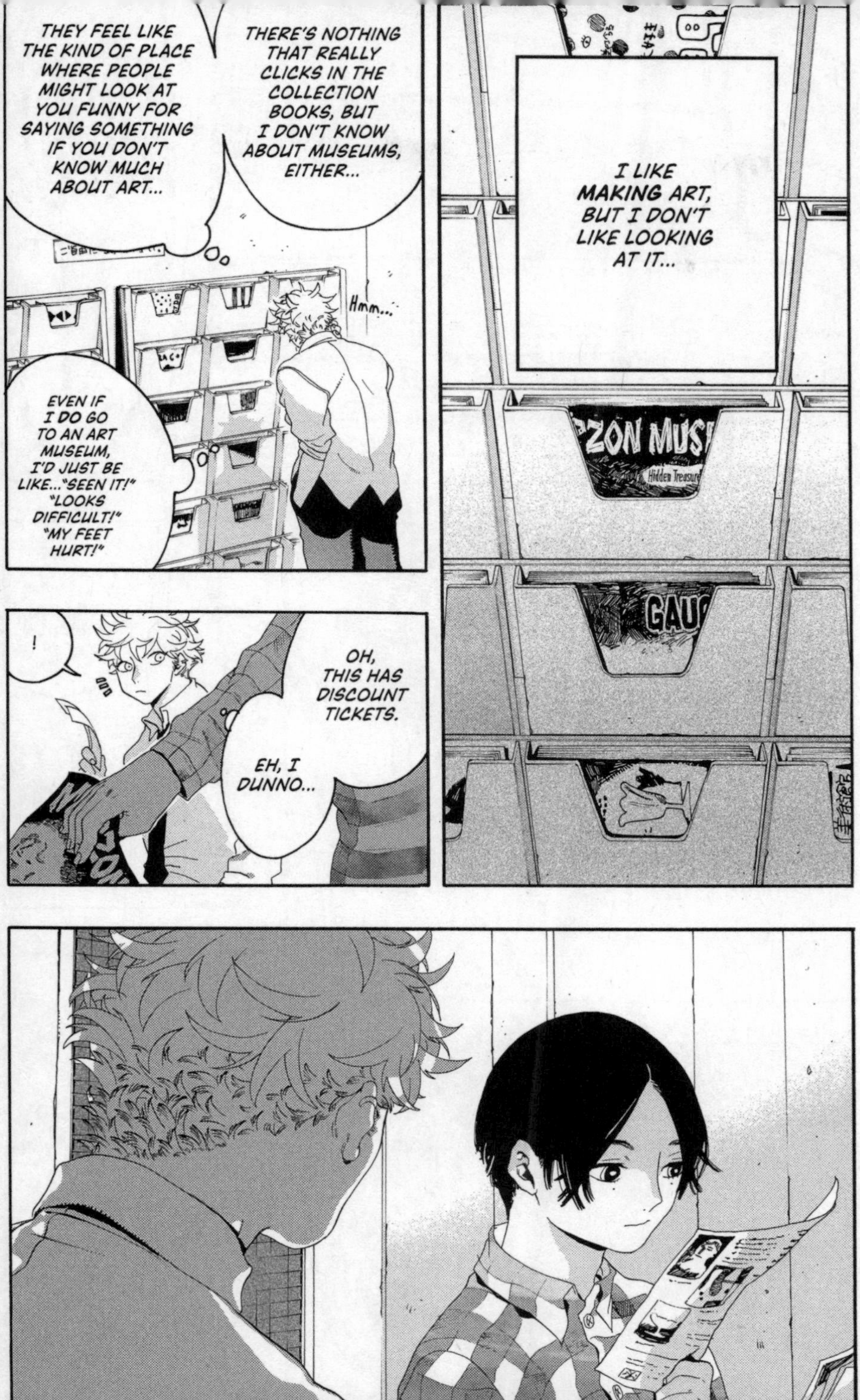
I LIKE MAKING ART, BUT I DON'T LIKE LOOKING AT IT...
THERE'S NOTHING THAT REALLY CLICKS IN THE COLLECTION BOOKS, BUT I DON'T KNOW ABOUT MUSEUMS, EITHER...
THEY FEEL LIKE THE KIND OF PLACE WHERE PEOPLE MIGHT LOOK AT YOU FUNNY FOR SAYING SOMETHING IF YOU DON'T KNOW MUCH ABOUT ART...
Hmm...
EVEN IF I DO GO TO AN ART MUSEUM, I'D JUST BE LIKE..."SEEN IT!" "LOOKS DIFFICULT!" "MY FEET HURT!"
OH, THIS HAS DISCOUNT TICKETS.
EH, I DUNNO...
!

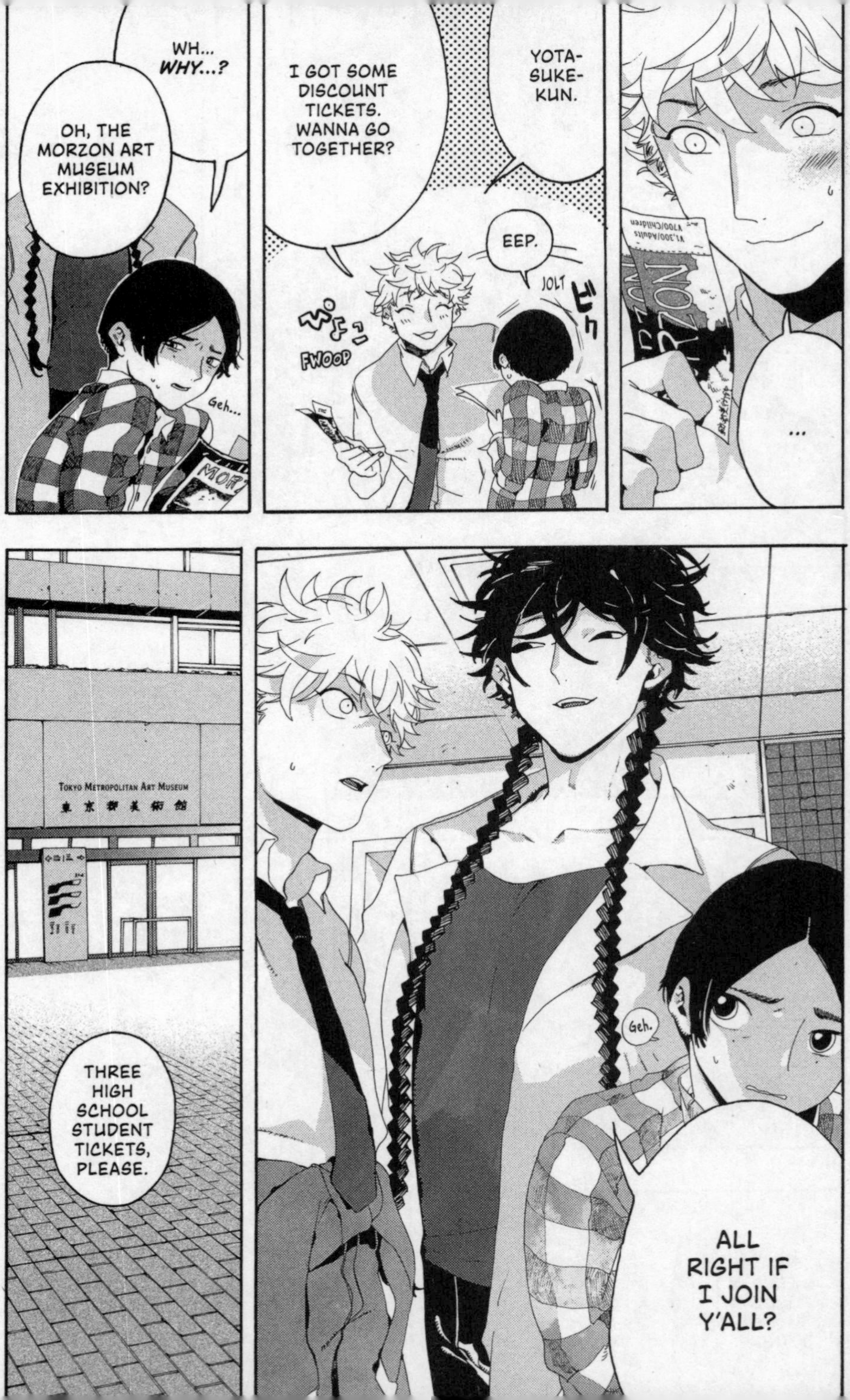
...
YOTA-SUKE-KUN.
I GOT SOME DISCOUNT TICKETS. WANNA GO TOGETHER?
EEP.
JOLT
FWOOP
WH... WHY...?
OH, THE MORZON ART MUSEUM EXHIBITION?
Geh...
ALL RIGHT IF I JOIN Y'ALL?
Geh.
TOKYO METROPOLITAN ART MUSEUM
東京都美術館
THREE HIGH SCHOOL STUDENT TICKETS, PLEASE.

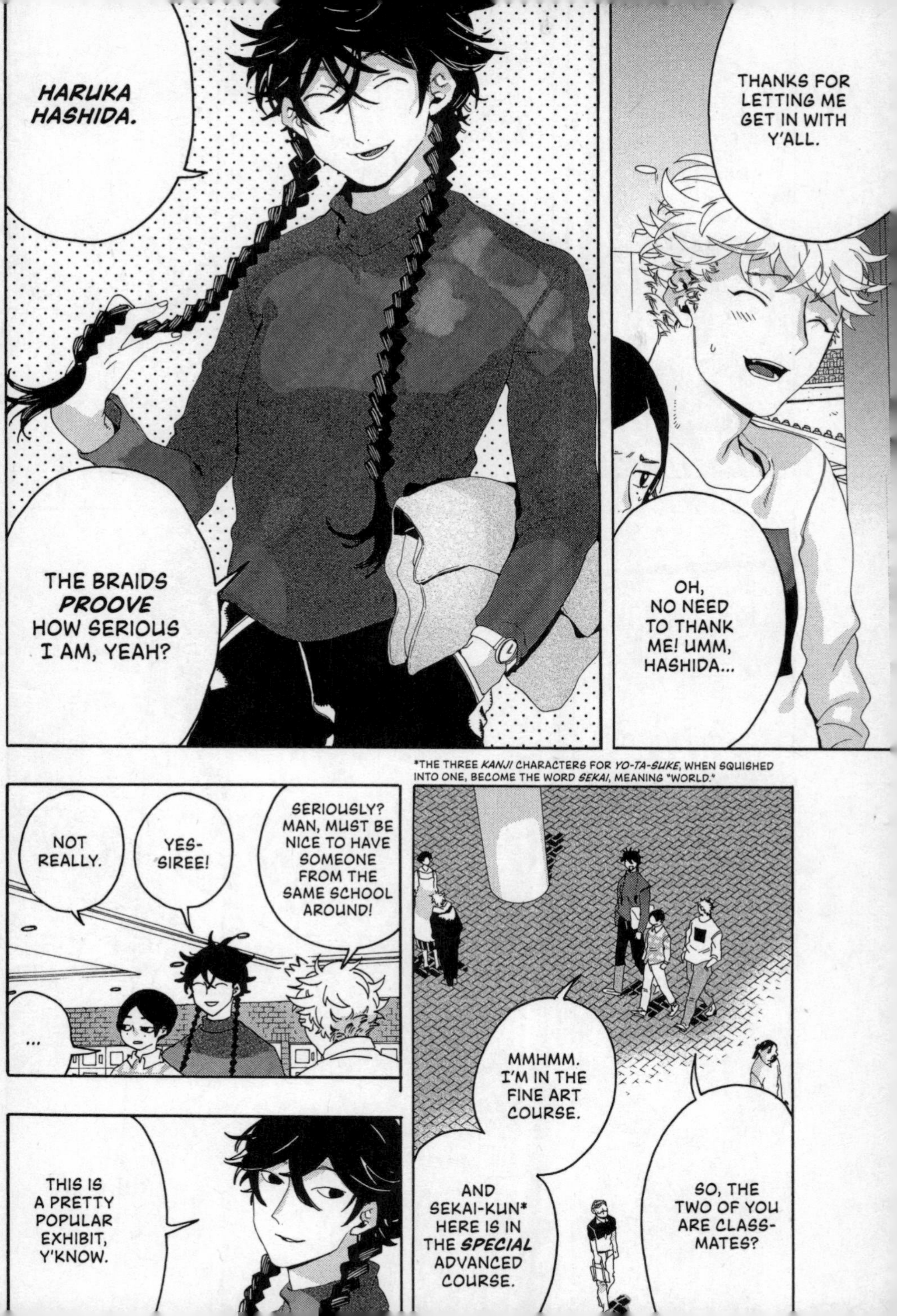
THANKS FOR LETTING ME GET IN WITH Y'ALL.
OH, NO NEED TO THANK ME! UMM, HASHIDA...
HARUKA HASHIDA.
THE BRAIDS PROOVE HOW SERIOUS I AM, YEAH?
SO, THE TWO OF YOU ARE CLASS-MATES?
MMHMM. I'M IN THE FINE ART COURSE.
AND SEKAI-KUN* HERE IS IN THE SPECIAL ADVANCED COURSE.
SERIOUSLY? MAN, MUST BE NICE TO HAVE SOMEONE FROM THE SAME SCHOOL AROUND!
YES-SIREE!
NOT REALLY.
...
THIS IS A PRETTY POPULAR EXHIBIT, Y'KNOW.

*THE THREE KANJI CHARACTERS FOR YO-TA-SUKE, WHEN SQUISHED INTO ONE, BECOME THE WORD SEKAI, MEANING "WORLD."

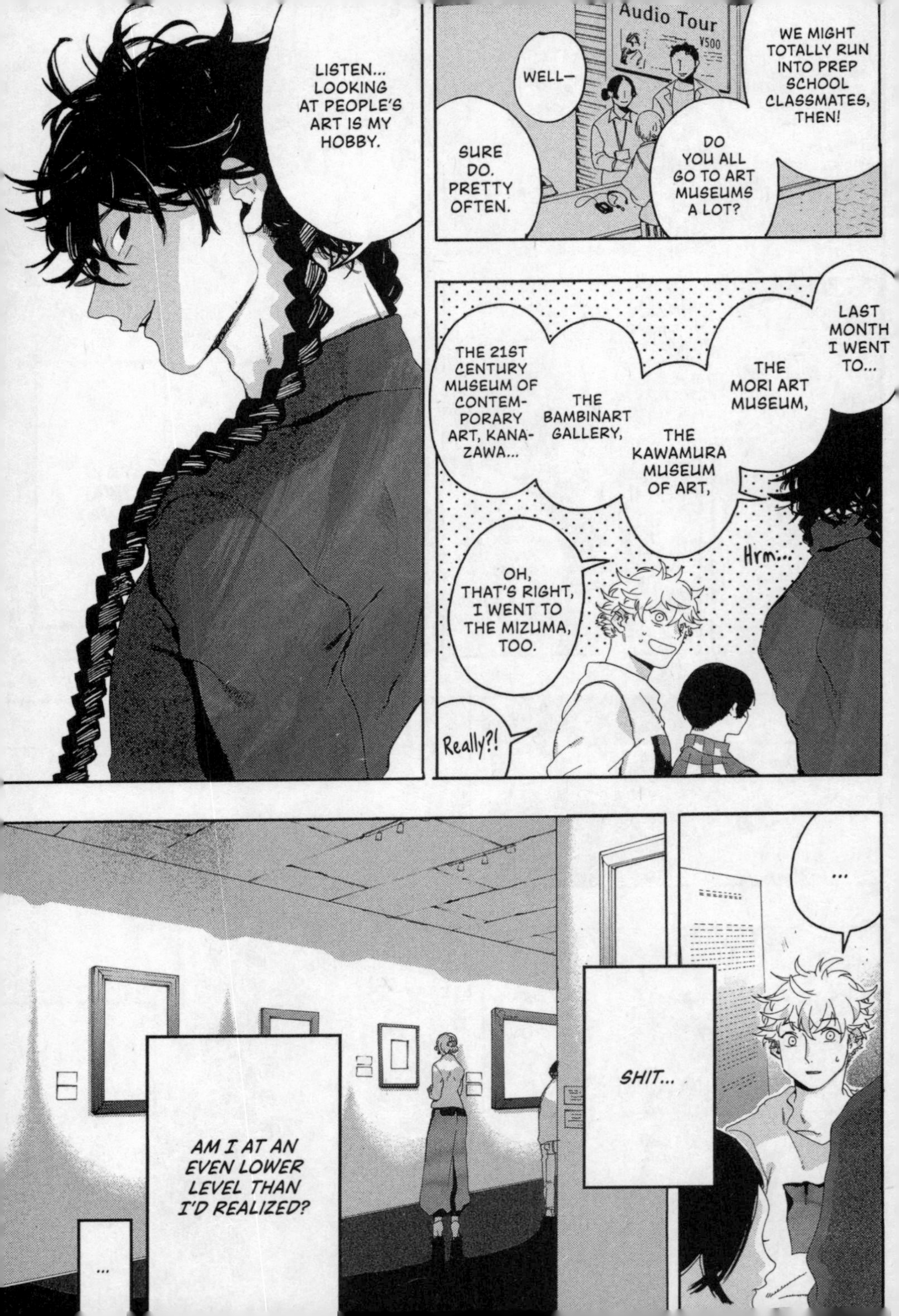
Audio Tour
¥500
WE MIGHT TOTALLY RUN INTO PREP SCHOOL CLASSMATES, THEN!
DO YOU ALL GO TO ART MUSEUMS A LOT?
WELL—
SURE DO. PRETTY OFTEN.
LAST MONTH I WENT TO...
THE MORI ART MUSEUM,
THE KAWAMURA MUSEUM OF ART,
THE BAMBINART GALLERY,
THE 21ST CENTURY MUSEUM OF CONTEMPORARY ART, KANAZAWA...
Hrm...
OH, THAT'S RIGHT, I WENT TO THE MIZUMA, TOO.
Really?!
LISTEN... LOOKING AT PEOPLE'S ART IS MY HOBBY.
...
SHIT...
AM I AT AN EVEN LOWER LEVEL THAN I'D REALIZED?
...

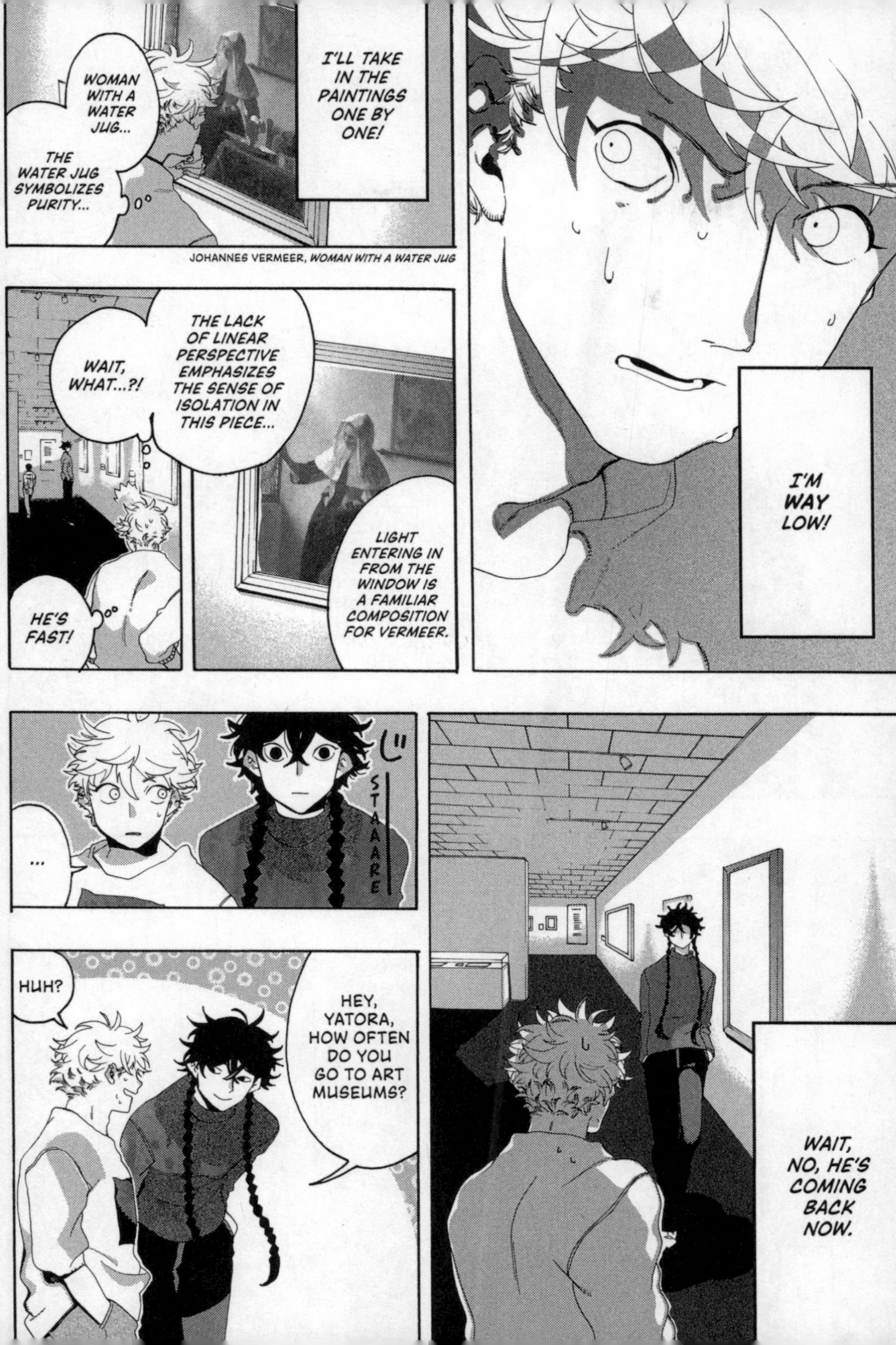
I'M WAY LOW!
I'LL TAKE IN THE PAINTINGS ONE BY ONE!
WOMAN WITH A WATER JUG...
THE WATER JUG SYMBOLIZES PURITY...
JOHANNES VERMEER, WOMAN WITH A WATER JUG
THE LACK OF LINEAR PERSPECTIVE EMPHASIZES THE SENSE OF ISOLATION IN THIS PIECE...
LIGHT ENTERING IN FROM THE WINDOW IS A FAMILIAR COMPOSITION FOR VERMEER.
WAIT, WHAT...?!
HE'S FAST!
WAIT, NO, HE'S COMING BACK NOW.
じ
STAAAARE
...
HEY, YATORA, HOW OFTEN DO YOU GO TO ART MUSEUMS?
HUH?

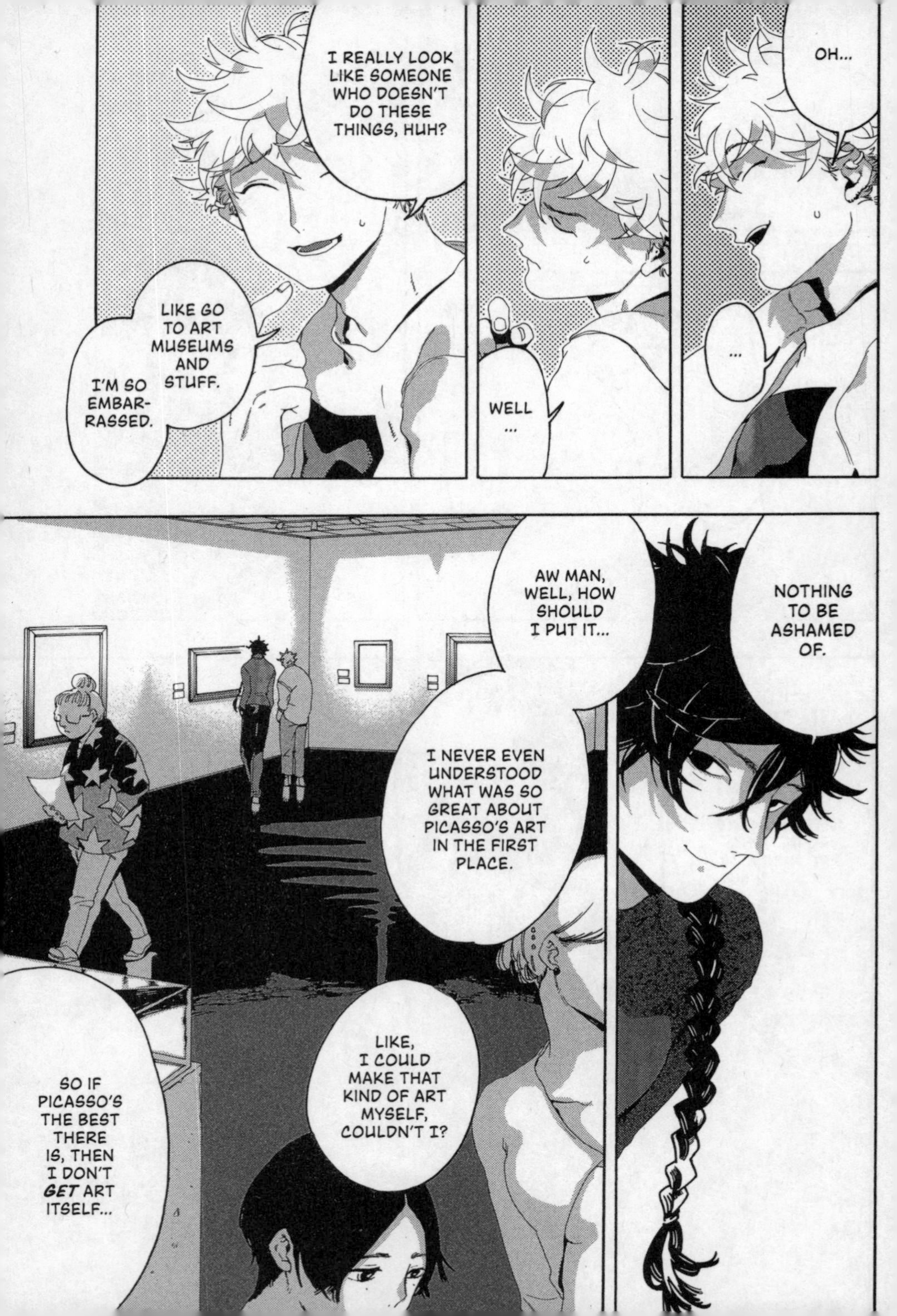
OH...
...
WELL ...
I REALLY LOOK LIKE SOMEONE WHO DOESN'T DO THESE THINGS, HUH?
LIKE GO TO ART MUSEUMS AND STUFF.
I'M SO EMBARRASSED.
NOTHING TO BE ASHAMED OF.
AW MAN, WELL, HOW SHOULD I PUT IT...
I NEVER EVEN UNDERSTOOD WHAT WAS SO GREAT ABOUT PICASSO'S ART IN THE FIRST PLACE.
LIKE, I COULD MAKE THAT KIND OF ART MYSELF, COULDN'T I?
SO IF PICASSO'S THE BEST THERE IS, THEN I DON'T *GET* ART ITSELF...

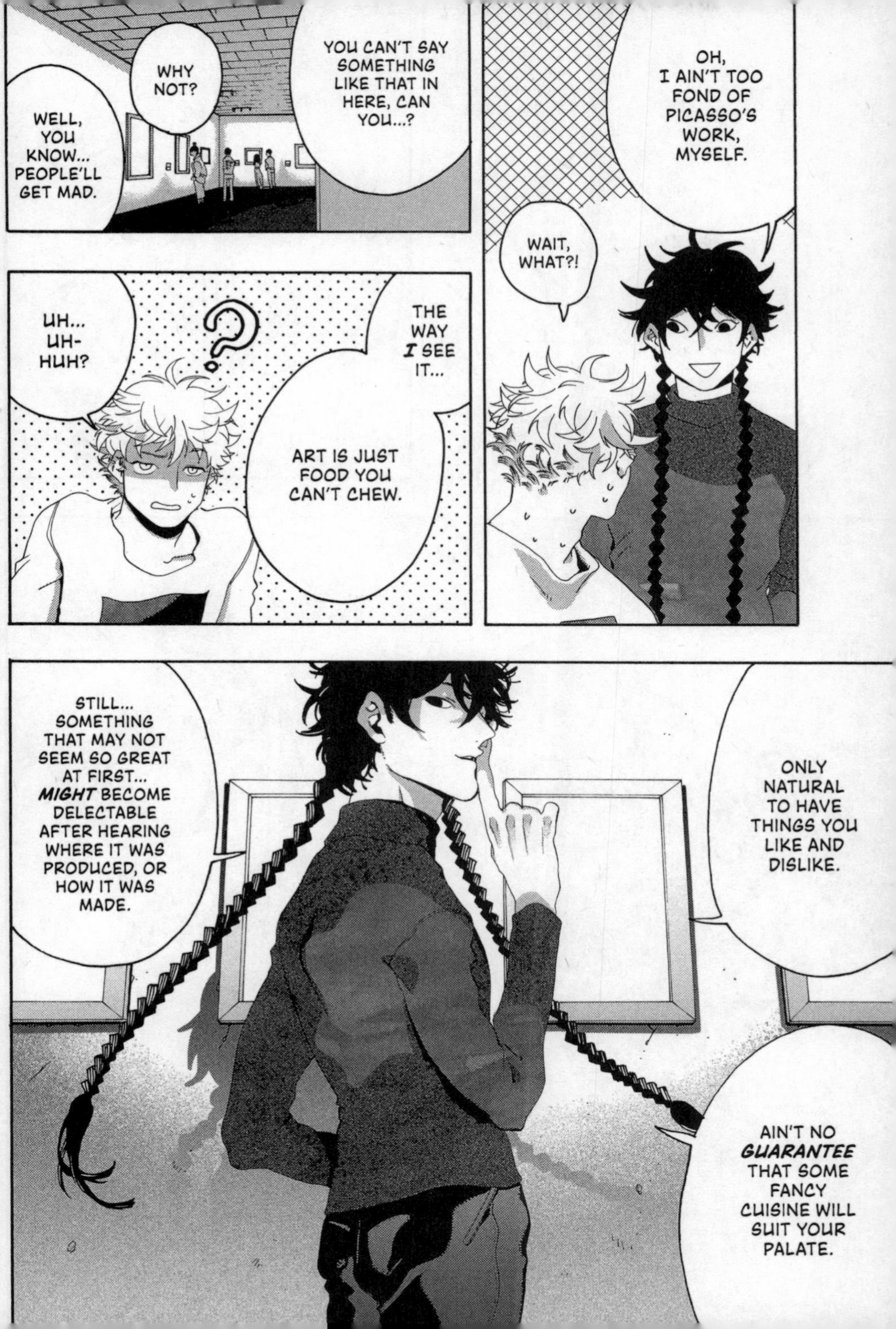
OH, I AIN'T TOO FOND OF PICASSO'S WORK, MYSELF.
WAIT, WHAT?!
YOU CAN'T SAY SOMETHING LIKE THAT IN HERE, CAN YOU...?
WHY NOT?
WELL, YOU KNOW... PEOPLE'LL GET MAD.
THE WAY *I* SEE IT...
ART IS JUST FOOD YOU CAN'T CHEW.
UH... UH-HUH?
ONLY NATURAL TO HAVE THINGS YOU LIKE AND DISLIKE.
AIN'T NO ***GUARANTEE*** THAT SOME FANCY CUISINE WILL SUIT YOUR PALATE.
STILL... SOMETHING THAT MAY NOT SEEM SO GREAT AT FIRST... ***MIGHT*** BECOME DELECTABLE AFTER HEARING WHERE IT WAS PRODUCED, OR HOW IT WAS MADE.

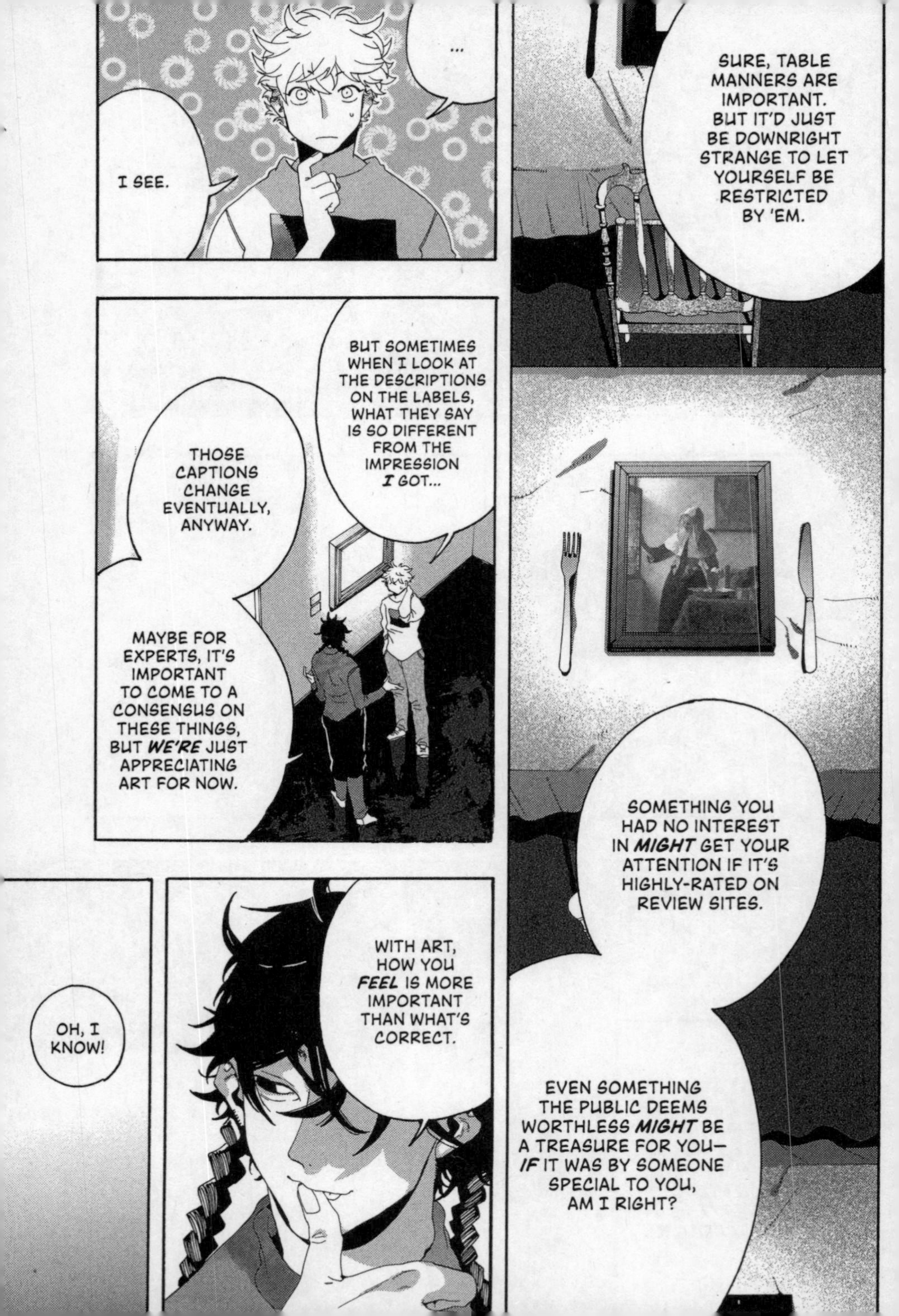
SURE, TABLE MANNERS ARE IMPORTANT. BUT IT'D JUST BE DOWNRIGHT STRANGE TO LET YOURSELF BE RESTRICTED BY 'EM.
...
I SEE.
SOMETHING YOU HAD NO INTEREST IN MIGHT GET YOUR ATTENTION IF IT'S HIGHLY-RATED ON REVIEW SITES.
BUT SOMETIMES WHEN I LOOK AT THE DESCRIPTIONS ON THE LABELS, WHAT THEY SAY IS SO DIFFERENT FROM THE IMPRESSION I GOT...
THOSE CAPTIONS CHANGE EVENTUALLY, ANYWAY.
MAYBE FOR EXPERTS, IT'S IMPORTANT TO COME TO A CONSENSUS ON THESE THINGS, BUT WE'RE JUST APPRECIATING ART FOR NOW.
EVEN SOMETHING THE PUBLIC DEEMS WORTHLESS MIGHT BE A TREASURE FOR YOU— IF IT WAS BY SOMEONE SPECIAL TO YOU, AM I RIGHT?
WITH ART, HOW YOU FEEL IS MORE IMPORTANT THAN WHAT'S CORRECT.
OH, I KNOW!

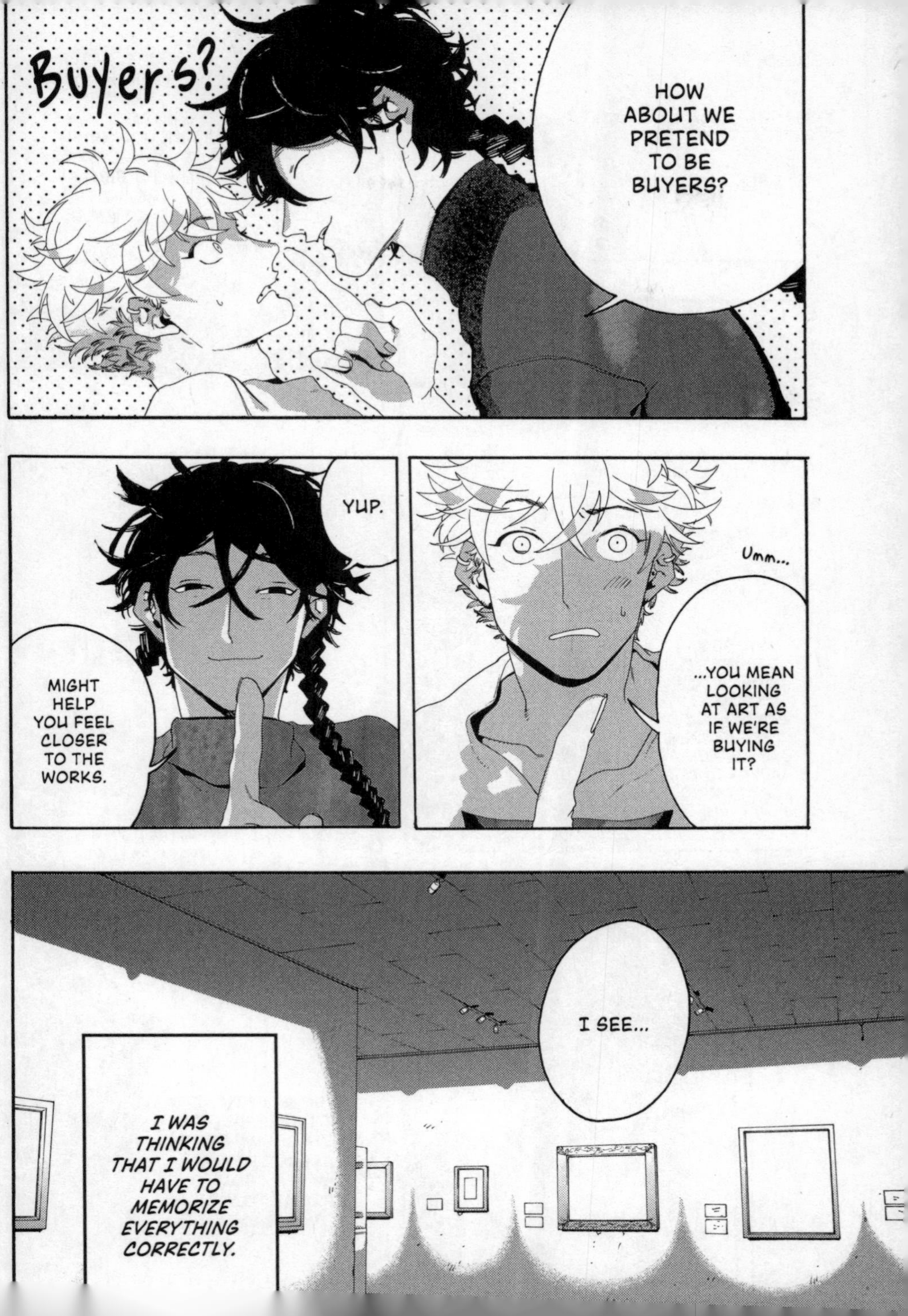
HOW ABOUT WE PRETEND TO BE BUYERS?
Buyers?
Umm...
...YOU MEAN LOOKING AT ART AS IF WE'RE BUYING IT?
YUP.
MIGHT HELP YOU FEEL CLOSER TO THE WORKS.
I SEE...
I WAS THINKING THAT I WOULD HAVE TO MEMORIZE EVERYTHING CORRECTLY.

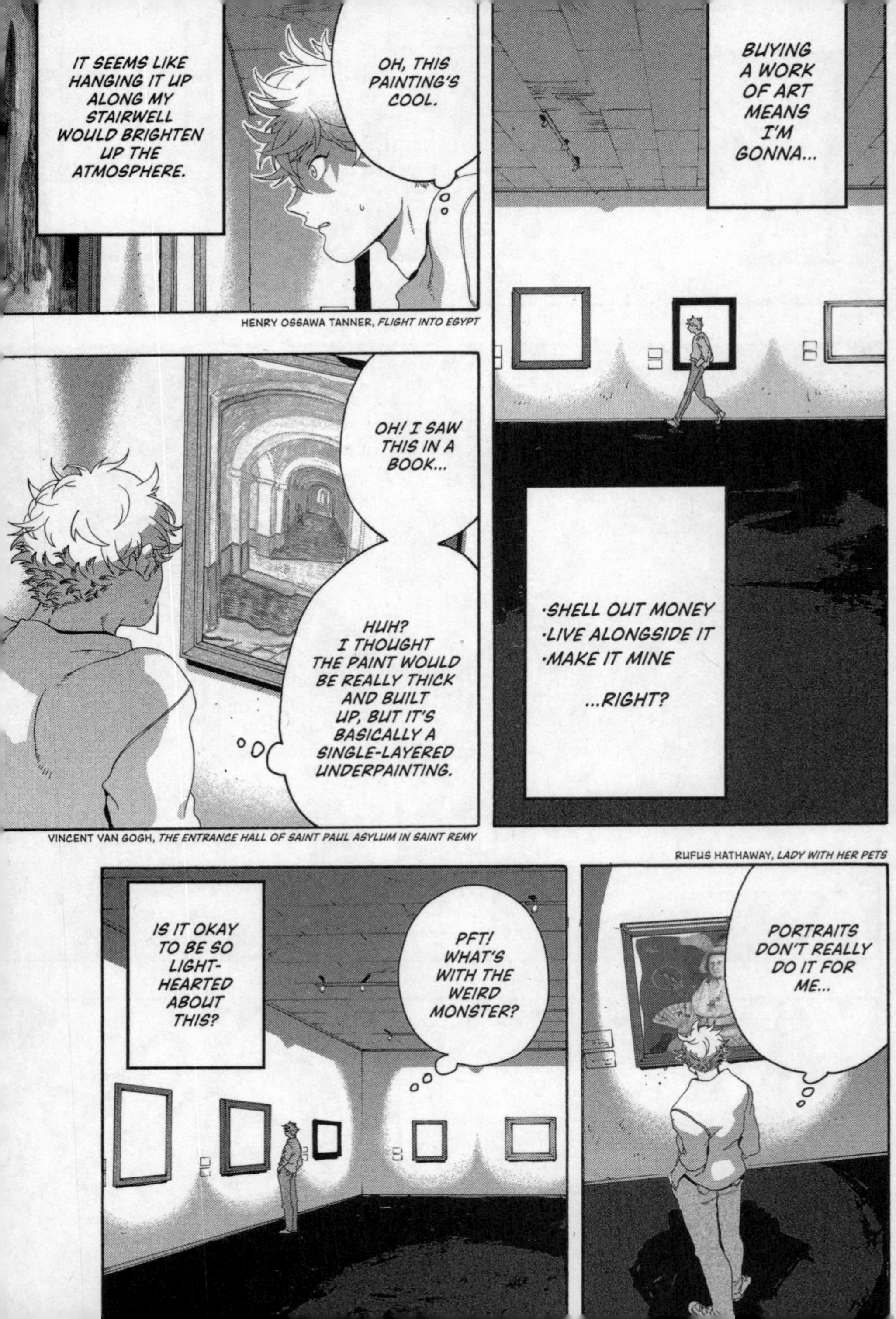
BUYING A WORK OF ART MEANS I'M GONNA...
·SHELL OUT MONEY
·LIVE ALONGSIDE IT
·MAKE IT MINE
...RIGHT?
OH, THIS PAINTING'S COOL.
IT SEEMS LIKE HANGING IT UP ALONG MY STAIRWELL WOULD BRIGHTEN UP THE ATMOSPHERE.
OH! I SAW THIS IN A BOOK...
HUH? I THOUGHT THE PAINT WOULD BE REALLY THICK AND BUILT UP, BUT IT'S BASICALLY A SINGLE-LAYERED UNDERPAINTING.
PORTRAITS DON'T REALLY DO IT FOR ME...
PFT! WHAT'S WITH THE WEIRD MONSTER?
IS IT OKAY TO BE SO LIGHT-HEARTED ABOUT THIS?
HENRY OSSAWA TANNER, *FLIGHT INTO EGYPT*
VINCENT VAN GOGH, *THE ENTRANCE HALL OF SAINT PAUL ASYLUM IN SAINT REMY*
RUFUS HATHAWAY, *LADY WITH HER PETS*

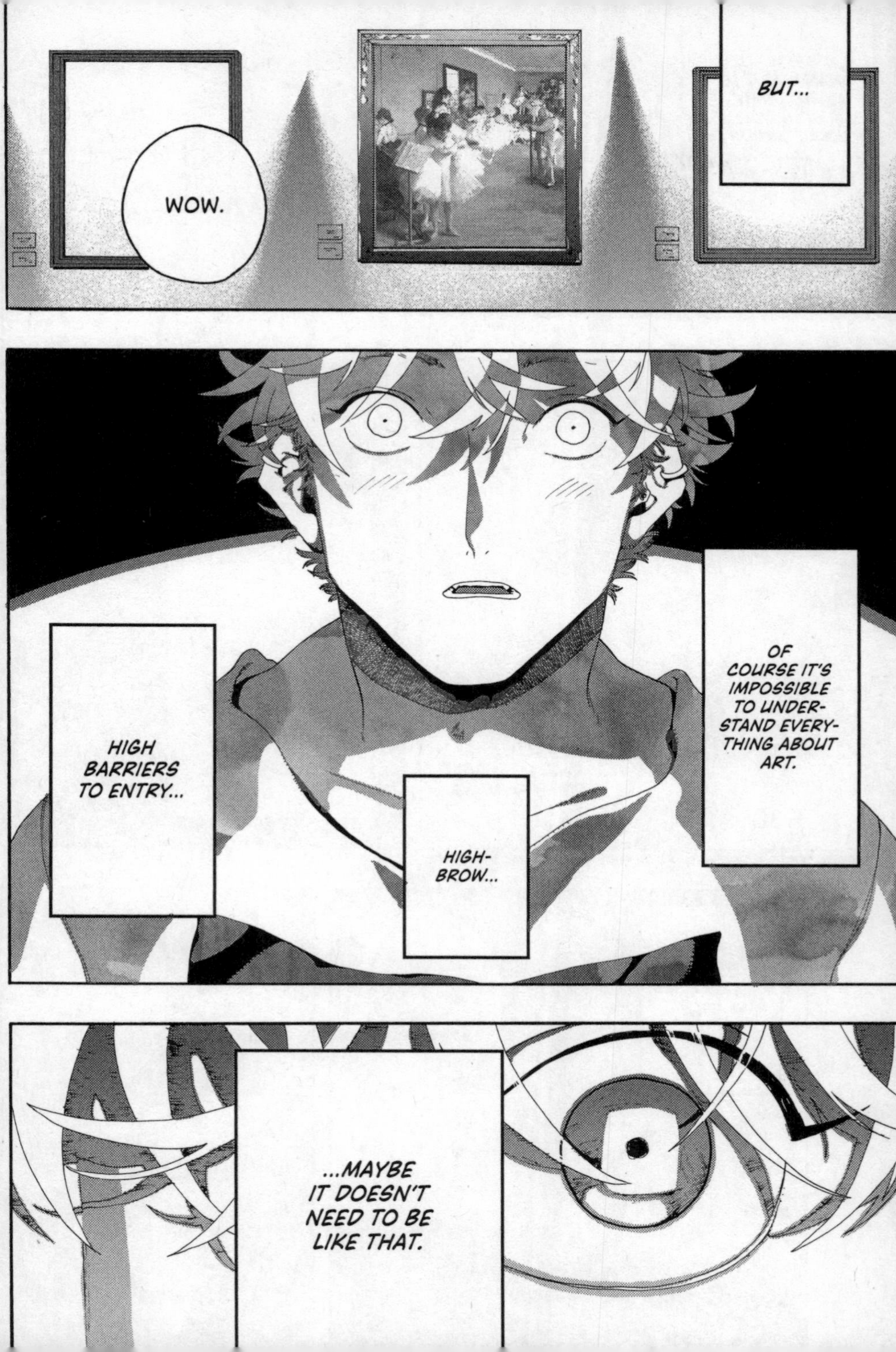
BUT...
WOW.
OF COURSE IT'S IMPOSSIBLE TO UNDER-STAND EVERY-THING ABOUT ART.
HIGH-BROW...
HIGH BARRIERS TO ENTRY...
...MAYBE IT DOESN'T NEED TO BE LIKE THAT.

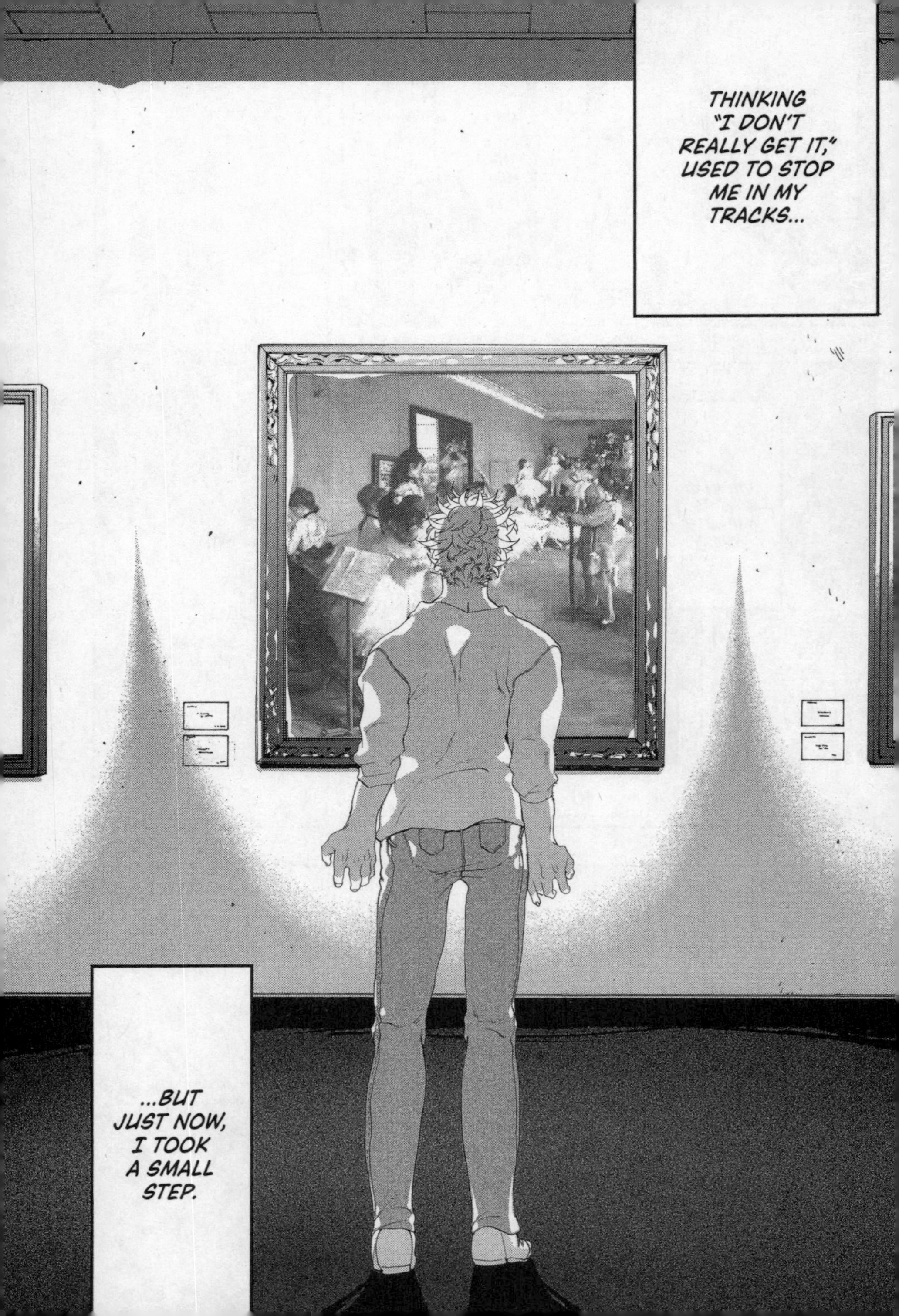
THINKING "I DON'T REALLY GET IT," USED TO STOP ME IN MY TRACKS...
...BUT JUST NOW, I TOOK A SMALL STEP.

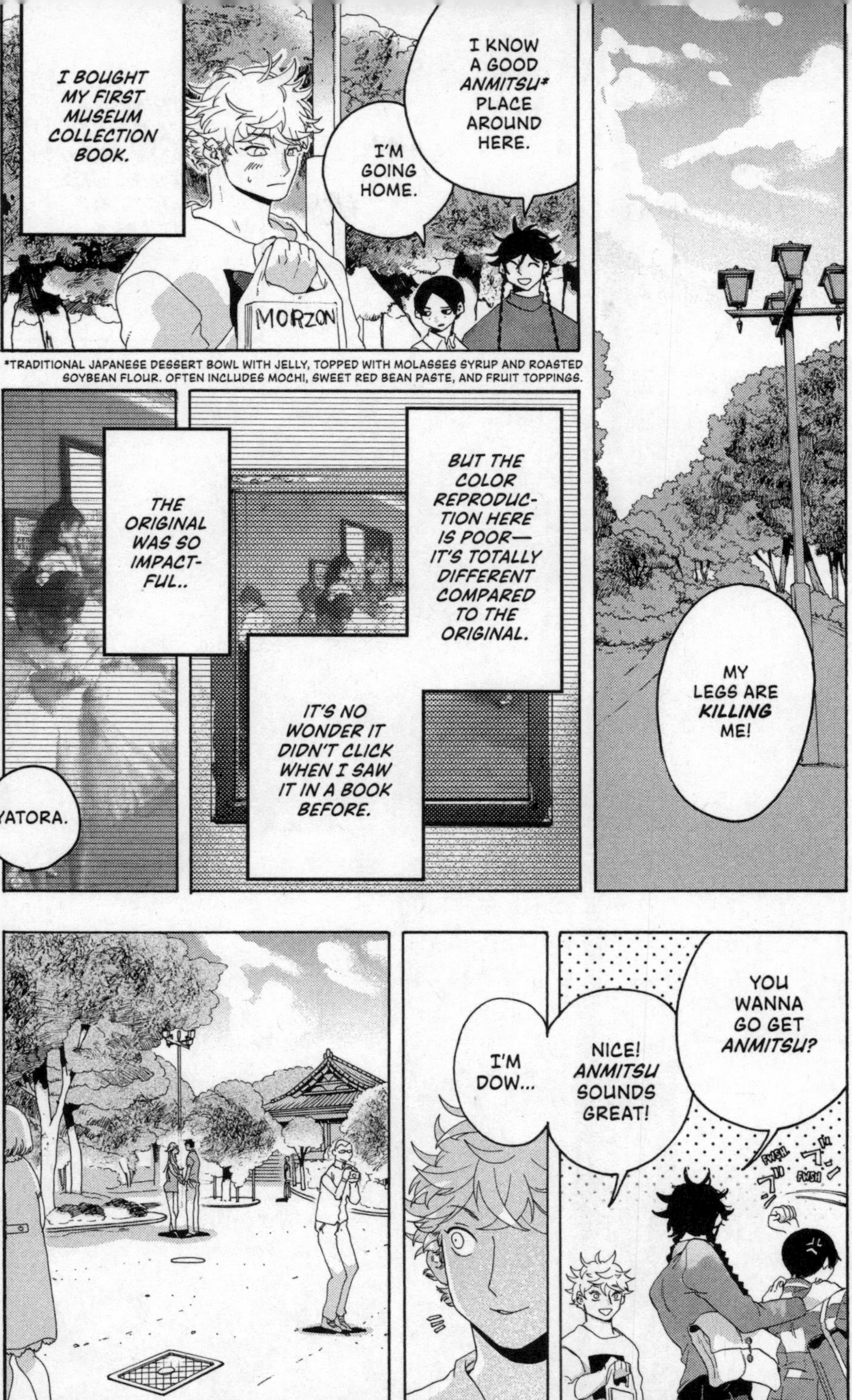
MY LEGS ARE KILLING ME!
I KNOW A GOOD ANMITSU* PLACE AROUND HERE.
I'M GOING HOME.
I BOUGHT MY FIRST MUSEUM COLLECTION BOOK.
MORZON
BUT THE COLOR REPRODUCTION HERE IS POOR—IT'S TOTALLY DIFFERENT COMPARED TO THE ORIGINAL.
IT'S NO WONDER IT DIDN'T CLICK WHEN I SAW IT IN A BOOK BEFORE.
THE ORIGINAL WAS SO IMPACTFUL..
YATORA.
YOU WANNA GO GET ANMITSU?
FWSH
FWSH
NICE! ANMITSU SOUNDS GREAT!
I'M DOW...

*TRADITIONAL JAPANESE DESSERT BOWL WITH JELLY, TOPPED WITH MOLASSES SYRUP AND ROASTED SOYBEAN FLOUR. OFTEN INCLUDES MOCHI, SWEET RED BEAN PASTE, AND FRUIT TOPPINGS.

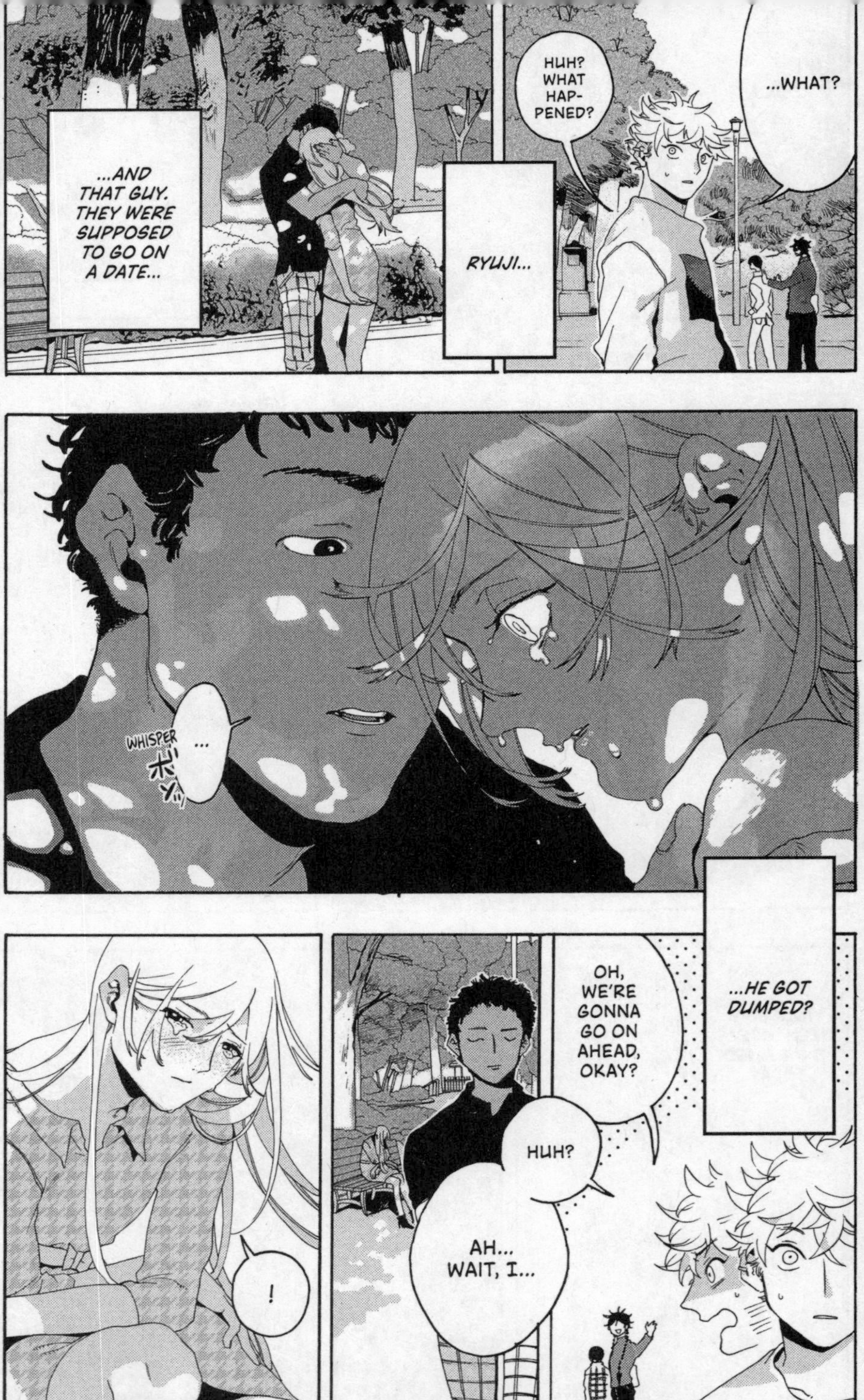
...WHAT?
HUH? WHAT HAP-PENED?
RYUJI...
...AND THAT GUY. THEY WERE SUPPOSED TO GO ON A DATE...
...
WHISPER
ボソッ
...HE GOT DUMPED?
OH, WE'RE GONNA GO ON AHEAD, OKAY?
HUH?
AH... WAIT, I...
!

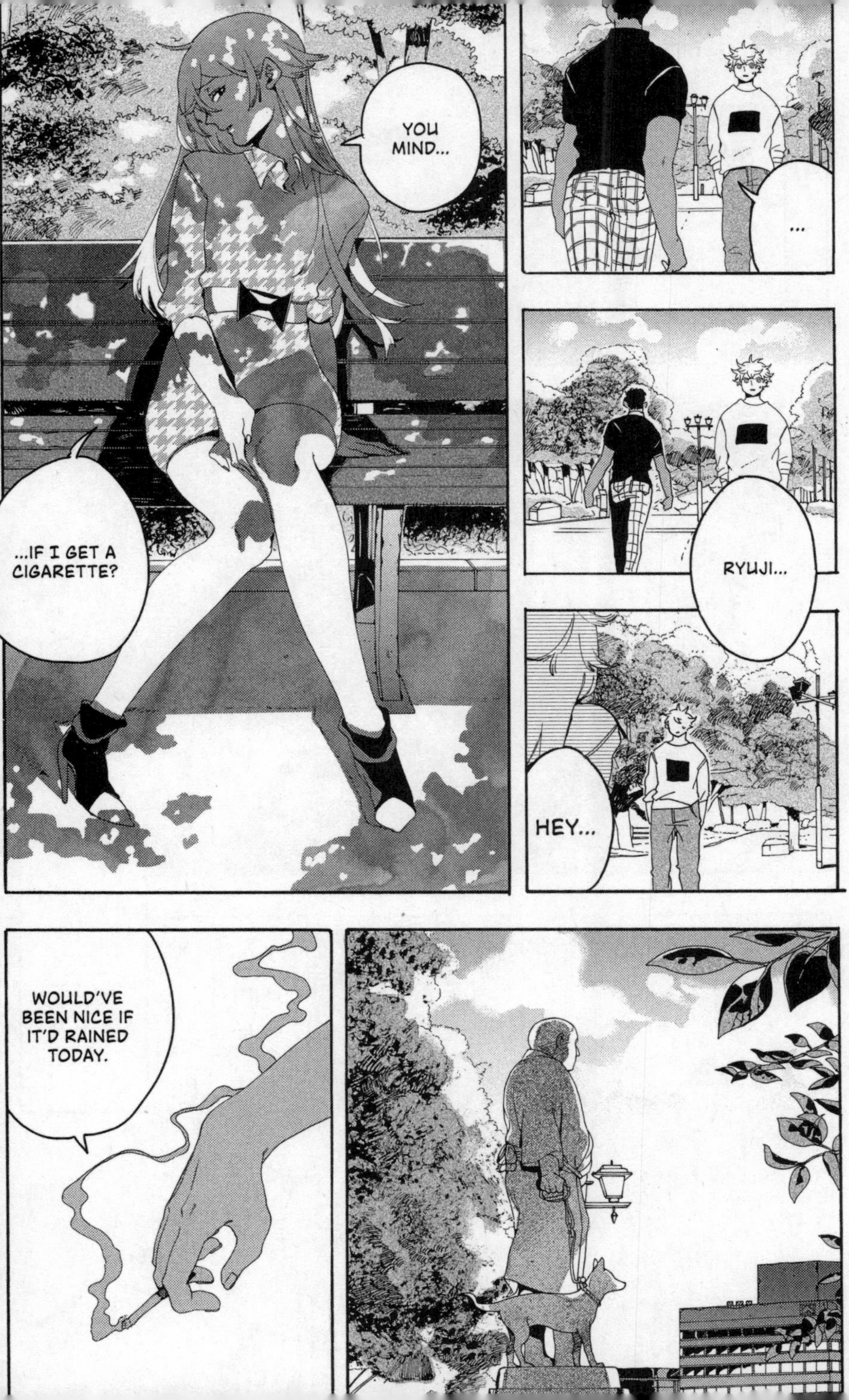
...
RYUJI...
HEY...
YOU MIND...
...IF I GET A CIGARETTE?
WOULD'VE BEEN NICE IF IT'D RAINED TODAY.

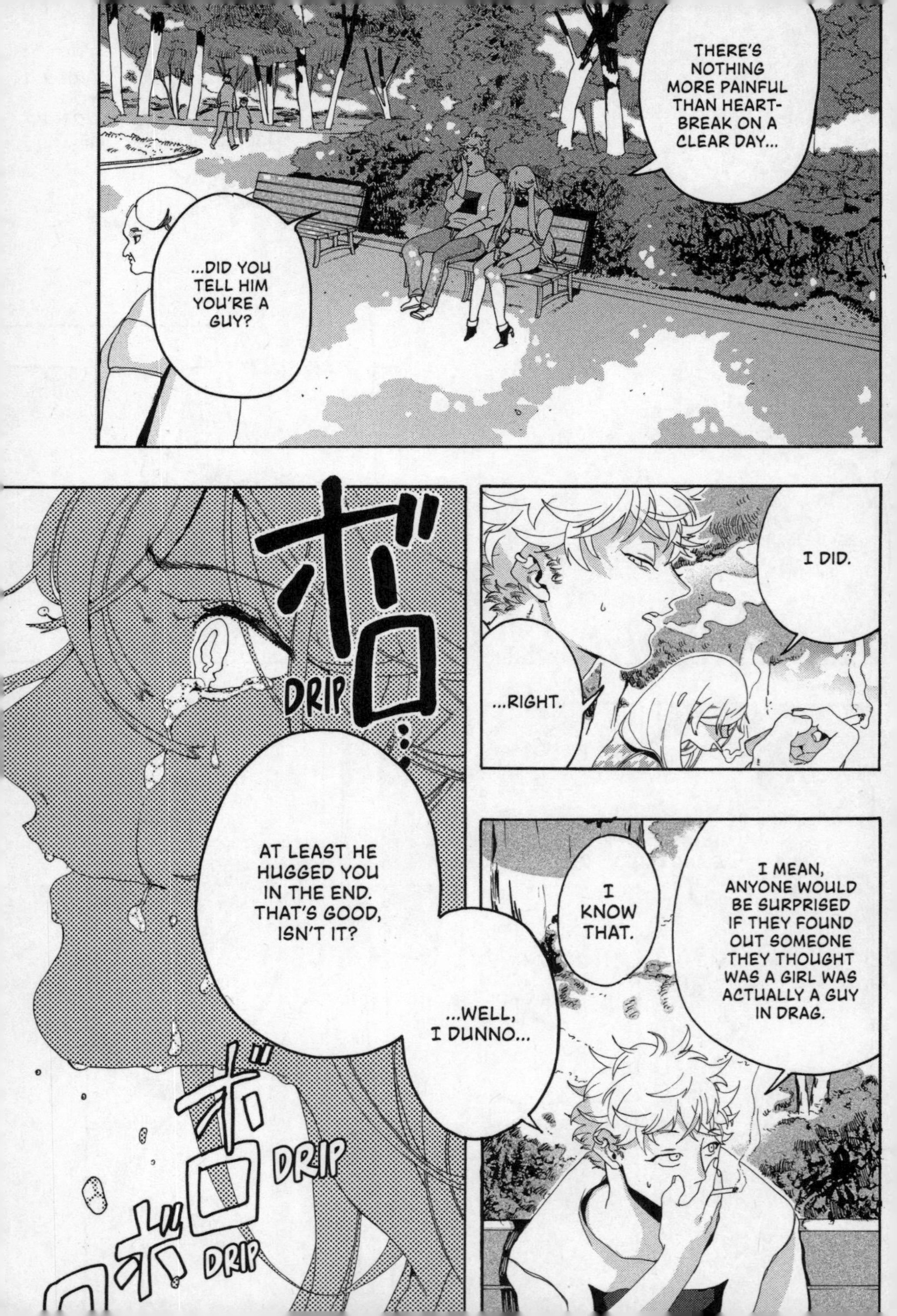
THERE'S NOTHING MORE PAINFUL THAN HEART-BREAK ON A CLEAR DAY...
...DID YOU TELL HIM YOU'RE A GUY?
I DID.
...RIGHT.
I MEAN, ANYONE WOULD BE SURPRISED IF THEY FOUND OUT SOMEONE THEY THOUGHT WAS A GIRL WAS ACTUALLY A GUY IN DRAG.
I KNOW THAT.
ボロ
DRIP
AT LEAST HE HUGGED YOU IN THE END. THAT'S GOOD, ISN'T IT?
...WELL, I DUNNO...
ボロボロ
DRIP
DRIP

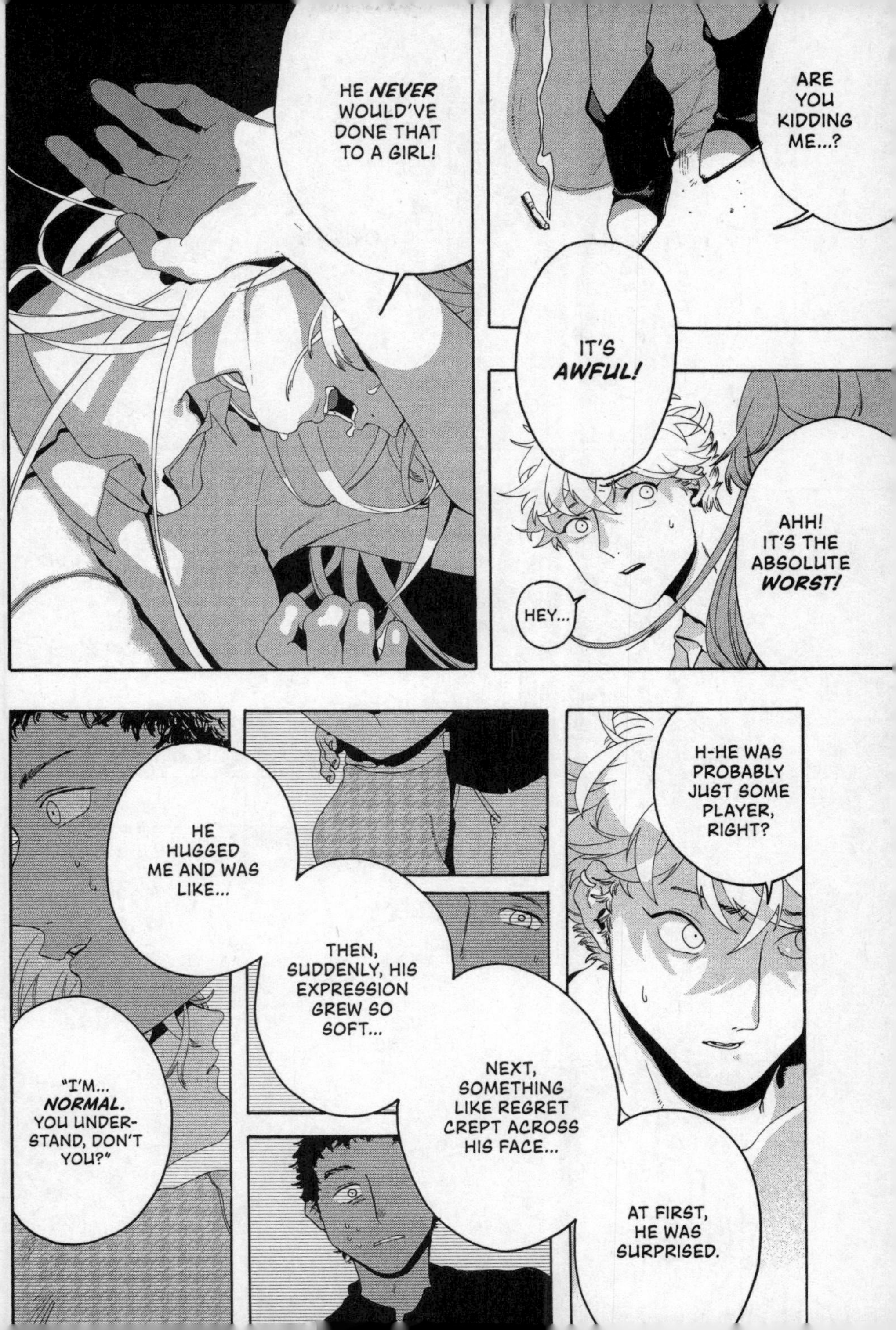
ARE YOU KIDDING ME...?
IT'S AWFUL!
AHH! IT'S THE ABSOLUTE WORST!
HEY...
HE NEVER WOULD'VE DONE THAT TO A GIRL!
H-HE WAS PROBABLY JUST SOME PLAYER, RIGHT?
AT FIRST, HE WAS SURPRISED.
THEN, SUDDENLY, HIS EXPRESSION GREW SO SOFT...
NEXT, SOMETHING LIKE REGRET CREPT ACROSS HIS FACE...
HE HUGGED ME AND WAS LIKE...
"I'M... NORMAL. YOU UNDER-STAND, DON'T YOU?"

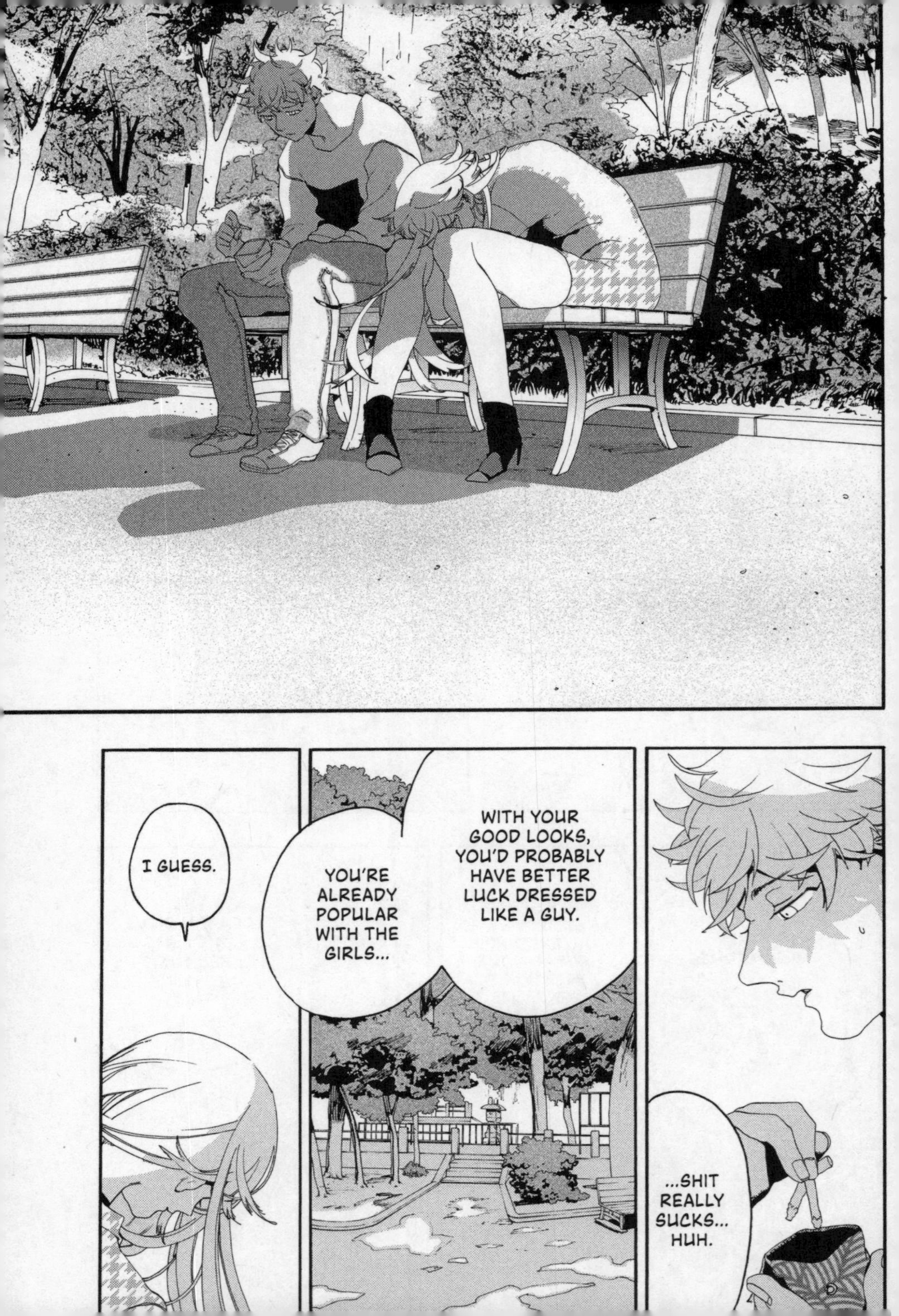
...SHIT REALLY SUCKS... HUH.
WITH YOUR GOOD LOOKS, YOU'D PROBABLY HAVE BETTER LUCK DRESSED LIKE A GUY.
YOU'RE ALREADY POPULAR WITH THE GIRLS...
I GUESS.

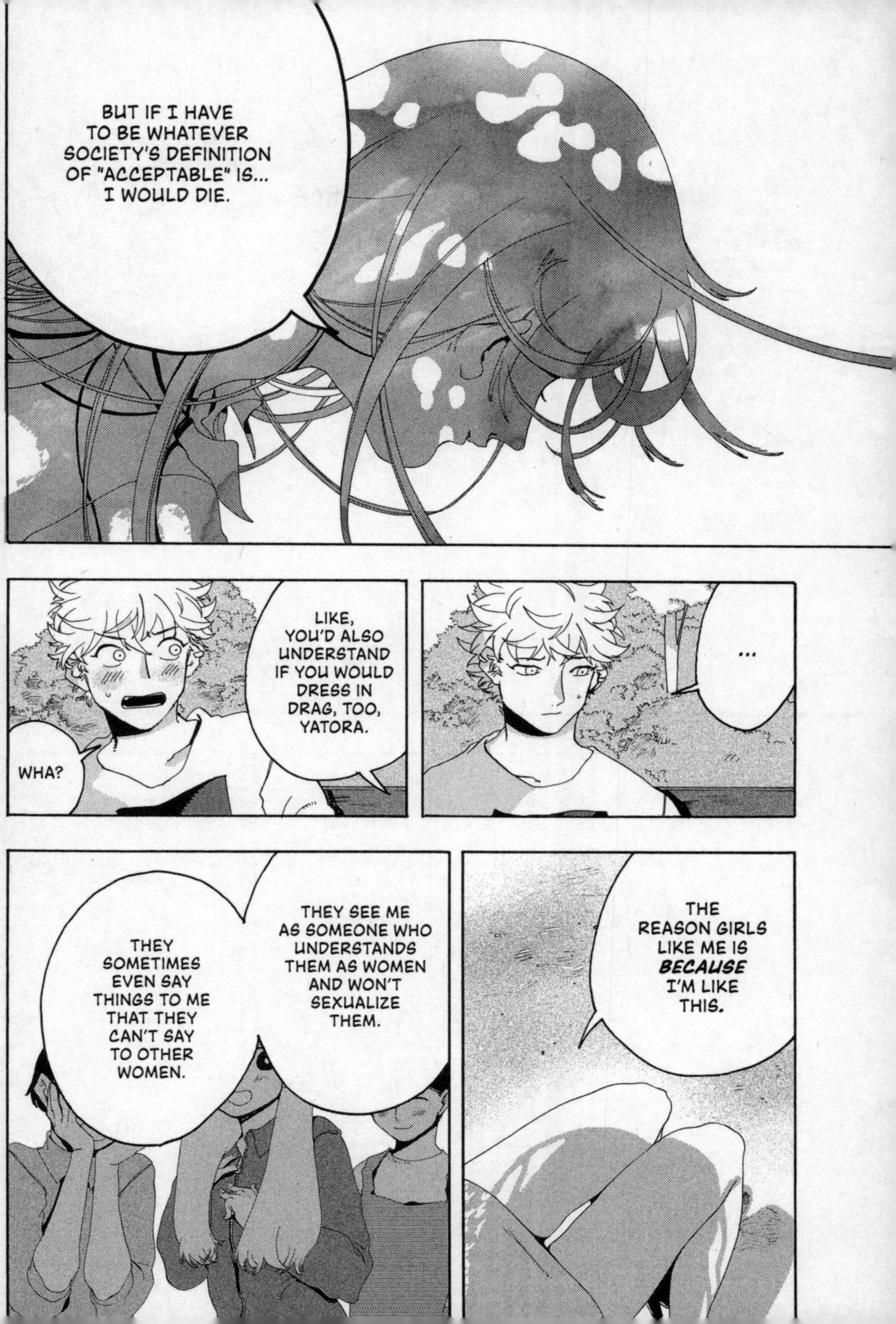
BUT IF I HAVE TO BE WHATEVER SOCIETY'S DEFINITION OF "ACCEPTABLE" IS... I WOULD DIE.
...
LIKE, YOU'D ALSO UNDERSTAND IF YOU WOULD DRESS IN DRAG, TOO, YATORA.
WHA?
THE REASON GIRLS LIKE ME IS *BECAUSE* I'M LIKE THIS.
THEY SEE ME AS SOMEONE WHO UNDERSTANDS THEM AS WOMEN AND WON'T SEXUALIZE THEM.
THEY SOMETIMES EVEN SAY THINGS TO ME THAT THEY CAN'T SAY TO OTHER WOMEN.

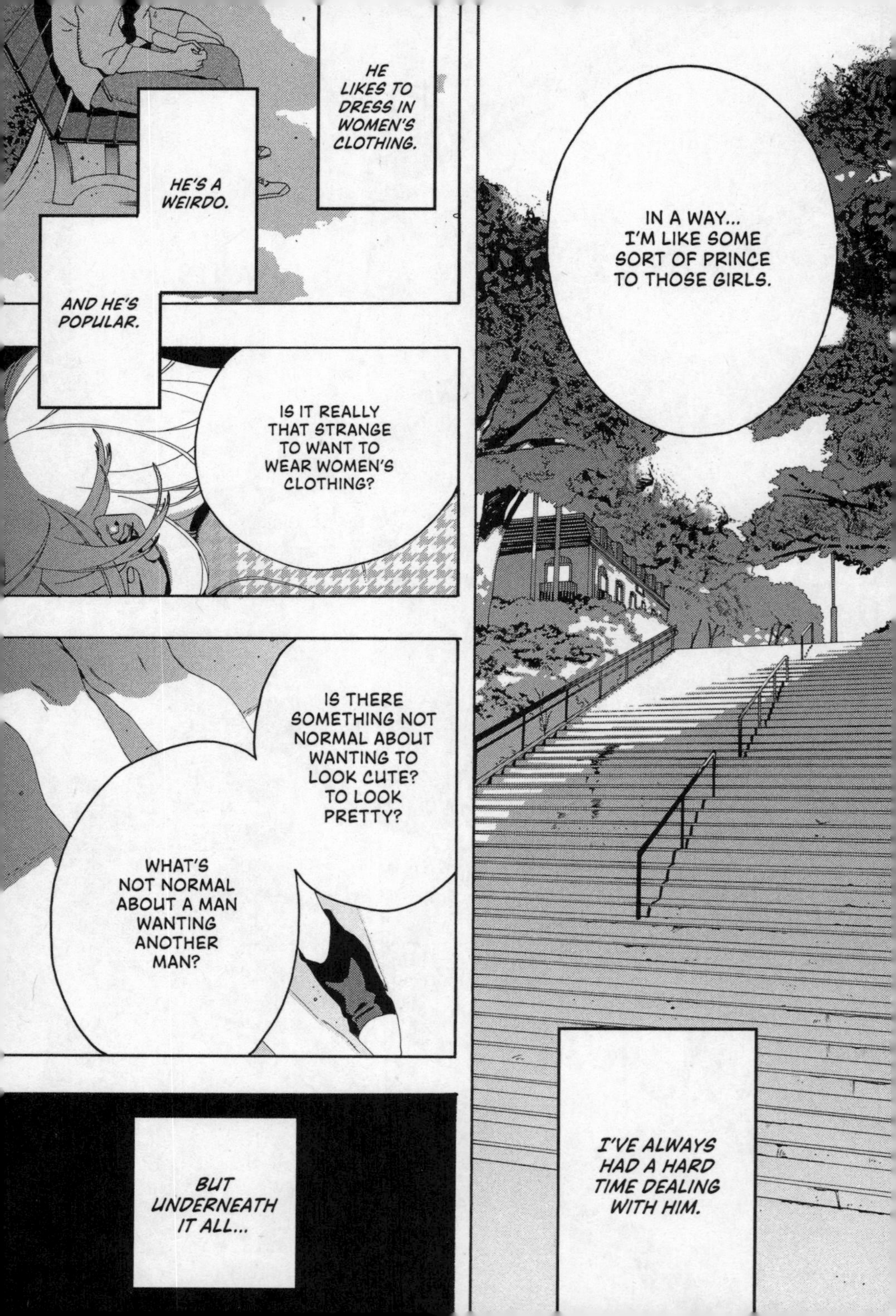
IN A WAY... I'M LIKE SOME SORT OF PRINCE TO THOSE GIRLS.
I'VE ALWAYS HAD A HARD TIME DEALING WITH HIM.
HE LIKES TO DRESS IN WOMEN'S CLOTHING.
HE'S A WEIRDO.
AND HE'S POPULAR.
IS IT REALLY THAT STRANGE TO WANT TO WEAR WOMEN'S CLOTHING?
IS THERE SOMETHING NOT NORMAL ABOUT WANTING TO LOOK CUTE? TO LOOK PRETTY?
WHAT'S NOT NORMAL ABOUT A MAN WANTING ANOTHER MAN?
BUT UNDERNEATH IT ALL...

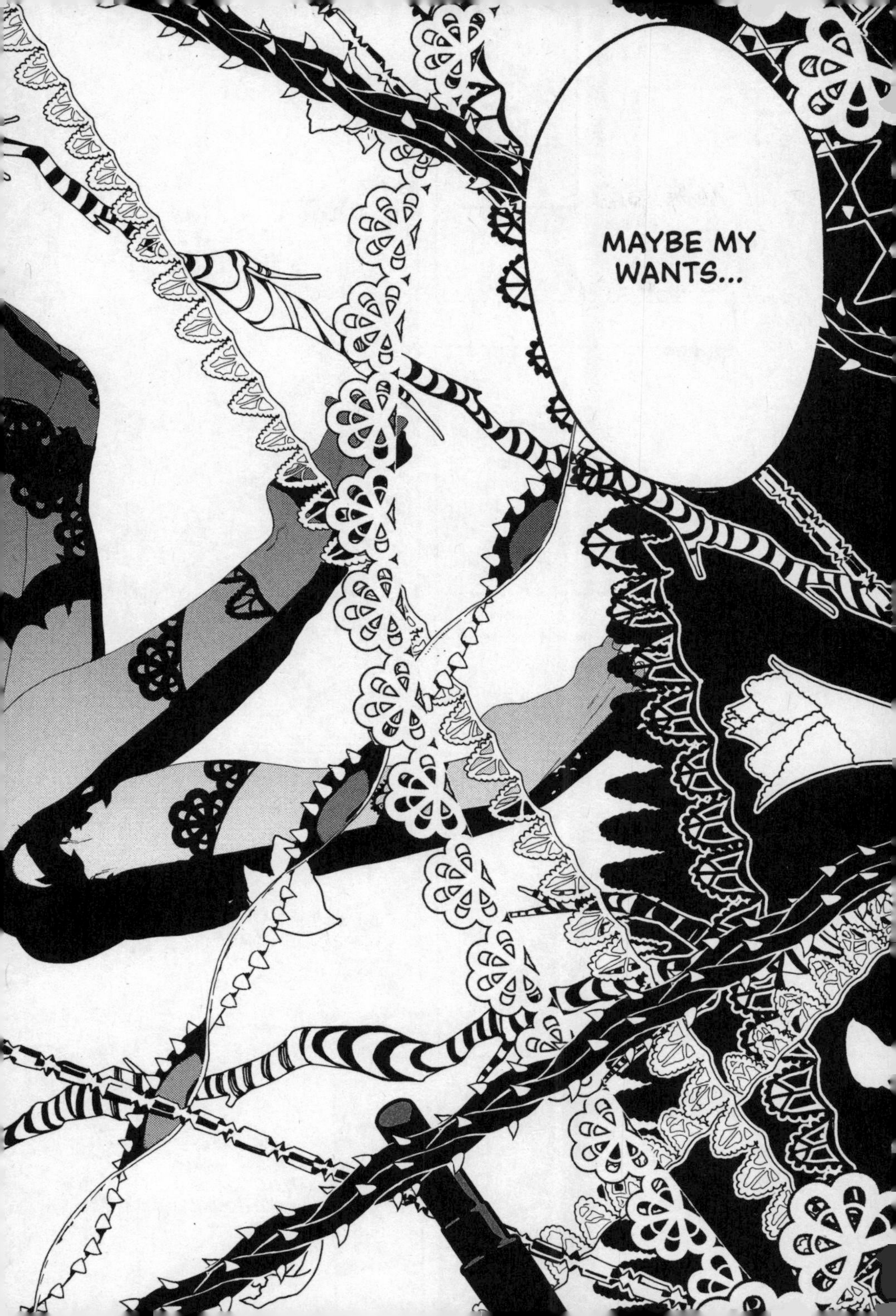
MAYBE MY WANTS...

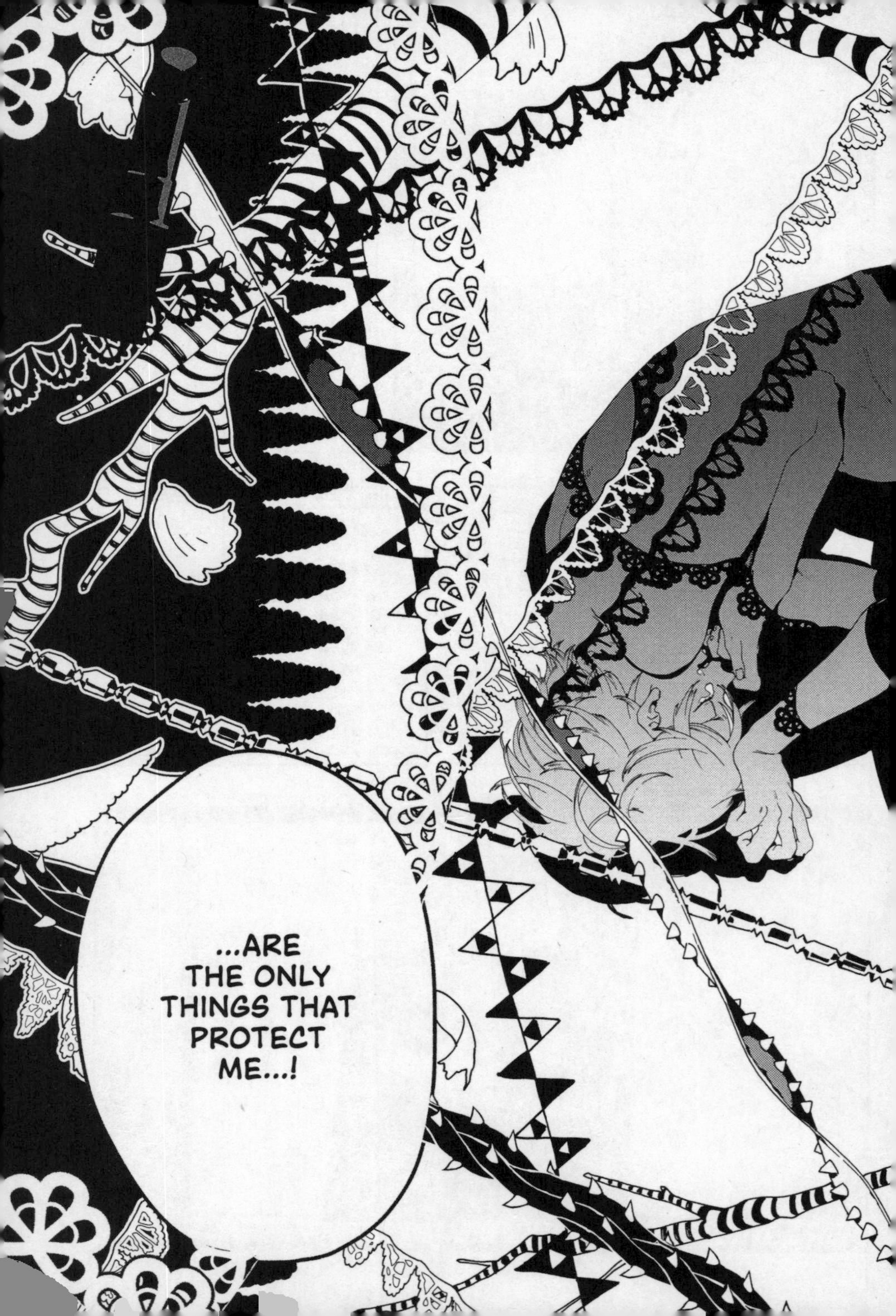
...ARE THE ONLY THINGS THAT PROTECT ME...!

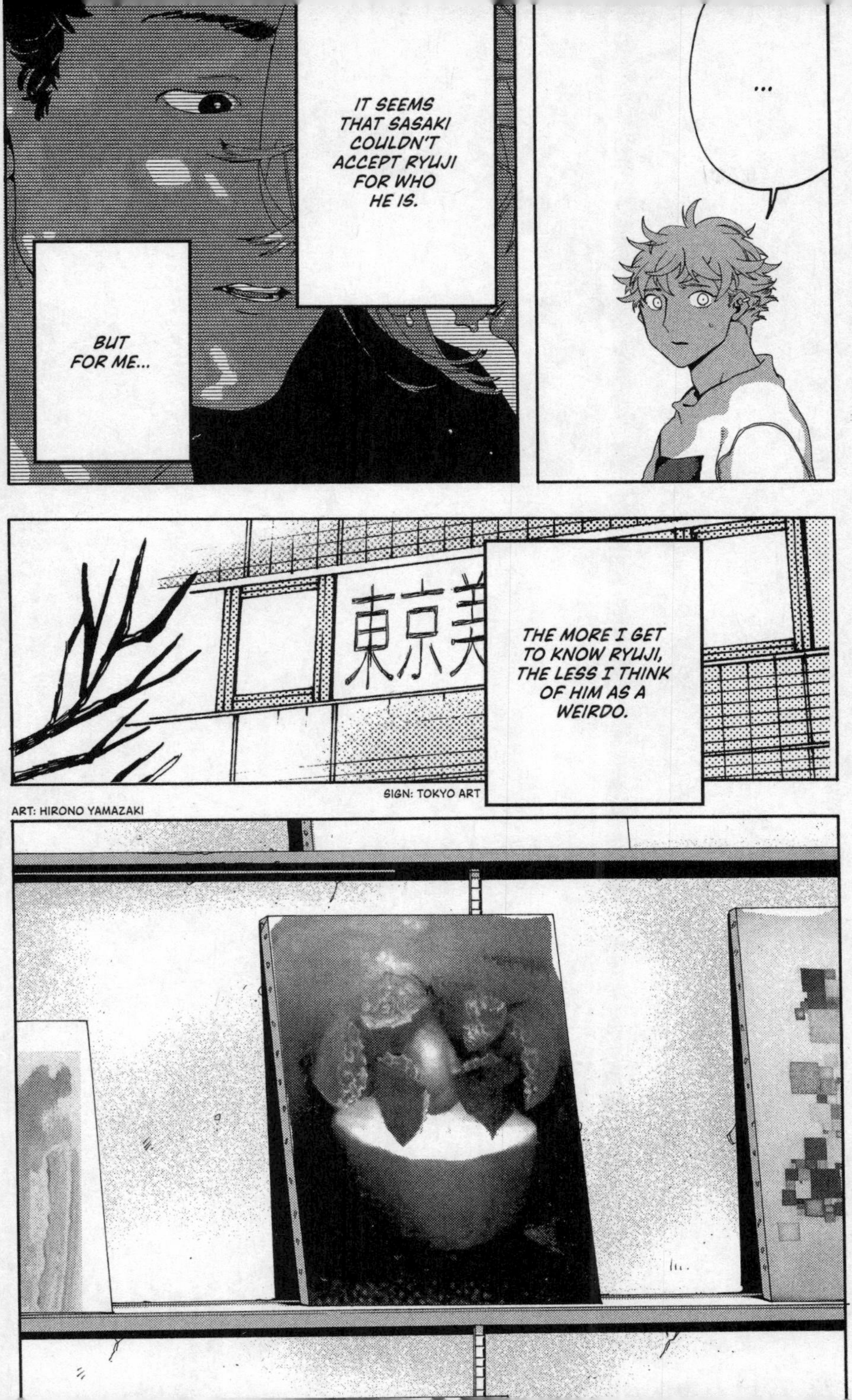
...
IT SEEMS THAT SASAKI COULDN'T ACCEPT RYUJI FOR WHO HE IS.
BUT FOR ME...
東京美
THE MORE I GET TO KNOW RYUJI, THE LESS I THINK OF HIM AS A WEIRDO.
SIGN: TOKYO ART
ART: HIRONO YAMAZAKI

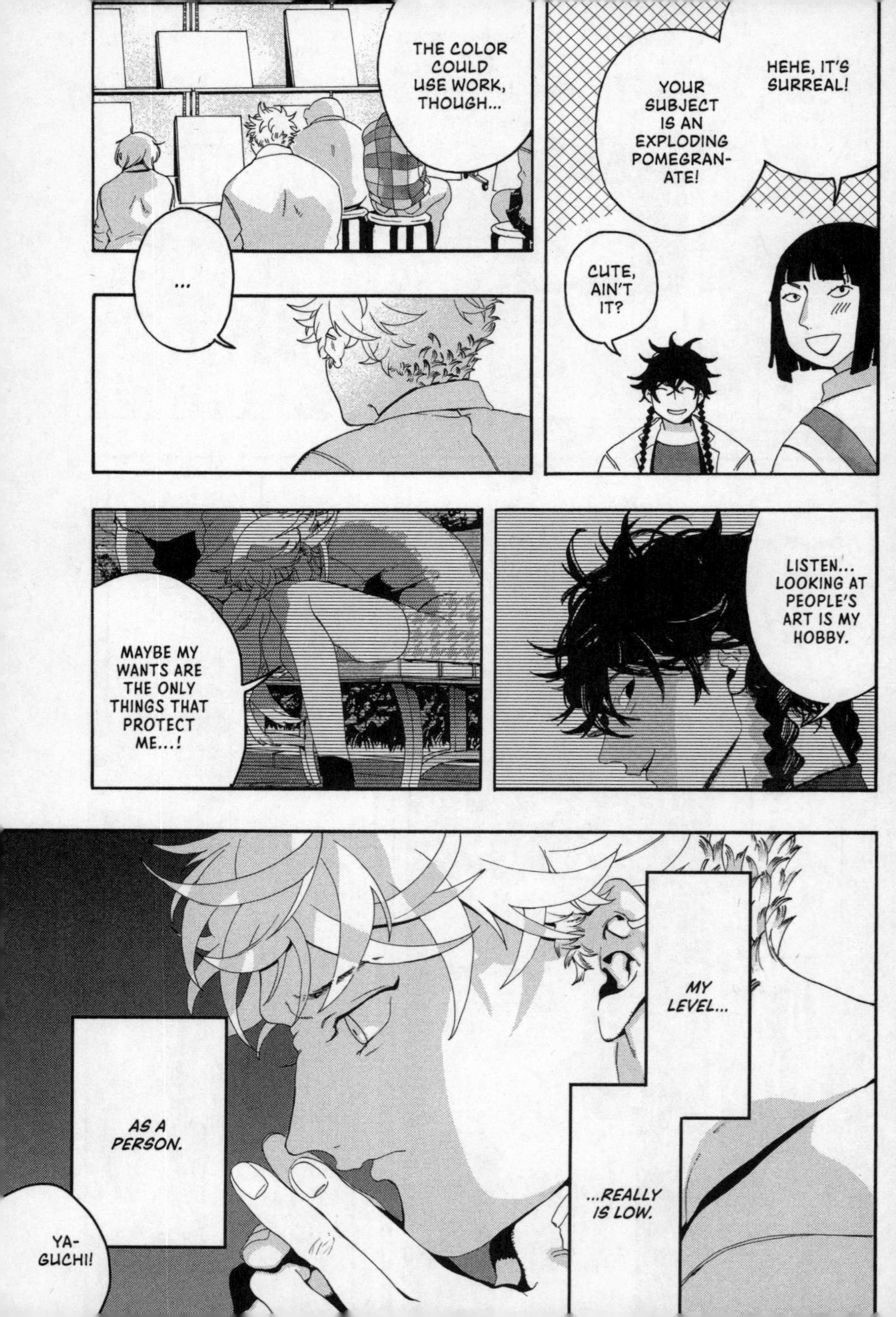
HEHE, IT'S SURREAL!
YOUR SUBJECT IS AN EXPLODING POMEGRANATE!
CUTE, AIN'T IT?
THE COLOR COULD USE WORK, THOUGH...
...
LISTEN... LOOKING AT PEOPLE'S ART IS MY HOBBY.
MAYBE MY WANTS ARE THE ONLY THINGS THAT PROTECT ME...!
MY LEVEL...
...REALLY IS LOW.
AS A PERSON.
YA-GUCHI!

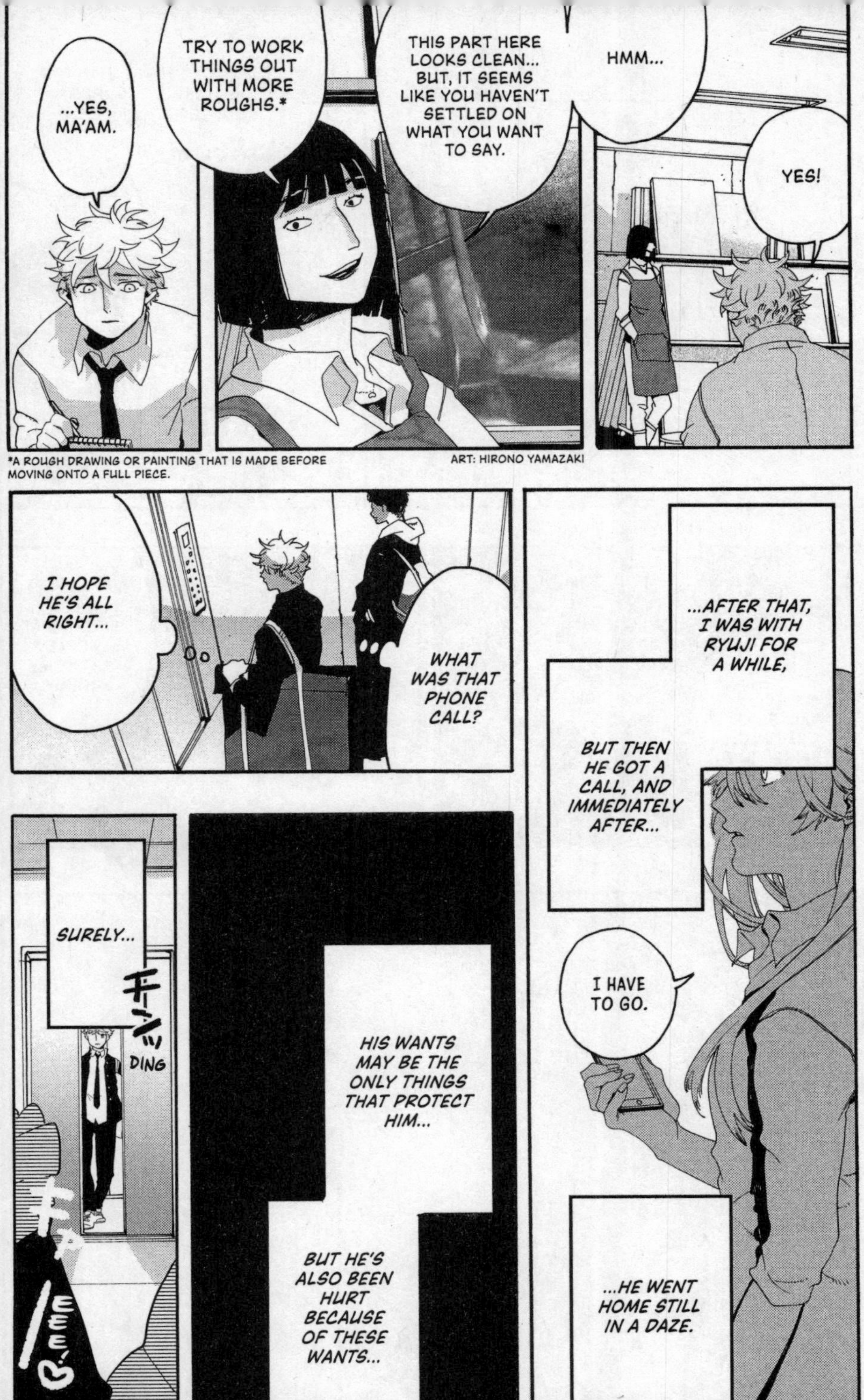
HMM...
YES!
THIS PART HERE LOOKS CLEAN... BUT, IT SEEMS LIKE YOU HAVEN'T SETTLED ON WHAT YOU WANT TO SAY.
TRY TO WORK THINGS OUT WITH MORE ROUGHS.*
...YES, MA'AM.
...AFTER THAT, I WAS WITH RYUJI FOR A WHILE,
BUT THEN HE GOT A CALL, AND IMMEDIATELY AFTER...
I HAVE TO GO.
...HE WENT HOME STILL IN A DAZE.
WHAT WAS THAT PHONE CALL?
I HOPE HE'S ALL RIGHT...
HIS WANTS MAY BE THE ONLY THINGS THAT PROTECT HIM...
BUT HE'S ALSO BEEN HURT BECAUSE OF THESE WANTS...
SURELY...
DING
EEE

*A ROUGH DRAWING OR PAINTING THAT IS MADE BEFORE MOVING ONTO A FULL PIECE.

ART: HIRONO YAMAZAKI

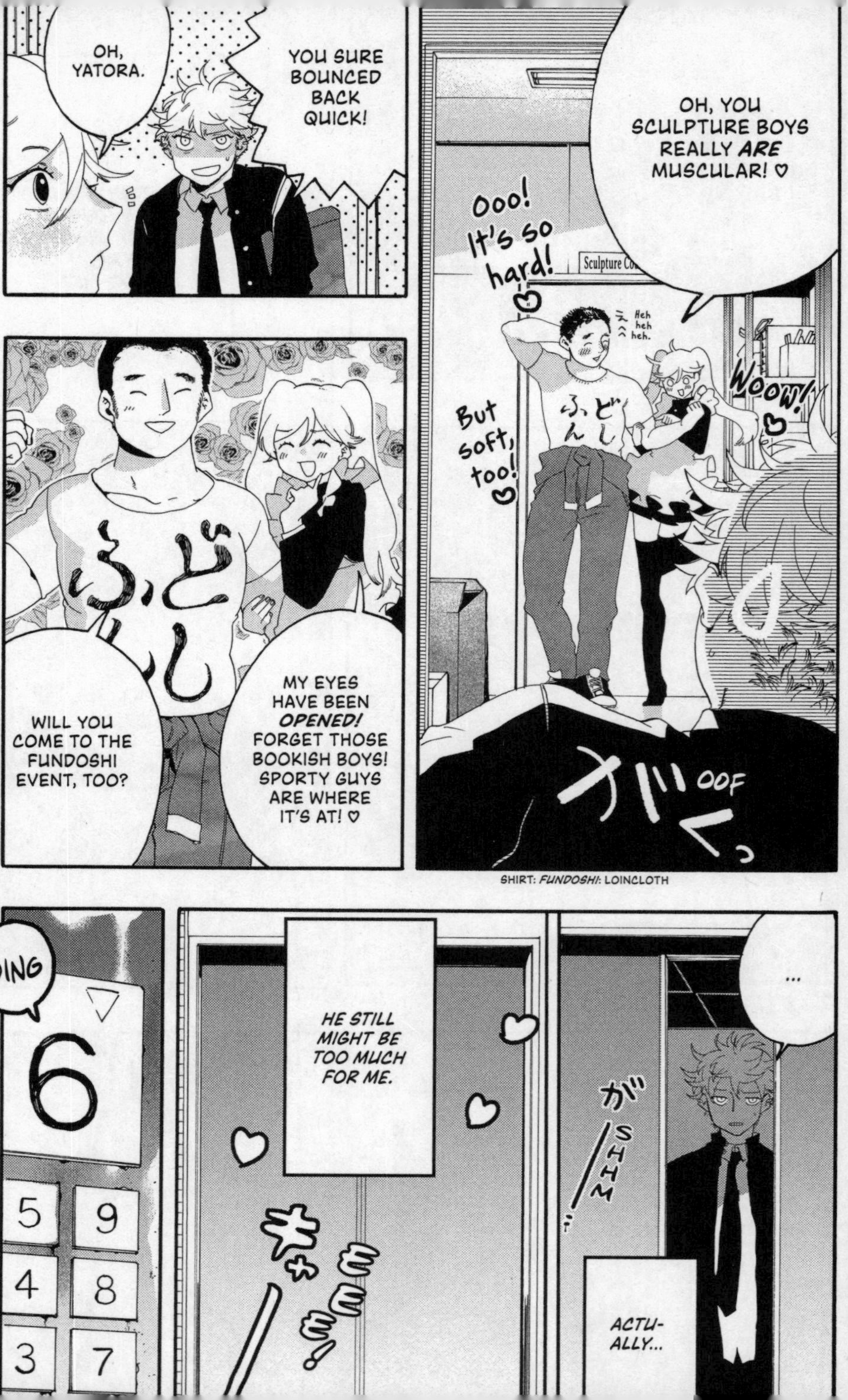
OH, YOU SCULPTURE BOYS REALLY *ARE* MUSCULAR! ♡
Ooo! It's so hard! ♡
Heh heh heh.
But soft, too! ♡
Woow! ♡
OOF
OH, YATORA.
YOU SURE BOUNCED BACK QUICK!
MY EYES HAVE BEEN *OPENED!* FORGET THOSE BOOKISH BOYS! SPORTY GUYS ARE WHERE IT'S AT! ♡
WILL YOU COME TO THE FUNDOSHI EVENT, TOO?
SHIRT: *FUNDOSHI*: LOINCLOTH
...
SHHM
ACTU-ALLY...
HE STILL MIGHT BE TOO MUCH FOR ME.
DING
6
5
9
4
8
3
7

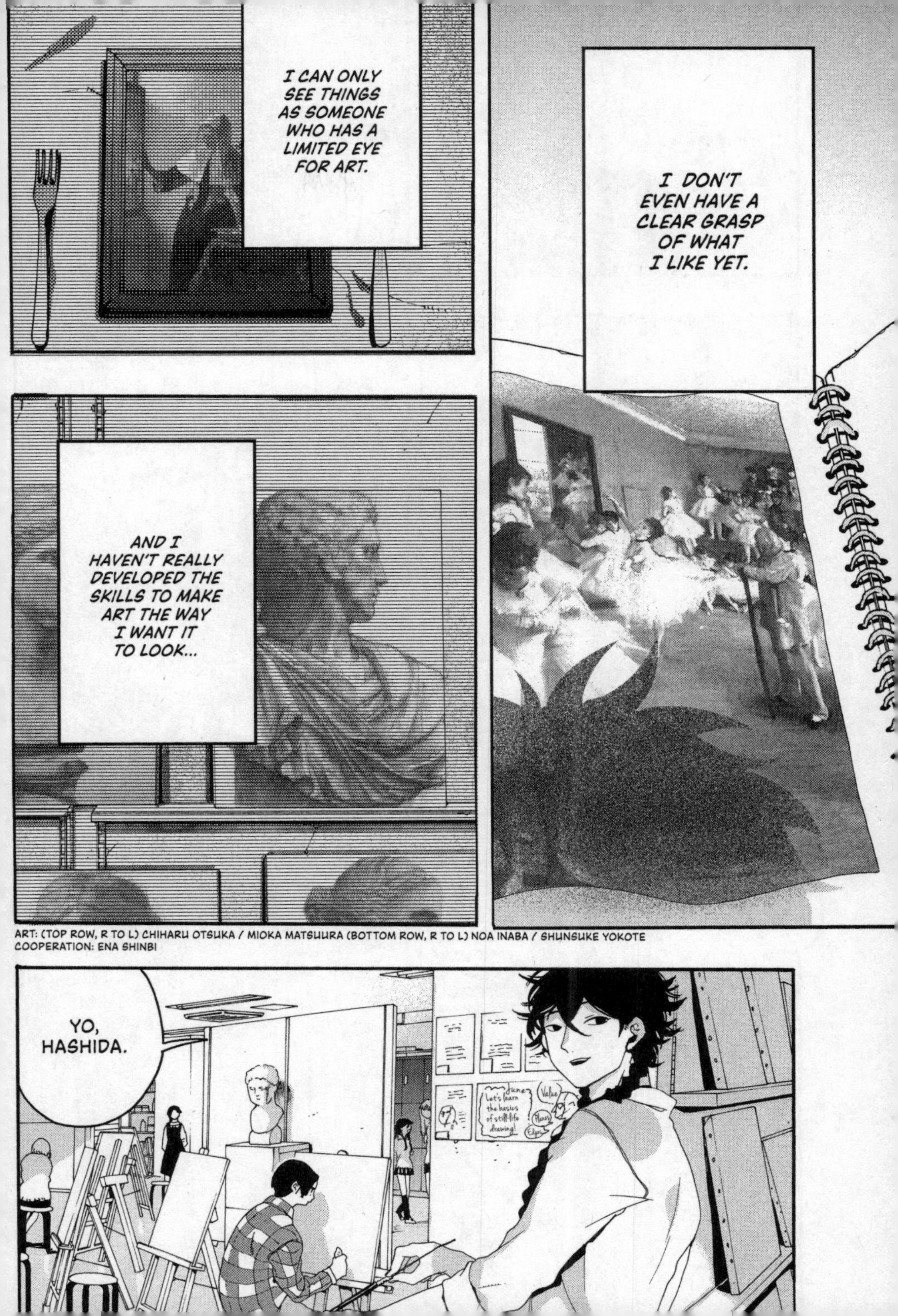
I DON'T EVEN HAVE A CLEAR GRASP OF WHAT I LIKE YET.
I CAN ONLY SEE THINGS AS SOMEONE WHO HAS A LIMITED EYE FOR ART.
AND I HAVEN'T REALLY DEVELOPED THE SKILLS TO MAKE ART THE WAY I WANT IT TO LOOK...
YO, HASHIDA.
June
Let's learn the basics of still-life drawing!
Value
Planes
Edges
ART: (TOP ROW, R TO L) CHIHARU OTSUKA / MIOKA MATSUURA (BOTTOM ROW, R TO L) NOA INABA / SHUNSUKE YOKOTE
COOPERATION: ENA SHINBI

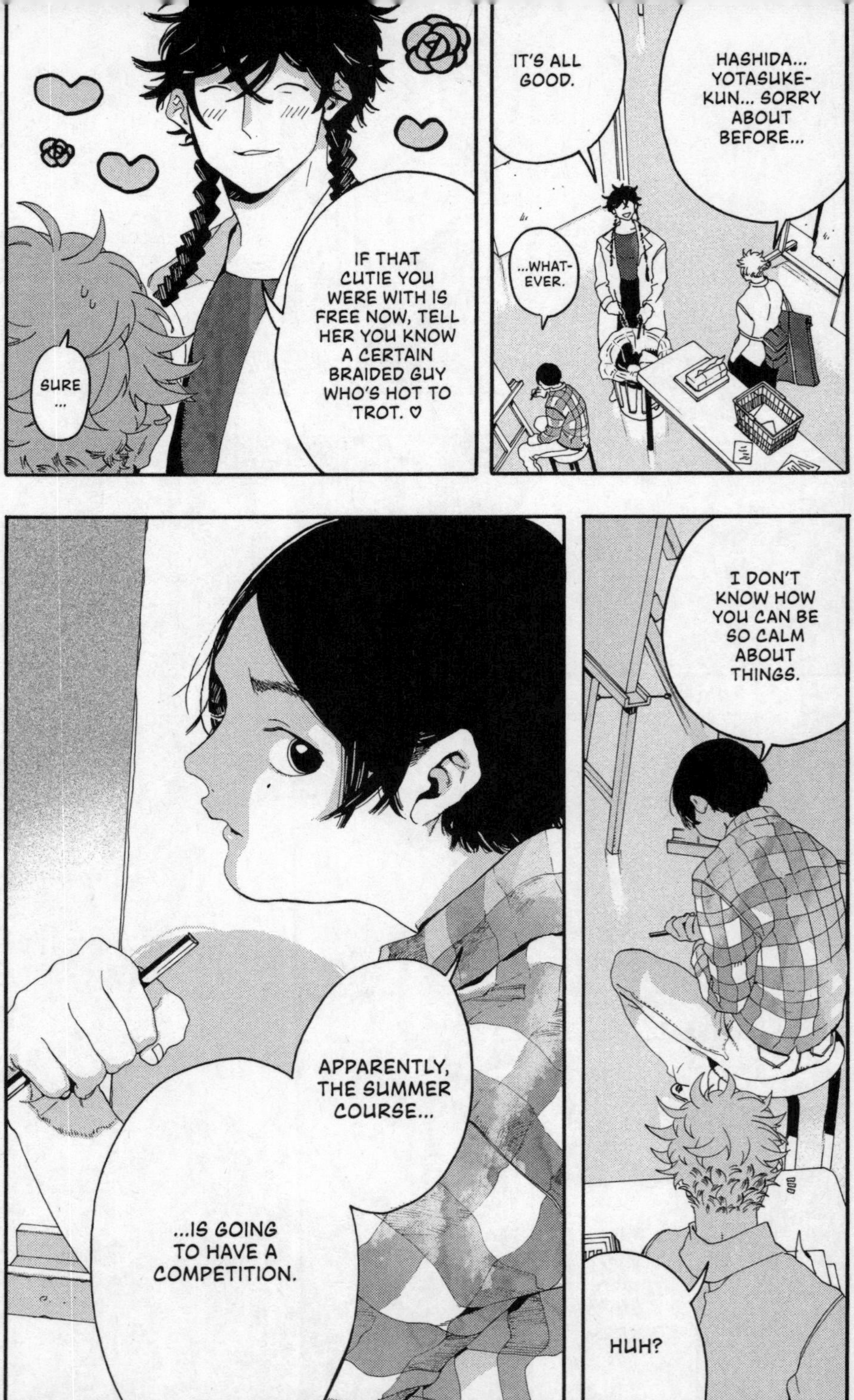
HASHIDA... YOTASUKE-KUN... SORRY ABOUT BEFORE...
IT'S ALL GOOD.
...WHAT-EVER.
IF THAT CUTIE YOU WERE WITH IS FREE NOW, TELL HER YOU KNOW A CERTAIN BRAIDED GUY WHO'S HOT TO TROT. ♡
SURE...
I DON'T KNOW HOW YOU CAN BE SO CALM ABOUT THINGS.
HUH?
APPARENTLY, THE SUMMER COURSE...
...IS GOING TO HAVE A COMPETITION.

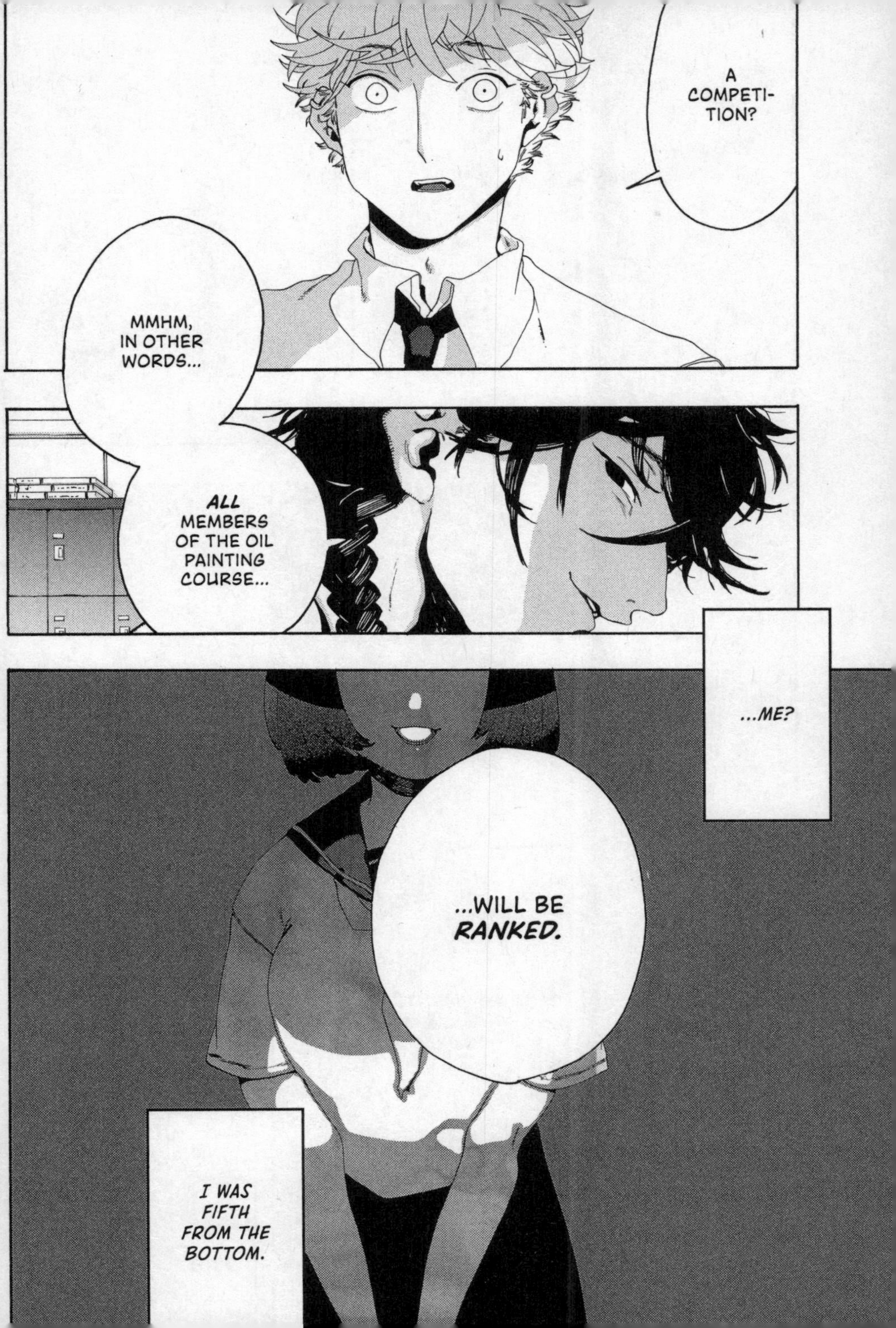
A COMPETI- TION?
MMHM, IN OTHER WORDS...
ALL MEMBERS OF THE OIL PAINTING COURSE...
...ME?
...WILL BE RANKED.
I WAS FIFTH FROM THE BOTTOM.

BLUE PERIOD

BLUE PERIOD

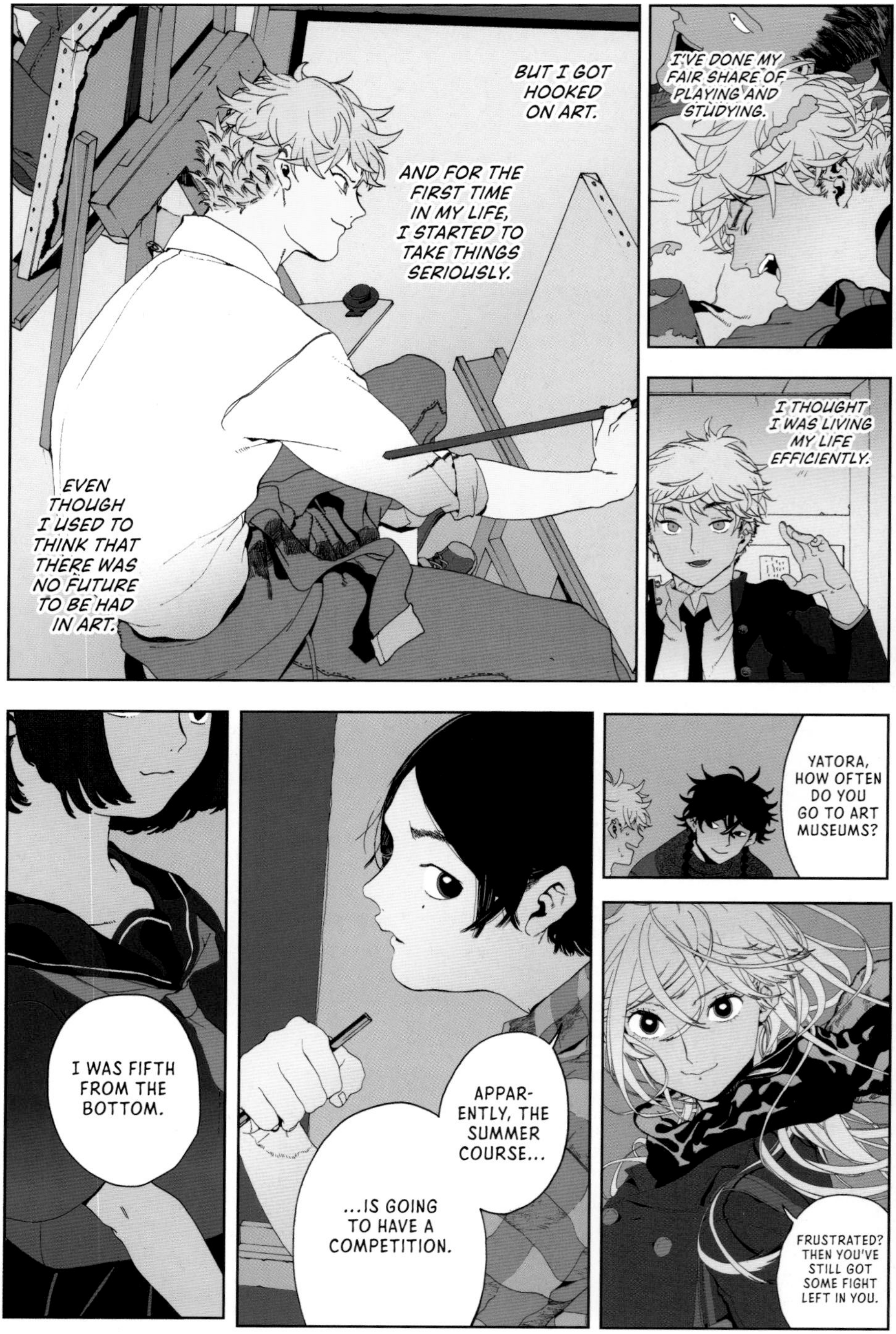
I'VE DONE MY FAIR SHARE OF PLAYING AND STUDYING.
I THOUGHT I WAS LIVING MY LIFE EFFICIENTLY.
BUT I GOT HOOKED ON ART.
AND FOR THE FIRST TIME IN MY LIFE, I STARTED TO TAKE THINGS SERIOUSLY.
EVEN THOUGH I USED TO THINK THAT THERE WAS NO FUTURE TO BE HAD IN ART.
YATORA, HOW OFTEN DO YOU GO TO ART MUSEUMS?
FRUSTRATED? THEN YOU'VE STILL GOT SOME FIGHT LEFT IN YOU.
APPAR- ENTLY, THE SUMMER COURSE...
...IS GOING TO HAVE A COMPETITION.
I WAS FIFTH FROM THE BOTTOM.

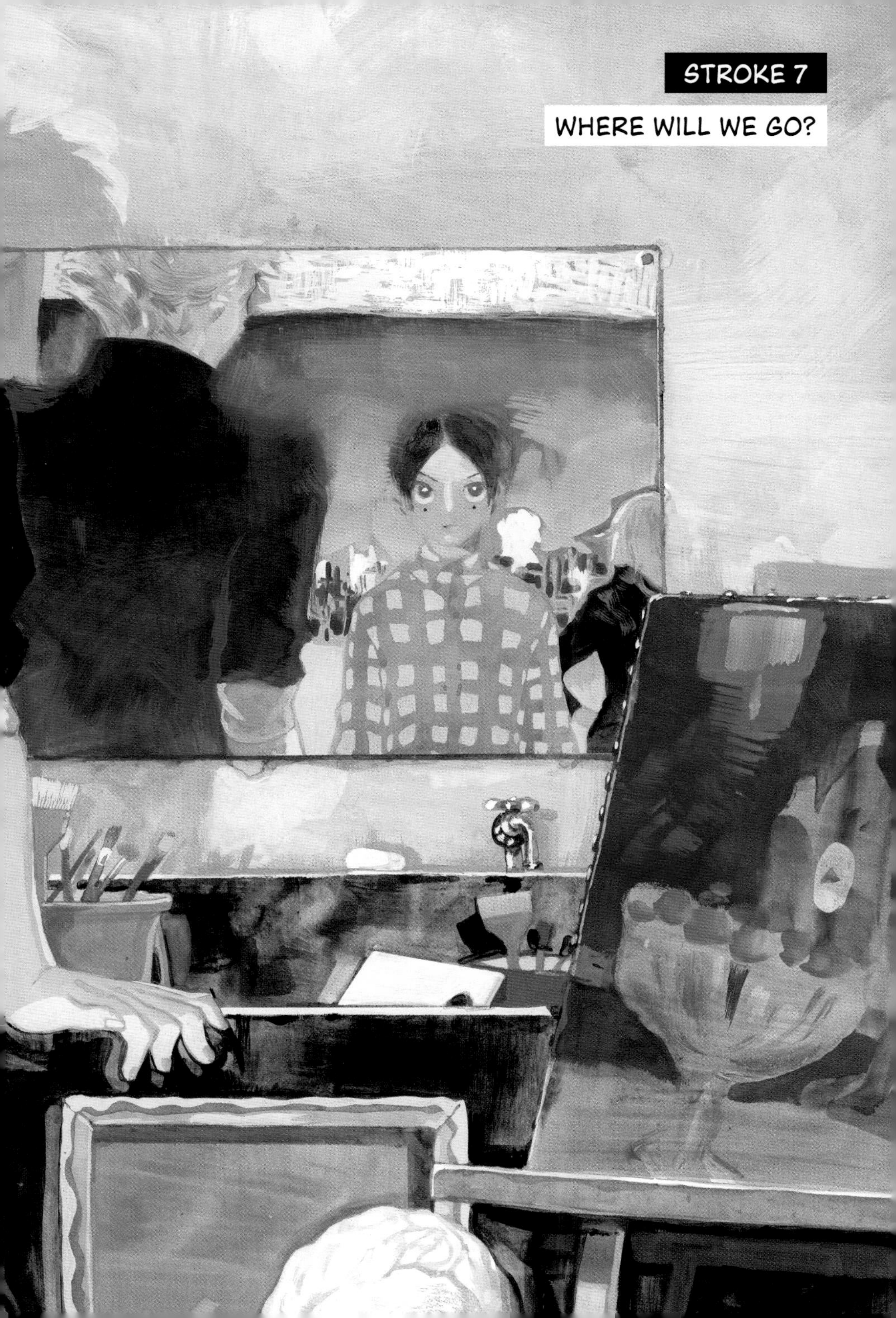
STROKE 7
WHERE WILL WE GO?

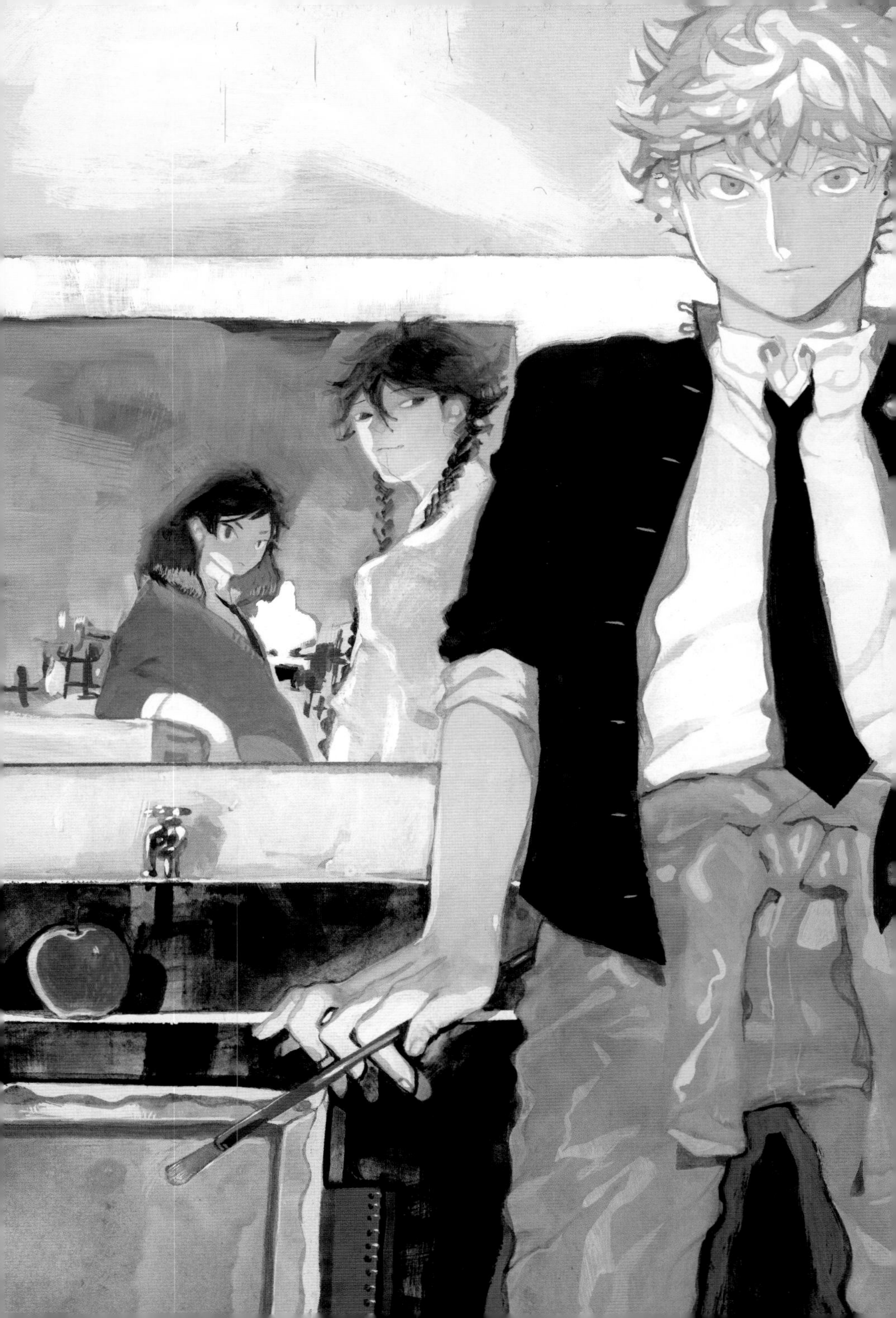

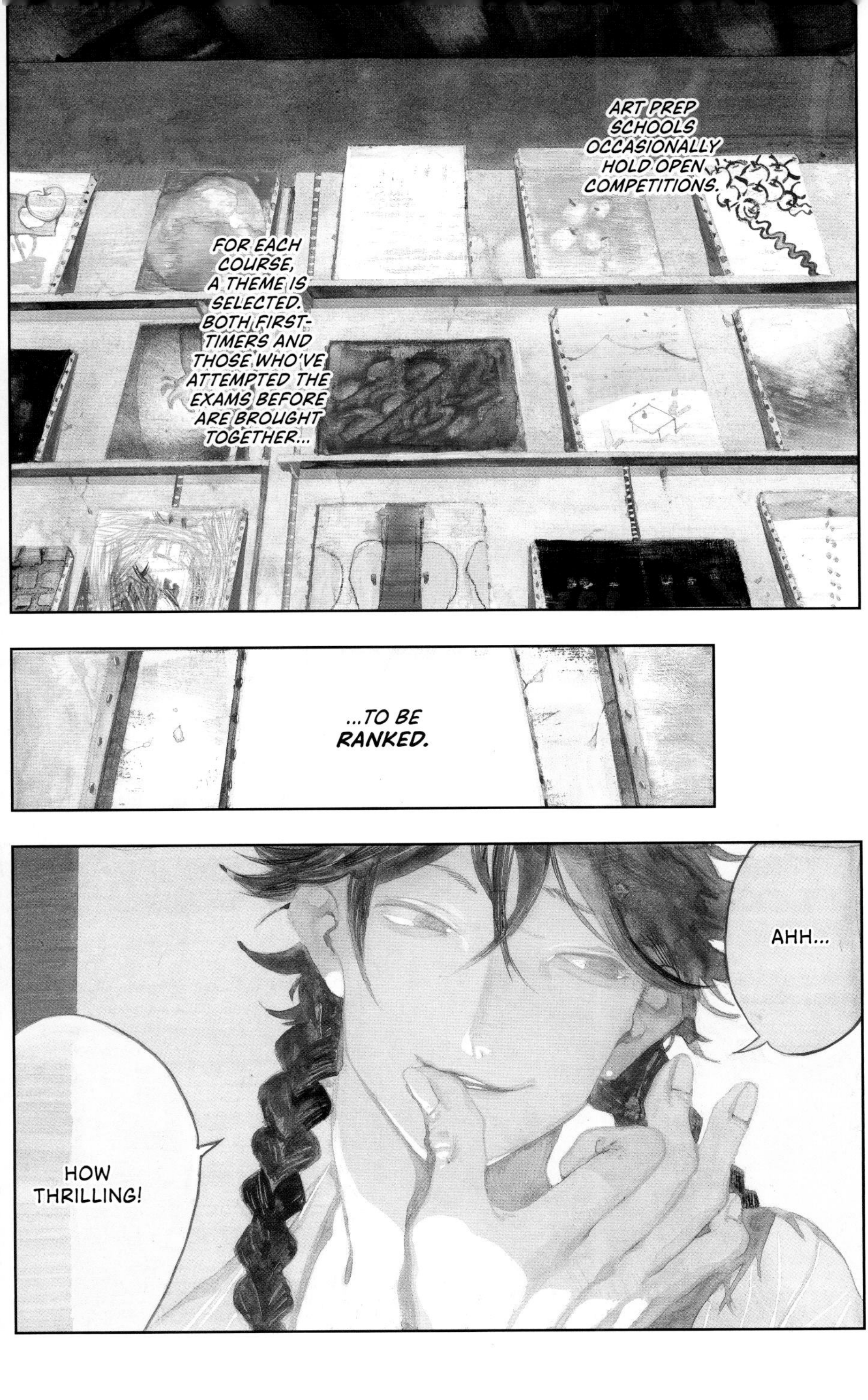
ART PREP SCHOOLS OCCASIONALLY HOLD OPEN COMPETITIONS.
FOR EACH COURSE, A THEME IS SELECTED. BOTH FIRST-TIMERS AND THOSE WHO'VE ATTEMPTED THE EXAMS BEFORE ARE BROUGHT TOGETHER...
...TO BE RANKED.
AHH...
HOW THRILLING!

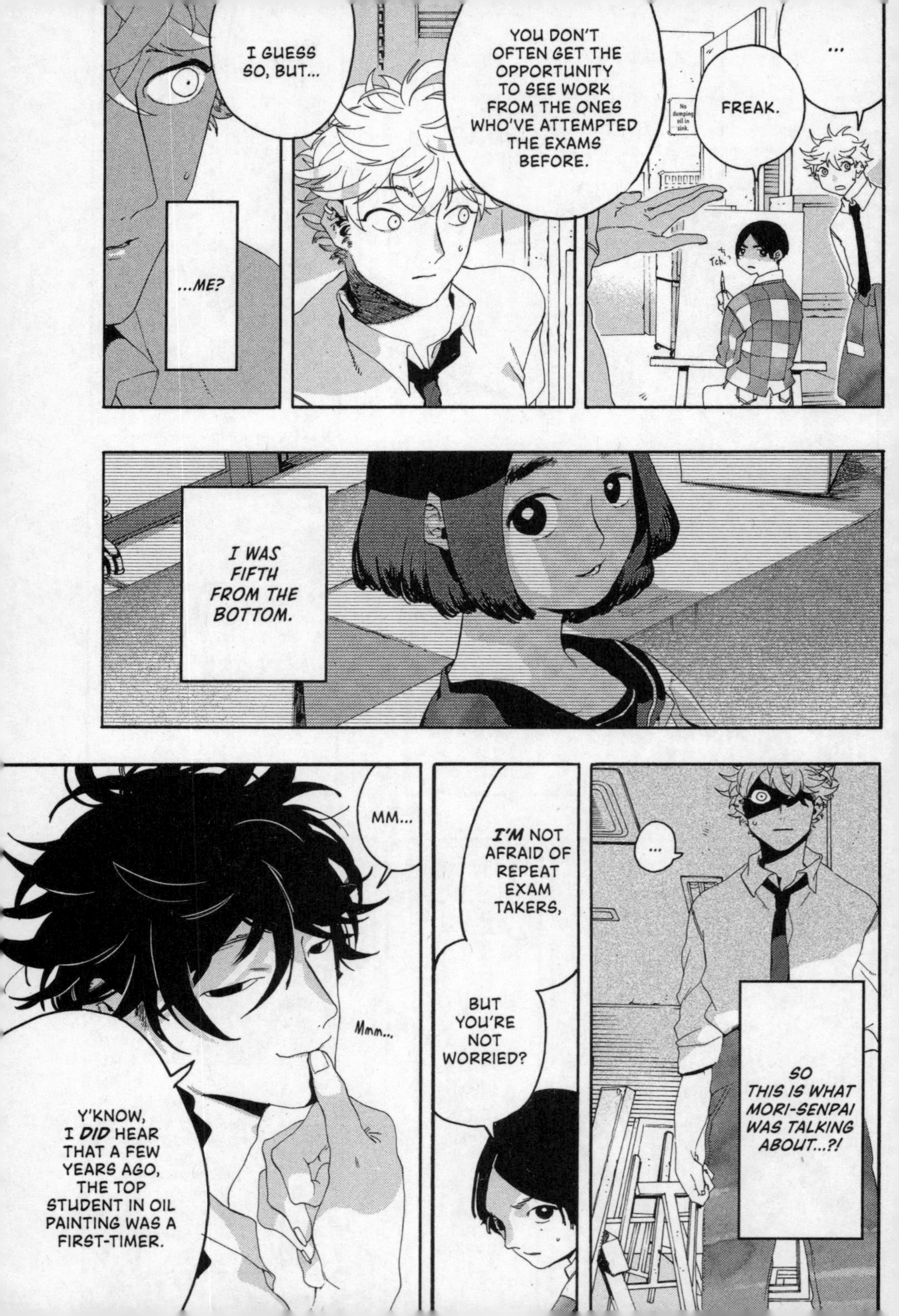
...
FREAK.
No dumping oil in sink.
Tch.
YOU DON'T OFTEN GET THE OPPORTUNITY TO SEE WORK FROM THE ONES WHO'VE ATTEMPTED THE EXAMS BEFORE.
I GUESS SO, BUT...
...ME?
I WAS FIFTH FROM THE BOTTOM.
...
SO THIS IS WHAT MORI-SENPAI WAS TALKING ABOUT...?!
I'M NOT AFRAID OF REPEAT EXAM TAKERS,
BUT YOU'RE NOT WORRIED?
MM...
Mmm...
Y'KNOW, I DID HEAR THAT A FEW YEARS AGO, THE TOP STUDENT IN OIL PAINTING WAS A FIRST-TIMER.

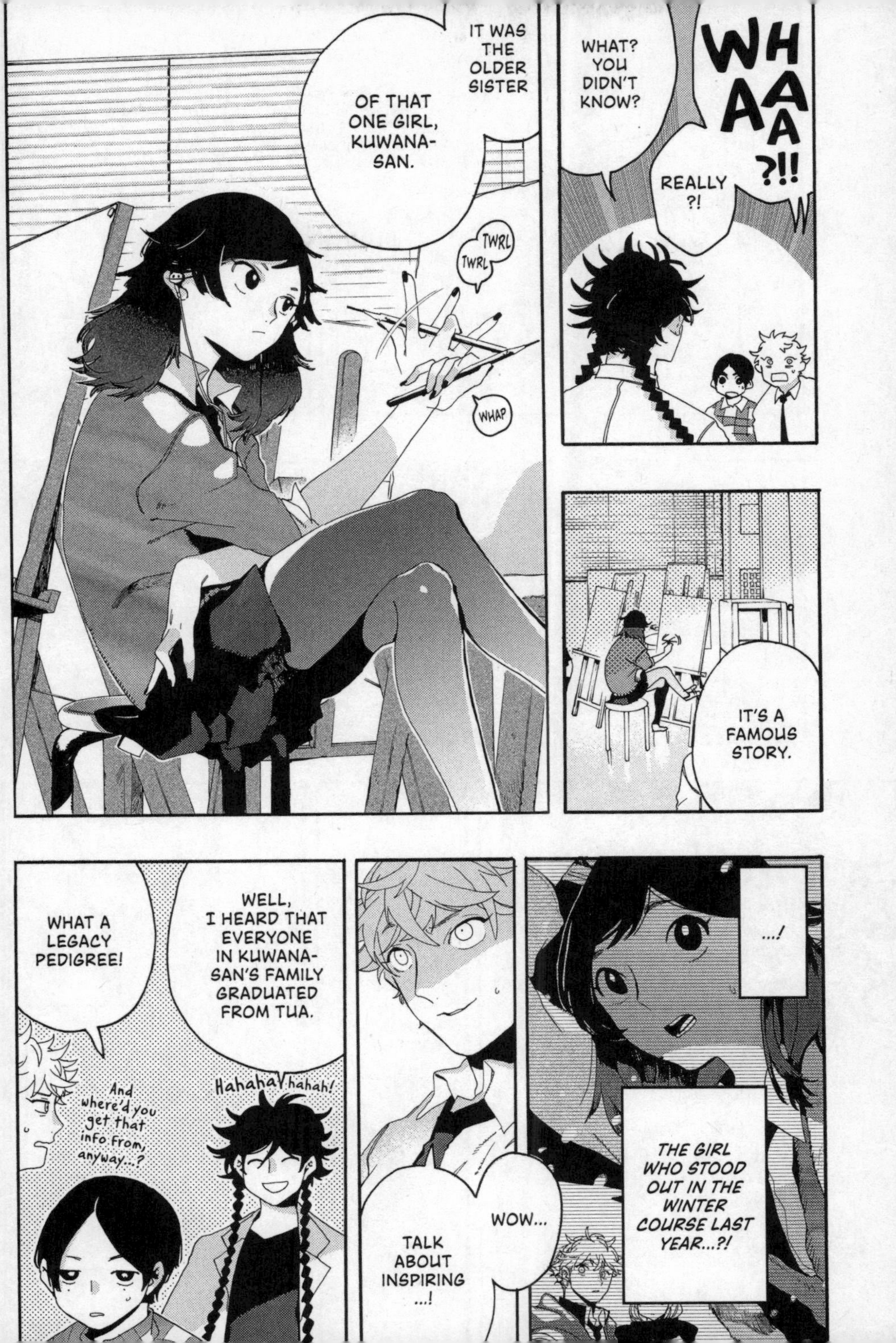
WHAAA?!!
WHAT? YOU DIDN'T KNOW?
REALLY?!
IT'S A FAMOUS STORY.
IT WAS THE OLDER SISTER
OF THAT ONE GIRL, KUWANA-SAN.
TWRL TWRL
WHAP
...!
THE GIRL WHO STOOD OUT IN THE WINTER COURSE LAST YEAR...?!
WOW...
TALK ABOUT INSPIRING ...!
WELL, I HEARD THAT EVERYONE IN KUWANA-SAN'S FAMILY GRADUATED FROM TUA.
WHAT A LEGACY PEDIGREE!
Hahaha hahah!
And where'd you get that info from, anyway...?

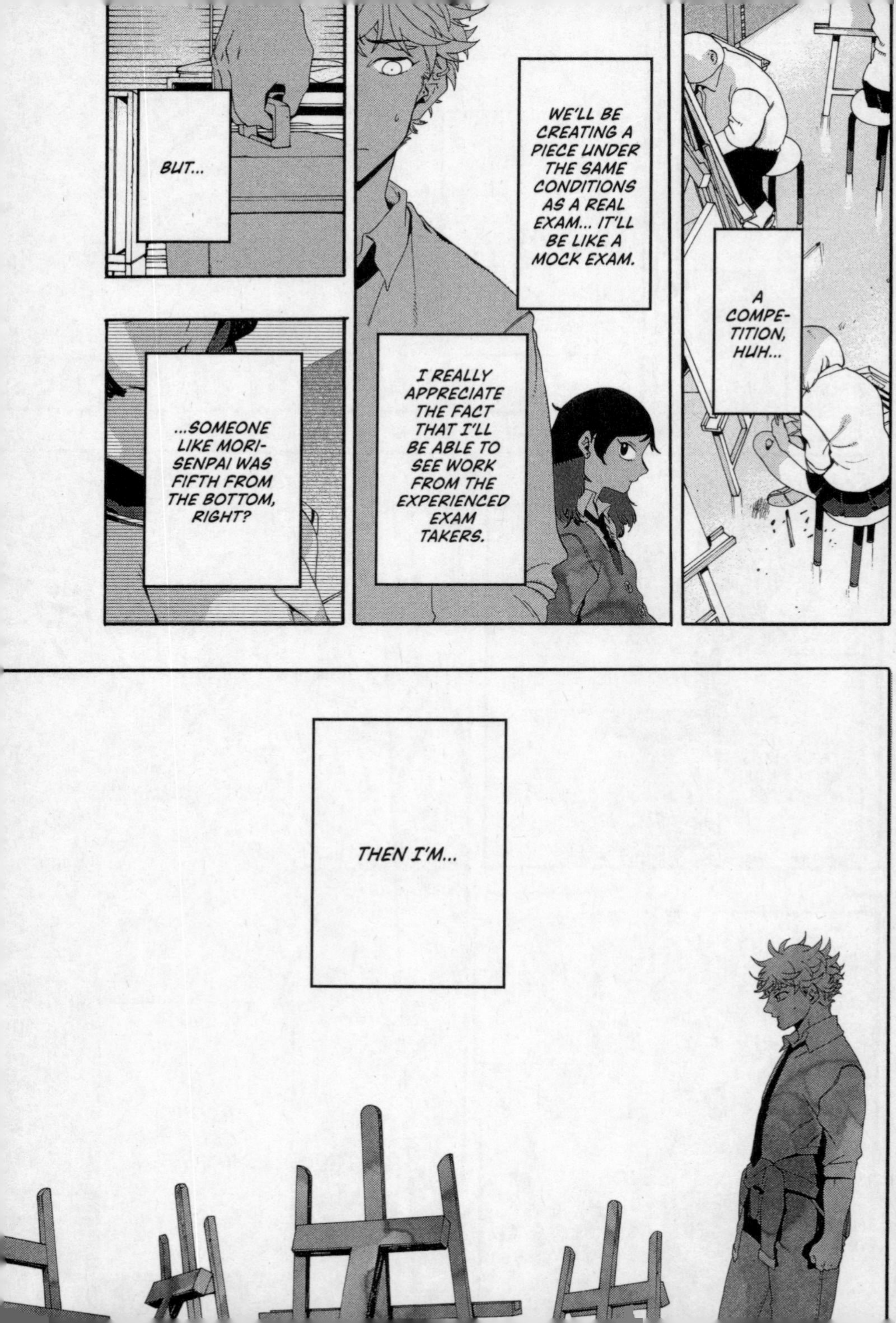
A COMPETITION, HUH...
WE'LL BE CREATING A PIECE UNDER THE SAME CONDITIONS AS A REAL EXAM... IT'LL BE LIKE A MOCK EXAM.
I REALLY APPRECIATE THE FACT THAT I'LL BE ABLE TO SEE WORK FROM THE EXPERIENCED EXAM TAKERS.
BUT...
...SOMEONE LIKE MORI-SENPAI WAS FIFTH FROM THE BOTTOM, RIGHT?
THEN I'M...

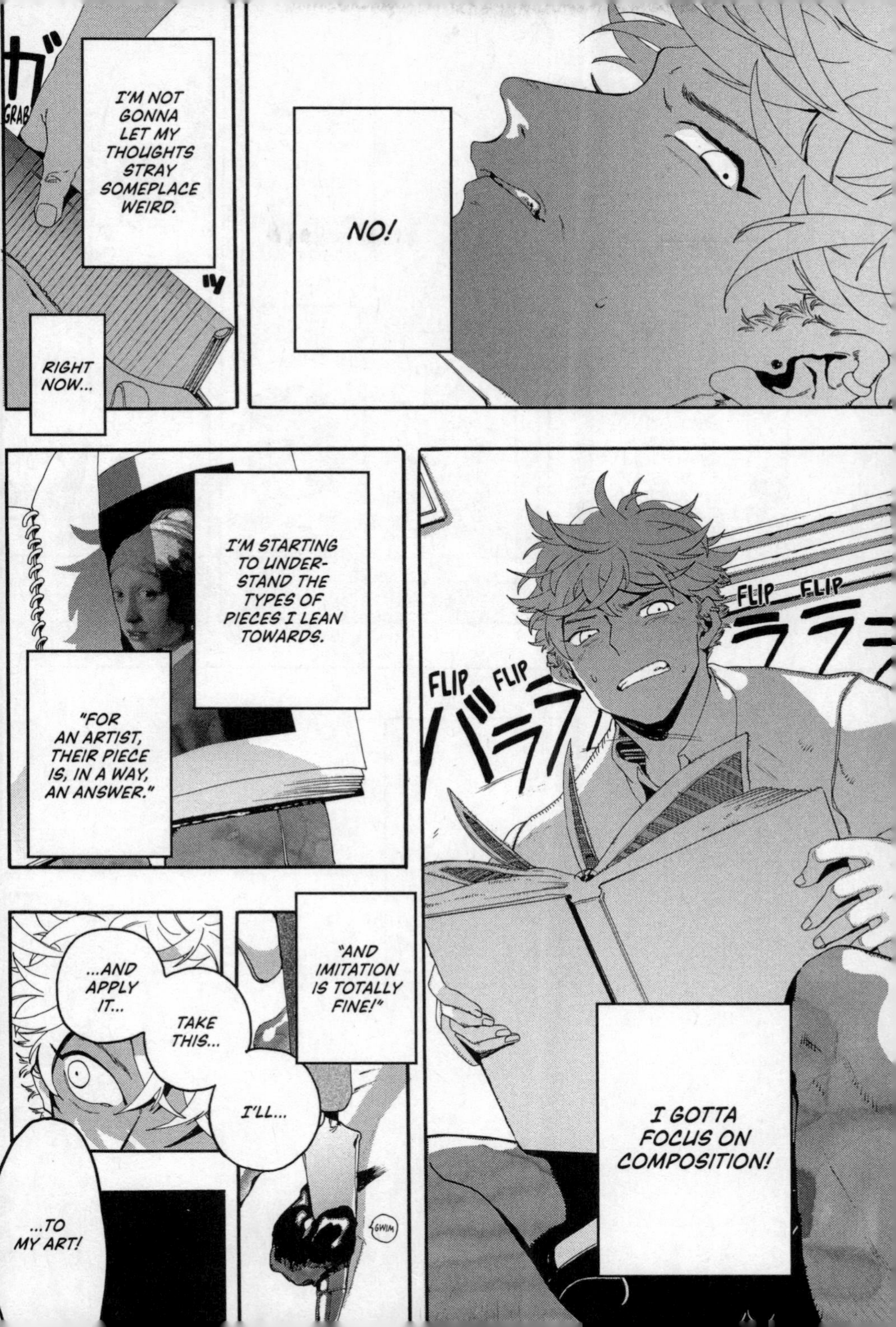

NO!
GRAB
I'M NOT GONNA LET MY THOUGHTS STRAY SOMEPLACE WEIRD.
RIGHT NOW...
FLIP FLIP
FLIP FLIP
I GOTTA FOCUS ON COMPOSITION!
I'M STARTING TO UNDER-STAND THE TYPES OF PIECES I LEAN TOWARDS.
"FOR AN ARTIST, THEIR PIECE IS, IN A WAY, AN ANSWER."
"AND IMITATION IS TOTALLY FINE!"
GWIM
I'LL...
TAKE THIS...
...AND APPLY IT...
...TO MY ART!

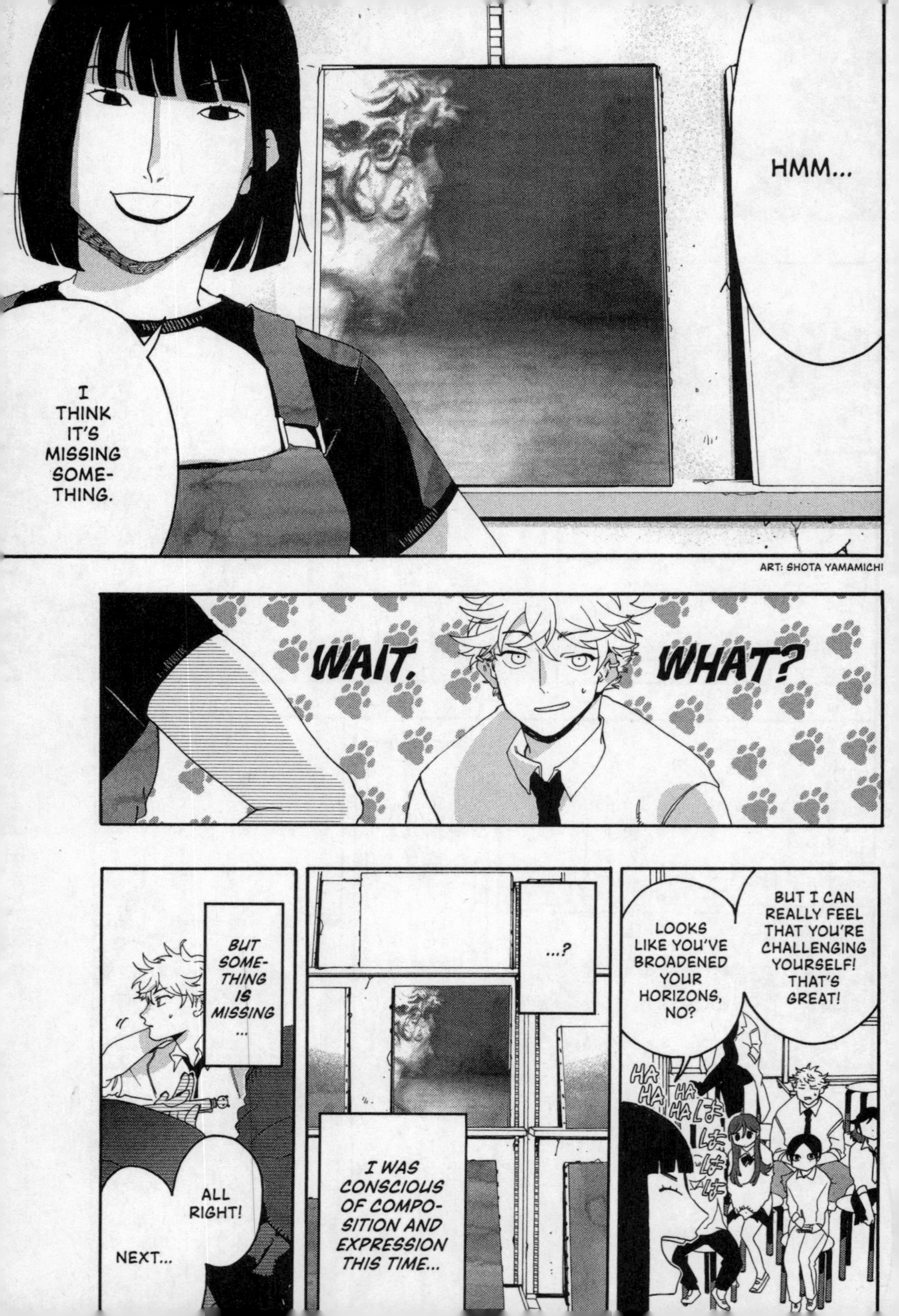
HMM...
I THINK IT'S MISSING SOME-THING.
WAIT.
WHAT?
LOOKS LIKE YOU'VE BROADENED YOUR HORIZONS, NO?
BUT I CAN REALLY FEEL THAT YOU'RE CHALLENGING YOURSELF! THAT'S GREAT!
HA HA HA HA
ははははは
...?
I WAS CONSCIOUS OF COMPO-SITION AND EXPRESSION THIS TIME...
BUT SOME-THING IS MISSING ...
ALL RIGHT!
NEXT...

ART: SHOTA YAMAMICHI

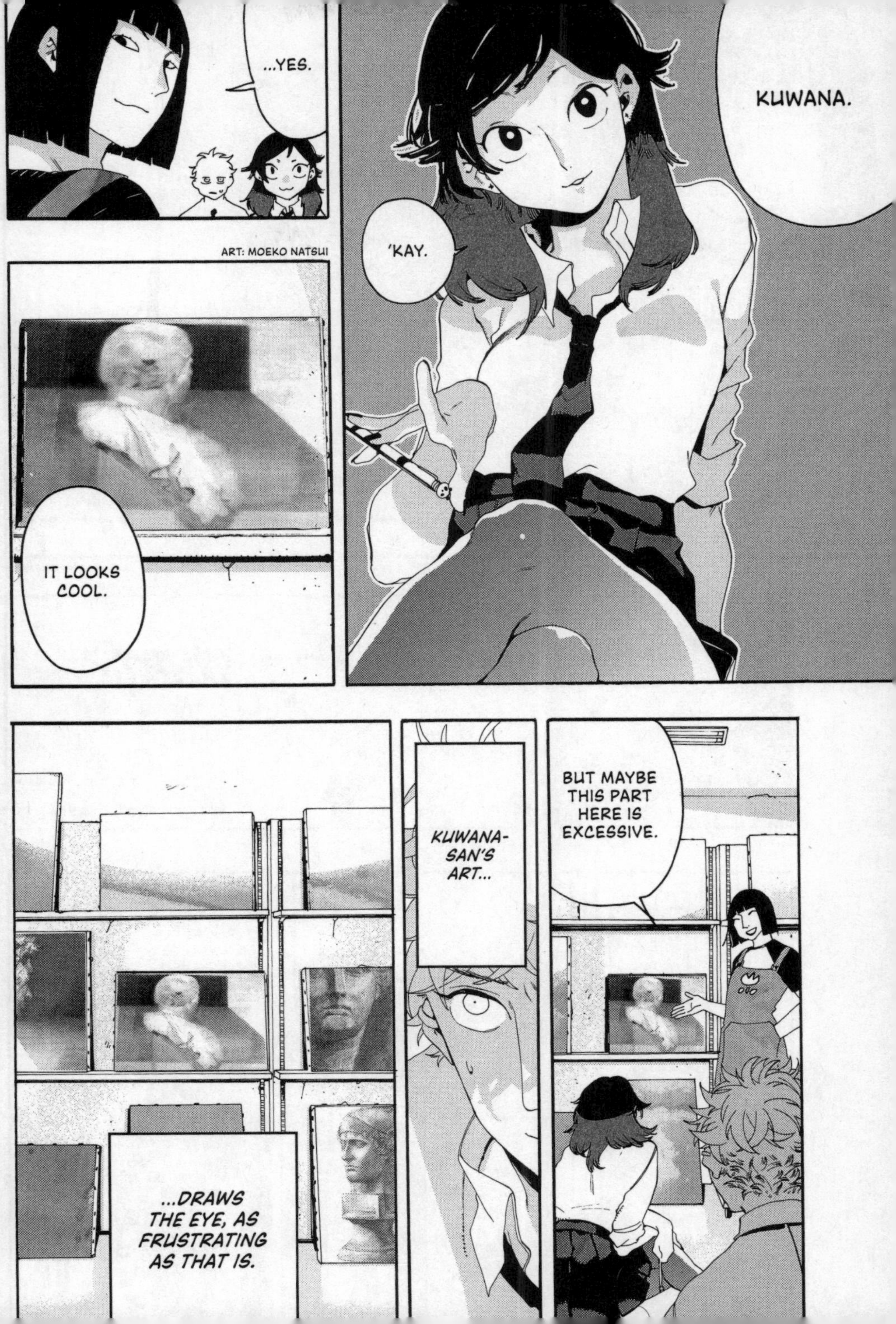

KUWANA.
'KAY.
...YES.
ART: MOEKO NATSUI
IT LOOKS COOL.
BUT MAYBE THIS PART HERE IS EXCESSIVE.
KUWANA-SAN'S ART...
...DRAWS THE EYE, AS FRUSTRATING AS THAT IS.

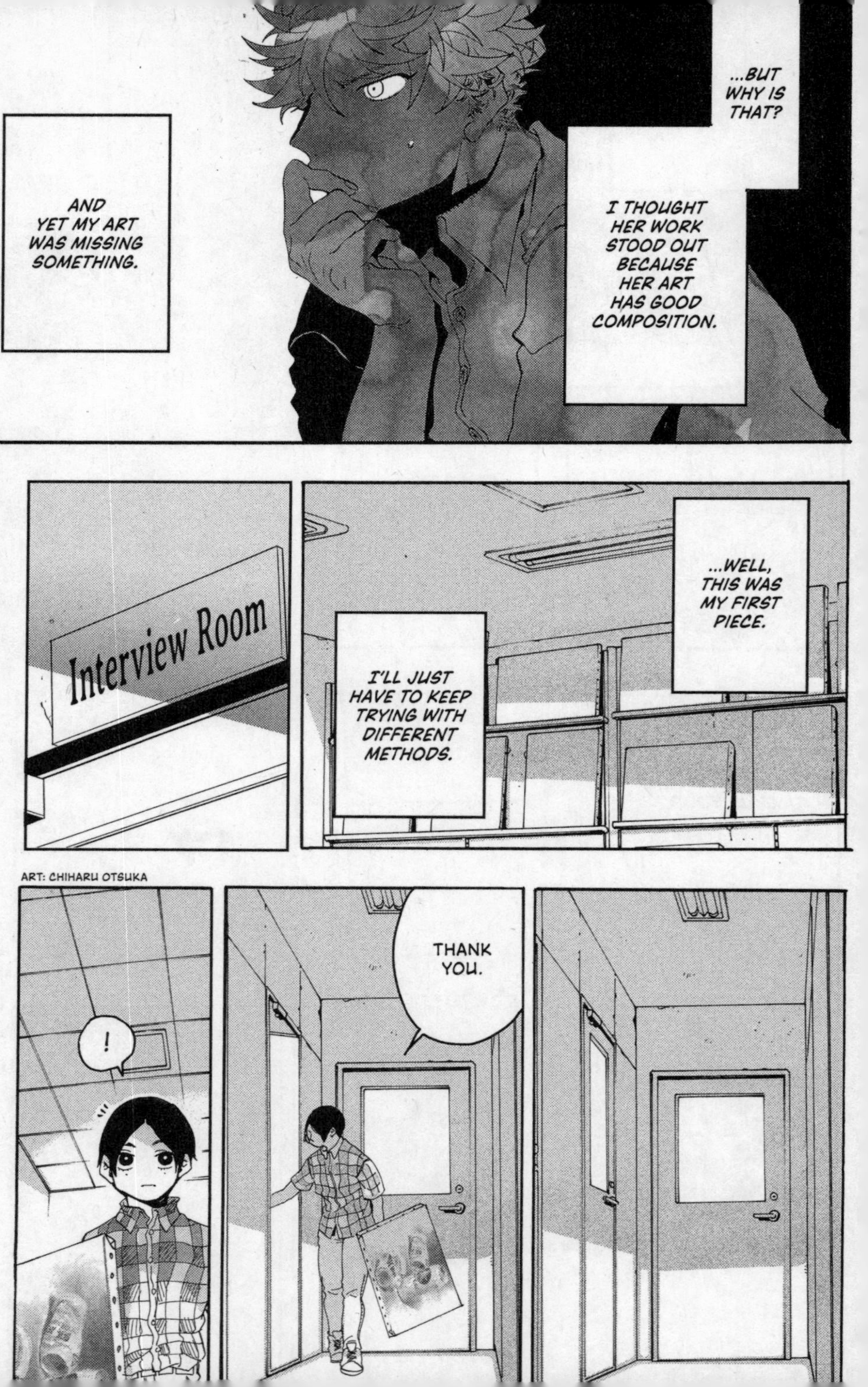
...BUT WHY IS THAT?
I THOUGHT HER WORK STOOD OUT BECAUSE HER ART HAS GOOD COMPOSITION.
AND YET MY ART WAS MISSING SOMETHING.
...WELL, THIS WAS MY FIRST PIECE.
I'LL JUST HAVE TO KEEP TRYING WITH DIFFERENT METHODS.
Interview Room
ART: CHIHARU OTSUKA
THANK YOU.
!

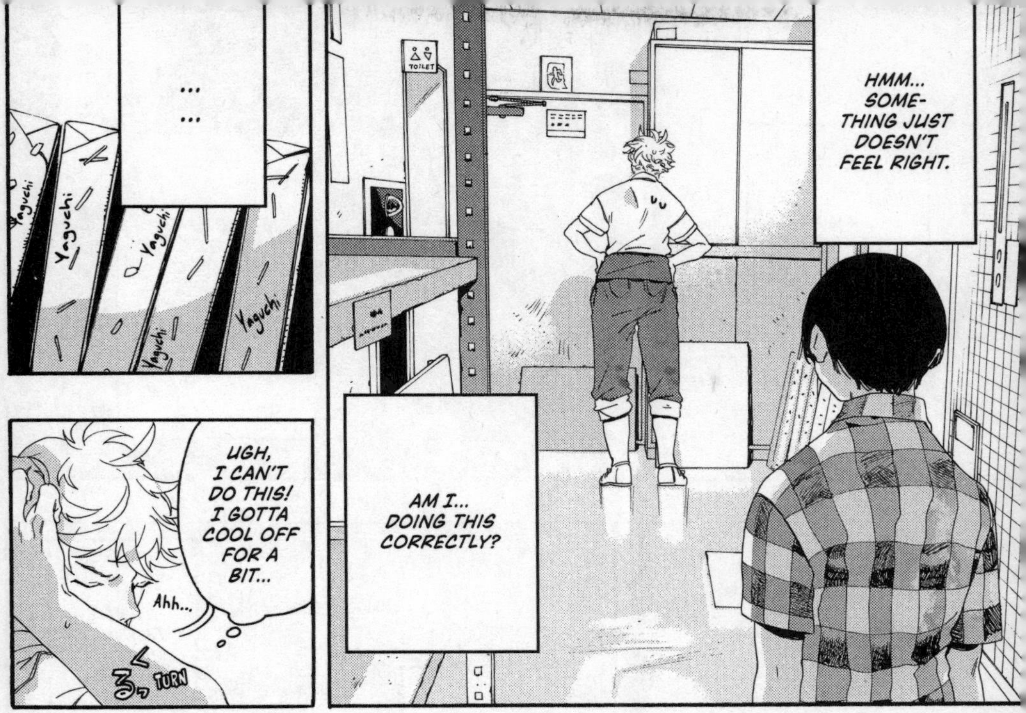
HMM... SOME-THING JUST DOESN'T FEEL RIGHT.
AM I... DOING THIS CORRECTLY?
...
...
UGH, I CAN'T DO THIS! I GOTTA COOL OFF FOR A BIT...
Ahh...
TURN

ART: (L) TAMANA MOTEKI (R) SHOTA YAMAMICHI

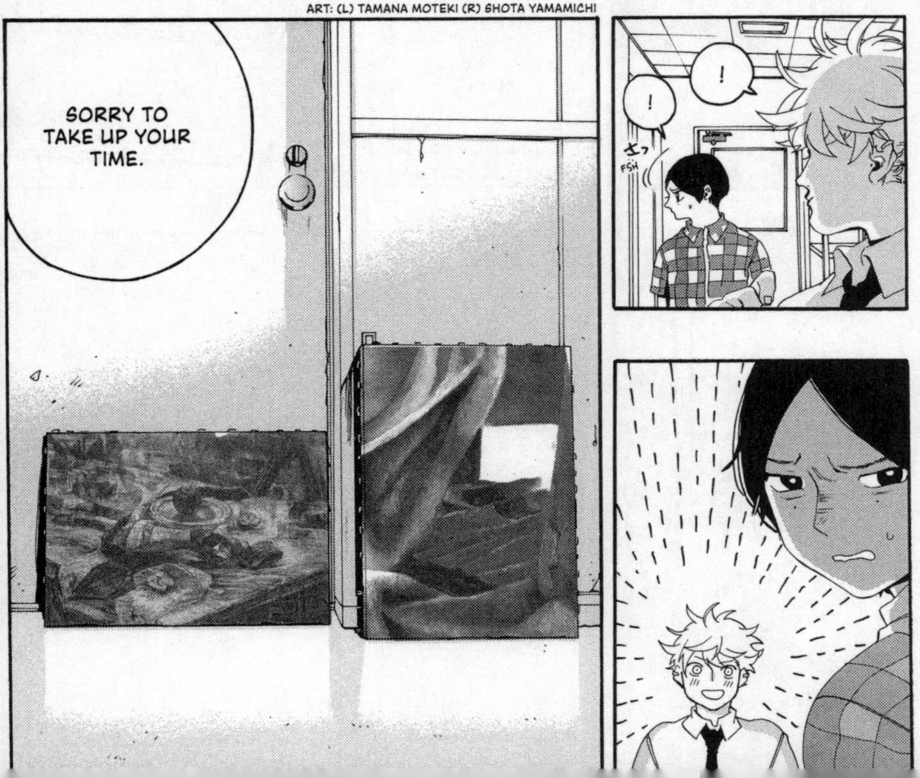
!
!
FSH
SORRY TO TAKE UP YOUR TIME.

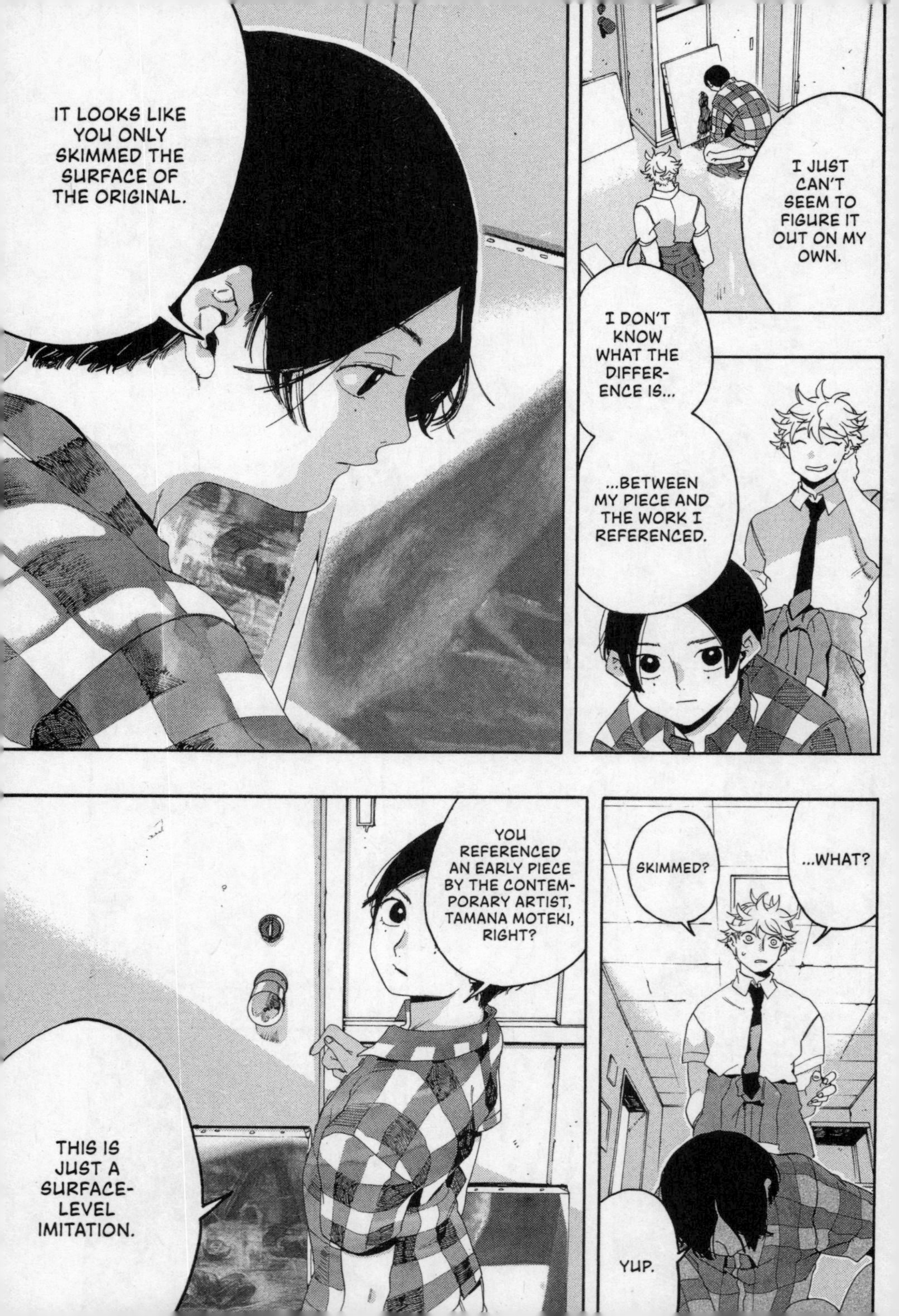
I JUST CAN'T SEEM TO FIGURE IT OUT ON MY OWN.
I DON'T KNOW WHAT THE DIFFERENCE IS...
...BETWEEN MY PIECE AND THE WORK I REFERENCED.
IT LOOKS LIKE YOU ONLY SKIMMED THE SURFACE OF THE ORIGINAL.
...WHAT?
SKIMMED?
YUP.
YOU REFERENCED AN EARLY PIECE BY THE CONTEMPORARY ARTIST, TAMANA MOTEKI, RIGHT?
THIS IS JUST A SURFACE-LEVEL IMITATION.

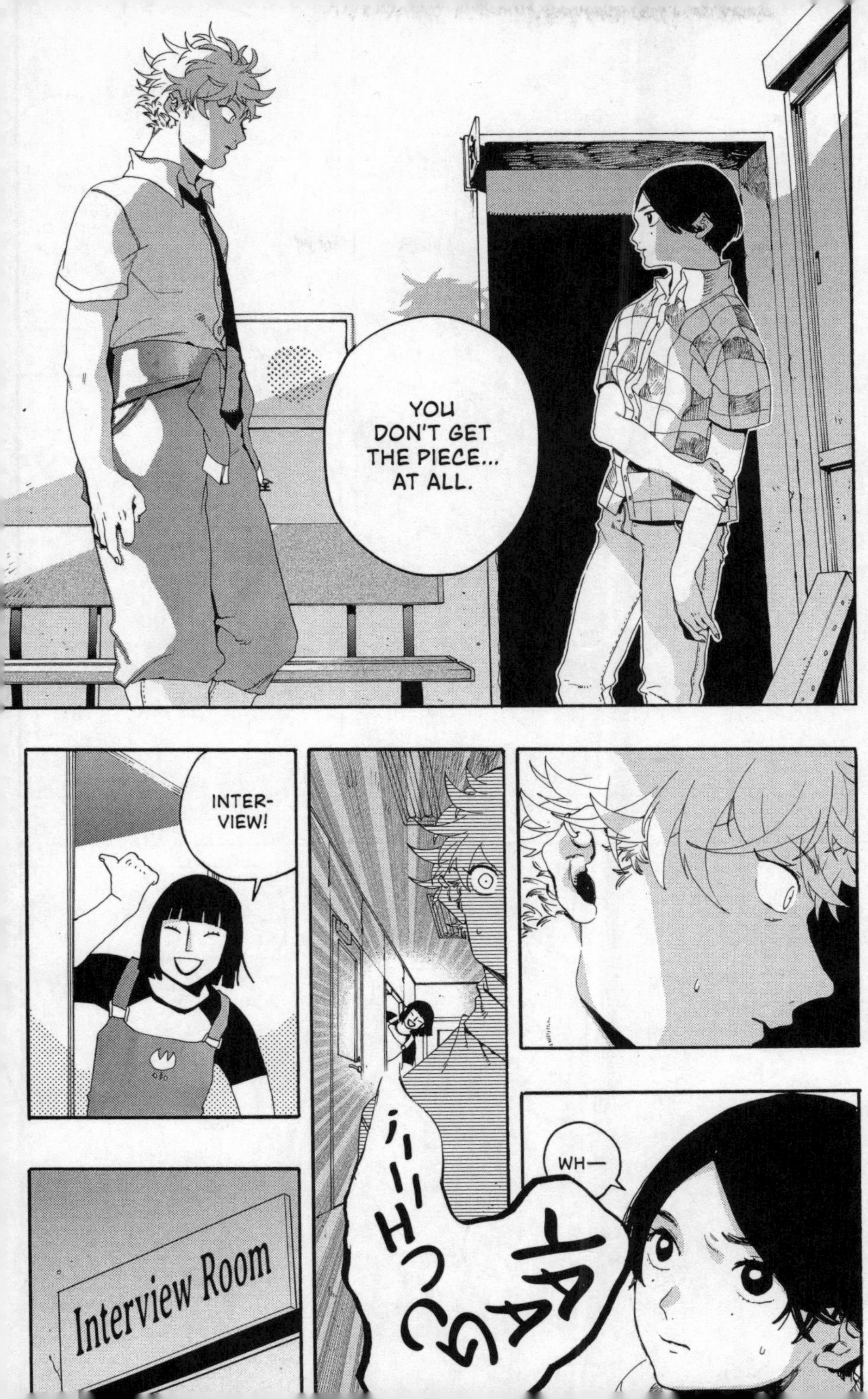
YOU DON'T GET THE PIECE... AT ALL.
WH—
AAHっっっ!!!!
INTER-VIEW!
Interview Room

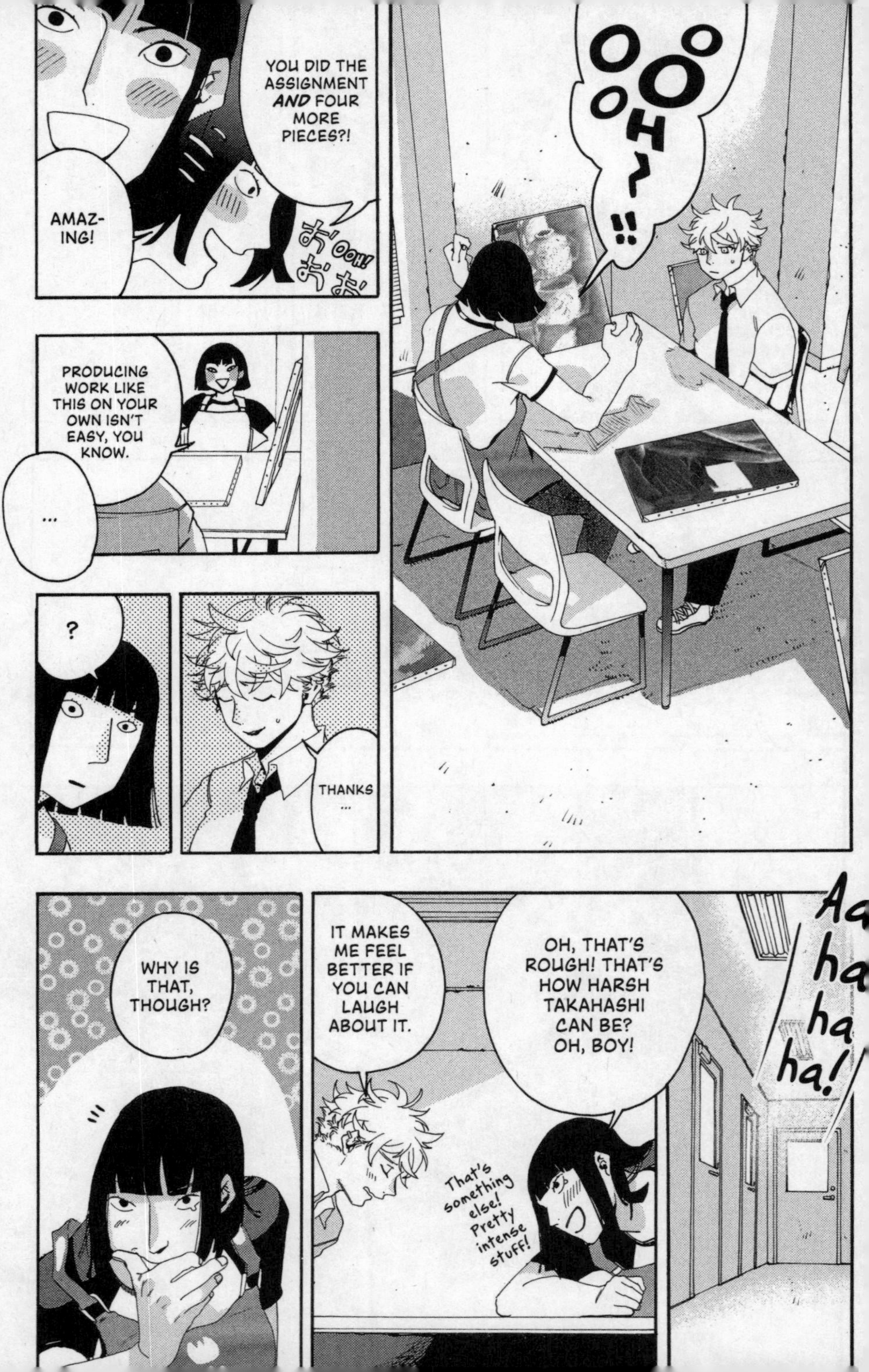
OOOOH~!!
YOU DID THE ASSIGNMENT AND FOUR MORE PIECES?!
OOH!
AMAZ-ING!
PRODUCING WORK LIKE THIS ON YOUR OWN ISN'T EASY, YOU KNOW.
...
THANKS...
?
Aahahaha!
OH, THAT'S ROUGH! THAT'S HOW HARSH TAKAHASHI CAN BE? OH, BOY!
IT MAKES ME FEEL BETTER IF YOU CAN LAUGH ABOUT IT.
That's something else! Pretty intense stuff!
WHY IS THAT, THOUGH?

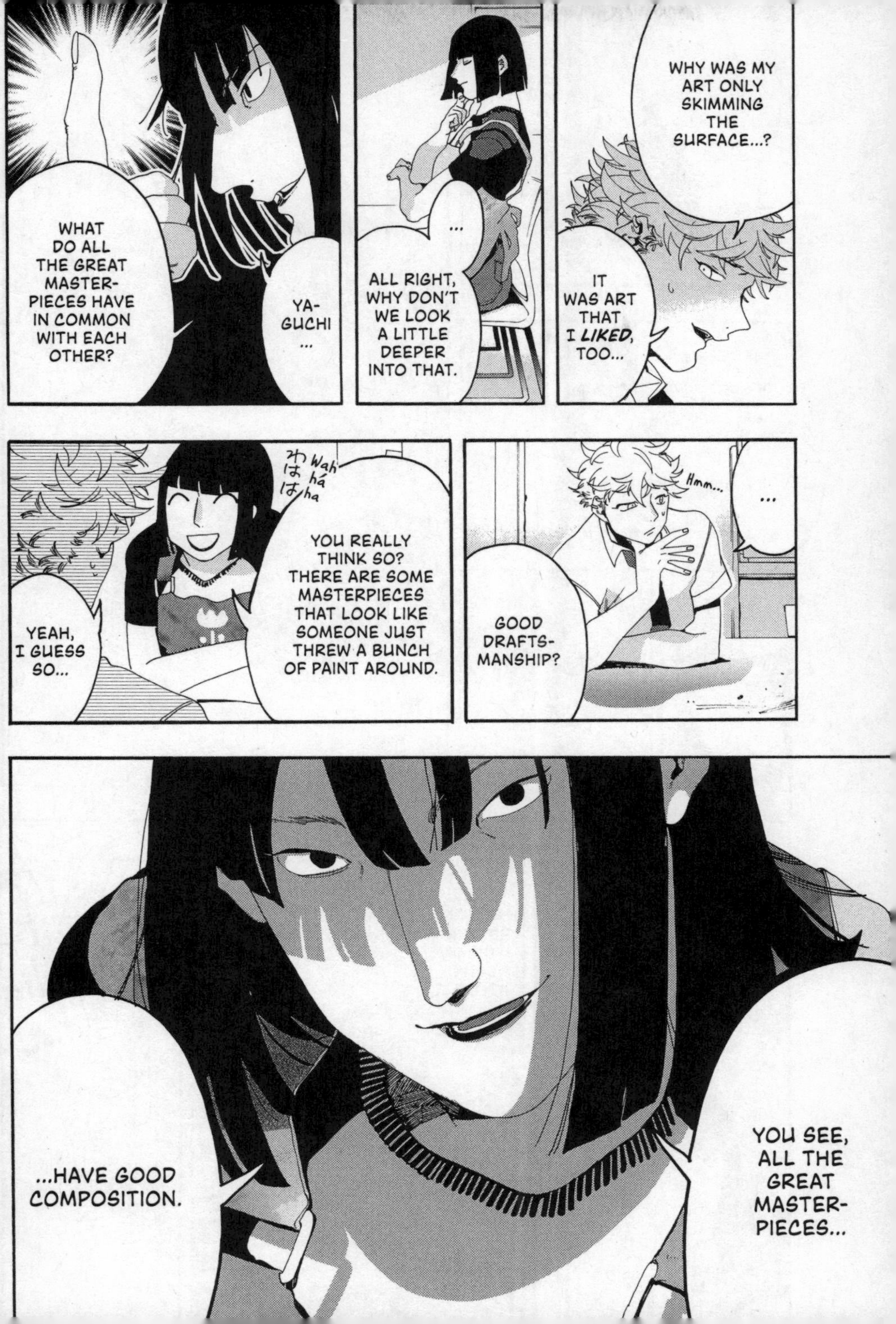
WHY WAS MY ART ONLY SKIMMING THE SURFACE...?
IT WAS ART THAT I *LIKED*, TOO...
...
ALL RIGHT, WHY DON'T WE LOOK A LITTLE DEEPER INTO THAT.
YA-GUCHI ...
WHAT DO ALL THE GREAT MASTER-PIECES HAVE IN COMMON WITH EACH OTHER?
Hmm...
...
GOOD DRAFTS-MANSHIP?
わはは Wah há ha
YOU REALLY THINK SO? THERE ARE SOME MASTERPIECES THAT LOOK LIKE SOMEONE JUST THREW A BUNCH OF PAINT AROUND.
YEAH, I GUESS SO...
YOU SEE, ALL THE GREAT MASTER-PIECES...
...HAVE GOOD COMPOSITION.

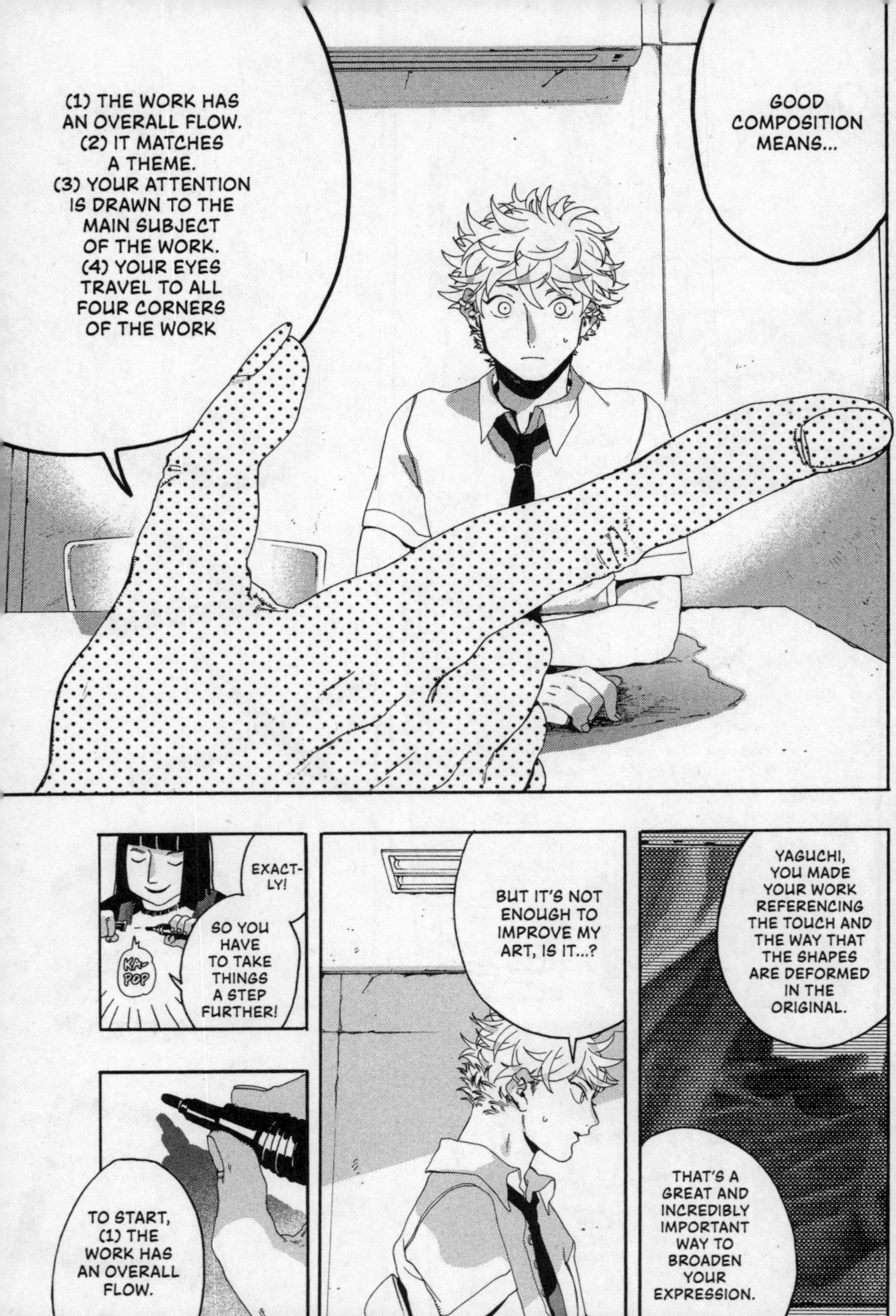
GOOD COMPOSITION MEANS...
(1) THE WORK HAS AN OVERALL FLOW. (2) IT MATCHES A THEME. (3) YOUR ATTENTION IS DRAWN TO THE MAIN SUBJECT OF THE WORK. (4) YOUR EYES TRAVEL TO ALL FOUR CORNERS OF THE WORK
YAGUCHI, YOU MADE YOUR WORK REFERENCING THE TOUCH AND THE WAY THAT THE SHAPES ARE DEFORMED IN THE ORIGINAL.
THAT'S A GREAT AND INCREDIBLY IMPORTANT WAY TO BROADEN YOUR EXPRESSION.
BUT IT'S NOT ENOUGH TO IMPROVE MY ART, IS IT...?
EXACT-LY!
SO YOU HAVE TO TAKE THINGS A STEP FURTHER!
KA-POP
TO START, (1) THE WORK HAS AN OVERALL FLOW.

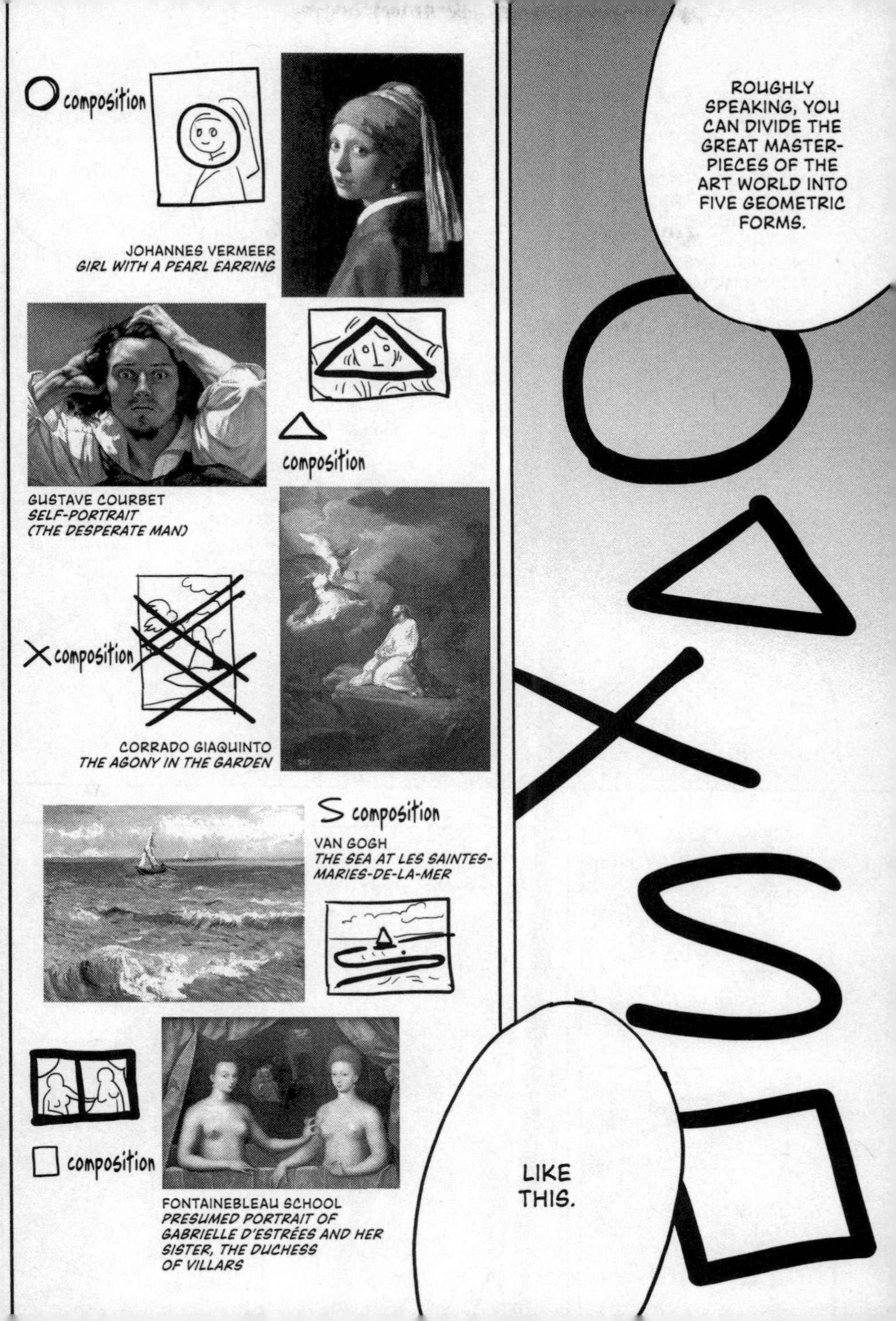
ROUGHLY SPEAKING, YOU CAN DIVIDE THE GREAT MASTER-PIECES OF THE ART WORLD INTO FIVE GEOMETRIC FORMS.
LIKE THIS.
composition
JOHANNES VERMEER
GIRL WITH A PEARL EARRING
composition
GUSTAVE COURBET
SELF-PORTRAIT
(THE DESPERATE MAN)
composition
CORRADO GIAQUINTO
THE AGONY IN THE GARDEN
S composition
VAN GOGH
THE SEA AT LES SAINTES-MARIES-DE-LA-MER
composition
FONTAINEBLEAU SCHOOL
PRESUMED PORTRAIT OF GABRIELLE D'ESTRÉES AND HER SISTER, THE DUCHESS OF VILLARS

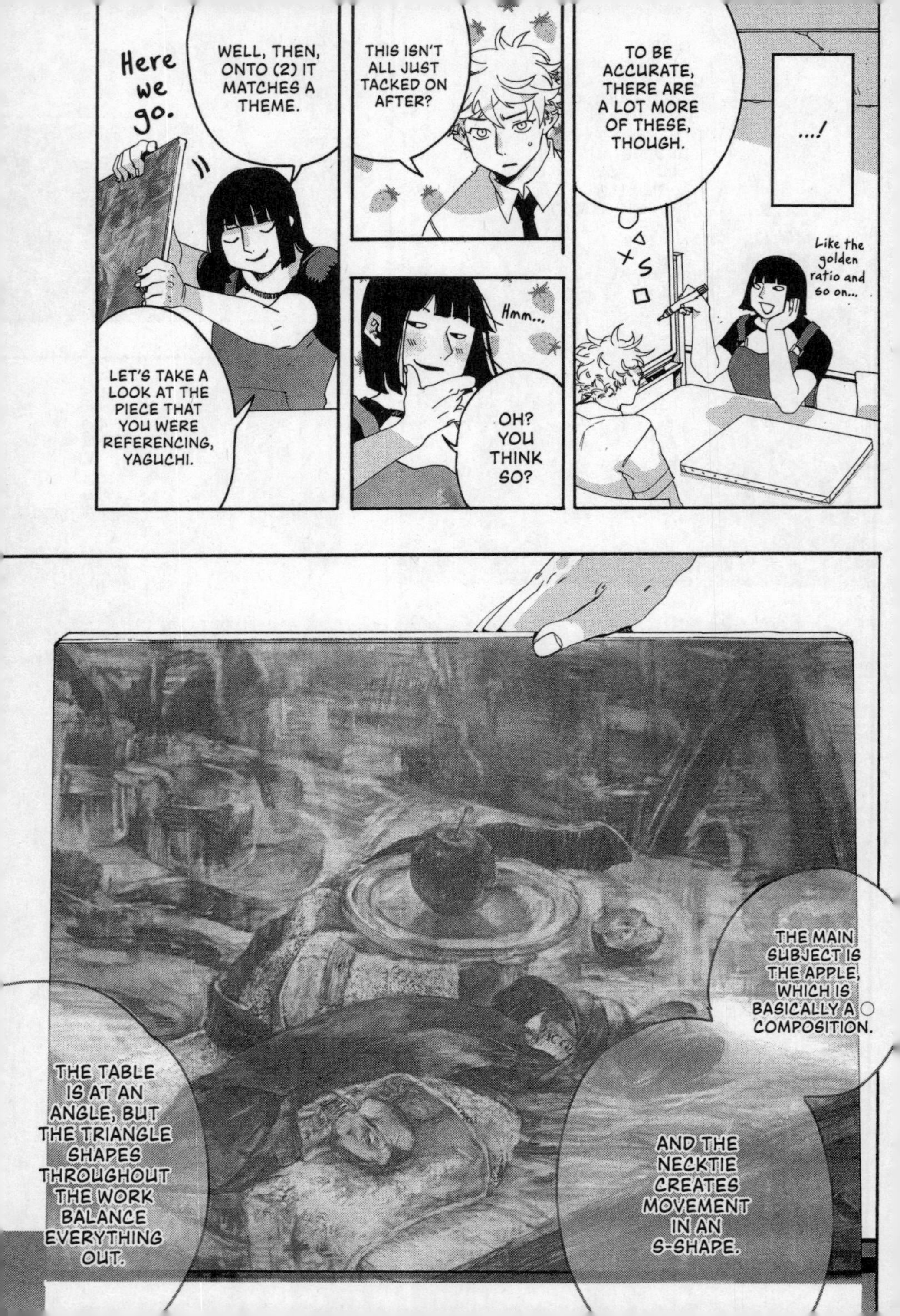

...!
TO BE ACCURATE, THERE ARE A LOT MORE OF THESE, THOUGH.
Like the golden ratio and so on...
THIS ISN'T ALL JUST TACKED ON AFTER?
Hmm...
OH? YOU THINK SO?
Here we go.
WELL, THEN, ONTO (2) IT MATCHES A THEME.
LET'S TAKE A LOOK AT THE PIECE THAT YOU WERE REFERENCING, YAGUCHI.
THE MAIN SUBJECT IS THE APPLE, WHICH IS BASICALLY A ○ COMPOSITION.
AND THE NECKTIE CREATES MOVEMENT IN AN S-SHAPE.
THE TABLE IS AT AN ANGLE, BUT THE TRIANGLE SHAPES THROUGHOUT THE WORK BALANCE EVERYTHING OUT.

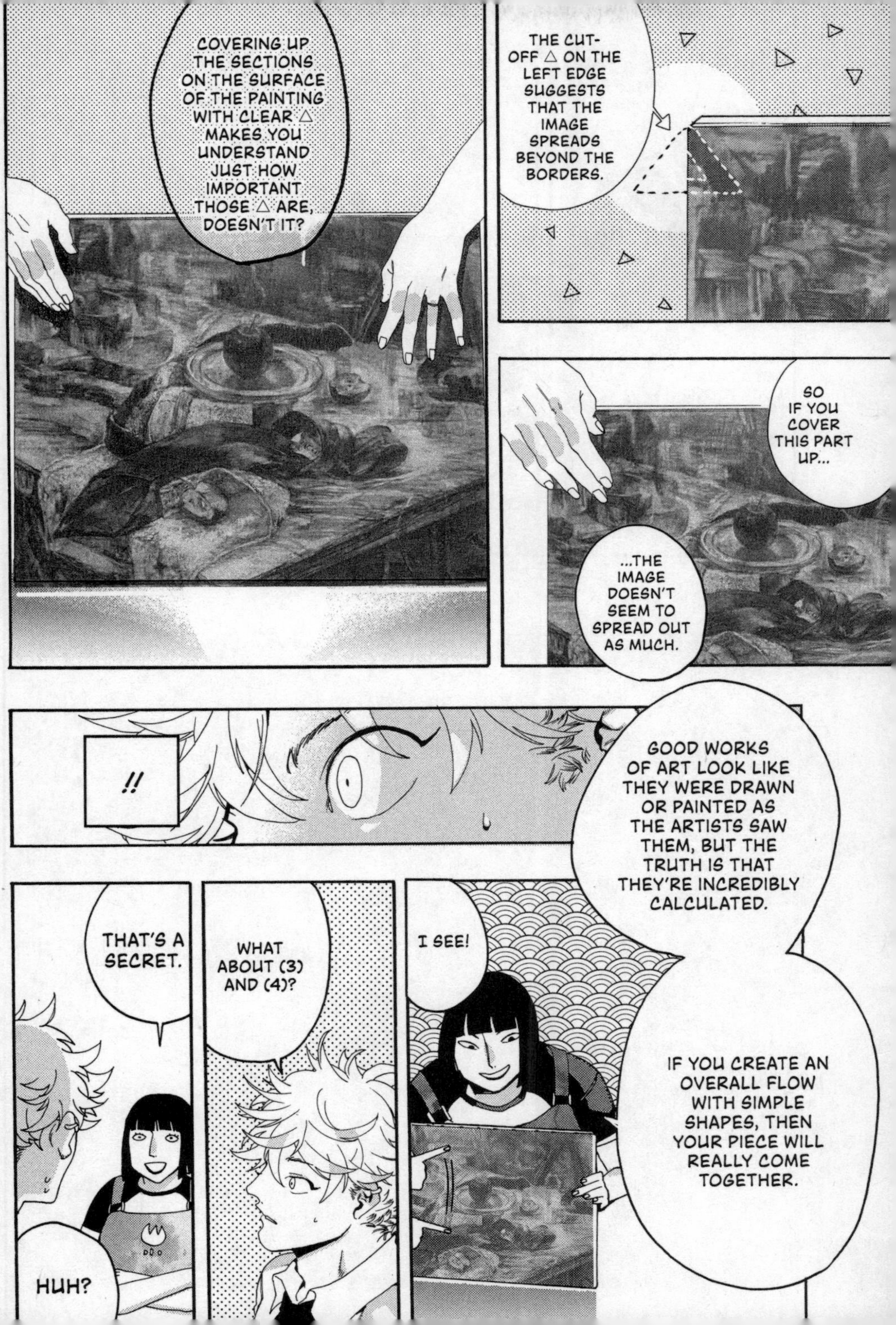
THE CUT-OFF △ ON THE LEFT EDGE SUGGESTS THAT THE IMAGE SPREADS BEYOND THE BORDERS.
SO IF YOU COVER THIS PART UP...
...THE IMAGE DOESN'T SEEM TO SPREAD OUT AS MUCH.
COVERING UP THE SECTIONS ON THE SURFACE OF THE PAINTING WITH CLEAR △ MAKES YOU UNDERSTAND JUST HOW IMPORTANT THOSE △ ARE, DOESN'T IT?
GOOD WORKS OF ART LOOK LIKE THEY WERE DRAWN OR PAINTED AS THE ARTISTS SAW THEM, BUT THE TRUTH IS THAT THEY'RE INCREDIBLY CALCULATED.
!!
I SEE!
IF YOU CREATE AN OVERALL FLOW WITH SIMPLE SHAPES, THEN YOUR PIECE WILL REALLY COME TOGETHER.
WHAT ABOUT (3) AND (4)?
THAT'S A SECRET.
HUH?

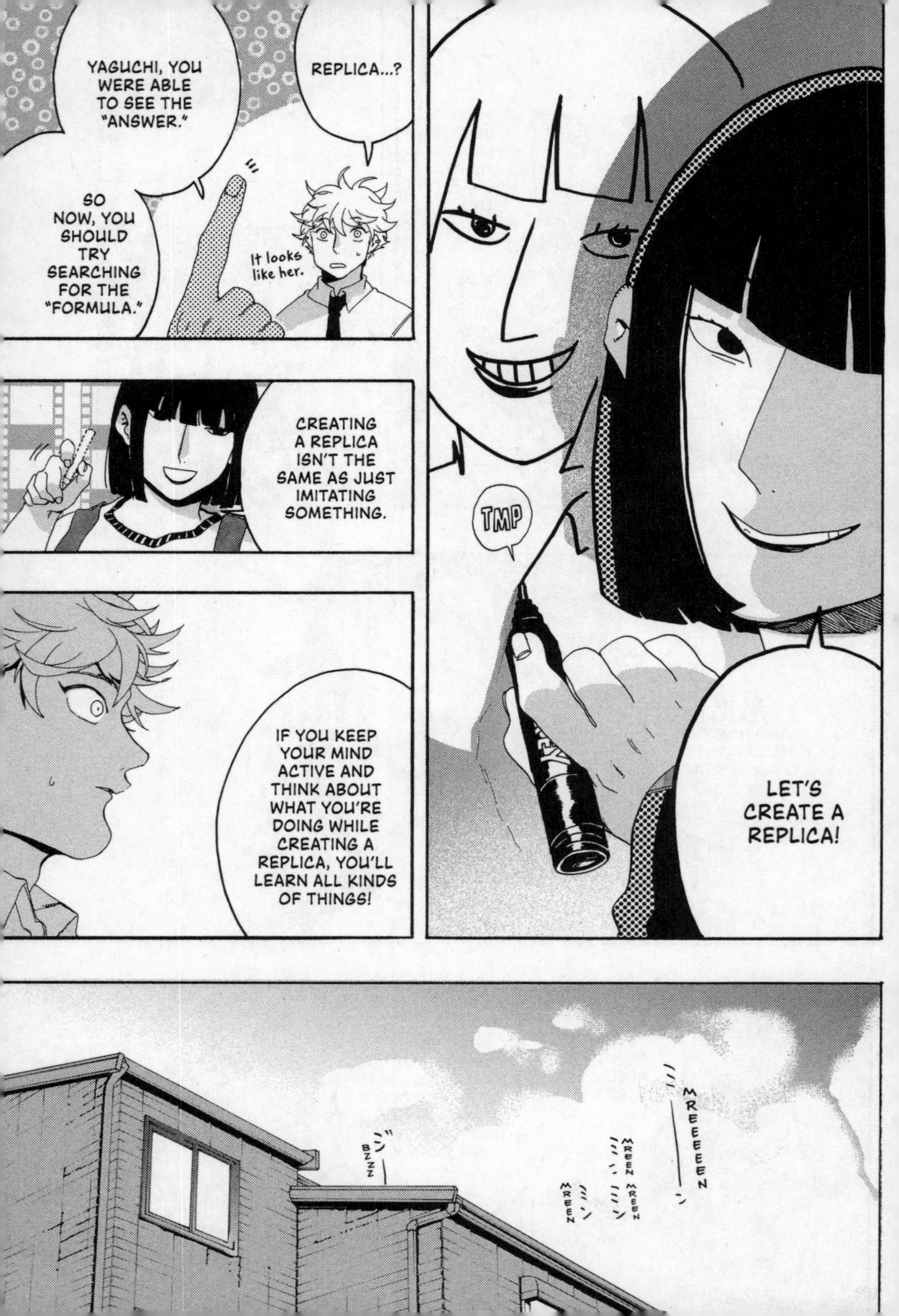
TMP
LET'S CREATE A REPLICA!
REPLICA...?
YAGUCHI, YOU WERE ABLE TO SEE THE "ANSWER."
It looks like her.
SO NOW, YOU SHOULD TRY SEARCHING FOR THE "FORMULA."
CREATING A REPLICA ISN'T THE SAME AS JUST IMITATING SOMETHING.
IF YOU KEEP YOUR MIND ACTIVE AND THINK ABOUT WHAT YOU'RE DOING WHILE CREATING A REPLICA, YOU'LL LEARN ALL KINDS OF THINGS!
MREEEEEN
MREEN MREEN
MREEN
BZZ

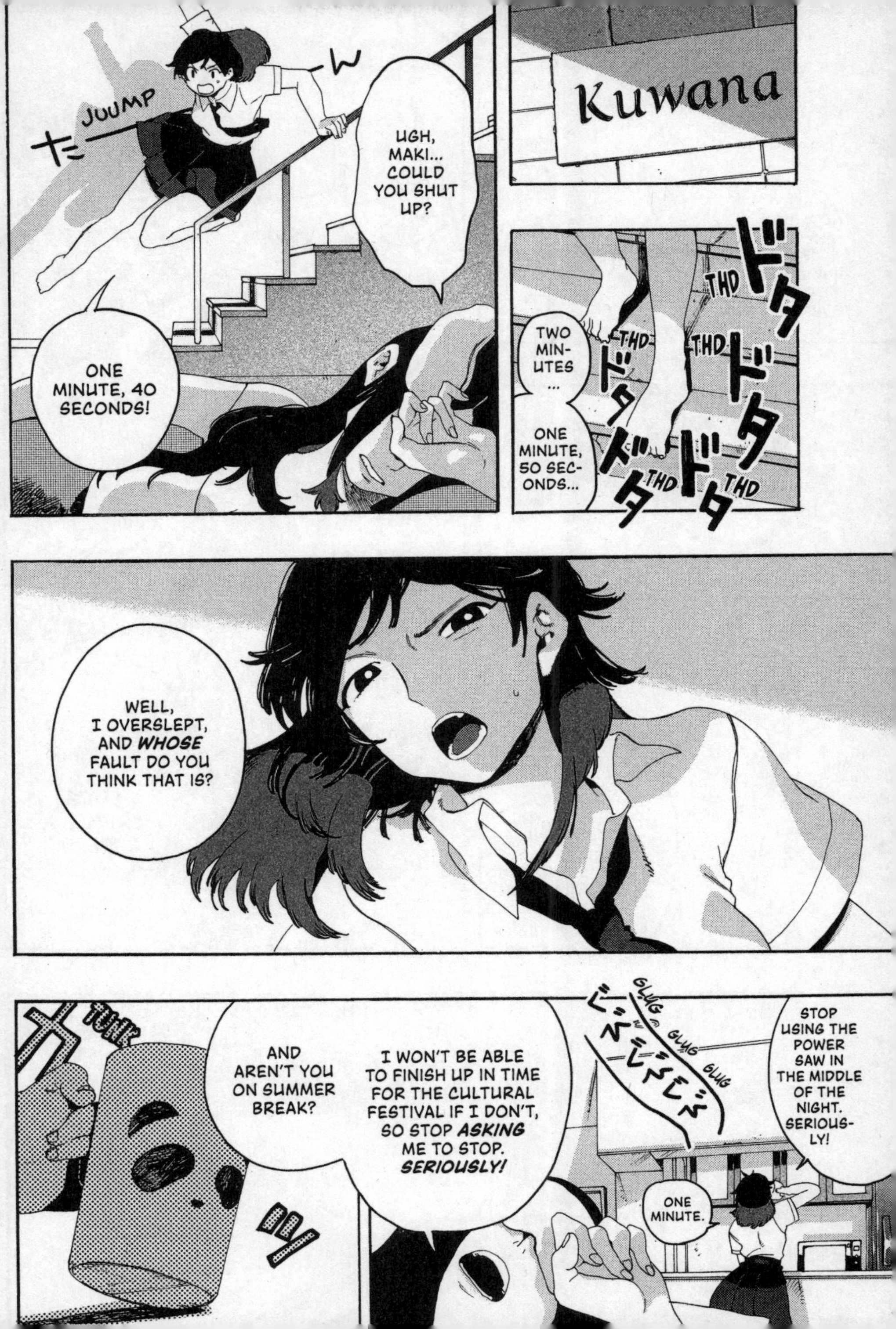
Kuwana
THD ドタ
THD ドタ
THD ドタ
THD ドタ
TWO MINUTES...
ONE MINUTE, 50 SECONDS...
UGH, MAKI... COULD YOU SHUT UP?
JUUMP
ONE MINUTE, 40 SECONDS!
WELL, I OVERSLEPT, AND ***WHOSE*** FAULT DO YOU THINK THAT IS?
STOP USING THE POWER SAW IN THE MIDDLE OF THE NIGHT. SERIOUSLY!
GLUG GLUG GLUG
ONE MINUTE.
I WON'T BE ABLE TO FINISH UP IN TIME FOR THE CULTURAL FESTIVAL IF I DON'T, SO STOP ***ASKING*** ME TO STOP. ***SERIOUSLY!***
AND AREN'T YOU ON SUMMER BREAK?

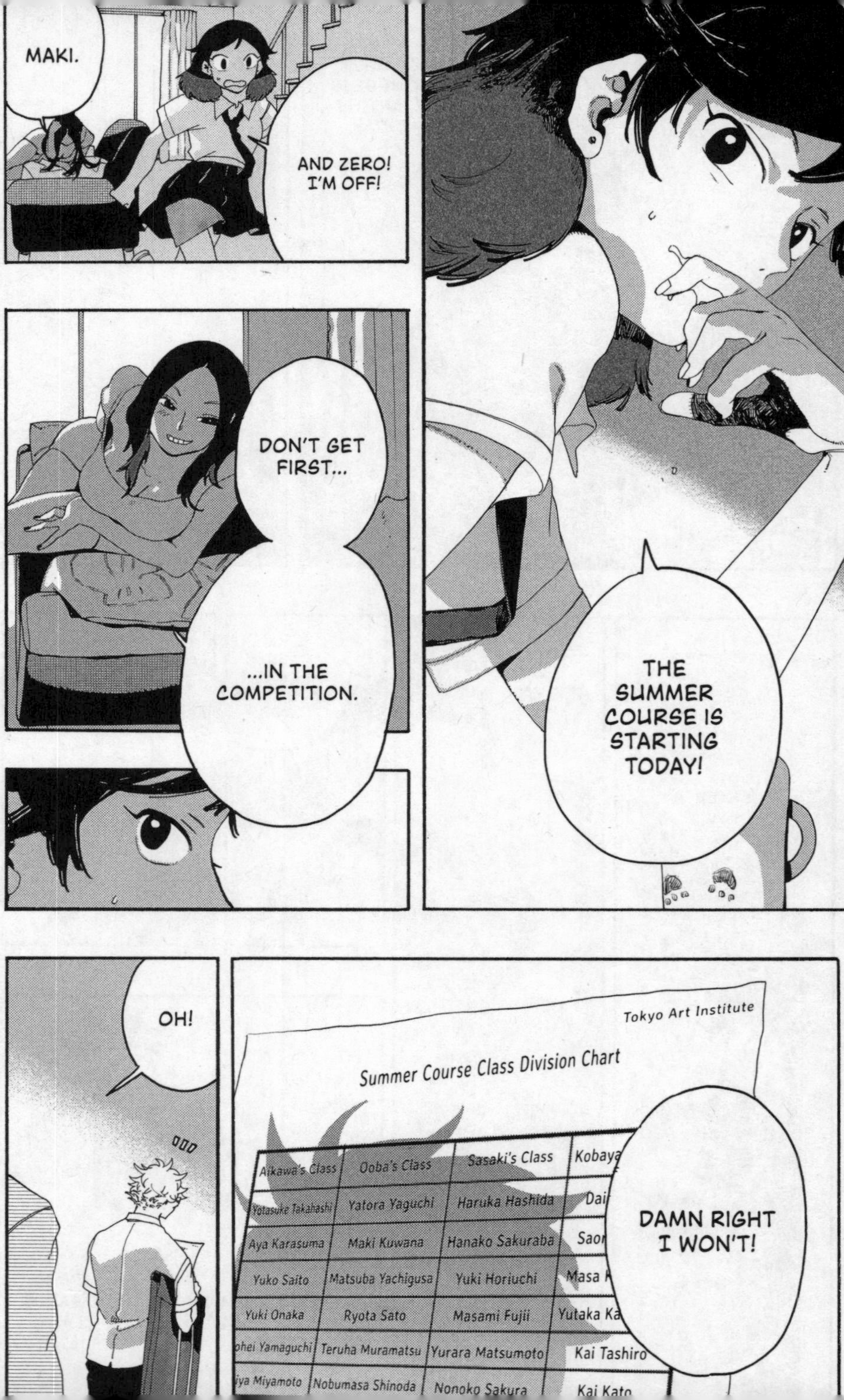
THE SUMMER COURSE IS STARTING TODAY!
MAKI.
AND ZERO! I'M OFF!
DON'T GET FIRST...
...IN THE COMPETITION.
Tokyo Art Institute
Summer Course Class Division Chart
Aikawa's Class
Ooba's Class
Sasaki's Class
Yotasuke Takahashi
Yatora Yaguchi
Haruka Hashida
Aya Karasuma
Maki Kuwana
Hanako Sakuraba
Yuko Saito
Matsuba Yachigusa
Yuki Horiuchi
Yuki Onaka
Ryota Sato
Masami Fujii
Teruha Muramatsu
Yurara Matsumoto
Kai Tashiro
Nobumasa Shinoda
Nonoko Sakura
Kai Kato
DAMN RIGHT I WON'T!
OH!

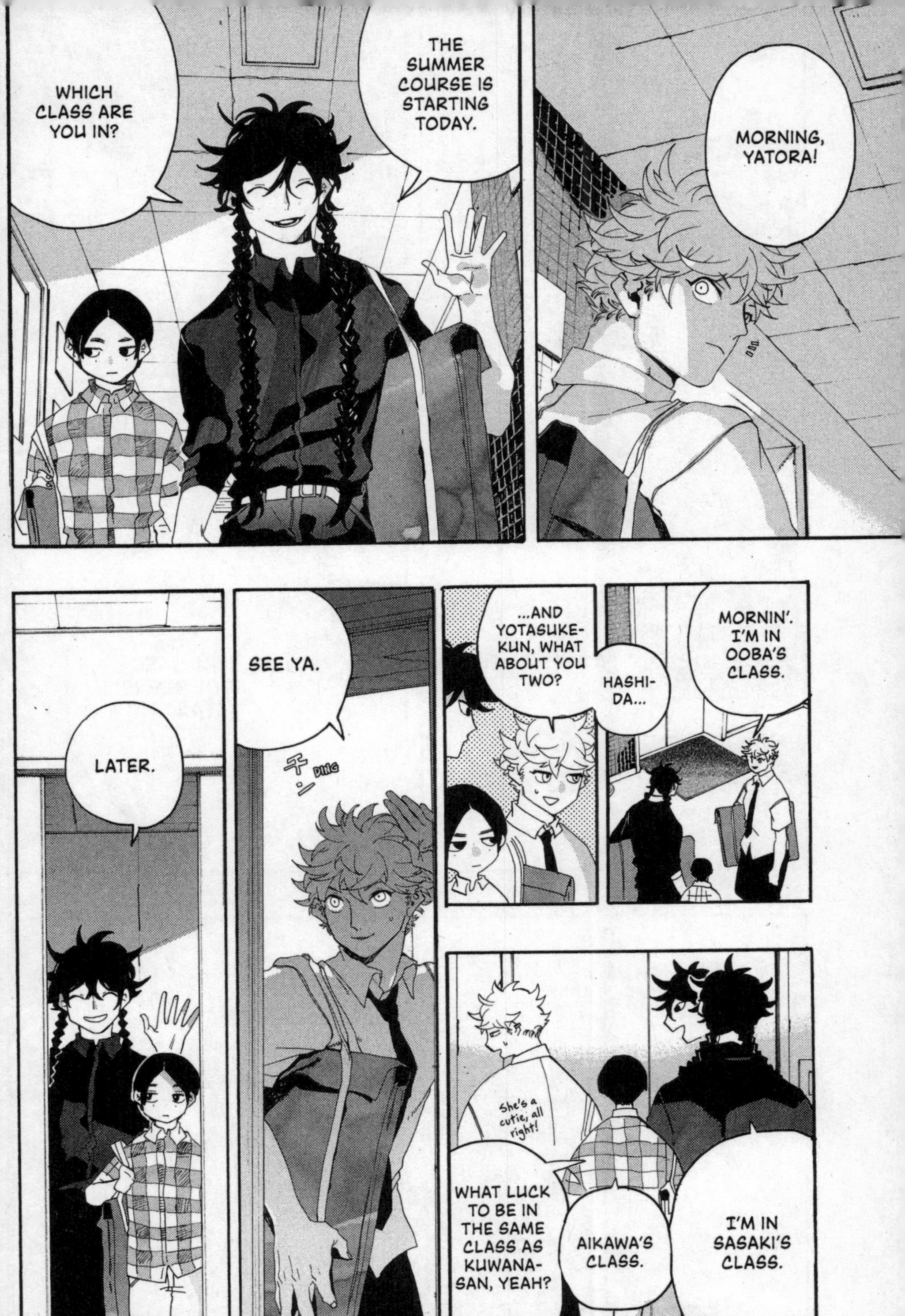
MORNING, YATORA!
THE SUMMER COURSE IS STARTING TODAY.
WHICH CLASS ARE YOU IN?
MORNIN'. I'M IN OOBA'S CLASS.
...AND YOTASUKE-KUN, WHAT ABOUT YOU TWO?
HASHI-DA...
I'M IN SASAKI'S CLASS.
AIKAWA'S CLASS.
She's a cutie, all right!
WHAT LUCK TO BE IN THE SAME CLASS AS KUWANA-SAN, YEAH?
SEE YA.
チン DING
LATER.

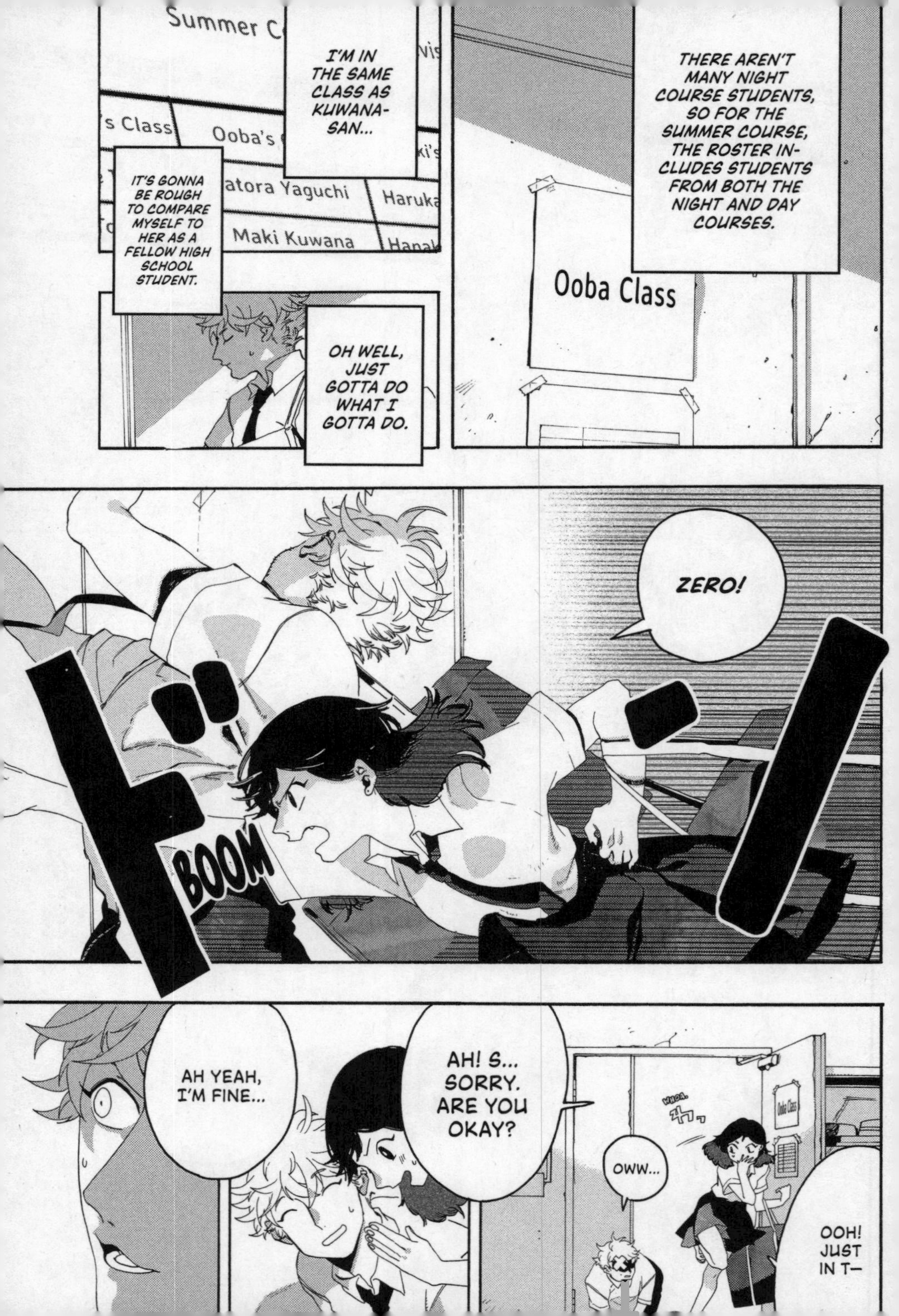
THERE AREN'T MANY NIGHT COURSE STUDENTS, SO FOR THE SUMMER COURSE, THE ROSTER INCLUDES STUDENTS FROM BOTH THE NIGHT AND DAY COURSES.
Ooba Class
I'M IN THE SAME CLASS AS KUWANA-SAN...
Maki Kuwana
IT'S GONNA BE ROUGH TO COMPARE MYSELF TO HER AS A FELLOW HIGH SCHOOL STUDENT.
OH WELL, JUST GOTTA DO WHAT I GOTTA DO.
ZERO!
BOOM
OOH! JUST IN T—
WHOA
OWW...
Ooba Class
AH! S... SORRY. ARE YOU OKAY?
AH YEAH, I'M FINE...

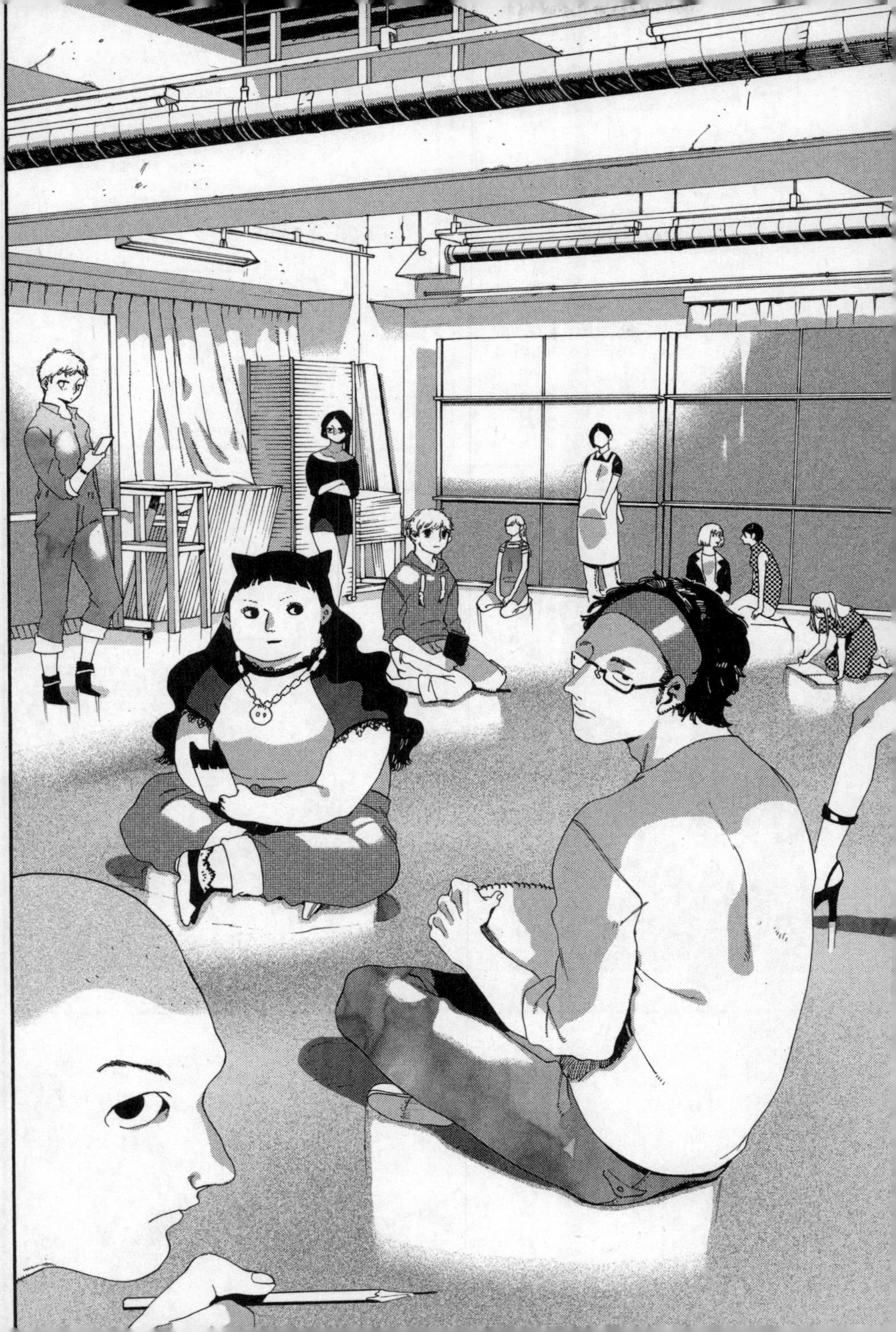

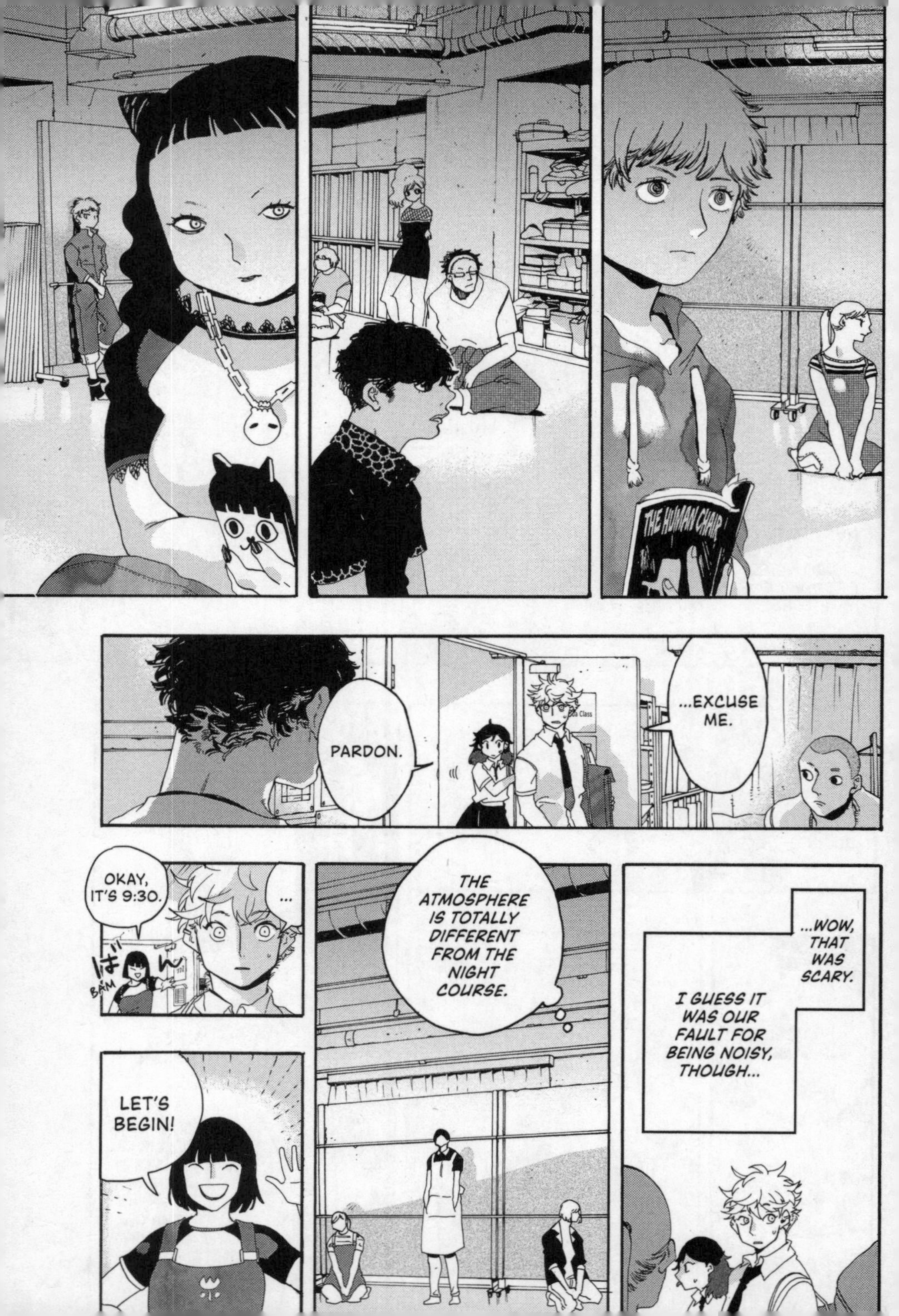
THE HUMAN CHAIR
...EXCUSE ME.
PARDON.
...WOW, THAT WAS SCARY.
I GUESS IT WAS OUR FAULT FOR BEING NOISY, THOUGH...
THE ATMOSPHERE IS TOTALLY DIFFERENT FROM THE NIGHT COURSE.
...
OKAY, IT'S 9:30.
ばん
BAM
LET'S BEGIN!

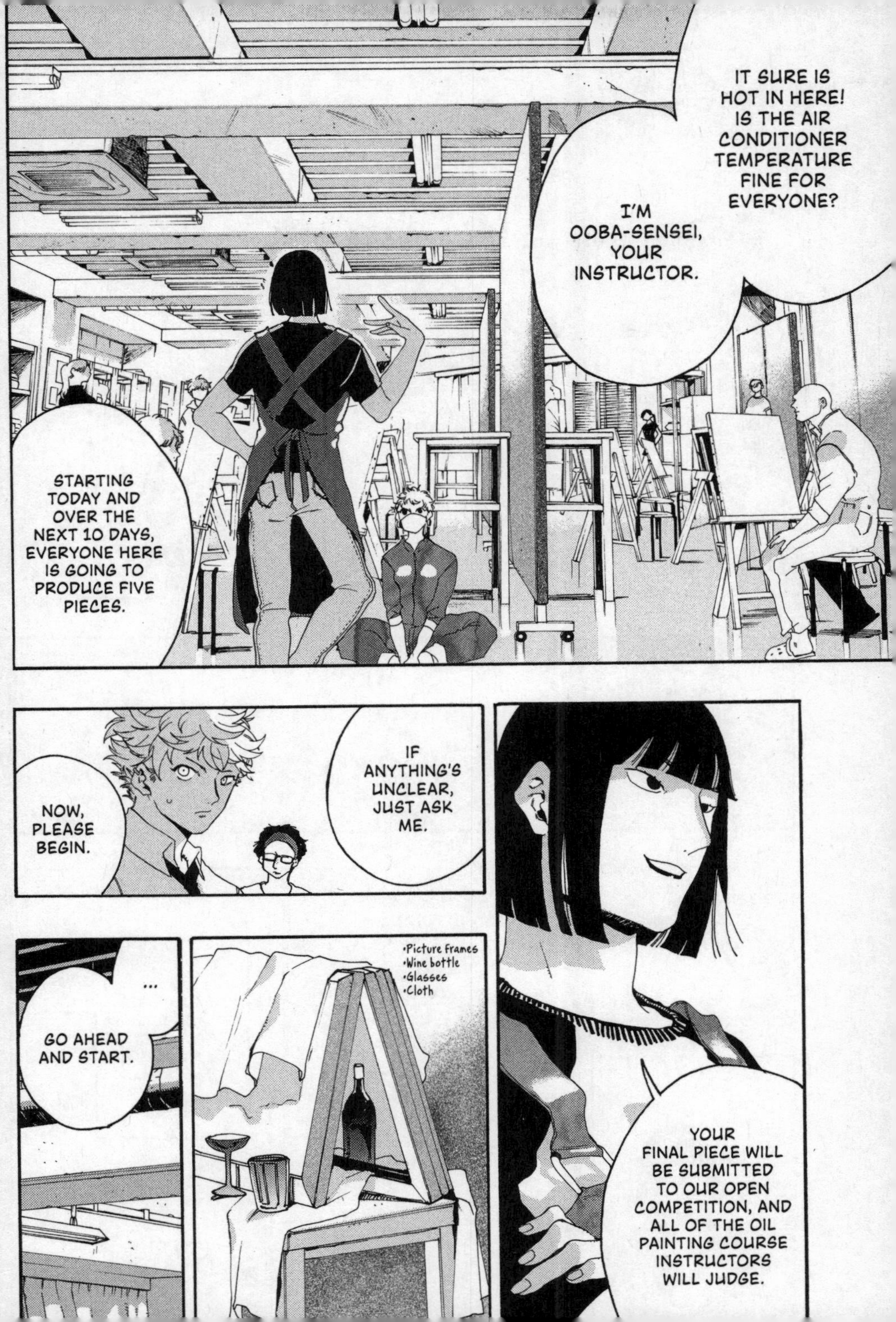
IT SURE IS HOT IN HERE! IS THE AIR CONDITIONER TEMPERATURE FINE FOR EVERYONE?
I'M OOBA-SENSEI, YOUR INSTRUCTOR.
STARTING TODAY AND OVER THE NEXT 10 DAYS, EVERYONE HERE IS GOING TO PRODUCE FIVE PIECES.
YOUR FINAL PIECE WILL BE SUBMITTED TO OUR OPEN COMPETITION, AND ALL OF THE OIL PAINTING COURSE INSTRUCTORS WILL JUDGE.
IF ANYTHING'S UNCLEAR, JUST ASK ME.
NOW, PLEASE BEGIN.
•Picture Frames
•Wine bottle
•Glasses
•Cloth
...
GO AHEAD AND START.

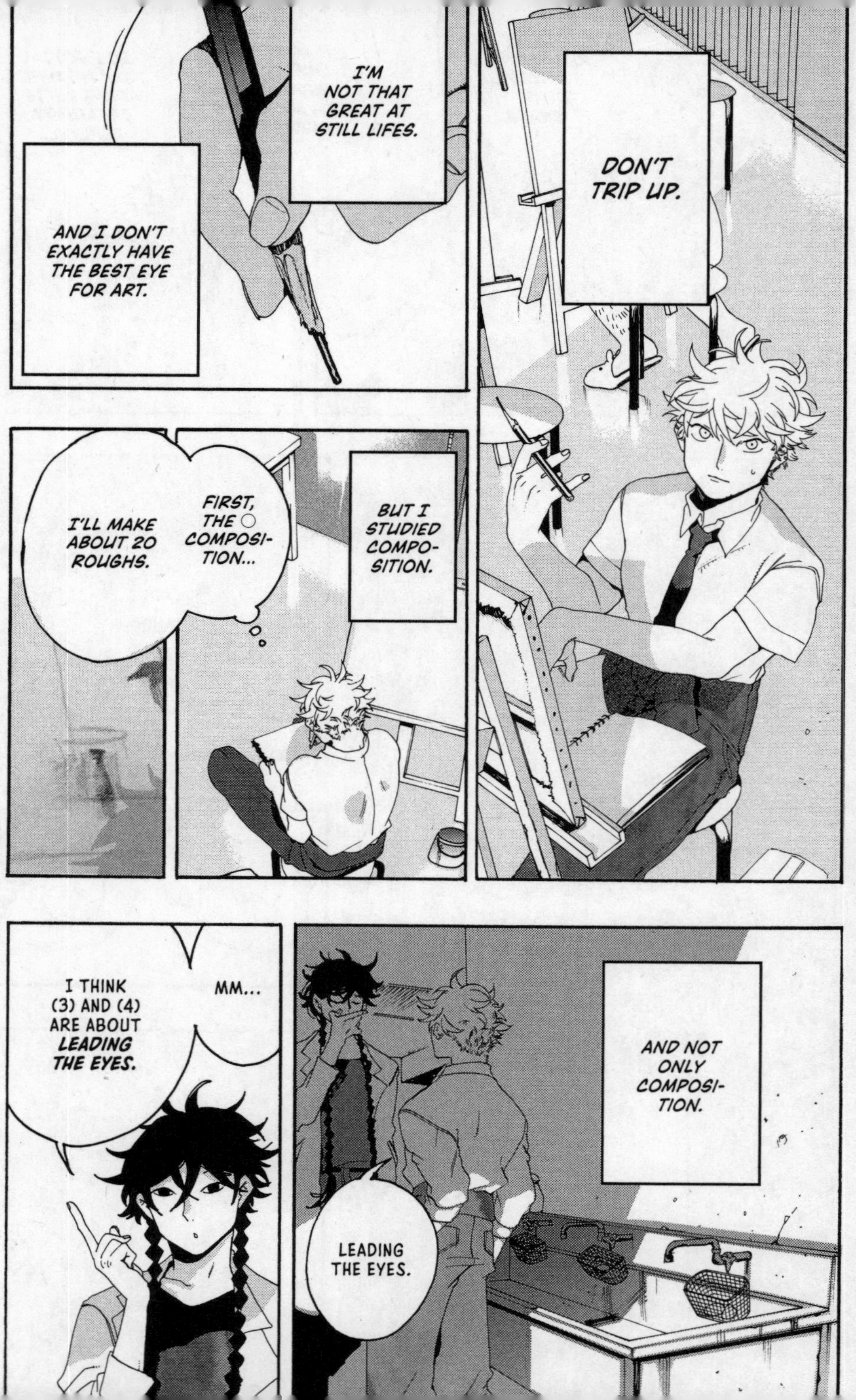
DON'T TRIP UP.
I'M NOT THAT GREAT AT STILL LIFES.
AND I DON'T EXACTLY HAVE THE BEST EYE FOR ART.
BUT I STUDIED COMPOSITION.
FIRST, THE ○ COMPOSITION...
I'LL MAKE ABOUT 20 ROUGHS.
AND NOT ONLY COMPOSITION.
LEADING THE EYES.
MM...
I THINK (3) AND (4) ARE ABOUT *LEADING THE EYES.*

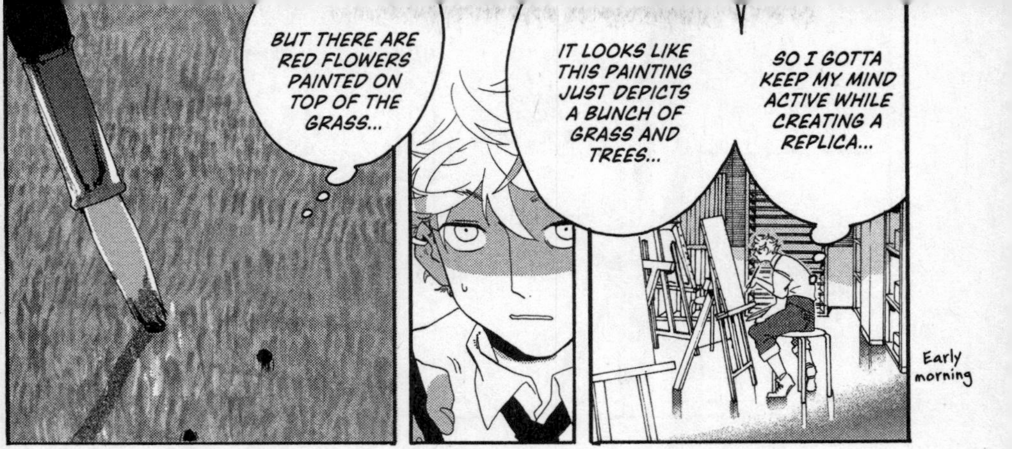
Early morning
IT LOOKS LIKE THIS PAINTING JUST DEPICTS A BUNCH OF GRASS AND TREES...
SO I GOTTA KEEP MY MIND ACTIVE WHILE CREATING A REPLICA...
BUT THERE ARE RED FLOWERS PAINTED ON TOP OF THE GRASS...

*A REPLICA OF GUSTAV KLIMT'S *FIELD OF POPPIES* BY MATSUBA YACHIGUSA.

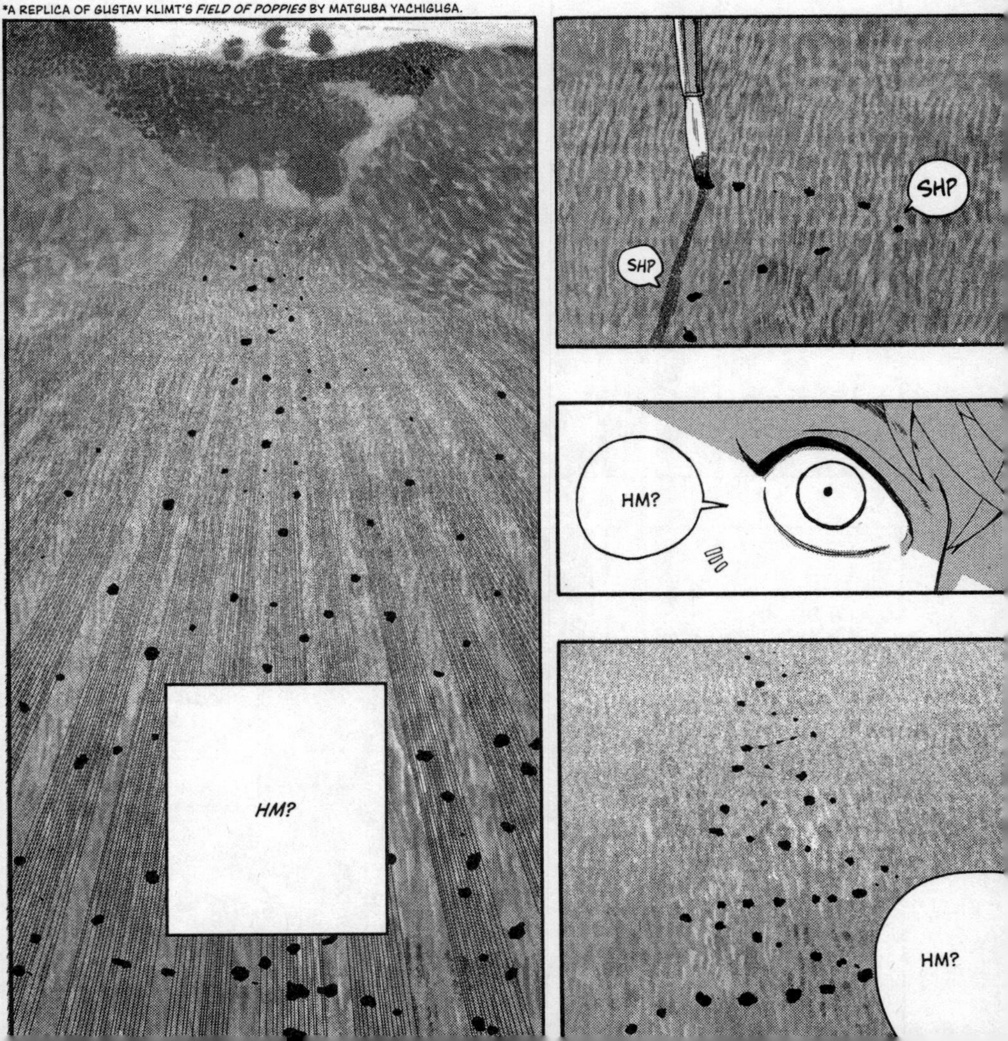
SHP
SHP
HM?
HM?
HM?

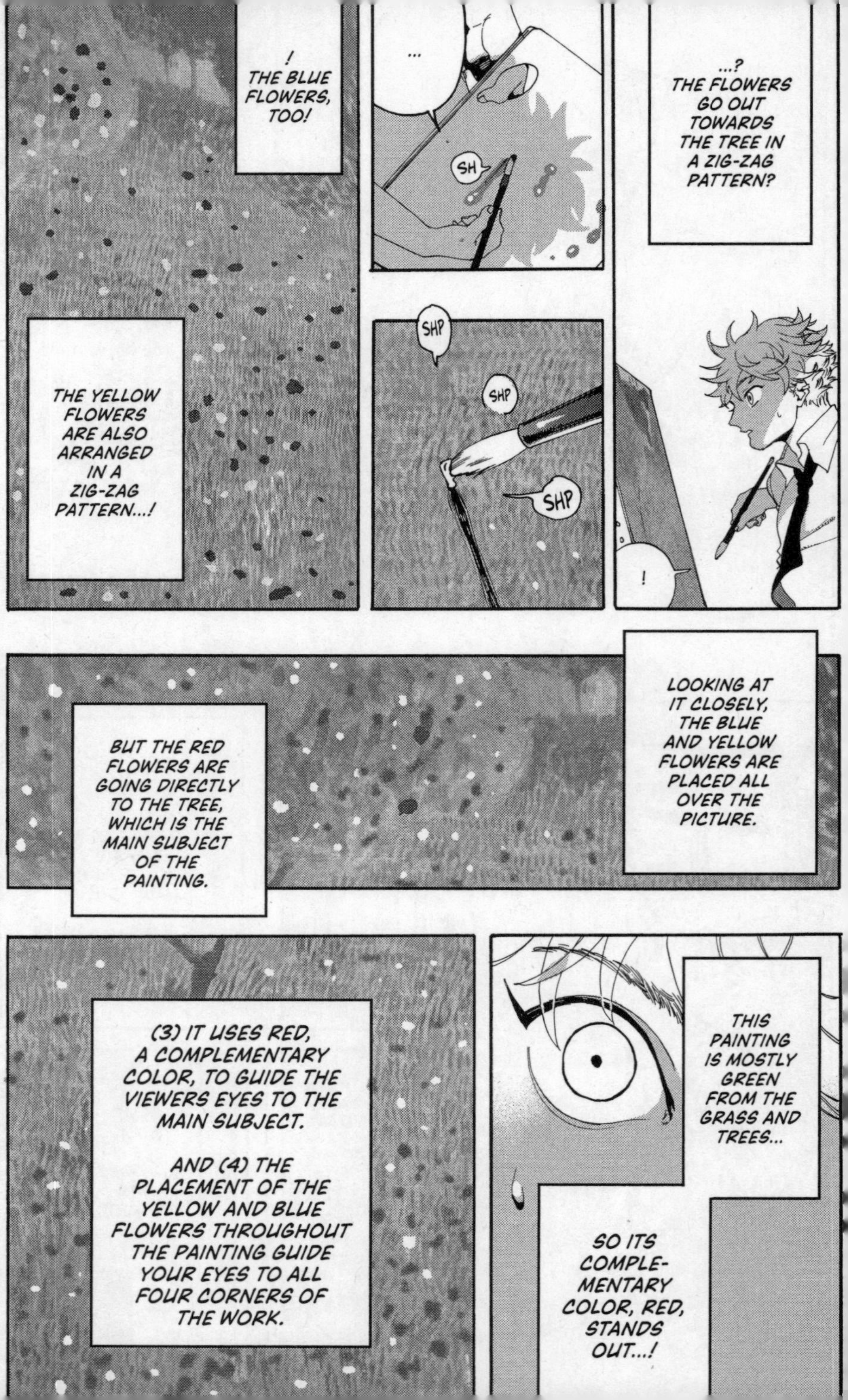
...? THE FLOWERS GO OUT TOWARDS THE TREE IN A ZIG-ZAG PATTERN?
!
...
SH
SHP
SHP
SHP
! THE BLUE FLOWERS, TOO!
THE YELLOW FLOWERS ARE ALSO ARRANGED IN A ZIG-ZAG PATTERN...!
LOOKING AT IT CLOSELY, THE BLUE AND YELLOW FLOWERS ARE PLACED ALL OVER THE PICTURE.
BUT THE RED FLOWERS ARE GOING DIRECTLY TO THE TREE, WHICH IS THE MAIN SUBJECT OF THE PAINTING.
THIS PAINTING IS MOSTLY GREEN FROM THE GRASS AND TREES...
SO ITS COMPLE-MENTARY COLOR, RED, STANDS OUT...!
(3) IT USES RED, A COMPLEMENTARY COLOR, TO GUIDE THE VIEWERS EYES TO THE MAIN SUBJECT.
AND (4) THE PLACEMENT OF THE YELLOW AND BLUE FLOWERS THROUGHOUT THE PAINTING GUIDE YOUR EYES TO ALL FOUR CORNERS OF THE WORK.

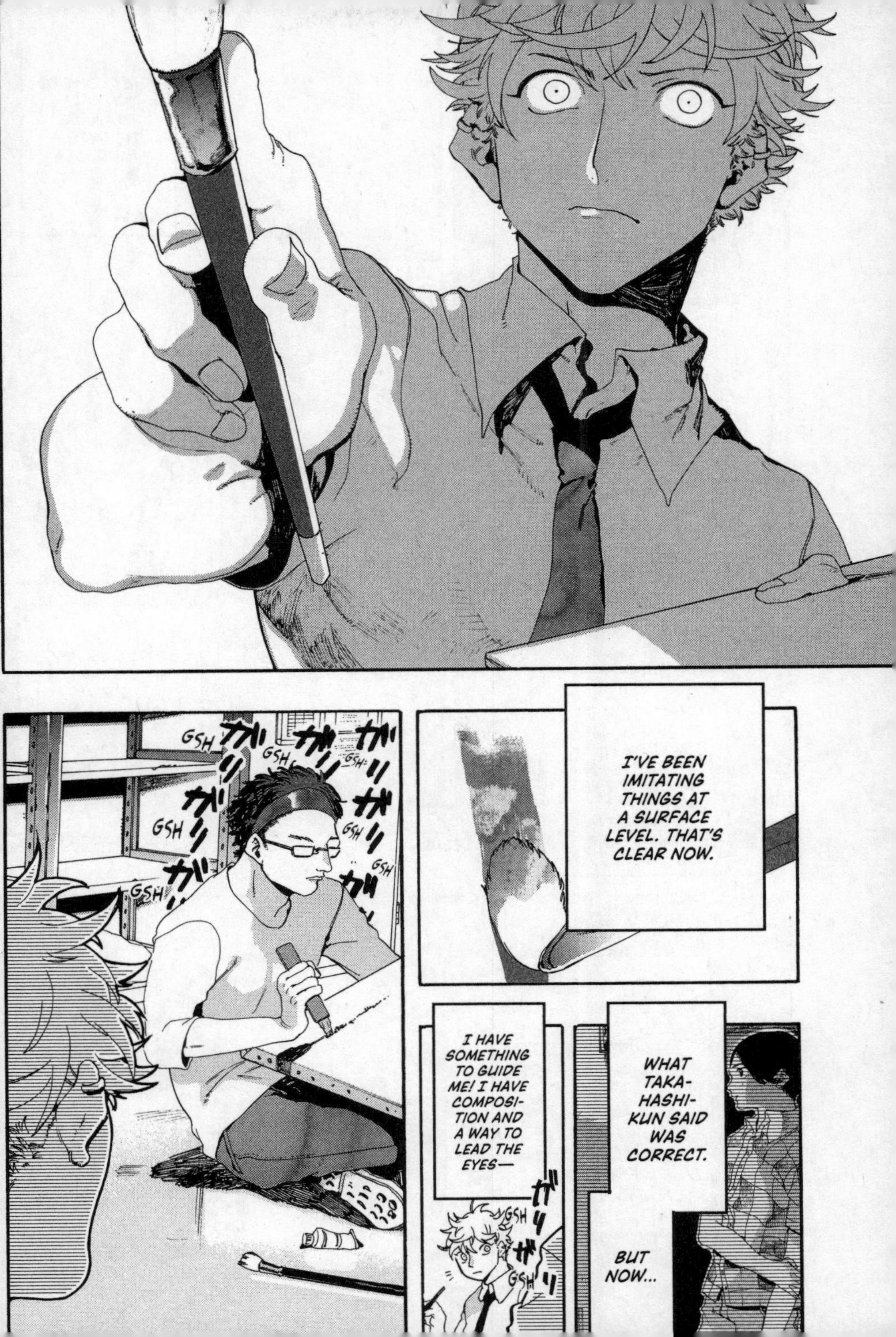
I'VE BEEN IMITATING THINGS AT A SURFACE LEVEL. THAT'S CLEAR NOW.
WHAT TAKA-HASHI-KUN SAID WAS CORRECT.
BUT NOW...
I HAVE SOMETHING TO GUIDE ME! I HAVE COMPOSI-TION AND A WAY TO LEAD THE EYES—
GSH
GSH
GSH
GSH
GSH
GSH
GSH
GSH

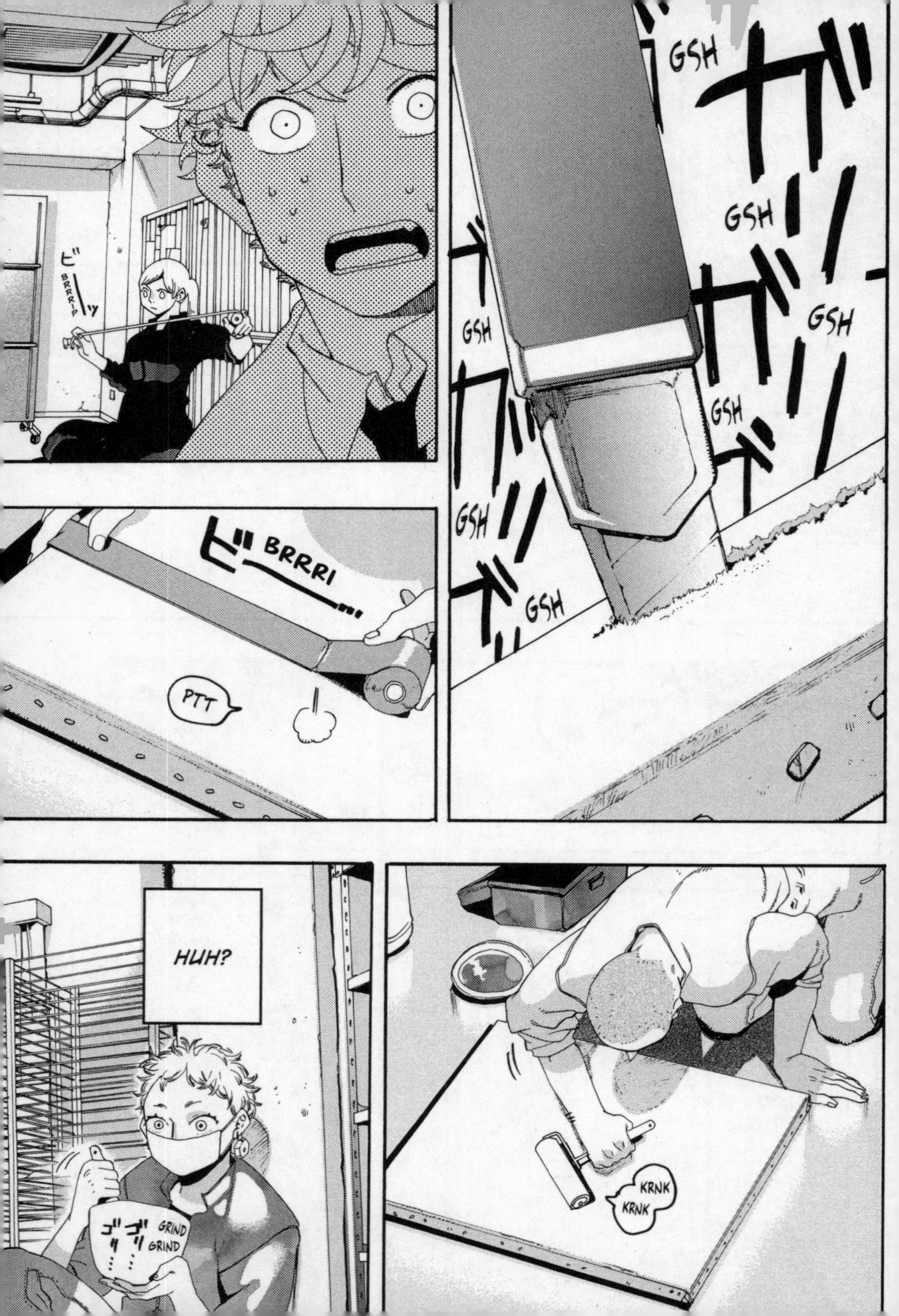

GSH
GSH
GSH
GSH
GSH
GSH
GSH
BRRRRIP
BRRRRI
PTT
KRNK
KRNK
HUH?
GRIND
GRIND

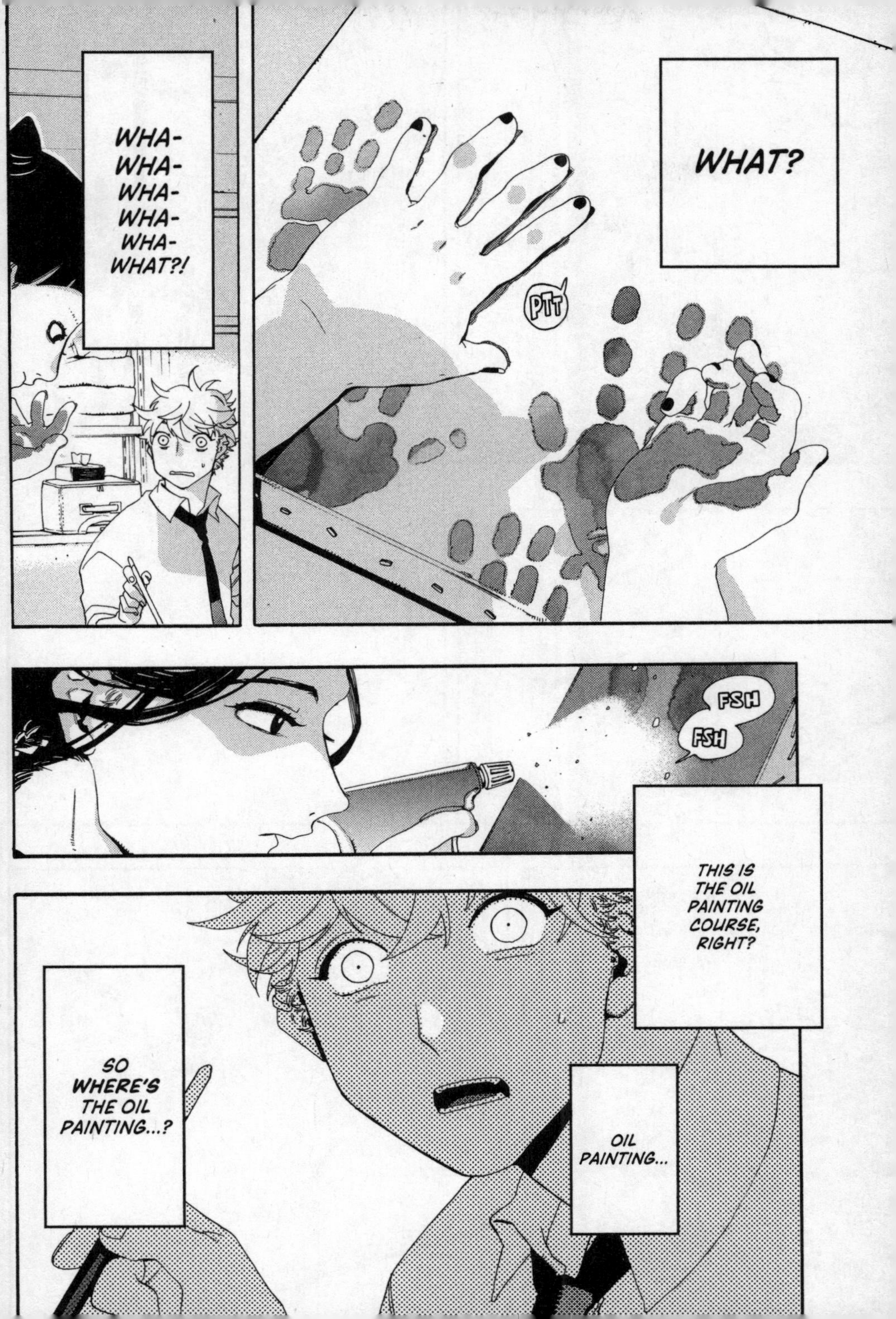
WHAT?
PTT
WHA-WHA-WHA-WHA-WHA-WHAT?!
FSH
FSH
THIS IS THE OIL PAINTING COURSE, RIGHT?
OIL PAINTING...
SO WHERE'S THE OIL PAINTING...?

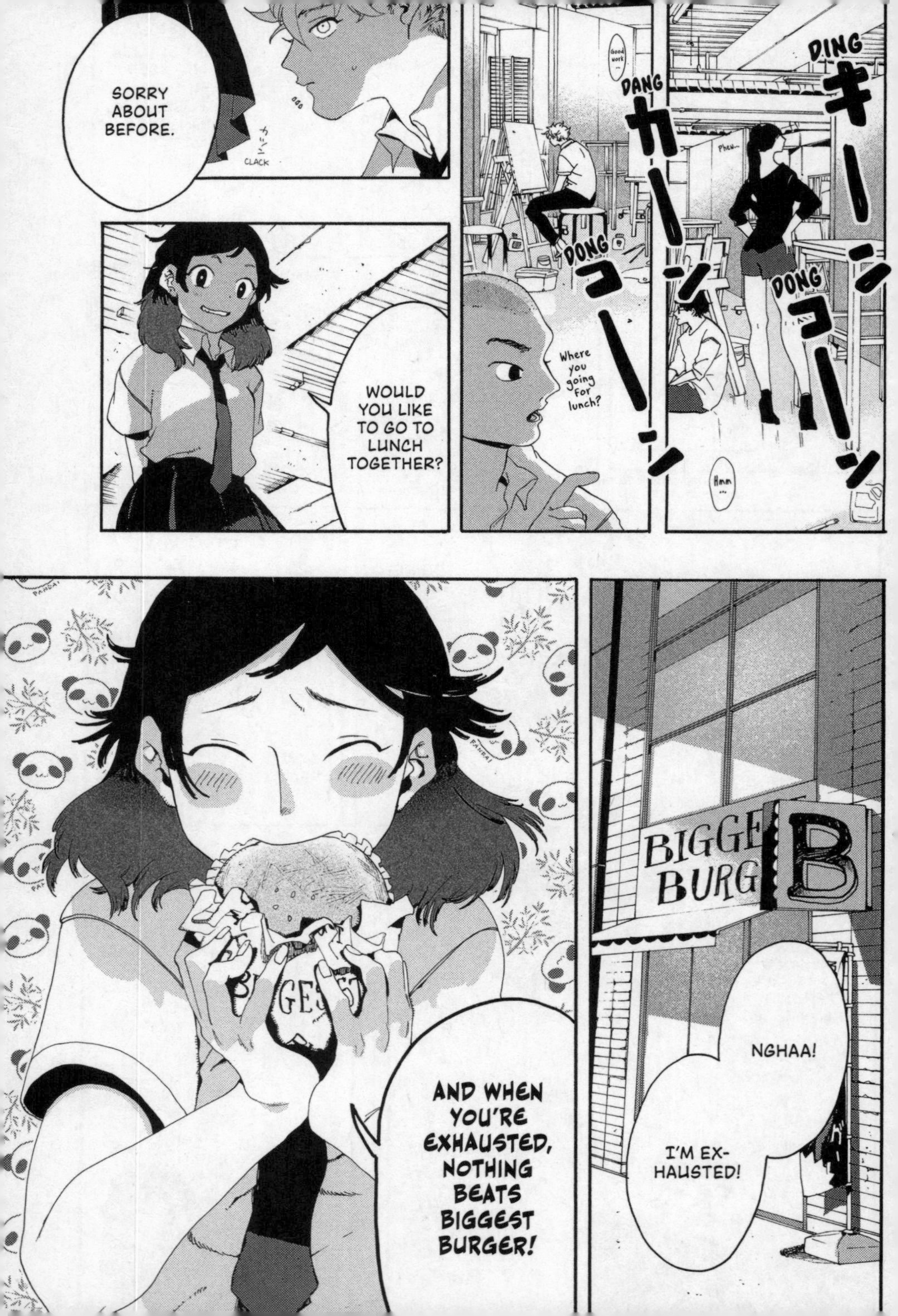
DING
DONG
Phew...
Hmm...
Good work...
DANG
DONG
Where you going for lunch?
SORRY ABOUT BEFORE.
CLACK
WOULD YOU LIKE TO GO TO LUNCH TOGETHER?
BIGGE
BURG
B
NGHAA!
I'M EX-HAUSTED!
AND WHEN YOU'RE EXHAUSTED, NOTHING BEATS BIGGEST BURGER!

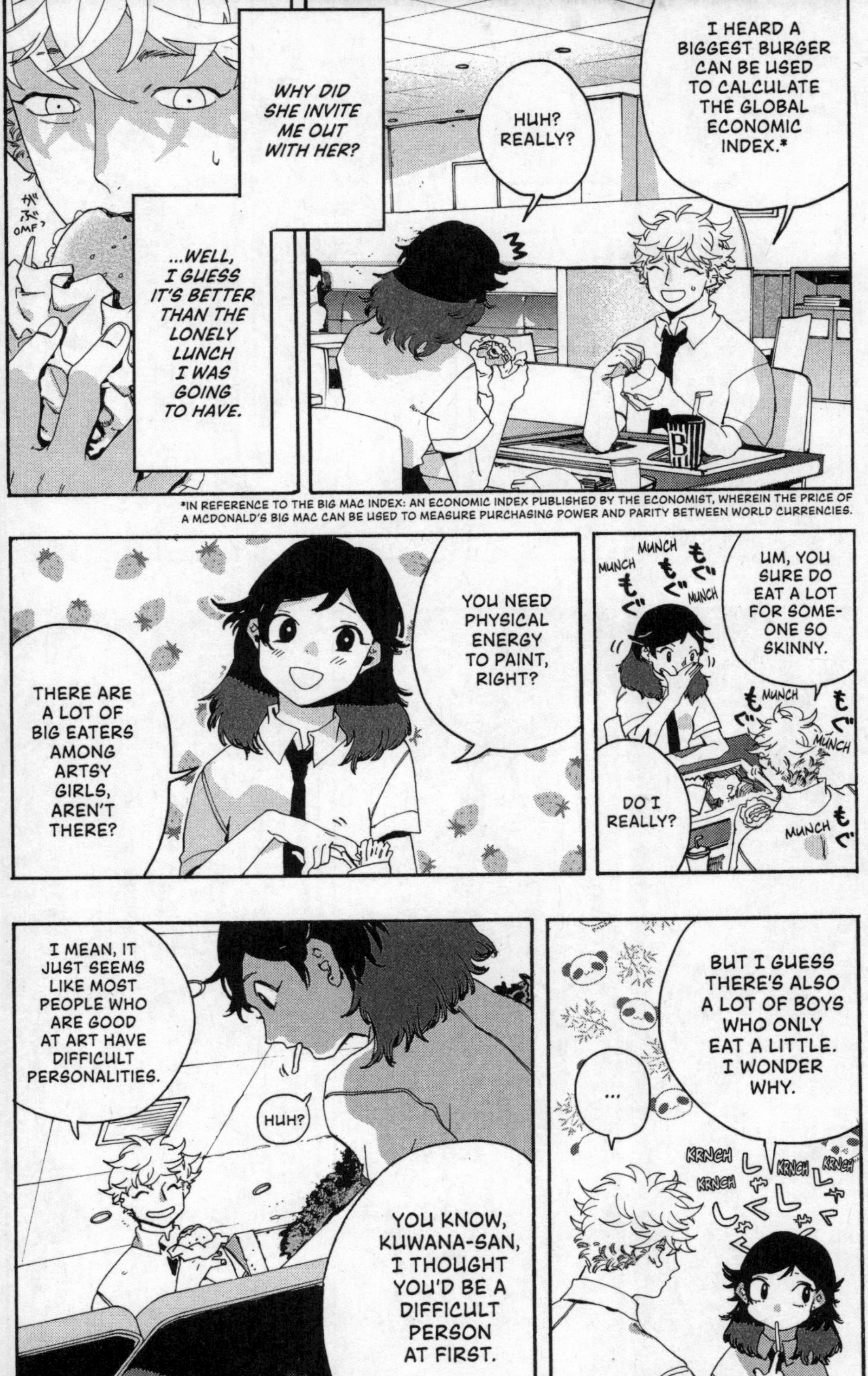
I HEARD A BIGGEST BURGER CAN BE USED TO CALCULATE THE GLOBAL ECONOMIC INDEX.*
HUH? REALLY?
WHY DID SHE INVITE ME OUT WITH HER?
...WELL, I GUESS IT'S BETTER THAN THE LONELY LUNCH I WAS GOING TO HAVE.
がぶ
OMF
MUNCH もぐ
MUNCH もぐ
MUNCH もぐ
MUNCH もぐ
UM, YOU SURE DO EAT A LOT FOR SOME-ONE SO SKINNY.
DO I REALLY?
YOU NEED PHYSICAL ENERGY TO PAINT, RIGHT?
THERE ARE A LOT OF BIG EATERS AMONG ARTSY GIRLS, AREN'T THERE?
BUT I GUESS THERE'S ALSO A LOT OF BOYS WHO ONLY EAT A LITTLE. I WONDER WHY.
...
KRNCH
KRNCH
KRNCH
KRNCH
YOU KNOW, KUWANA-SAN, I THOUGHT YOU'D BE A DIFFICULT PERSON AT FIRST.
HUH?
I MEAN, IT JUST SEEMS LIKE MOST PEOPLE WHO ARE GOOD AT ART HAVE DIFFICULT PERSONALITIES.

*IN REFERENCE TO THE BIG MAC INDEX: AN ECONOMIC INDEX PUBLISHED BY THE ECONOMIST, WHEREIN THE PRICE OF A MCDONALD'S BIG MAC CAN BE USED TO MEASURE PURCHASING POWER AND PARITY BETWEEN WORLD CURRENCIES.

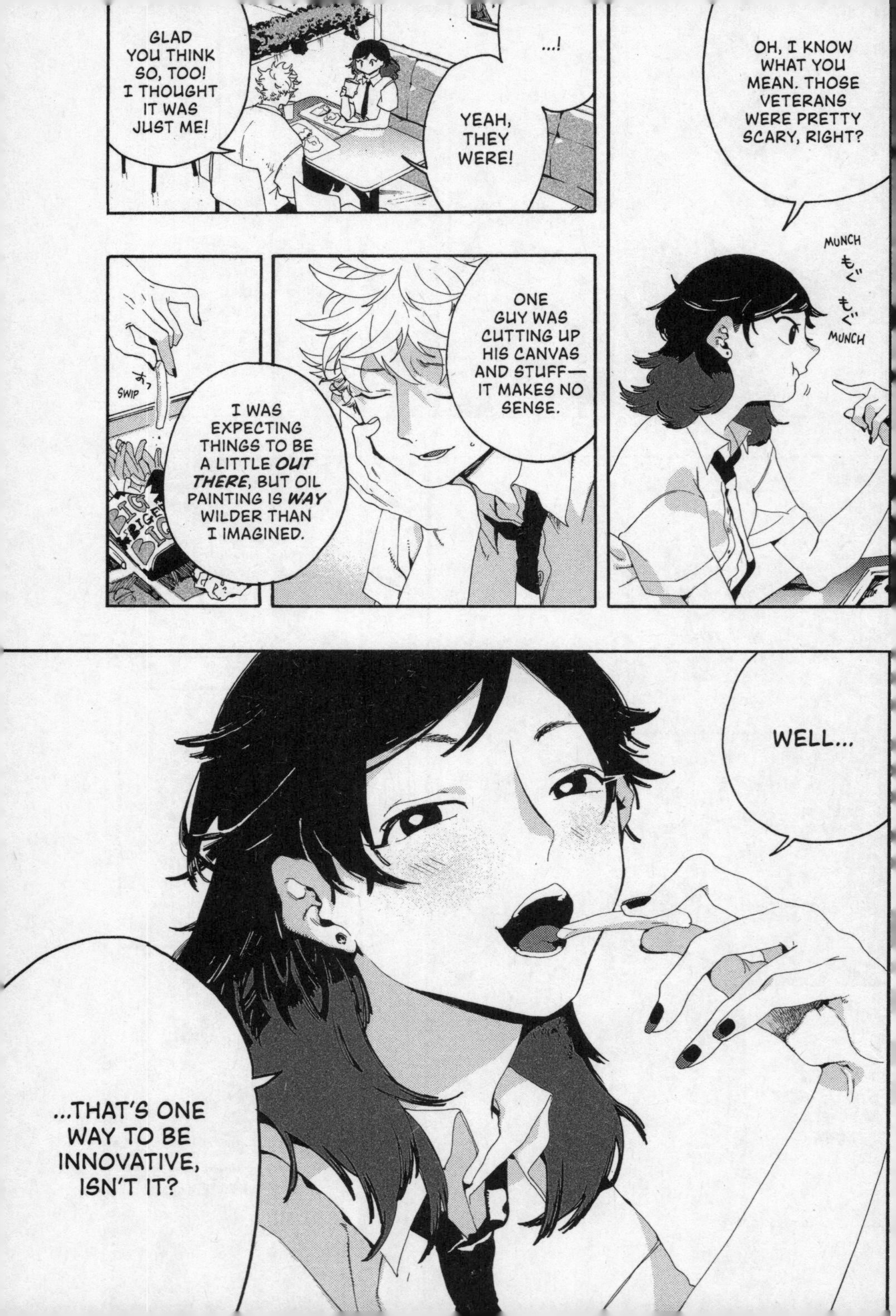
OH, I KNOW WHAT YOU MEAN. THOSE VETERANS WERE PRETTY SCARY, RIGHT?
MUNCH もぐ
もぐ MUNCH
...!
YEAH, THEY WERE!
GLAD YOU THINK SO, TOO! I THOUGHT IT WAS JUST ME!
ONE GUY WAS CUTTING UP HIS CANVAS AND STUFF—IT MAKES NO SENSE.
I WAS EXPECTING THINGS TO BE A LITTLE OUT THERE, BUT OIL PAINTING IS WAY WILDER THAN I IMAGINED.
あっ SWIP
WELL...
...THAT'S ONE WAY TO BE INNOVATIVE, ISN'T IT?

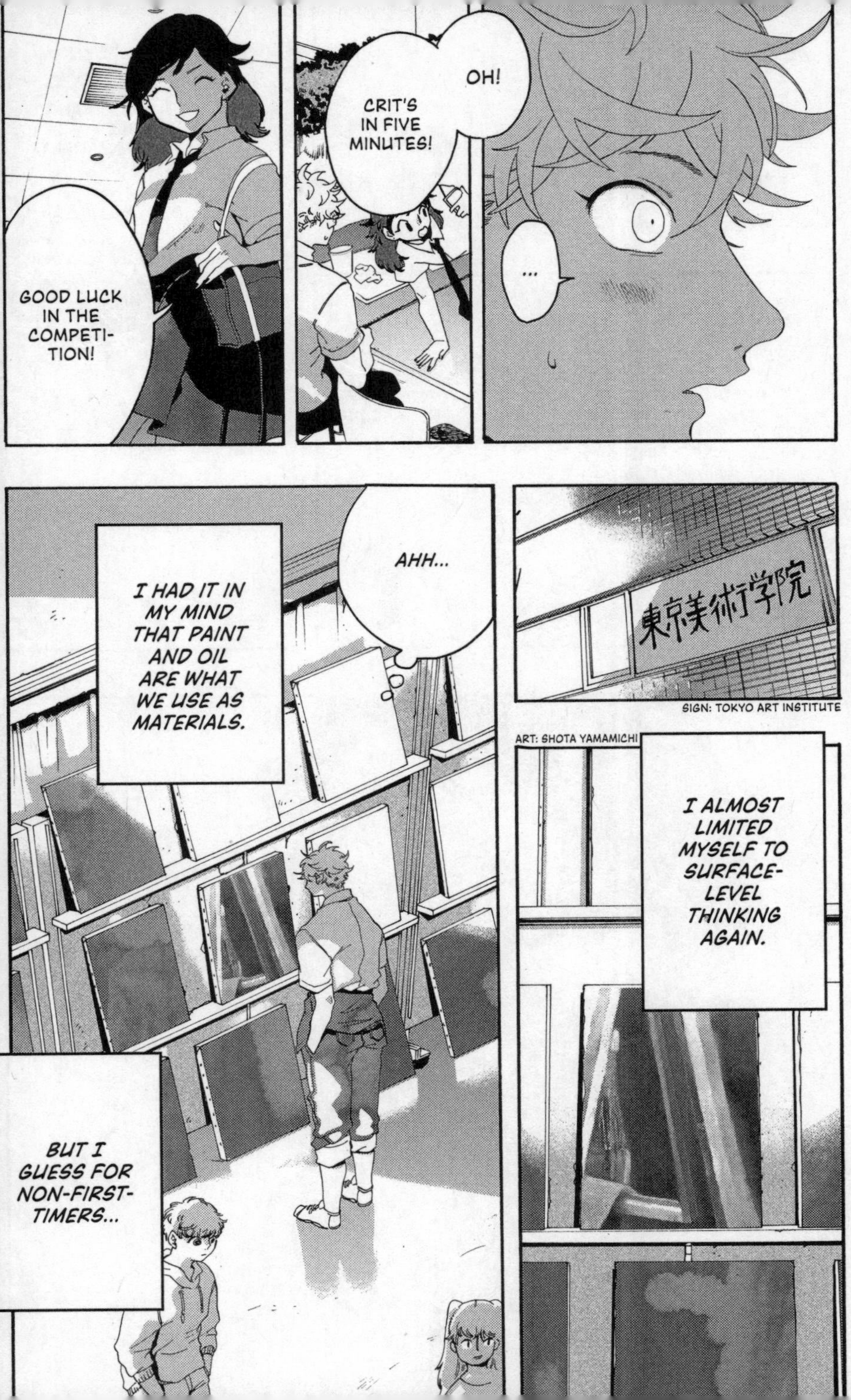
...
OH!
CRIT'S IN FIVE MINUTES!
GOOD LUCK IN THE COMPETITION!
東京美術学院
SIGN: TOKYO ART INSTITUTE
ART: SHOTA YAMAMICHI
I ALMOST LIMITED MYSELF TO SURFACE-LEVEL THINKING AGAIN.
AHH...
I HAD IT IN MY MIND THAT PAINT AND OIL ARE WHAT WE USE AS MATERIALS.
BUT I GUESS FOR NON-FIRST-TIMERS...

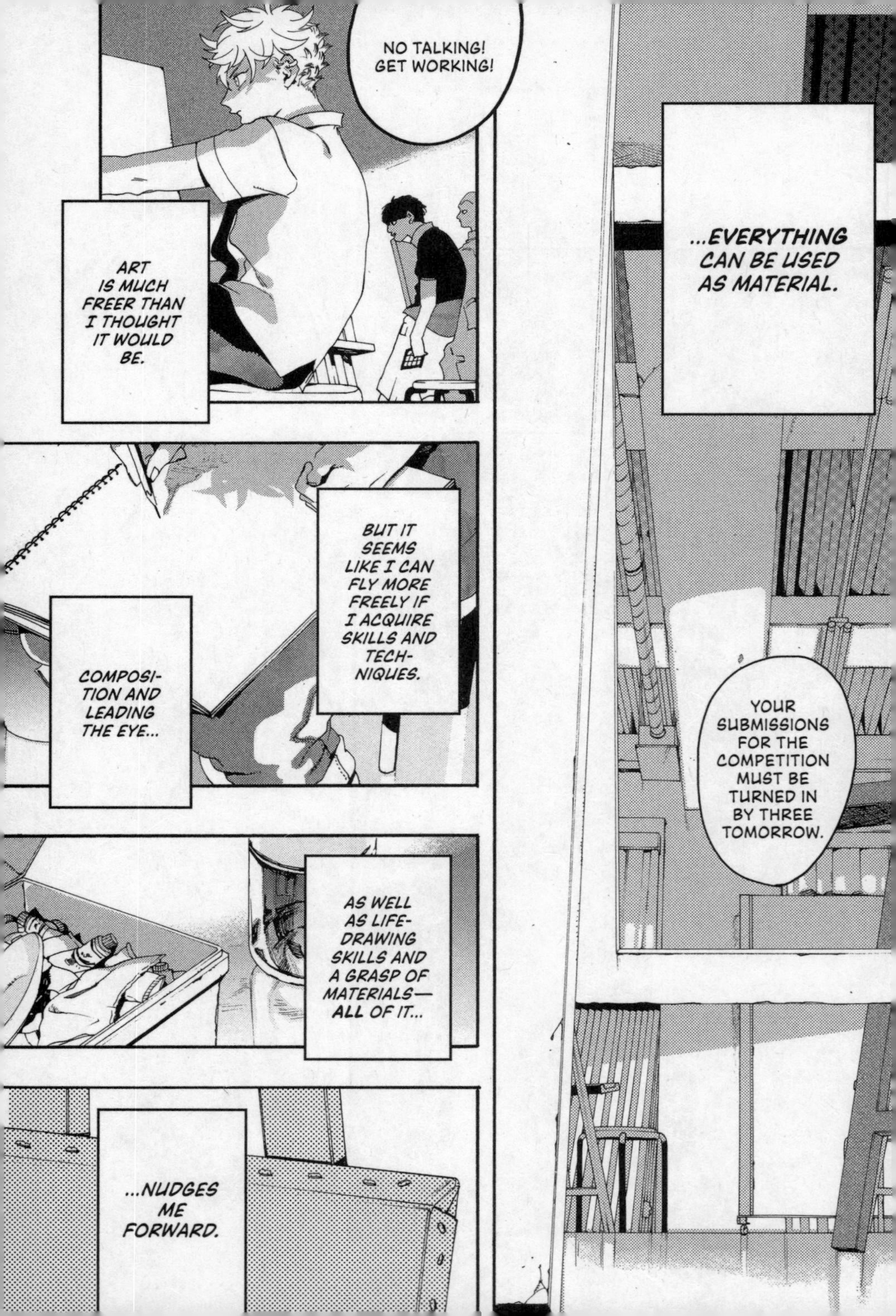
...EVERYTHING CAN BE USED AS MATERIAL.
YOUR SUBMISSIONS FOR THE COMPETITION MUST BE TURNED IN BY THREE TOMORROW.
NO TALKING! GET WORKING!
ART IS MUCH FREER THAN I THOUGHT IT WOULD BE.
BUT IT SEEMS LIKE I CAN FLY MORE FREELY IF I ACQUIRE SKILLS AND TECH-NIQUES.
COMPOSI-TION AND LEADING THE EYE...
AS WELL AS LIFE-DRAWING SKILLS AND A GRASP OF MATERIALS—ALL OF IT...
...NUDGES ME FORWARD.

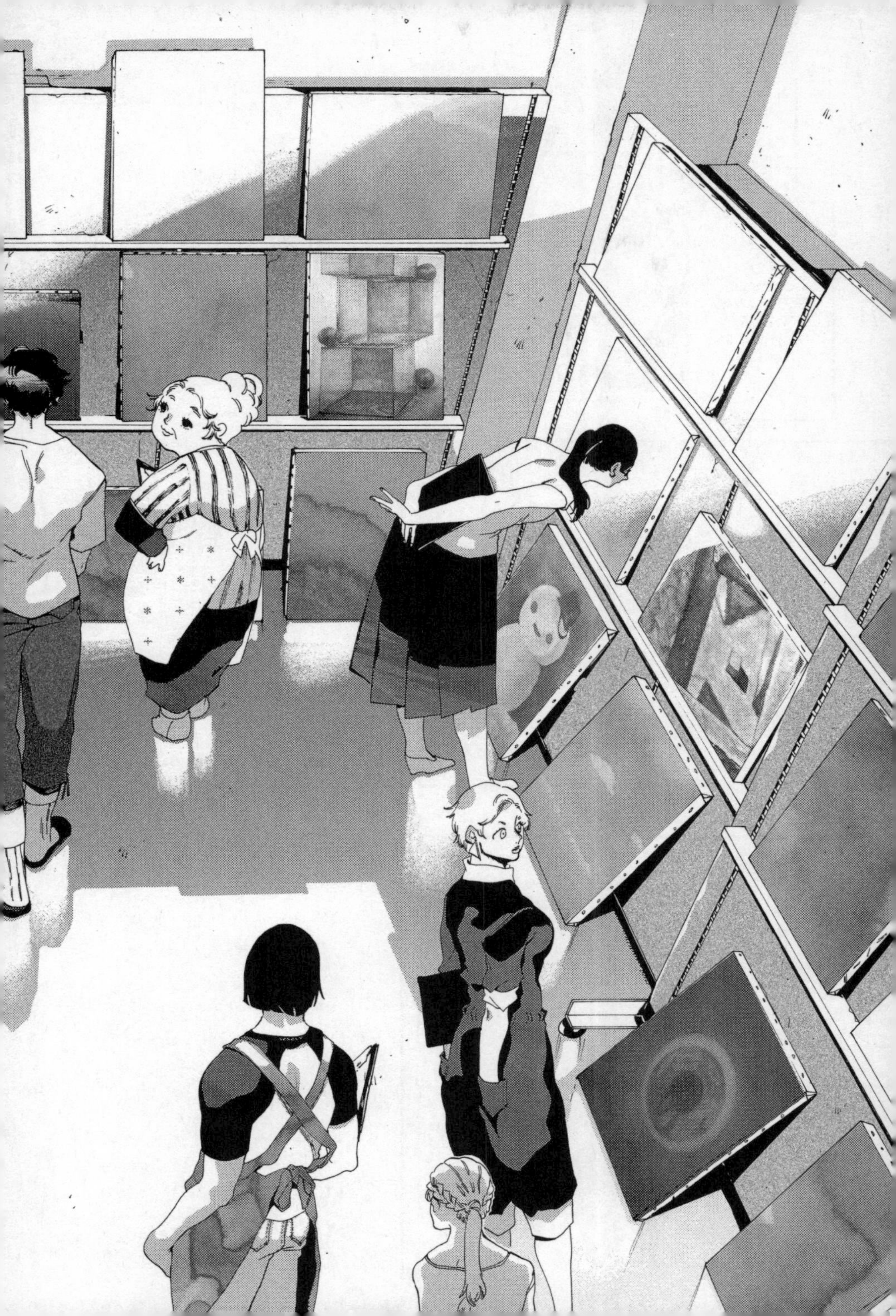

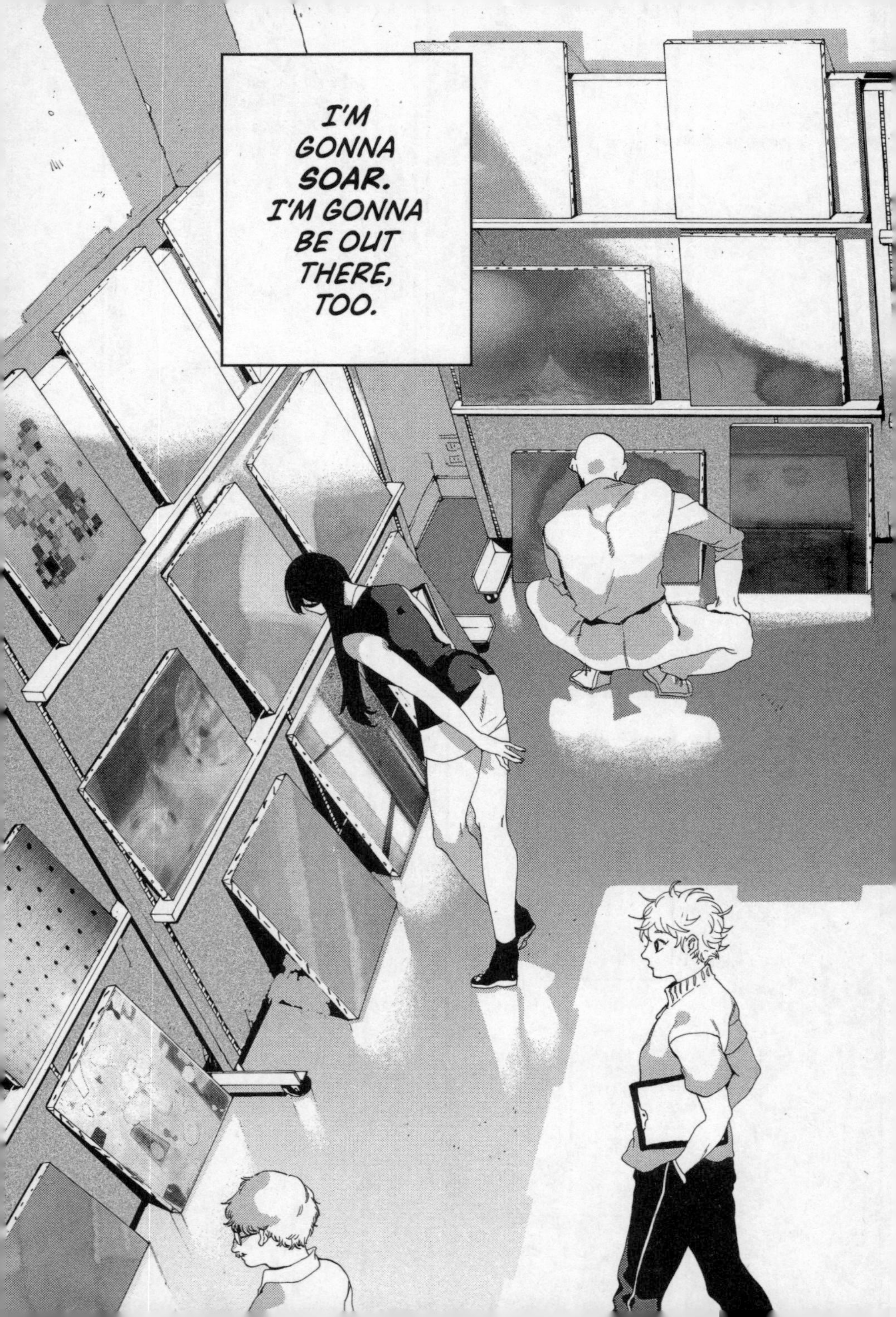
I'M GONNA SOAR. I'M GONNA BE OUT THERE, TOO.

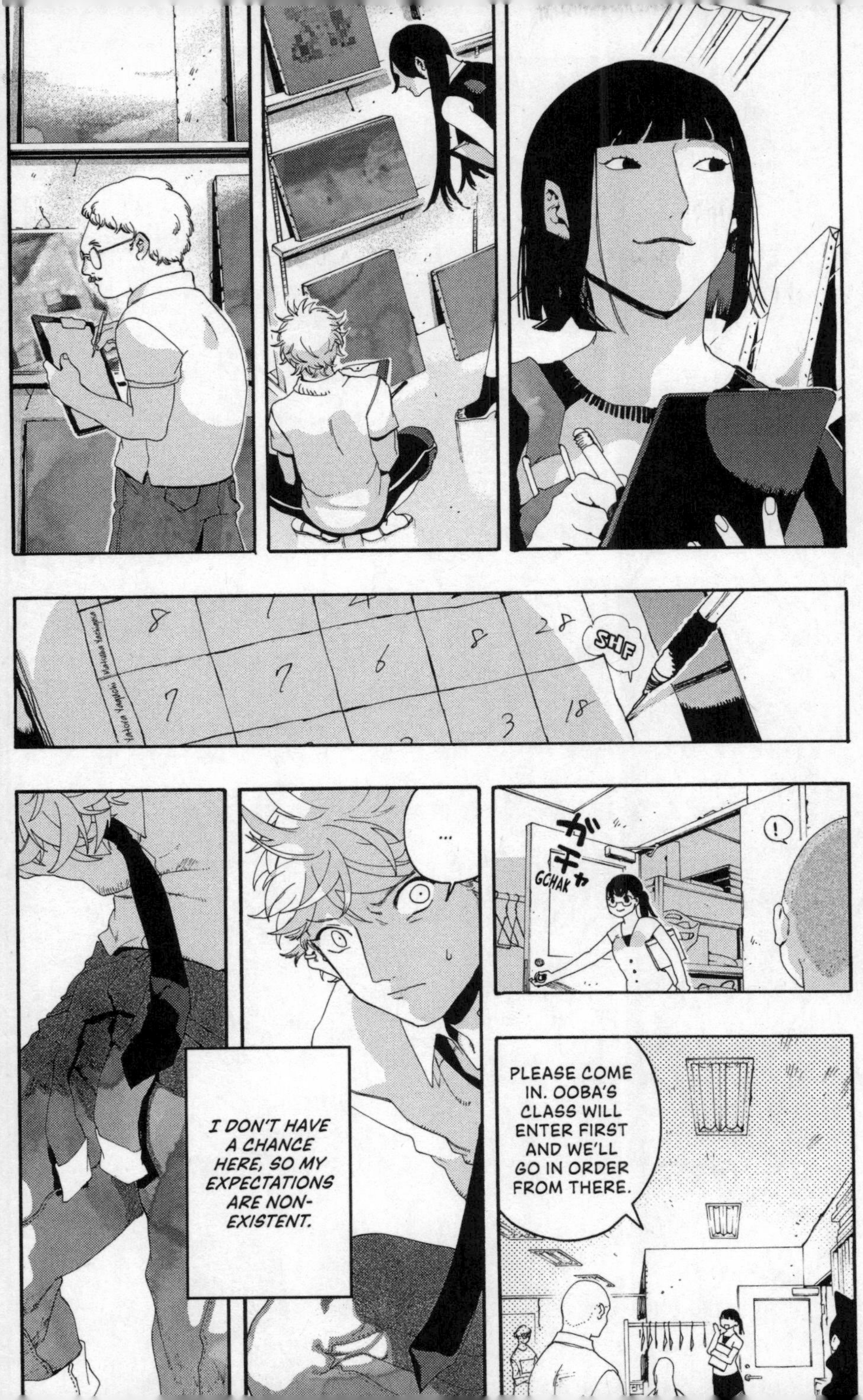
SHF
!
ガチャ
GCHAK
PLEASE COME IN. OOBA'S CLASS WILL ENTER FIRST AND WE'LL GO IN ORDER FROM THERE.
...
I DON'T HAVE A CHANCE HERE, SO MY EXPECTATIONS ARE NON-EXISTENT.

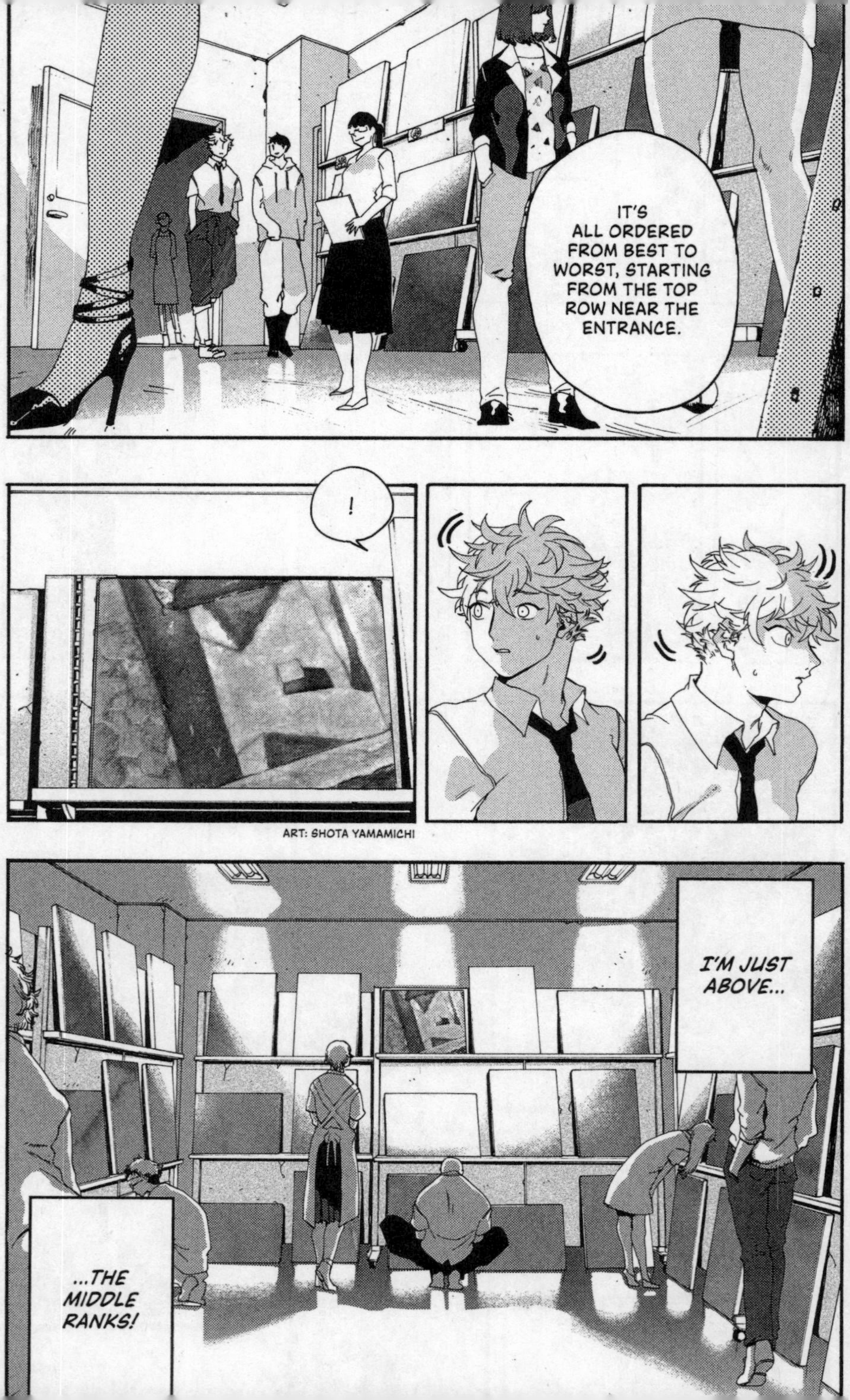
IT'S ALL ORDERED FROM BEST TO WORST, STARTING FROM THE TOP ROW NEAR THE ENTRANCE.
!
I'M JUST ABOVE...
...THE MIDDLE RANKS!
ART: SHOTA YAMAMICHI

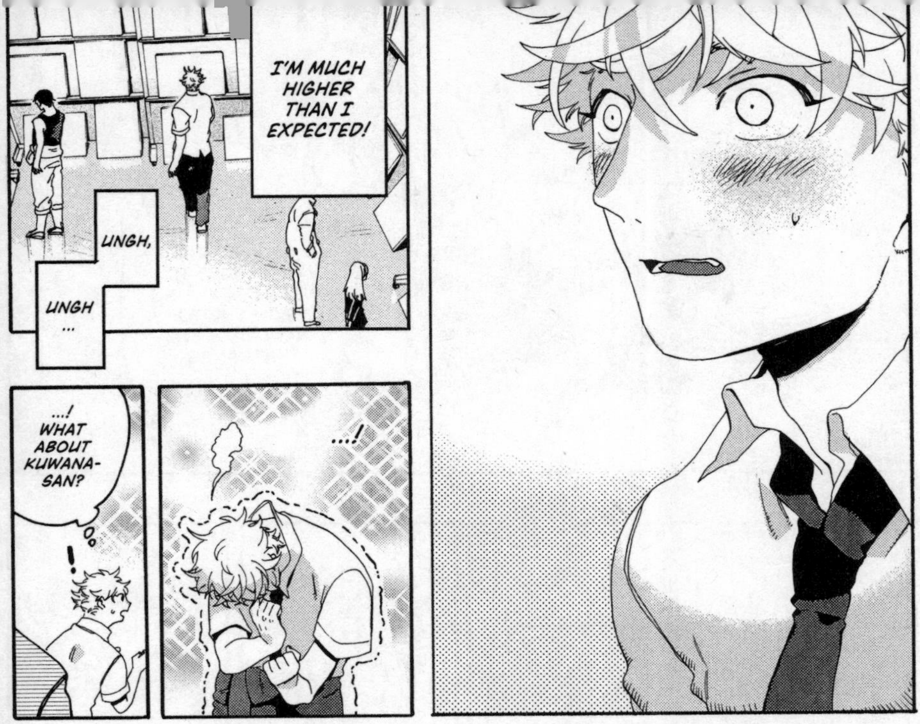
I'M MUCH HIGHER THAN I EXPECTED!
UNGH,
UNGH ...
...!
...! WHAT ABOUT KUWANA-SAN?

ART: MOEKO NATSUI

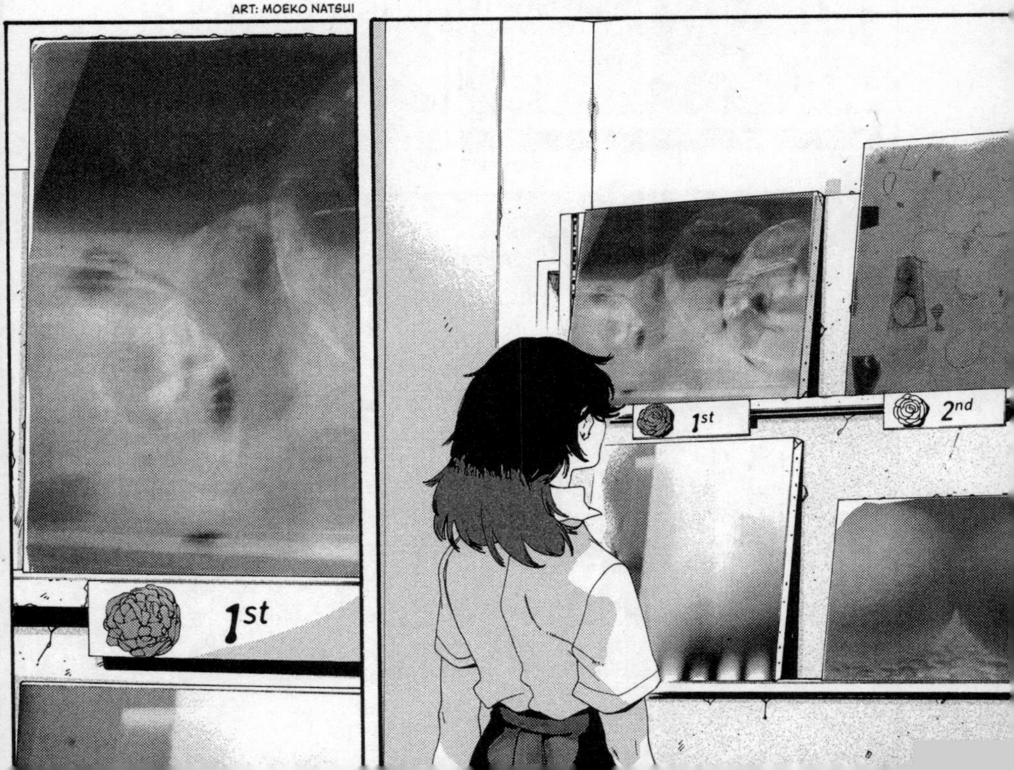
2nd
1st
1st

WOW! FOR REAL? AWESOME!

WHOA... WILD, HUH?!

FIRST?!

...DON'T YOU KNOW?

NO WAY...

THERE'S A CURSE WHERE ANYONE WHO'S RANKED FIRST...

...*FAILS* THEIR EXAMS THAT YEAR.

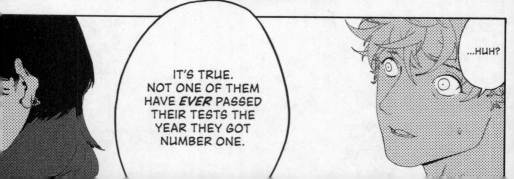

IT'S TRUE. NOT ONE OF THEM HAVE *EVER* PASSED THEIR TESTS THE YEAR THEY GOT NUMBER ONE.

...HUH?

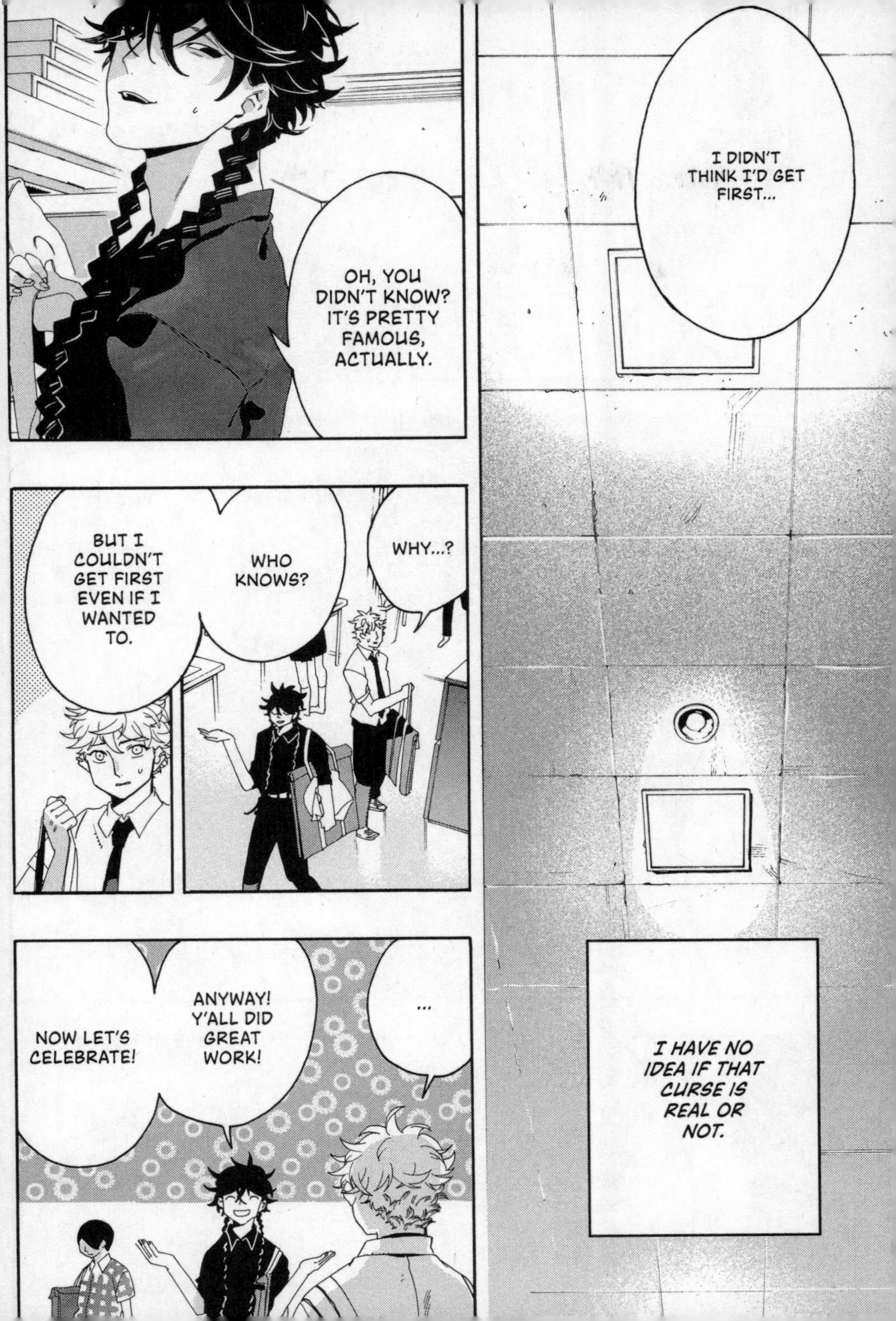
I DIDN'T THINK I'D GET FIRST...
I HAVE NO IDEA IF THAT CURSE IS REAL OR NOT.
OH, YOU DIDN'T KNOW? IT'S PRETTY FAMOUS, ACTUALLY.
WHY...?
WHO KNOWS?
BUT I COULDN'T GET FIRST EVEN IF I WANTED TO.
...
ANYWAY! Y'ALL DID GREAT WORK!
NOW LET'S CELEBRATE!

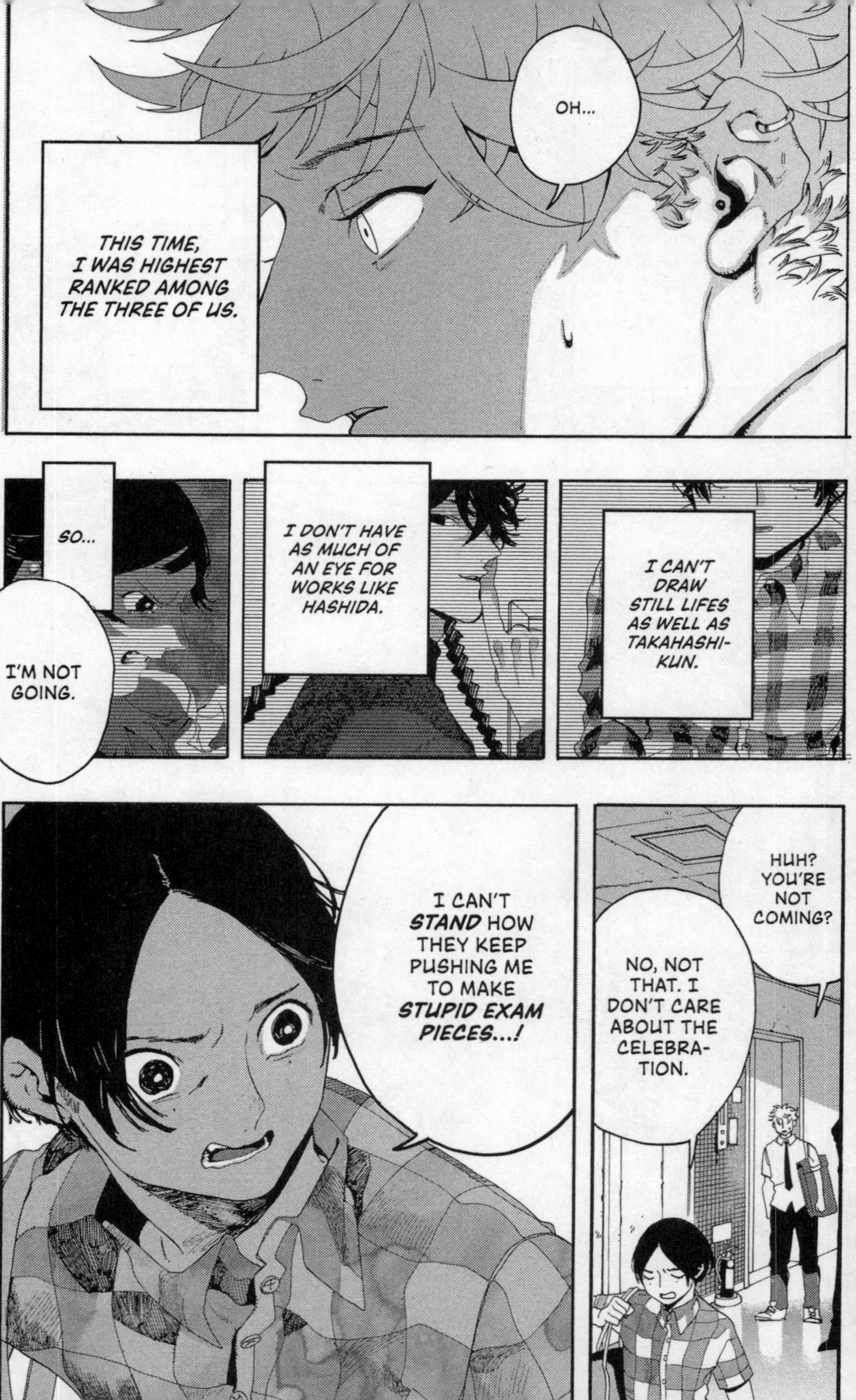
OH...
THIS TIME, I WAS HIGHEST RANKED AMONG THE THREE OF US.
I CAN'T DRAW STILL LIFES AS WELL AS TAKAHASHI-KUN.
I DON'T HAVE AS MUCH OF AN EYE FOR WORKS LIKE HASHIDA.
SO...
I'M NOT GOING.
HUH? YOU'RE NOT COMING?
NO, NOT THAT. I DON'T CARE ABOUT THE CELEBRATION.
I CAN'T STAND HOW THEY KEEP PUSHING ME TO MAKE STUPID EXAM PIECES...!

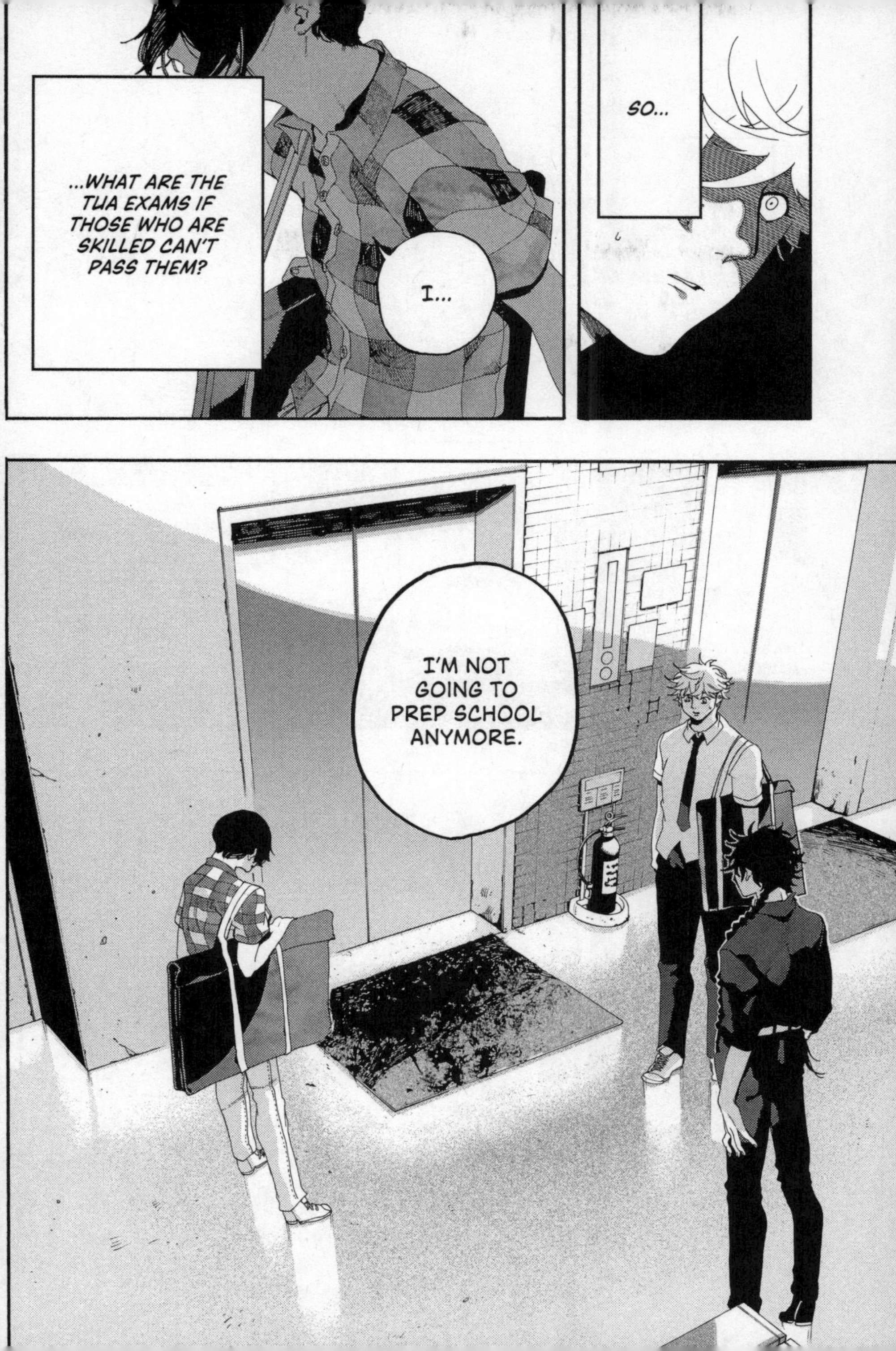
SO...
...WHAT ARE THE TUA EXAMS IF THOSE WHO ARE SKILLED CAN'T PASS THEM?
I...
I'M NOT GOING TO PREP SCHOOL ANYMORE.

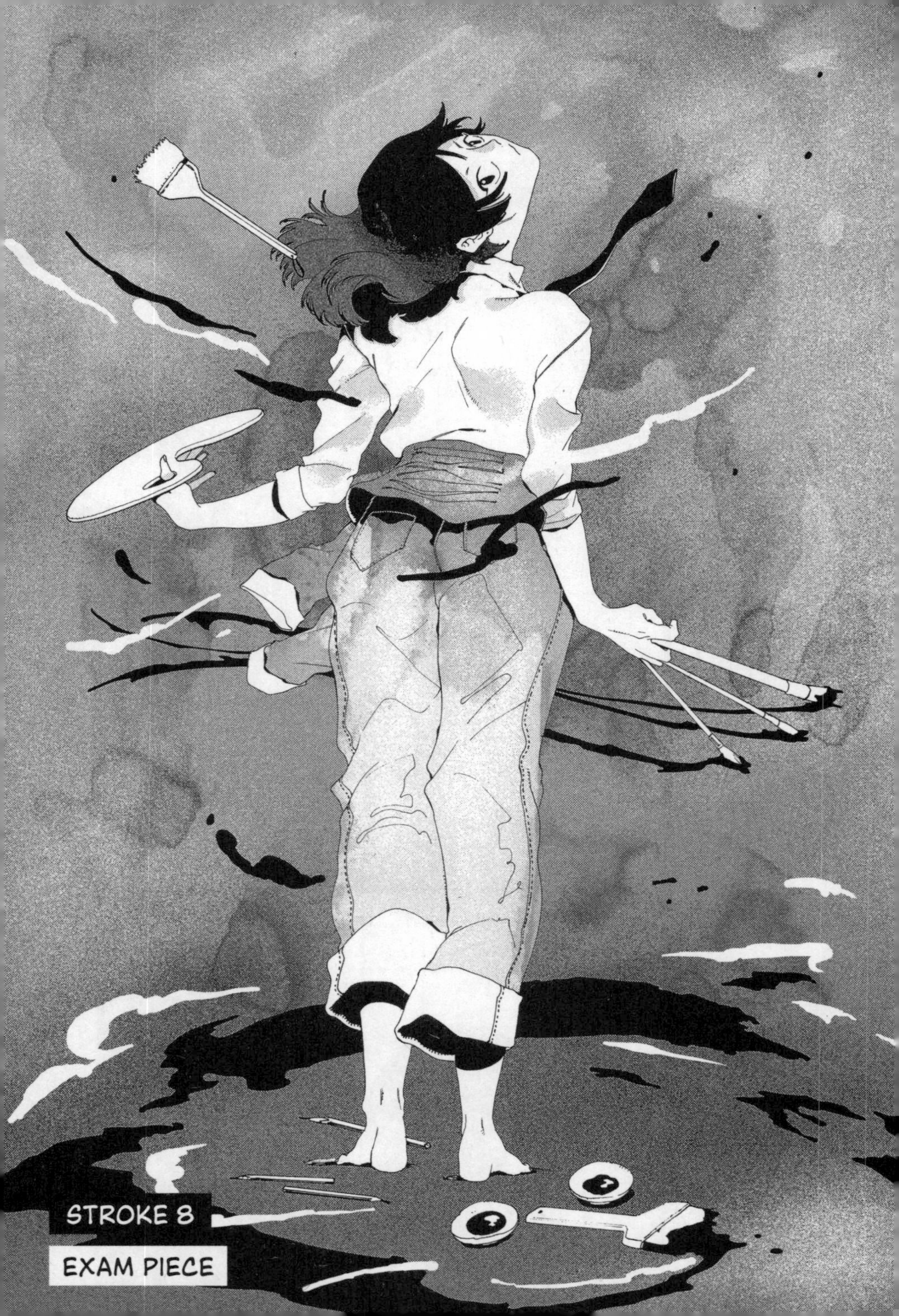
STROKE 8
EXAM PIECE

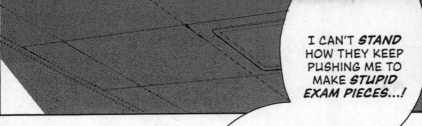

I CAN'T **STAND** HOW THEY KEEP PUSHING ME TO MAKE **STUPID EXAM PIECES**...!

I'M NOT GOING TO PREP SCHOOL ANYMORE.

...

EXAM PIECES?

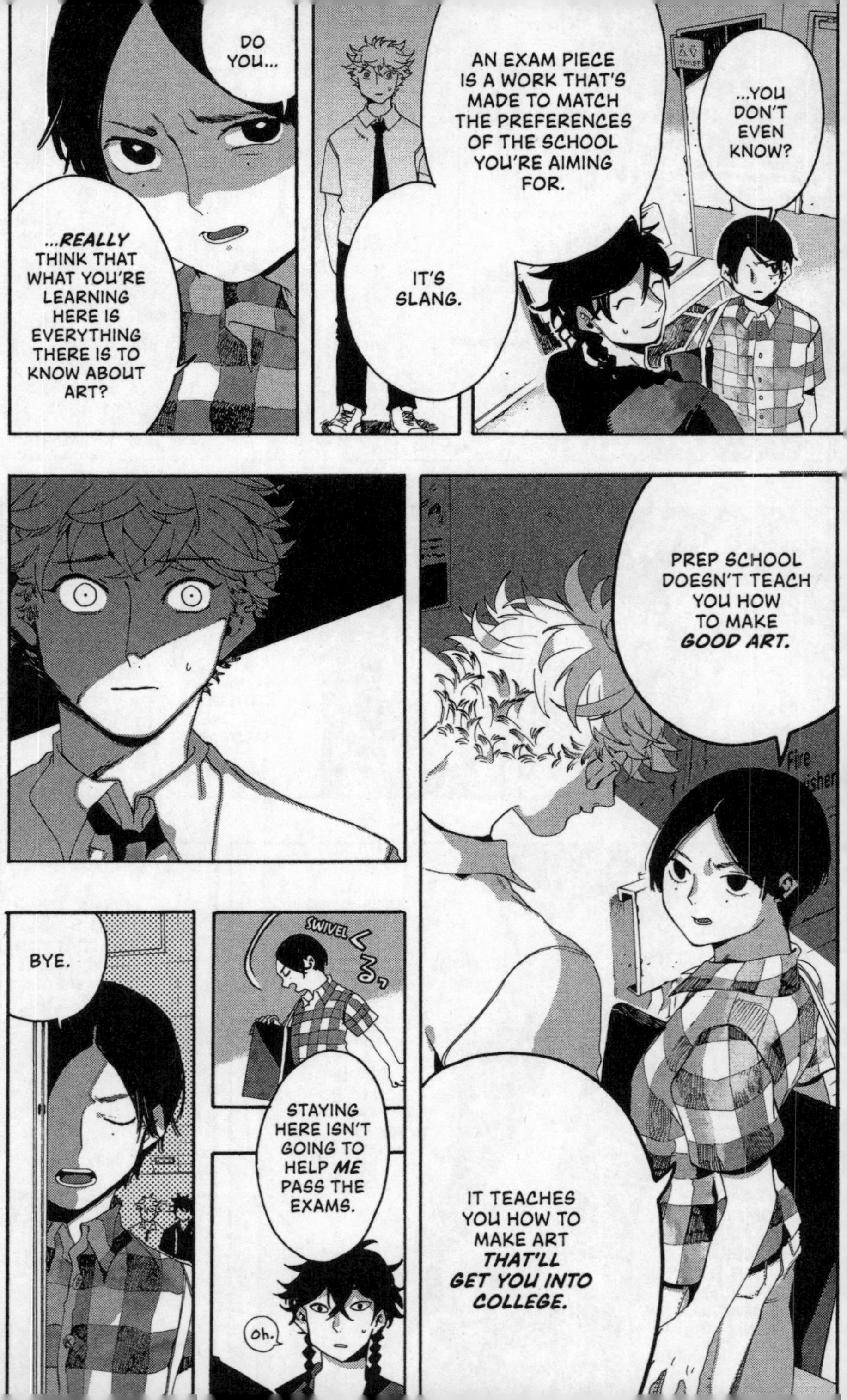
...YOU DON'T EVEN KNOW?
AN EXAM PIECE IS A WORK THAT'S MADE TO MATCH THE PREFERENCES OF THE SCHOOL YOU'RE AIMING FOR.
IT'S SLANG.
DO YOU...
...REALLY THINK THAT WHAT YOU'RE LEARNING HERE IS EVERYTHING THERE IS TO KNOW ABOUT ART?
PREP SCHOOL DOESN'T TEACH YOU HOW TO MAKE GOOD ART.
IT TEACHES YOU HOW TO MAKE ART THAT'LL GET YOU INTO COLLEGE.
SWIVEL くる
STAYING HERE ISN'T GOING TO HELP ME PASS THE EXAMS.
Oh.
BYE.

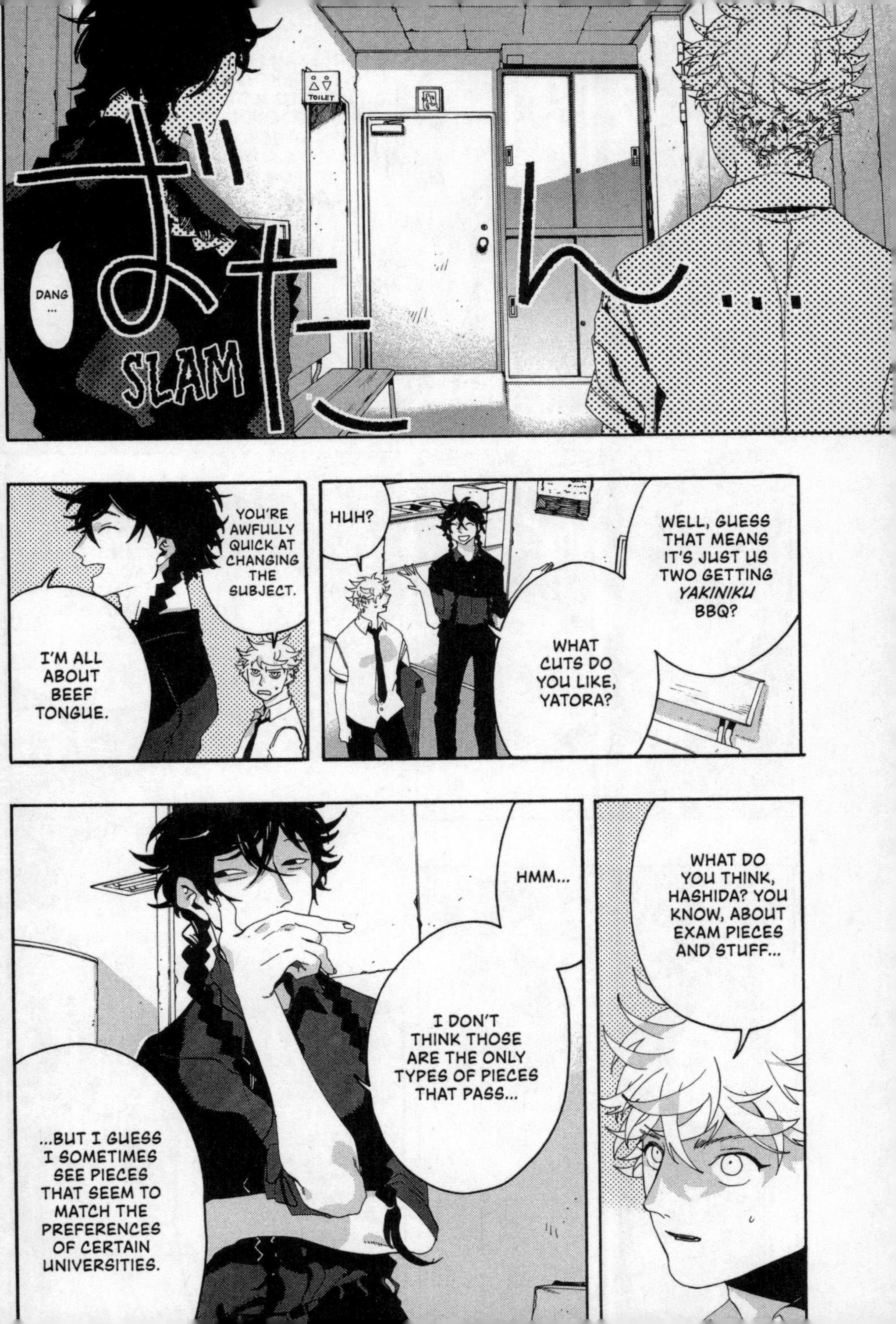
...
SLAM
DANG ...
WELL, GUESS THAT MEANS IT'S JUST US TWO GETTING *YAKINIKU* BBQ?
WHAT CUTS DO YOU LIKE, YATORA?
HUH?
YOU'RE AWFULLY QUICK AT CHANGING THE SUBJECT.
I'M ALL ABOUT BEEF TONGUE.
WHAT DO YOU THINK, HASHIDA? YOU KNOW, ABOUT EXAM PIECES AND STUFF...
HMM...
I DON'T THINK THOSE ARE THE ONLY TYPES OF PIECES THAT PASS...
...BUT I GUESS I SOMETIMES SEE PIECES THAT SEEM TO MATCH THE PREFERENCES OF CERTAIN UNIVERSITIES.

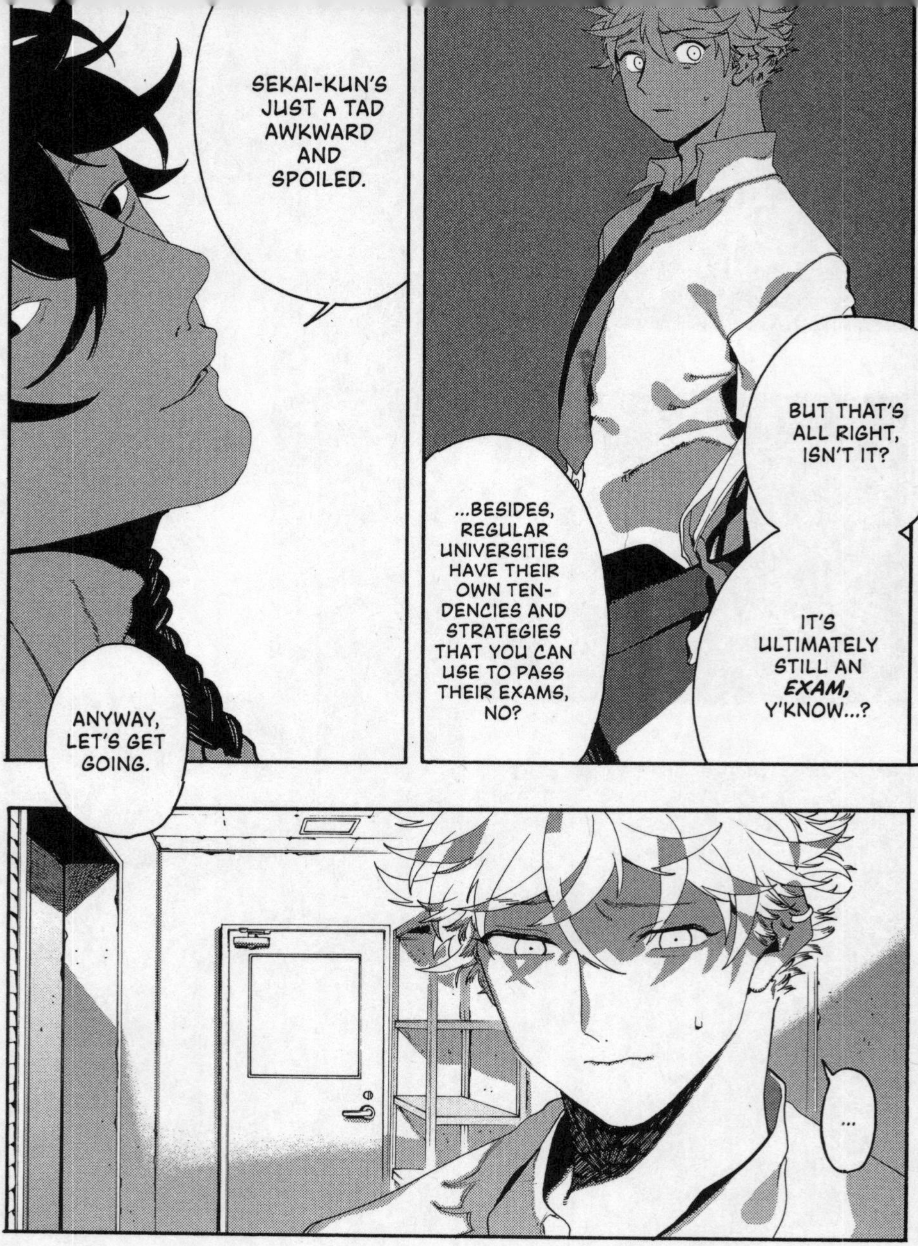
BUT THAT'S ALL RIGHT, ISN'T IT?
IT'S ULTIMATELY STILL AN *EXAM,* Y'KNOW...?
...BESIDES, REGULAR UNIVERSITIES HAVE THEIR OWN TEN-DENCIES AND STRATEGIES THAT YOU CAN USE TO PASS THEIR EXAMS, NO?
SEKAI-KUN'S JUST A TAD AWKWARD AND SPOILED.
ANYWAY, LET'S GET GOING.
...

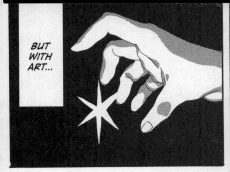

BUT
WITH
ART...

WITH
REGULAR
STUDIES,
I COULD SEE
WHERE I WAS
AIMING,
NO MATTER
HOW FAR
AWAY IT WAS.

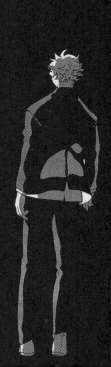

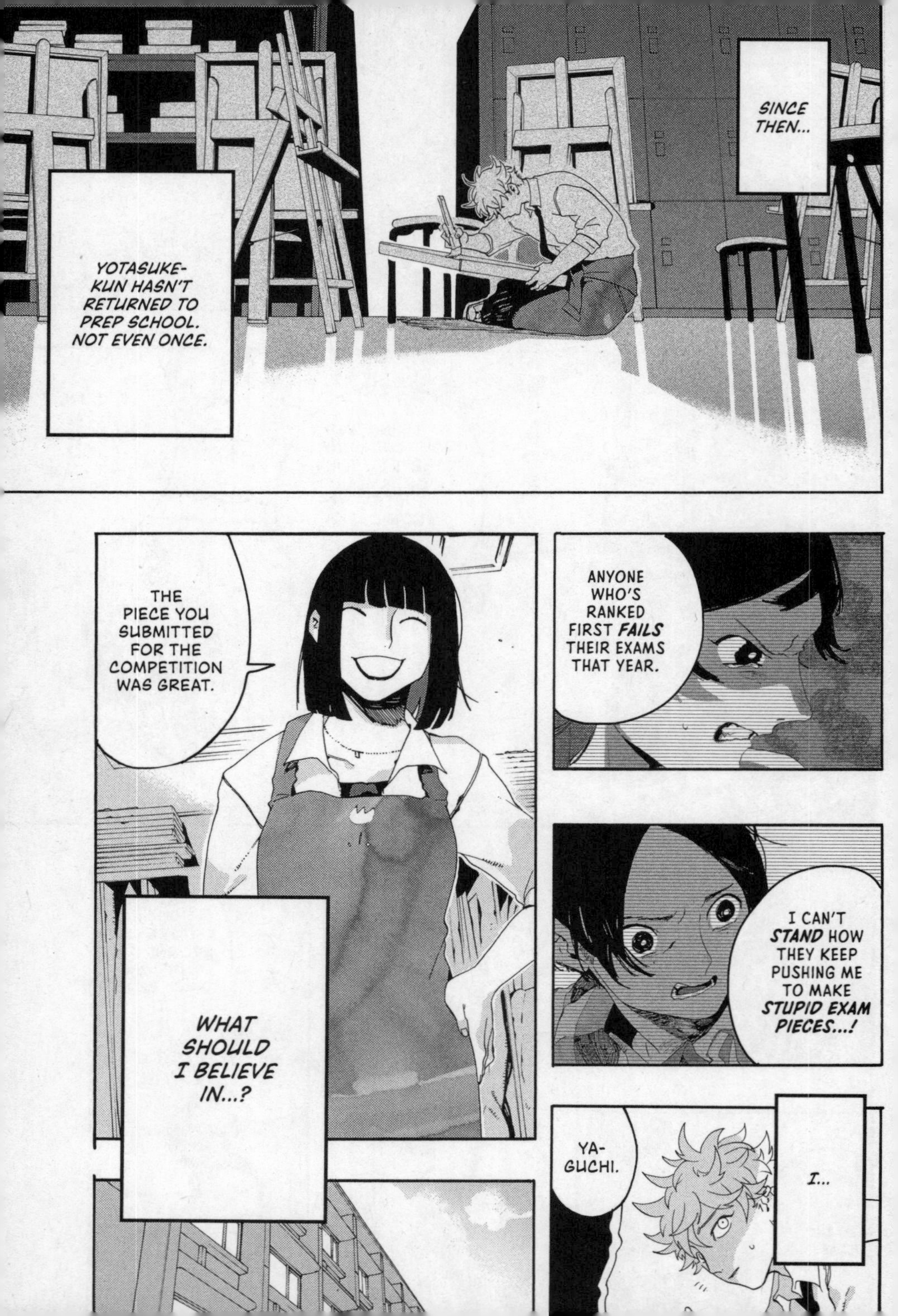
SINCE THEN...
YOTASUKE-KUN HASN'T RETURNED TO PREP SCHOOL. NOT EVEN ONCE.
ANYONE WHO'S RANKED FIRST FAILS THEIR EXAMS THAT YEAR.
I CAN'T STAND HOW THEY KEEP PUSHING ME TO MAKE STUPID EXAM PIECES...!
THE PIECE YOU SUBMITTED FOR THE COMPETITION WAS GREAT.
WHAT SHOULD I BELIEVE IN...?
I...
YA-GUCHI.

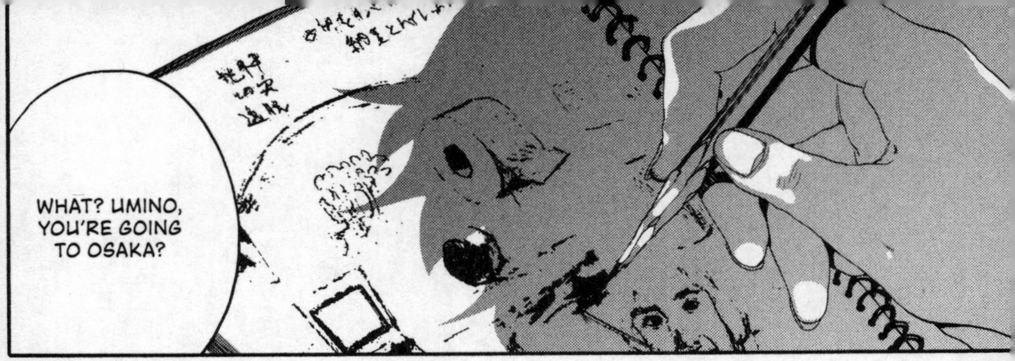
WHAT? UMINO, YOU'RE GOING TO OSAKA?

ART: SHOTA YAMAMICHI

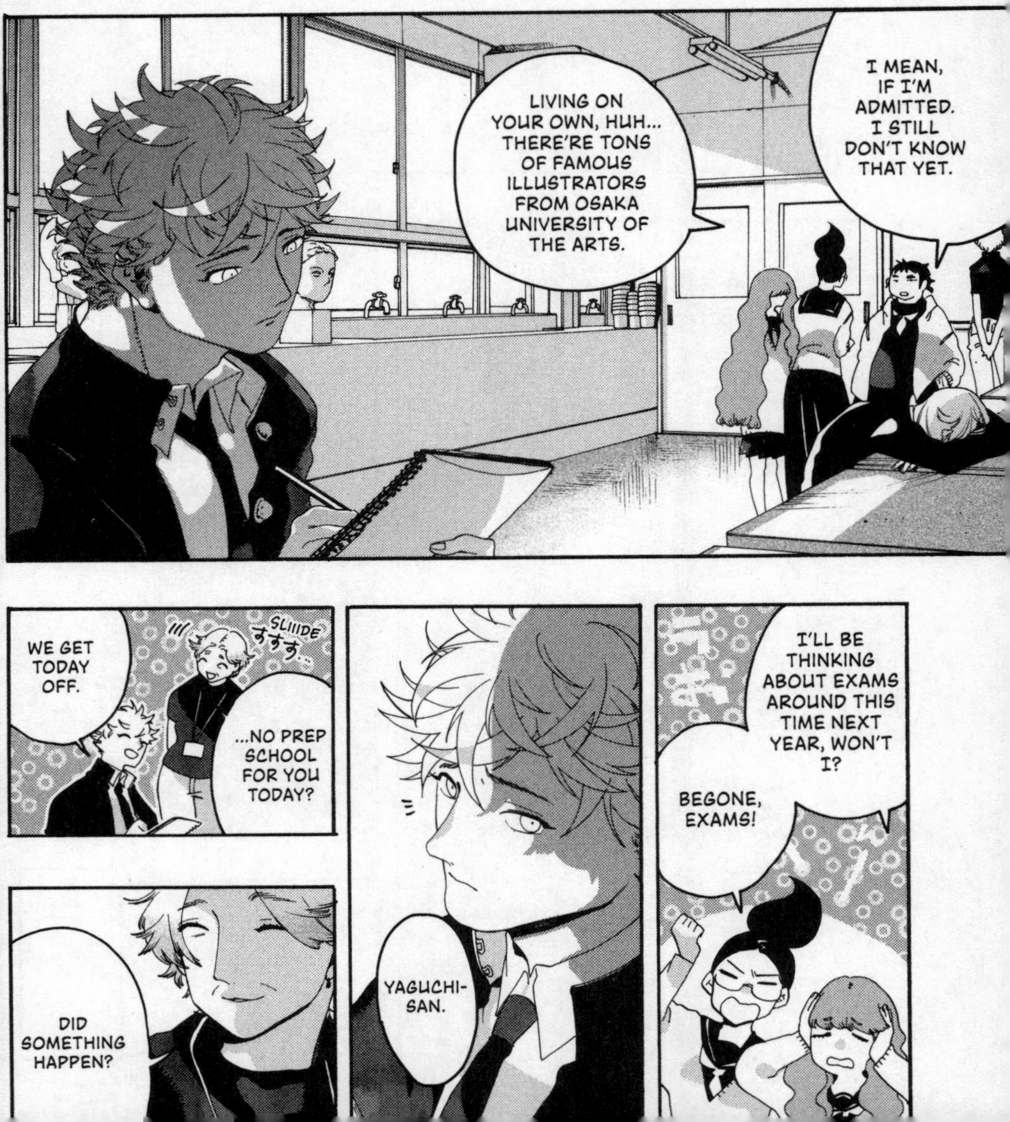
I MEAN, IF I'M ADMITTED. I STILL DON'T KNOW THAT YET.
LIVING ON YOUR OWN, HUH... THERE'RE TONS OF FAMOUS ILLUSTRATORS FROM OSAKA UNIVERSITY OF THE ARTS.
I'LL BE THINKING ABOUT EXAMS AROUND THIS TIME NEXT YEAR, WON'T I?
BEGONE, EXAMS!
YAGUCHI-SAN.
SLIIIDE すすす…
...NO PREP SCHOOL FOR YOU TODAY?
WE GET TODAY OFF.
DID SOMETHING HAPPEN?

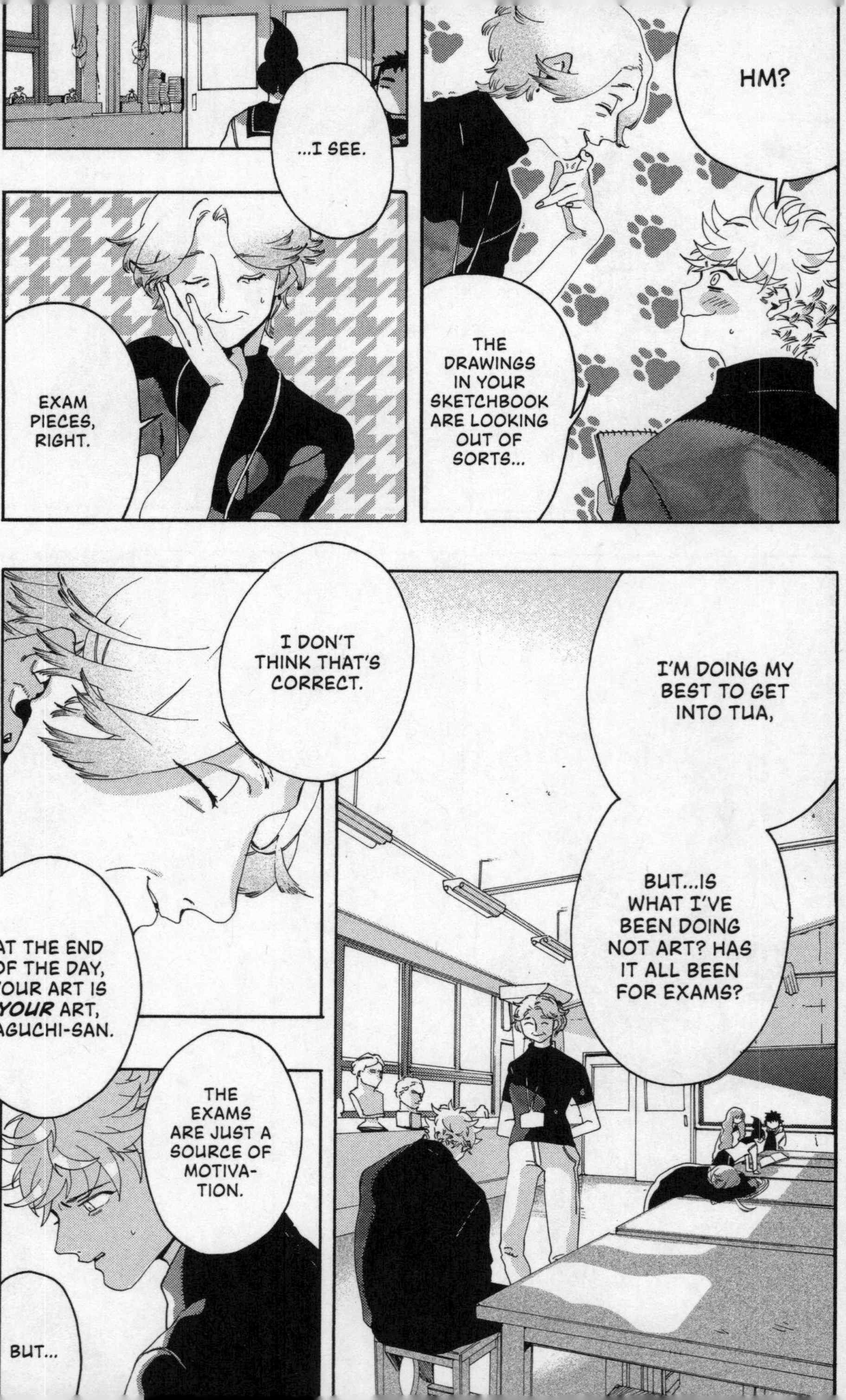
HM?
THE DRAWINGS IN YOUR SKETCHBOOK ARE LOOKING OUT OF SORTS...
...I SEE.
EXAM PIECES, RIGHT.
I'M DOING MY BEST TO GET INTO TUA,
BUT...IS WHAT I'VE BEEN DOING NOT ART? HAS IT ALL BEEN FOR EXAMS?
I DON'T THINK THAT'S CORRECT.
AT THE END OF THE DAY, YOUR ART IS *YOUR* ART, YAGUCHI-SAN.
THE EXAMS ARE JUST A SOURCE OF MOTIVATION.
BUT...

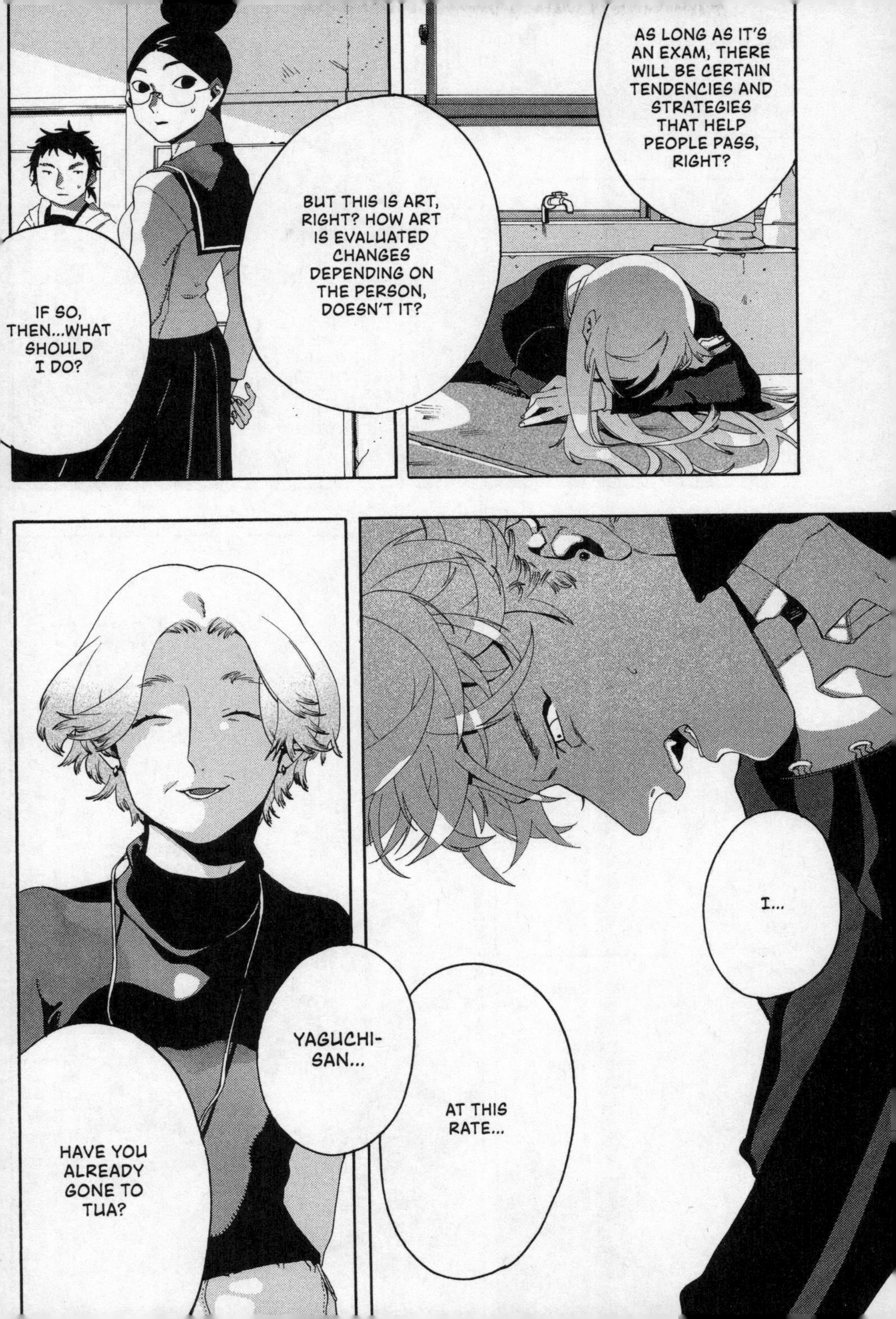
AS LONG AS IT'S AN EXAM, THERE WILL BE CERTAIN TENDENCIES AND STRATEGIES THAT HELP PEOPLE PASS, RIGHT?
BUT THIS IS ART, RIGHT? HOW ART IS EVALUATED CHANGES DEPENDING ON THE PERSON, DOESN'T IT?
IF SO, THEN...WHAT SHOULD I DO?
I...
AT THIS RATE...
YAGUCHI-SAN...
HAVE YOU ALREADY GONE TO TUA?

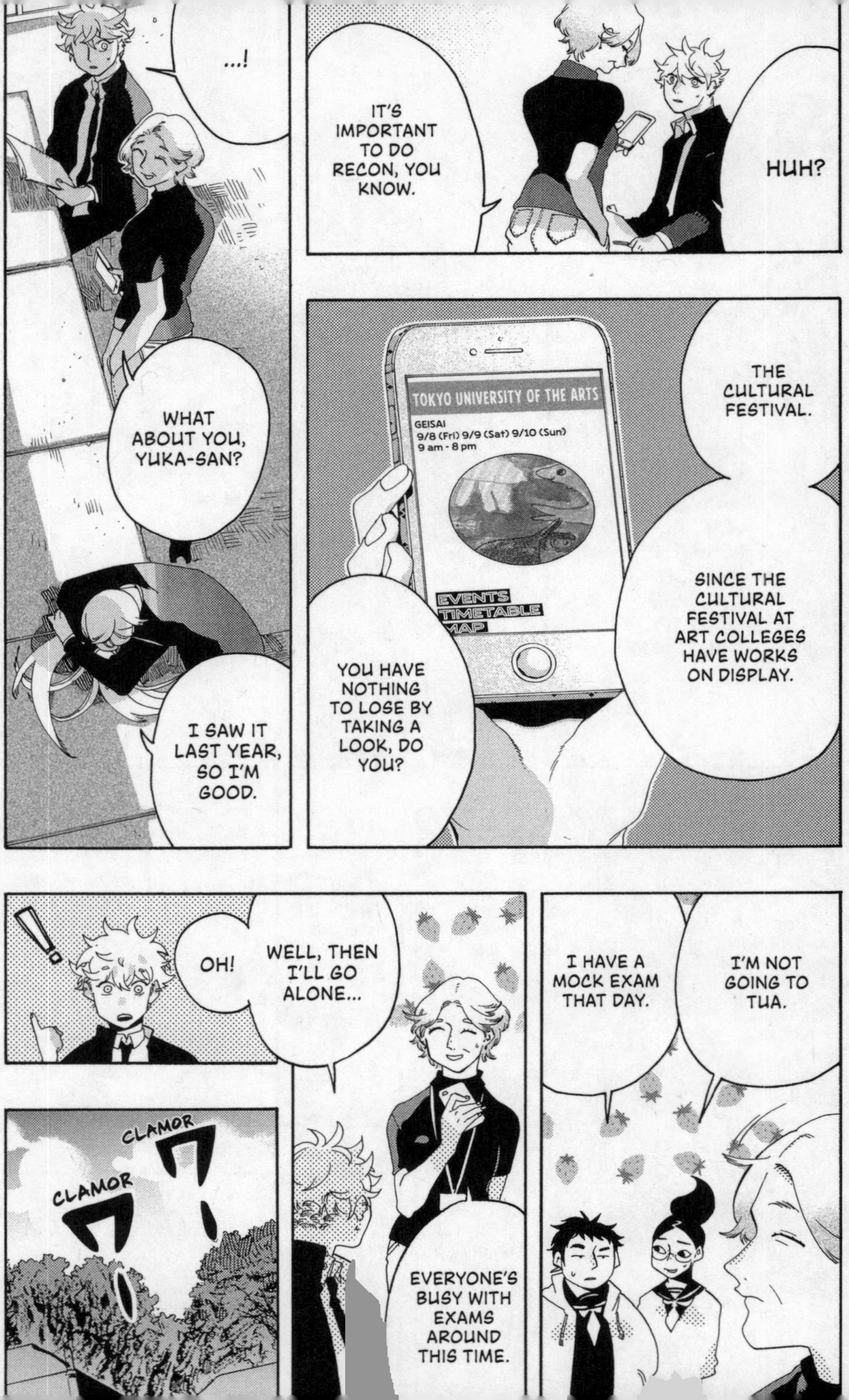
IT'S IMPORTANT TO DO RECON, YOU KNOW.
HUH?
THE CULTURAL FESTIVAL.
SINCE THE CULTURAL FESTIVAL AT ART COLLEGES HAVE WORKS ON DISPLAY.
TOKYO UNIVERSITY OF THE ARTS
GEISAI
9/8 (Fri) 9/9 (Sat) 9/10 (Sun)
9 am - 8 pm
EVENTS
TIMETABLE
MAP
YOU HAVE NOTHING TO LOSE BY TAKING A LOOK, DO YOU?
...!
WHAT ABOUT YOU, YUKA-SAN?
I SAW IT LAST YEAR, SO I'M GOOD.
I'M NOT GOING TO TUA.
I HAVE A MOCK EXAM THAT DAY.
WELL, THEN I'LL GO ALONE...
EVERYONE'S BUSY WITH EXAMS AROUND THIS TIME.
OH!
CLAMOR
CLAMOR

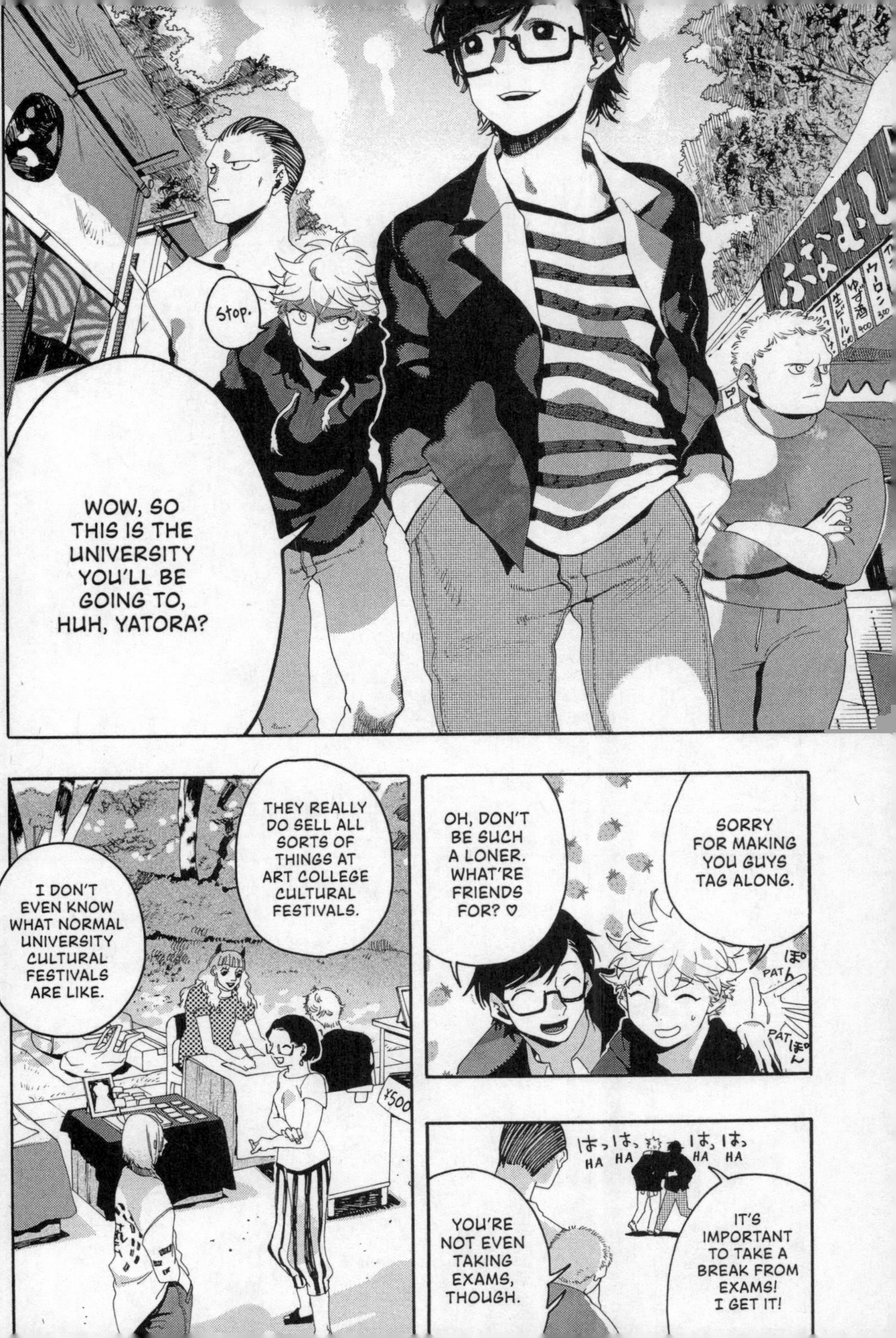
Stop.
WOW, SO THIS IS THE UNIVERSITY YOU'LL BE GOING TO, HUH, YATORA?
SORRY FOR MAKING YOU GUYS TAG ALONG.
OH, DON'T BE SUCH A LONER. WHAT'RE FRIENDS FOR? ♡
ぽん PAT
ぽん PAT
はっはっ HA HA はっはっ HA HA
IT'S IMPORTANT TO TAKE A BREAK FROM EXAMS! I GET IT!
YOU'RE NOT EVEN TAKING EXAMS, THOUGH.
THEY REALLY DO SELL ALL SORTS OF THINGS AT ART COLLEGE CULTURAL FESTIVALS.
I DON'T EVEN KNOW WHAT NORMAL UNIVERSITY CULTURAL FESTIVALS ARE LIKE.
¥500

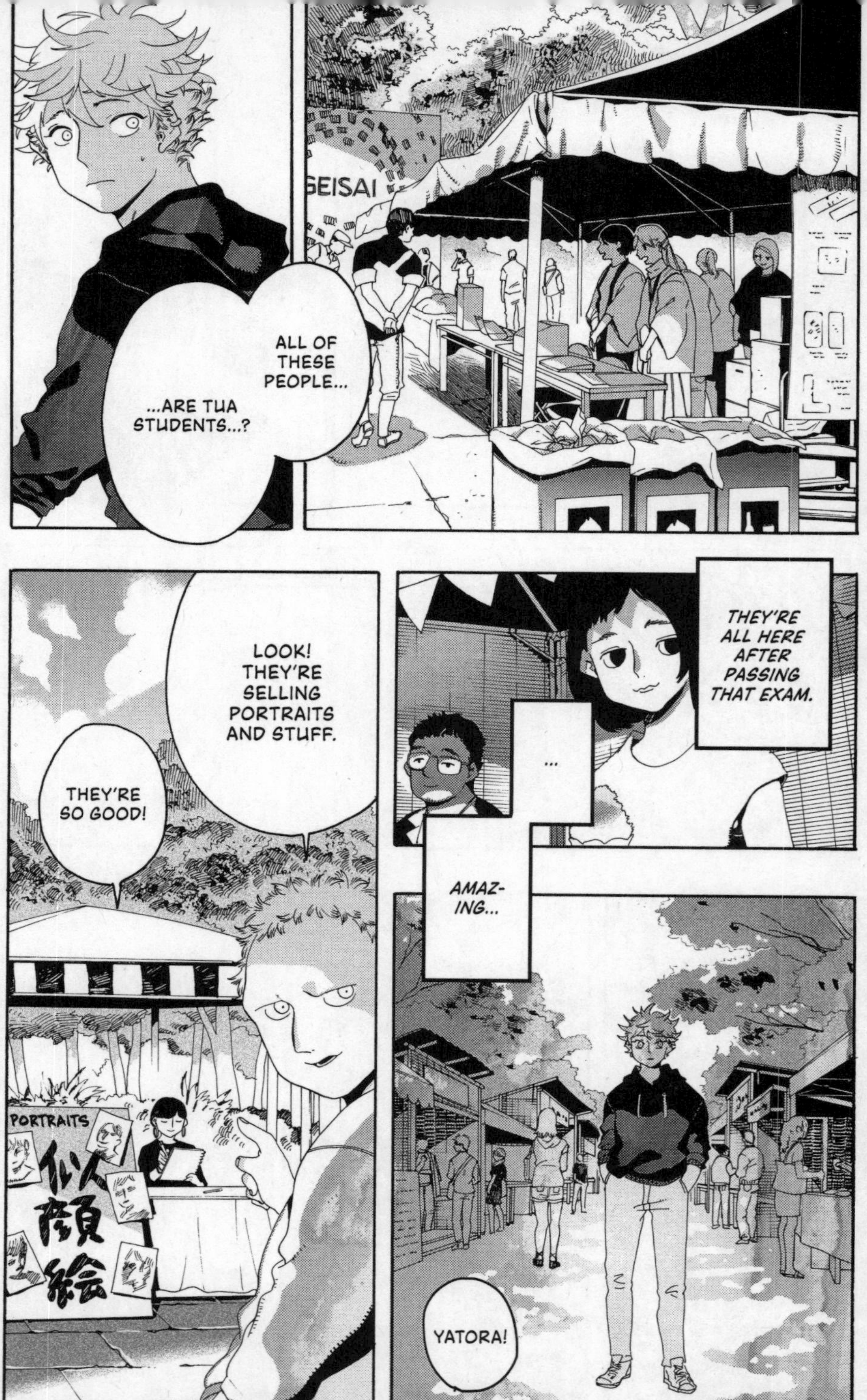
GEISAI
ALL OF THESE PEOPLE...
...ARE TUA STUDENTS...?
THEY'RE ALL HERE AFTER PASSING THAT EXAM.
...
AMAZ-ING...
YATORA!
LOOK! THEY'RE SELLING PORTRAITS AND STUFF.
THEY'RE SO GOOD!
PORTRAITS
似顔絵

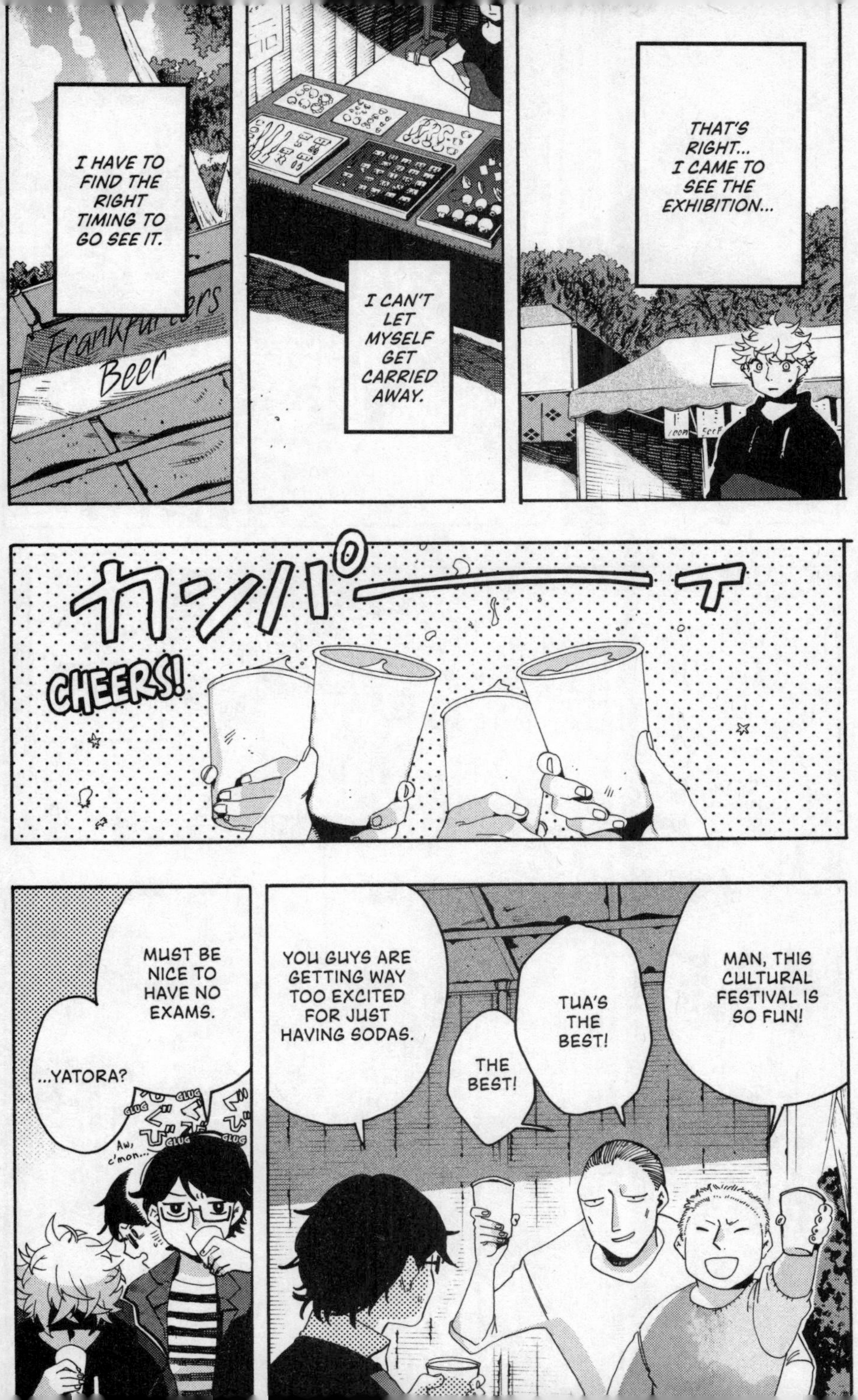
THAT'S RIGHT... I CAME TO SEE THE EXHIBITION...
I CAN'T LET MYSELF GET CARRIED AWAY.
I HAVE TO FIND THE RIGHT TIMING TO GO SEE IT.
Frankfurters
Beer
カンパーイ
CHEERS!
MAN, THIS CULTURAL FESTIVAL IS SO FUN!
TUA'S THE BEST!
THE BEST!
YOU GUYS ARE GETTING WAY TOO EXCITED FOR JUST HAVING SODAS.
MUST BE NICE TO HAVE NO EXAMS.
...YATORA?
GLUG
GLUG
GLUG
Aw, c'mon...

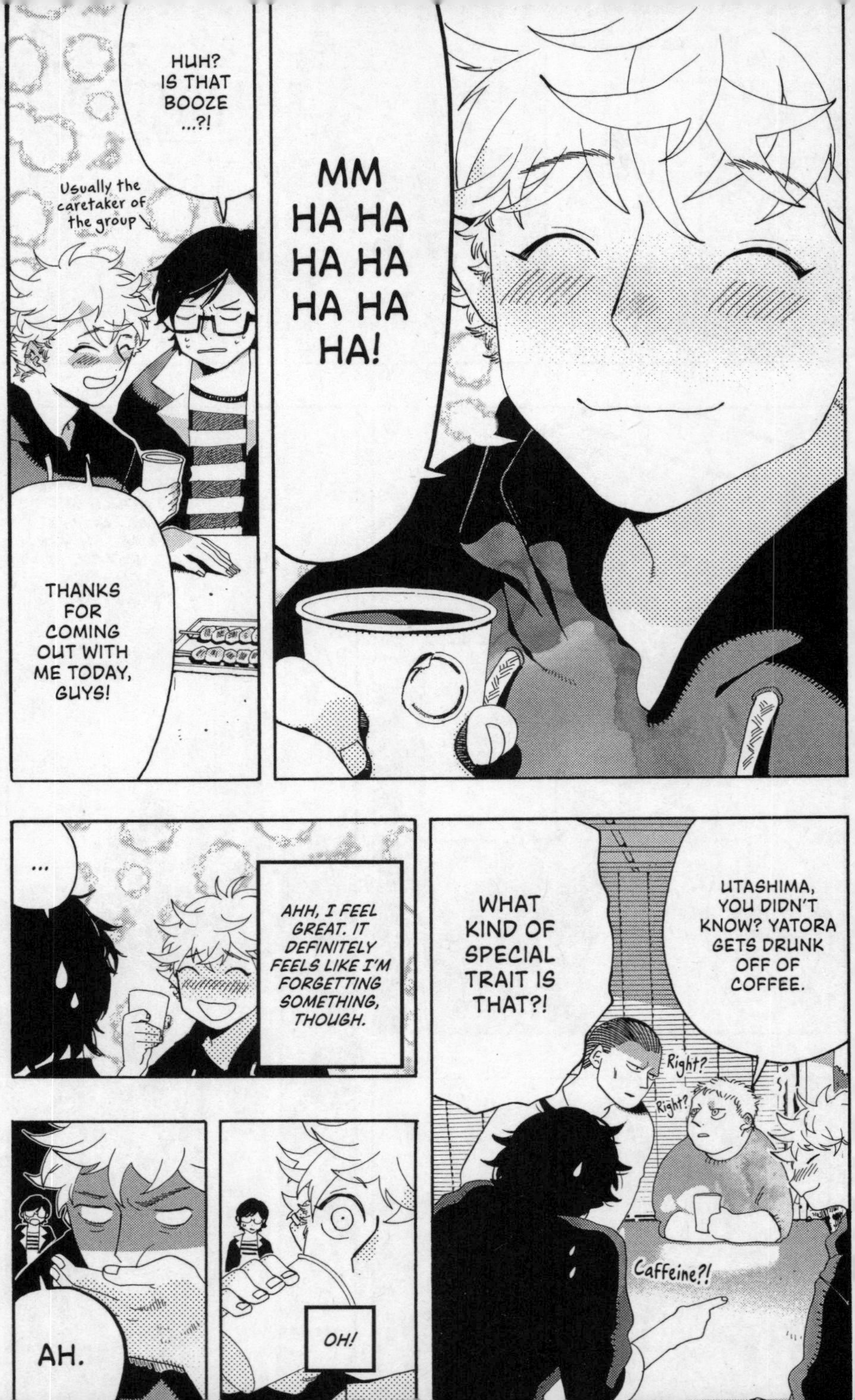
MM HA HA HA HA HA HA HA!
HUH? IS THAT BOOZE ...?!
Usually the caretaker of the group
THANKS FOR COMING OUT WITH ME TODAY, GUYS!
UTASHIMA, YOU DIDN'T KNOW? YATORA GETS DRUNK OFF OF COFFEE.
WHAT KIND OF SPECIAL TRAIT IS THAT?!
Right?
Right?
Caffeine?!
AHH, I FEEL GREAT. IT DEFINITELY FEELS LIKE I'M FORGETTING SOMETHING, THOUGH.
...
OH!
AH.

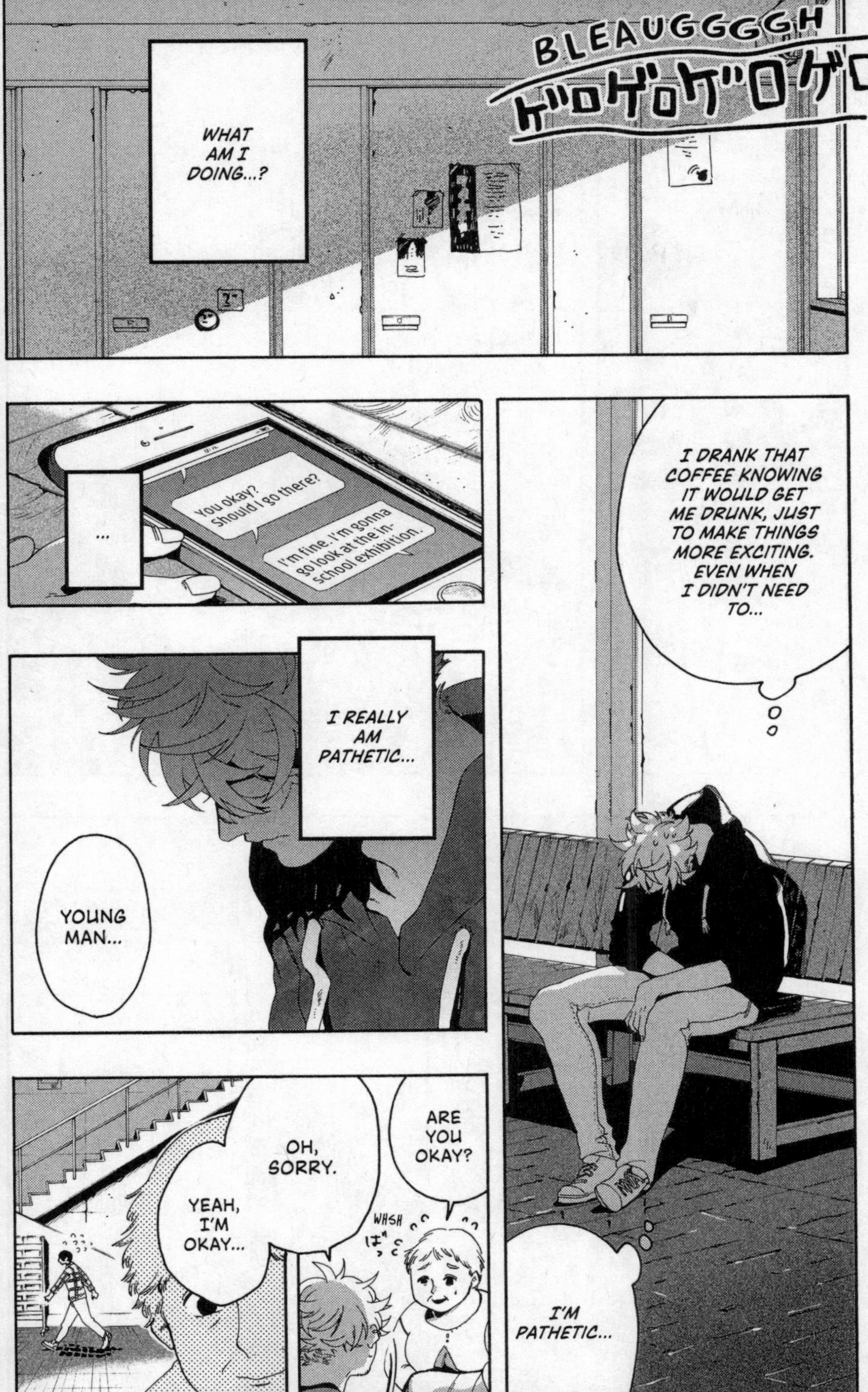
BLEAUGGGGH
ゲロゲロゲロゲロ
WHAT AM I DOING...?
I DRANK THAT COFFEE KNOWING IT WOULD GET ME DRUNK, JUST TO MAKE THINGS MORE EXCITING. EVEN WHEN I DIDN'T NEED TO...
I'M PATHETIC...
You okay? Should I go there?
I'm fine. I'm gonna go look at the in-school exhibition.
...
I REALLY AM PATHETIC...
YOUNG MAN...
ARE YOU OKAY?
WHSH
OH, SORRY.
YEAH, I'M OKAY...

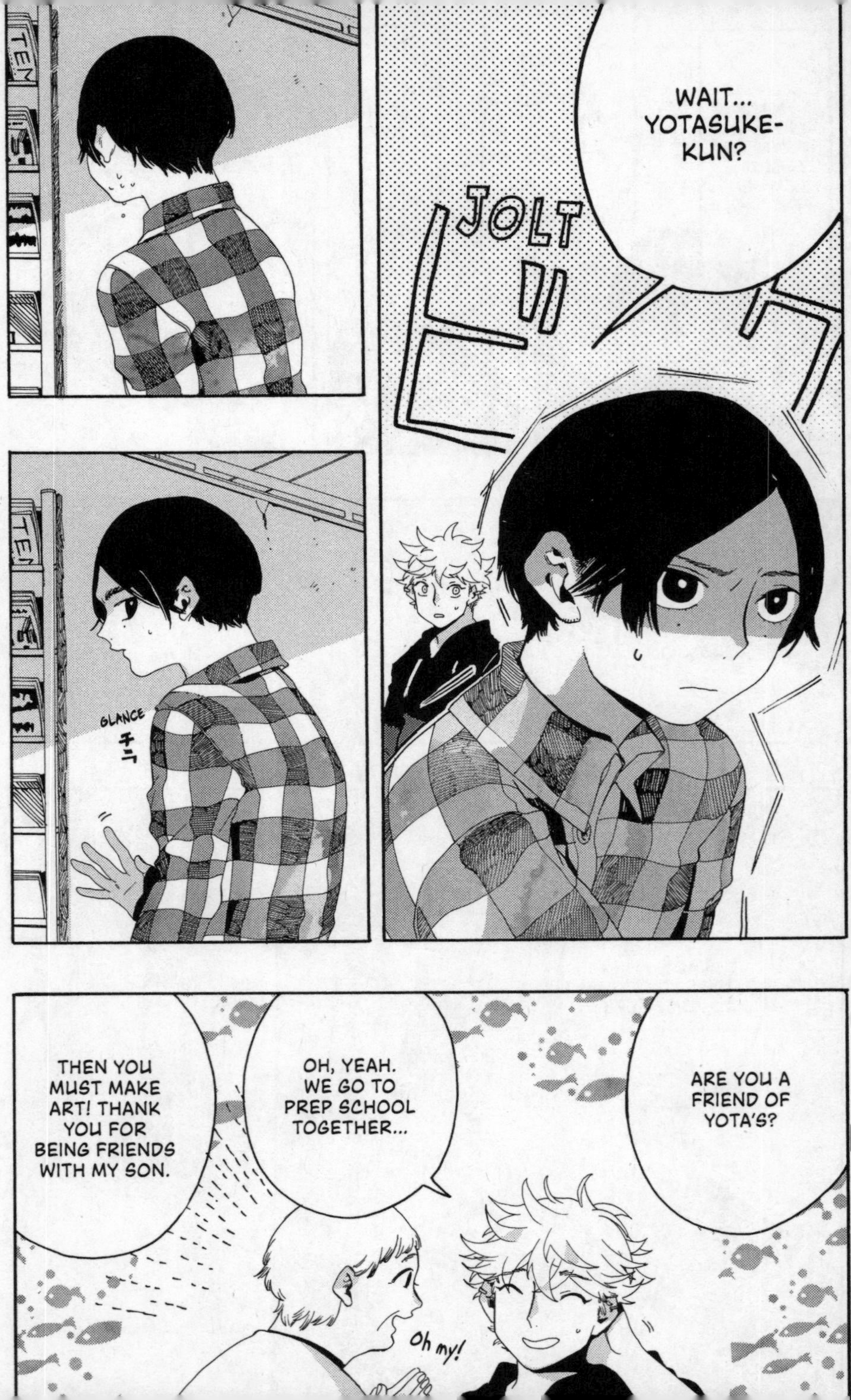
WAIT... YOTASUKE-KUN?
JOLT
GLANCE
チラ
ARE YOU A FRIEND OF YOTA'S?
OH, YEAH. WE GO TO PREP SCHOOL TOGETHER...
THEN YOU MUST MAKE ART! THANK YOU FOR BEING FRIENDS WITH MY SON.
Oh my!

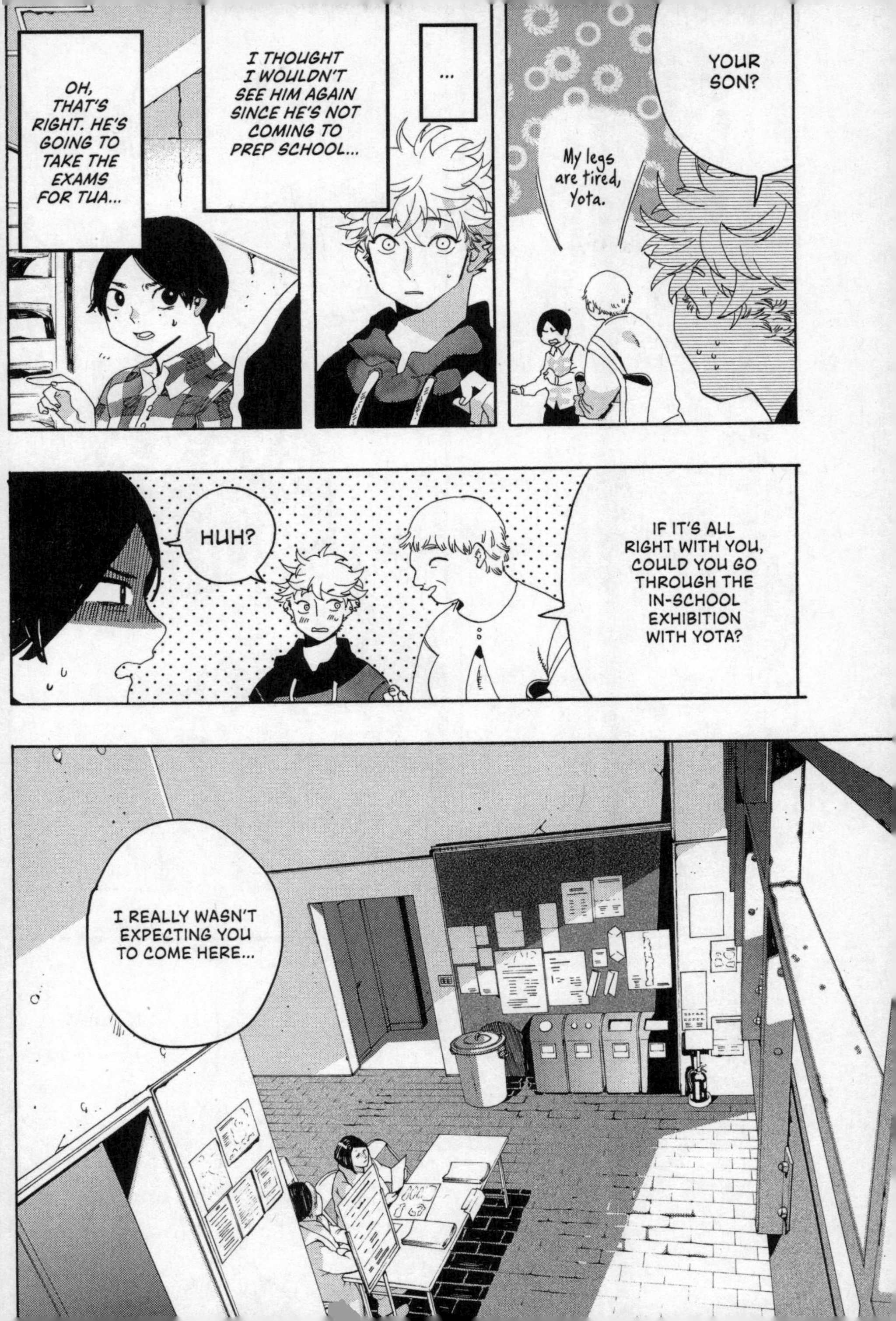
YOUR SON?
My legs are tired, Yota.
...
I THOUGHT I WOULDN'T SEE HIM AGAIN SINCE HE'S NOT COMING TO PREP SCHOOL...
OH, THAT'S RIGHT. HE'S GOING TO TAKE THE EXAMS FOR TUA...
IF IT'S ALL RIGHT WITH YOU, COULD YOU GO THROUGH THE IN-SCHOOL EXHIBITION WITH YOTA?
HUH?
I REALLY WASN'T EXPECTING YOU TO COME HERE...

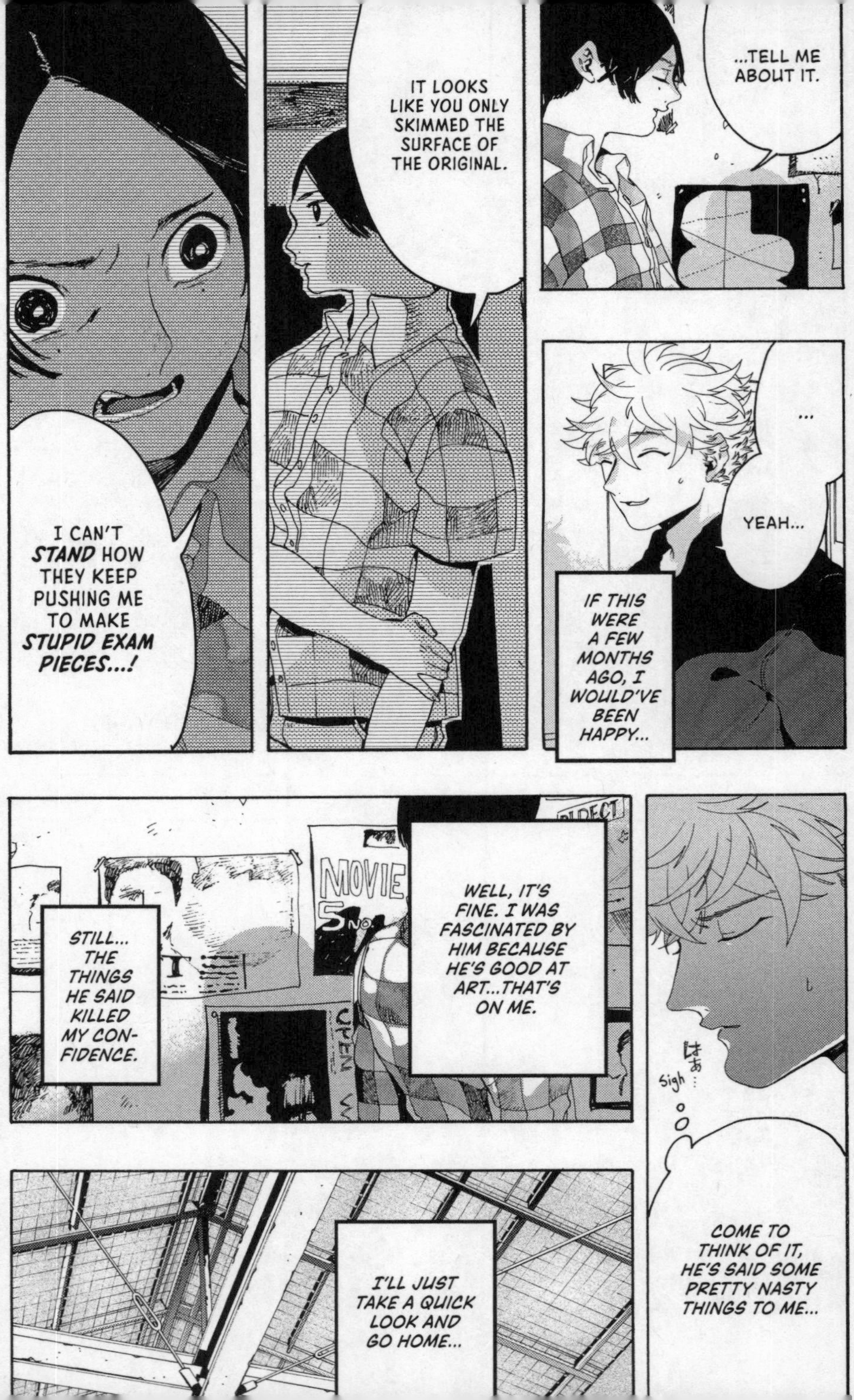
...TELL ME ABOUT IT.
...
YEAH...
IF THIS WERE A FEW MONTHS AGO, I WOULD'VE BEEN HAPPY...
IT LOOKS LIKE YOU ONLY SKIMMED THE SURFACE OF THE ORIGINAL.
I CAN'T ***STAND*** HOW THEY KEEP PUSHING ME TO MAKE ***STUPID EXAM PIECES...!***
はあ…
Sigh
COME TO THINK OF IT, HE'S SAID SOME PRETTY NASTY THINGS TO ME...
MOVIE
WELL, IT'S FINE. I WAS FASCINATED BY HIM BECAUSE HE'S GOOD AT ART...THAT'S ON ME.
STILL... THE THINGS HE SAID KILLED MY CON-FIDENCE.
I'LL JUST TAKE A QUICK LOOK AND GO HOME...

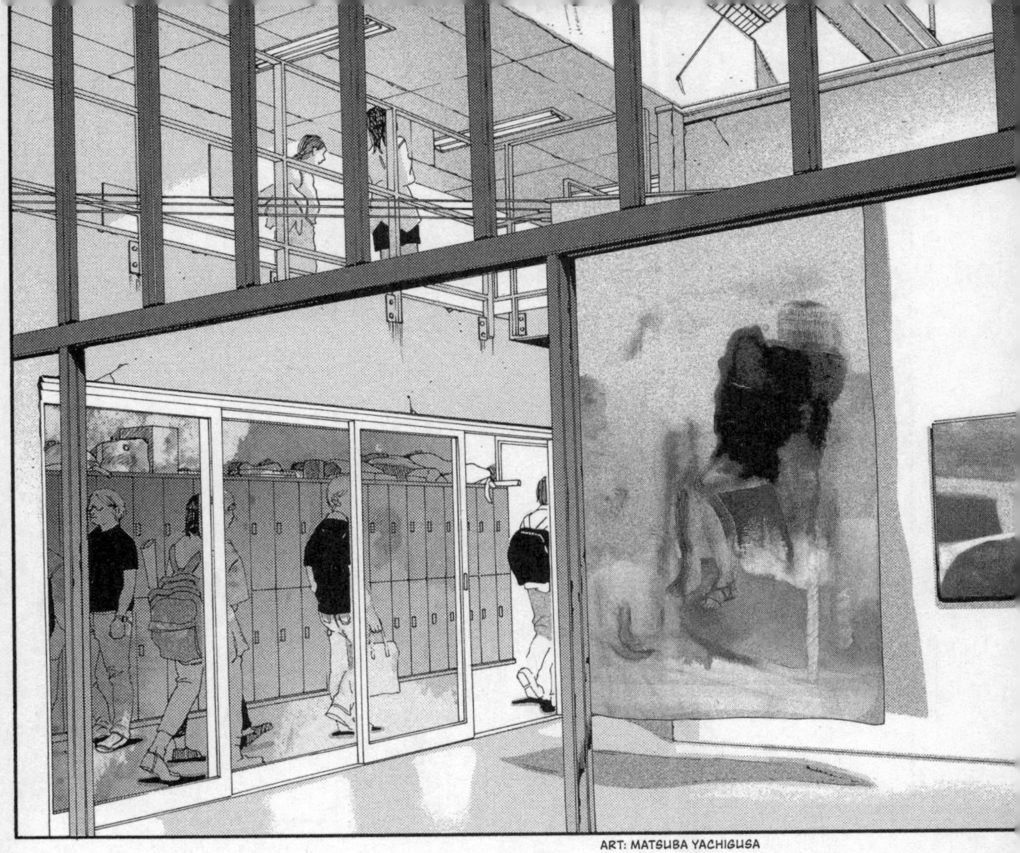

ART: MATSUBA YACHIGUSA

ART: MEI TANIMOTO

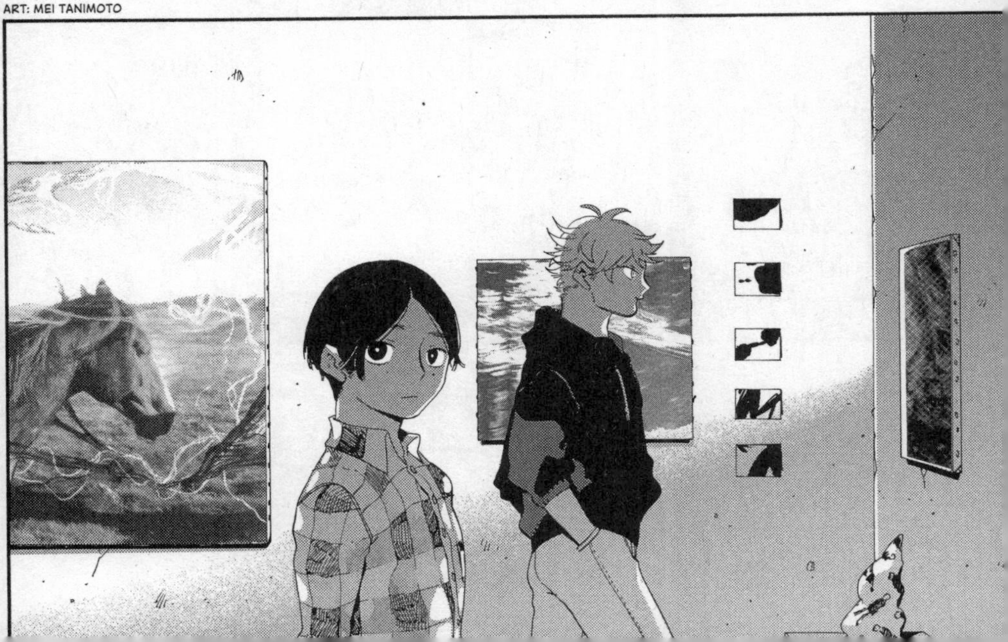

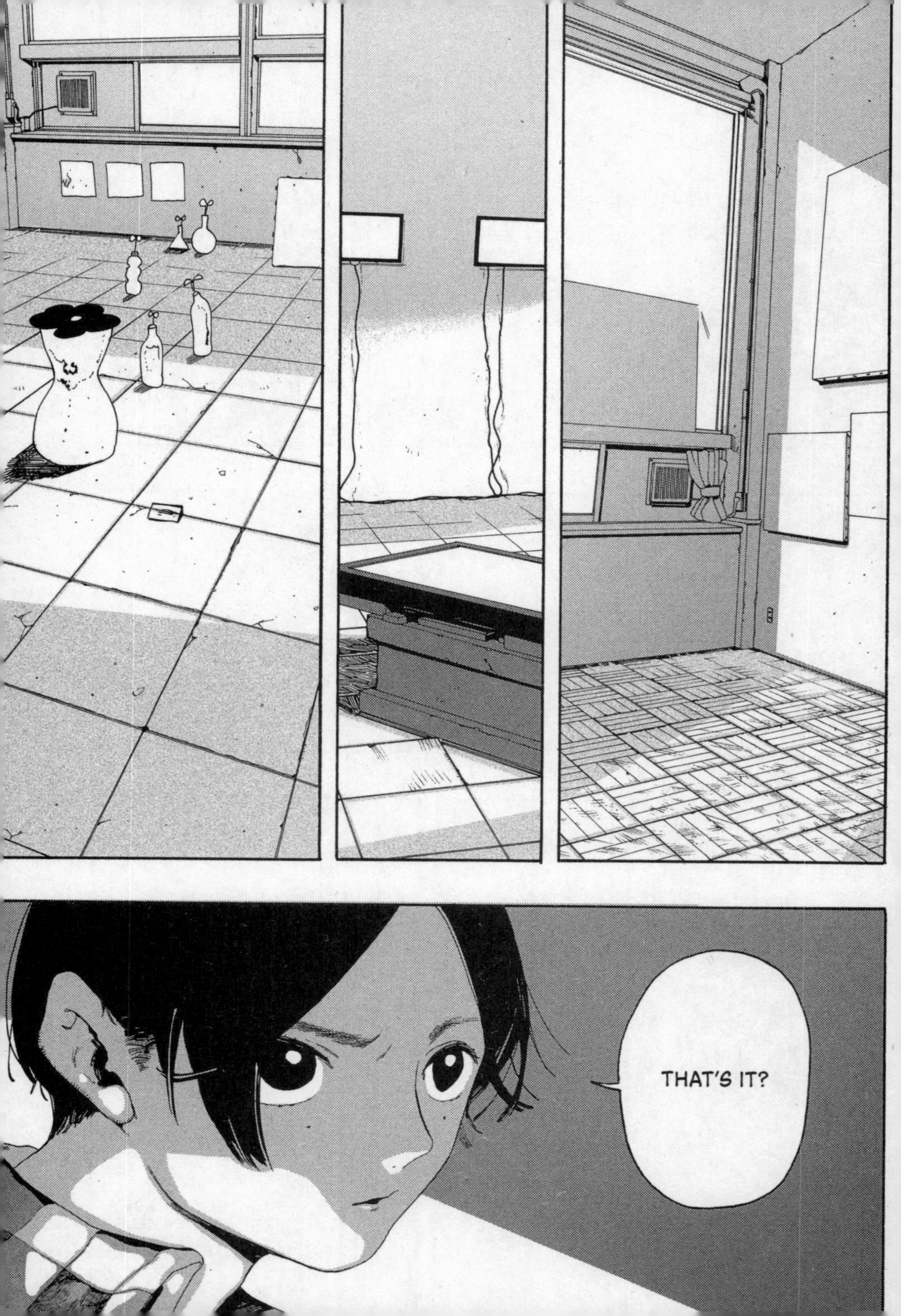
THAT'S IT?

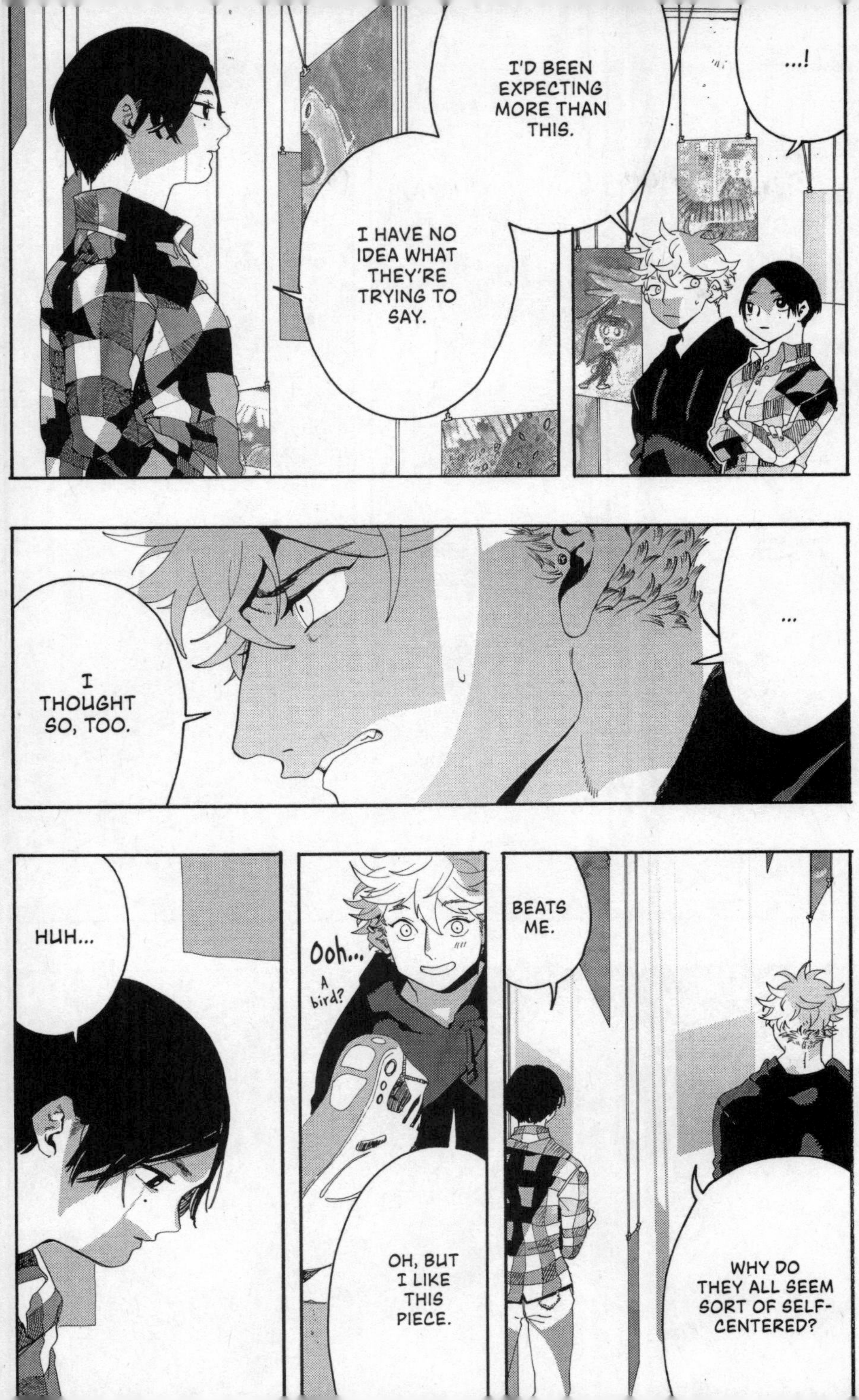
...!
I'D BEEN EXPECTING MORE THAN THIS.
I HAVE NO IDEA WHAT THEY'RE TRYING TO SAY.
...
I THOUGHT SO, TOO.
WHY DO THEY ALL SEEM SORT OF SELF-CENTERED?
BEATS ME.
Ooh...
A bird?
OH, BUT I LIKE THIS PIECE.
HUH...

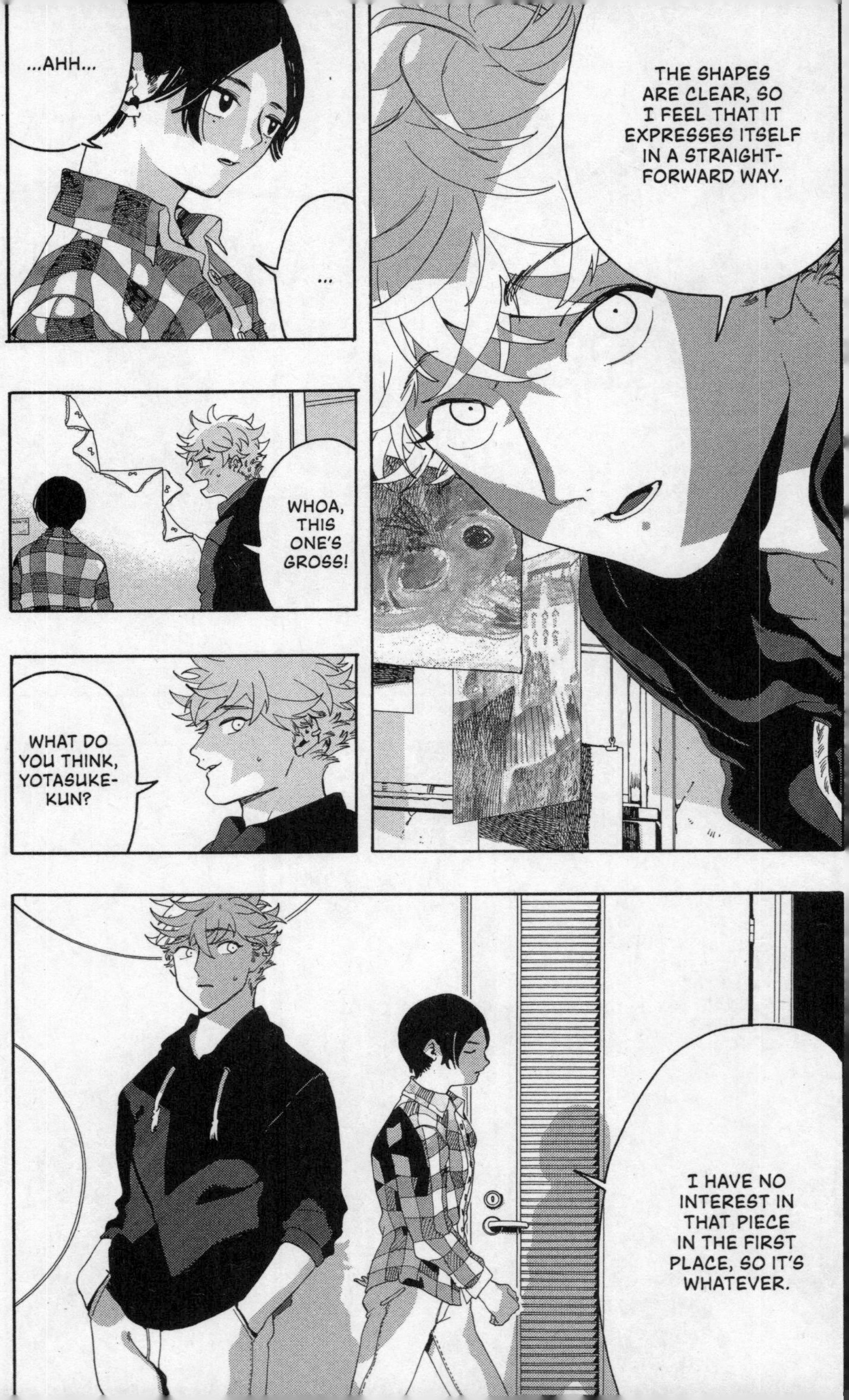

THE SHAPES ARE CLEAR, SO I FEEL THAT IT EXPRESSES ITSELF IN A STRAIGHT-FORWARD WAY.
...AHH...
...
WHOA, THIS ONE'S GROSS!
WHAT DO YOU THINK, YOTASUKE-KUN?
I HAVE NO INTEREST IN THAT PIECE IN THE FIRST PLACE, SO IT'S WHATEVER.

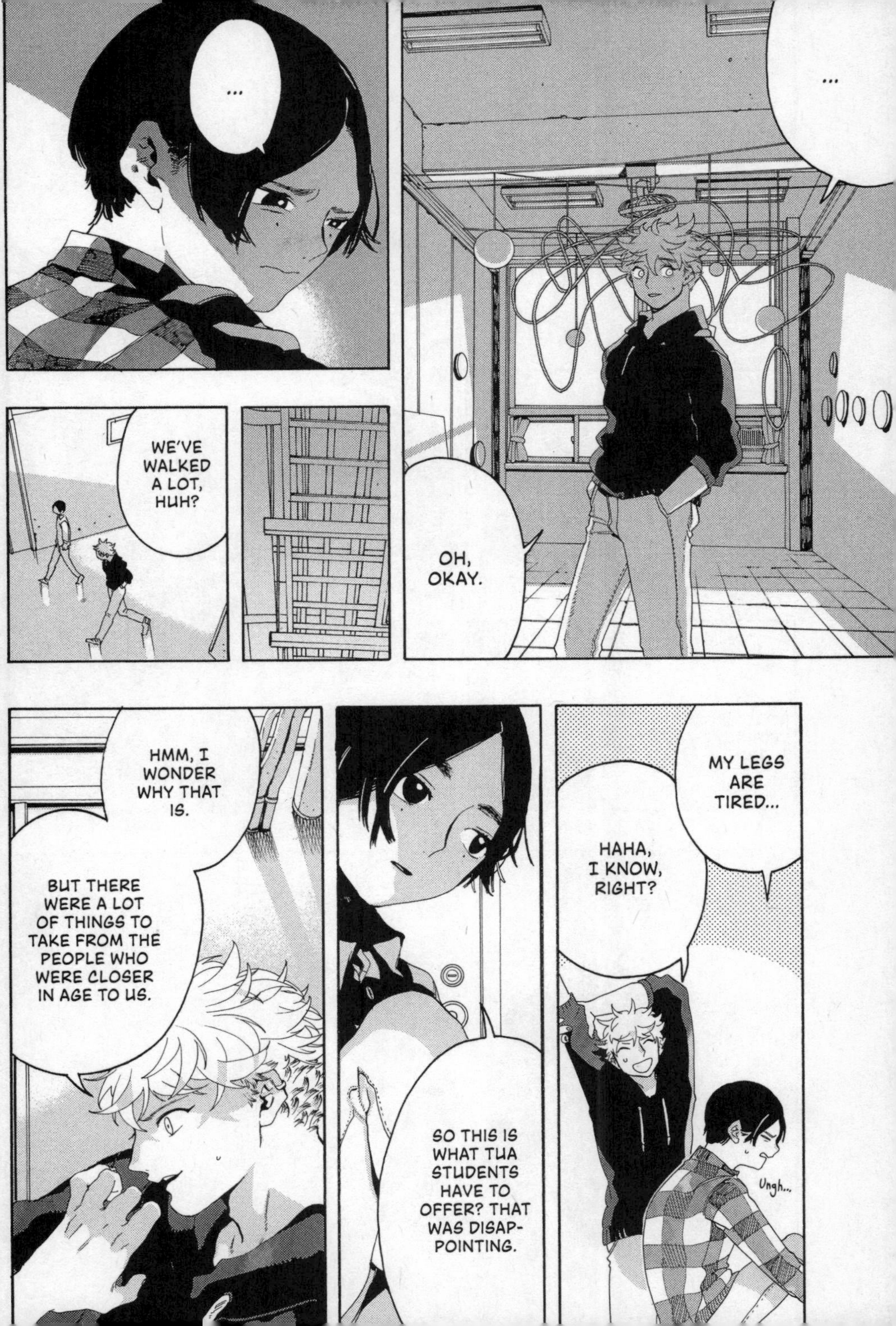
...
OH, OKAY.
...
WE'VE WALKED A LOT, HUH?
MY LEGS ARE TIRED...
HAHA, I KNOW, RIGHT?
Ungh...
SO THIS IS WHAT TUA STUDENTS HAVE TO OFFER? THAT WAS DISAP-POINTING.
HMM, I WONDER WHY THAT IS.
BUT THERE WERE A LOT OF THINGS TO TAKE FROM THE PEOPLE WHO WERE CLOSER IN AGE TO US.

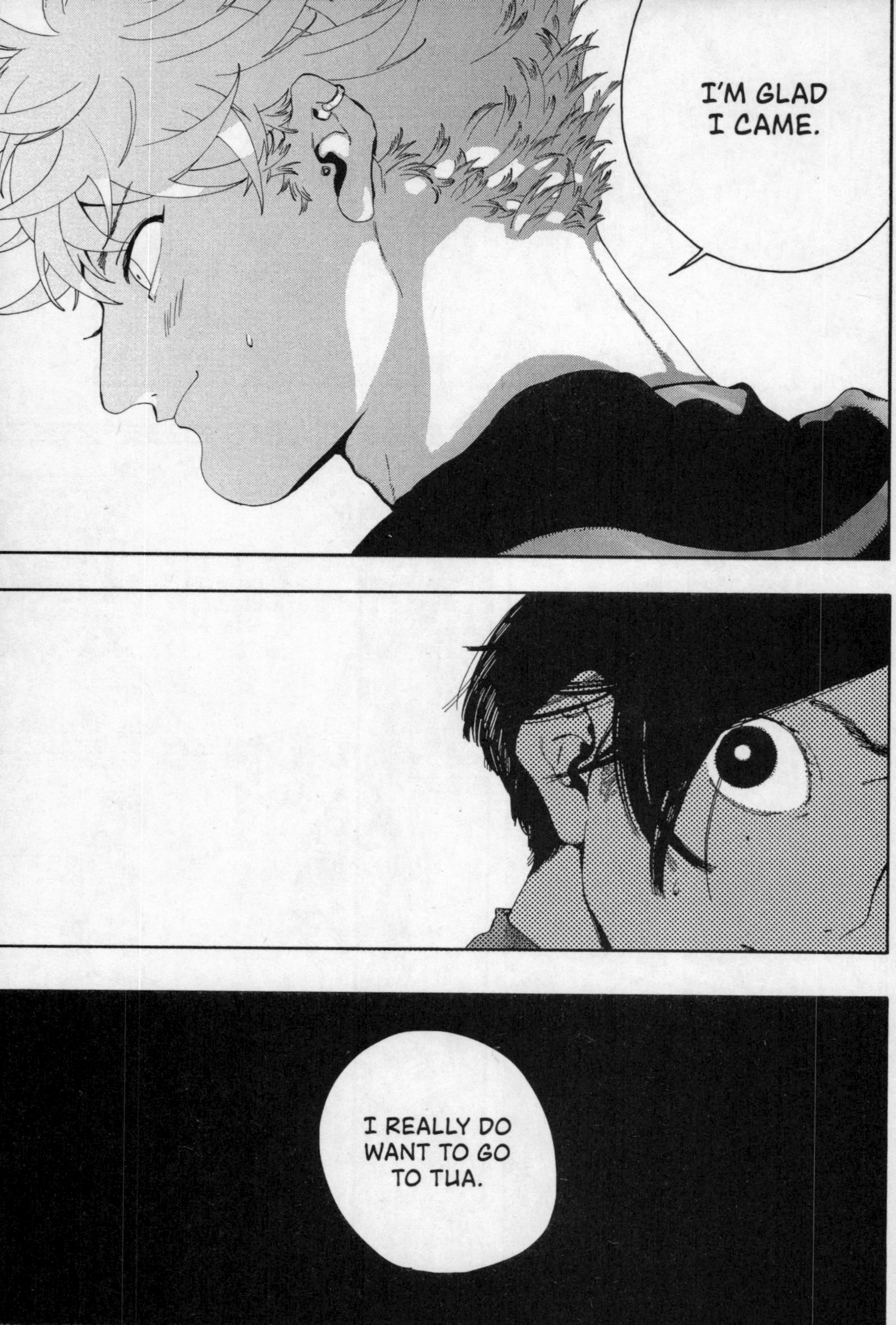
I'M GLAD I CAME.
I REALLY DO WANT TO GO TO TUA.

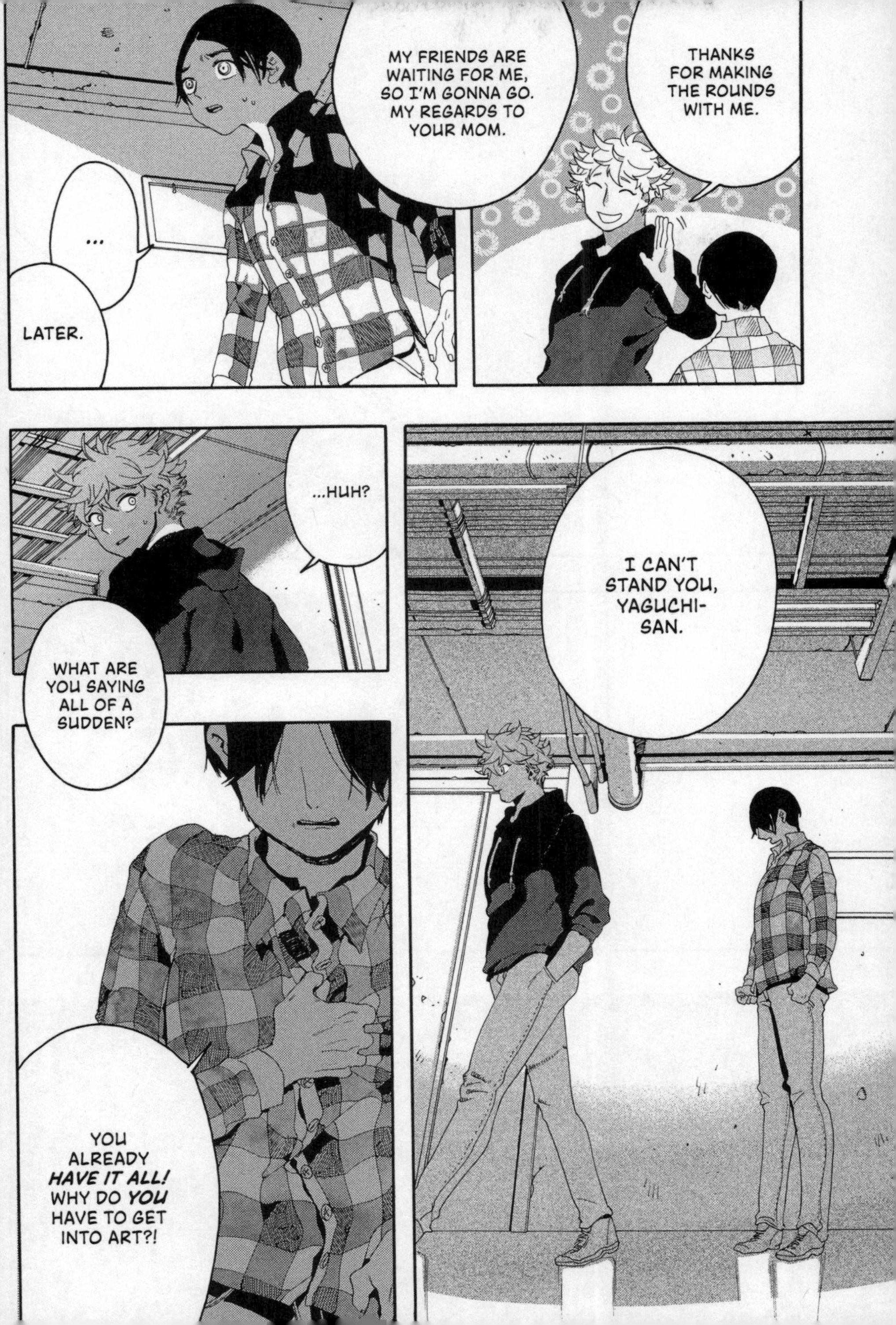
THANKS FOR MAKING THE ROUNDS WITH ME.
MY FRIENDS ARE WAITING FOR ME, SO I'M GONNA GO. MY REGARDS TO YOUR MOM.
...
LATER.
I CAN'T STAND YOU, YAGUCHI-SAN.
...HUH?
WHAT ARE YOU SAYING ALL OF A SUDDEN?
YOU ALREADY ***HAVE IT ALL!*** WHY DO ***YOU*** HAVE TO GET INTO ART?!

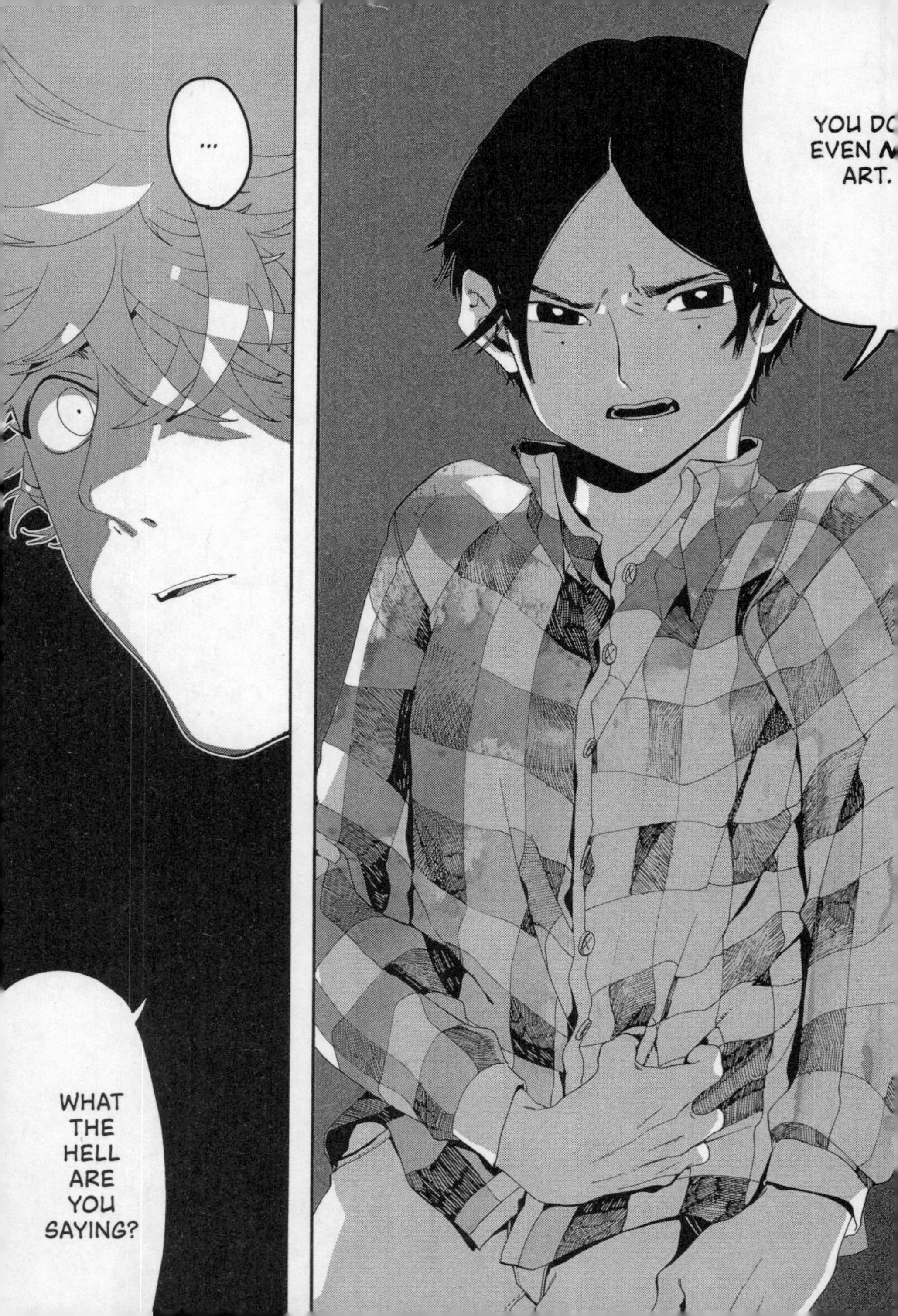
YOU DO EVEN ART.
...
WHAT THE HELL ARE YOU SAYING?

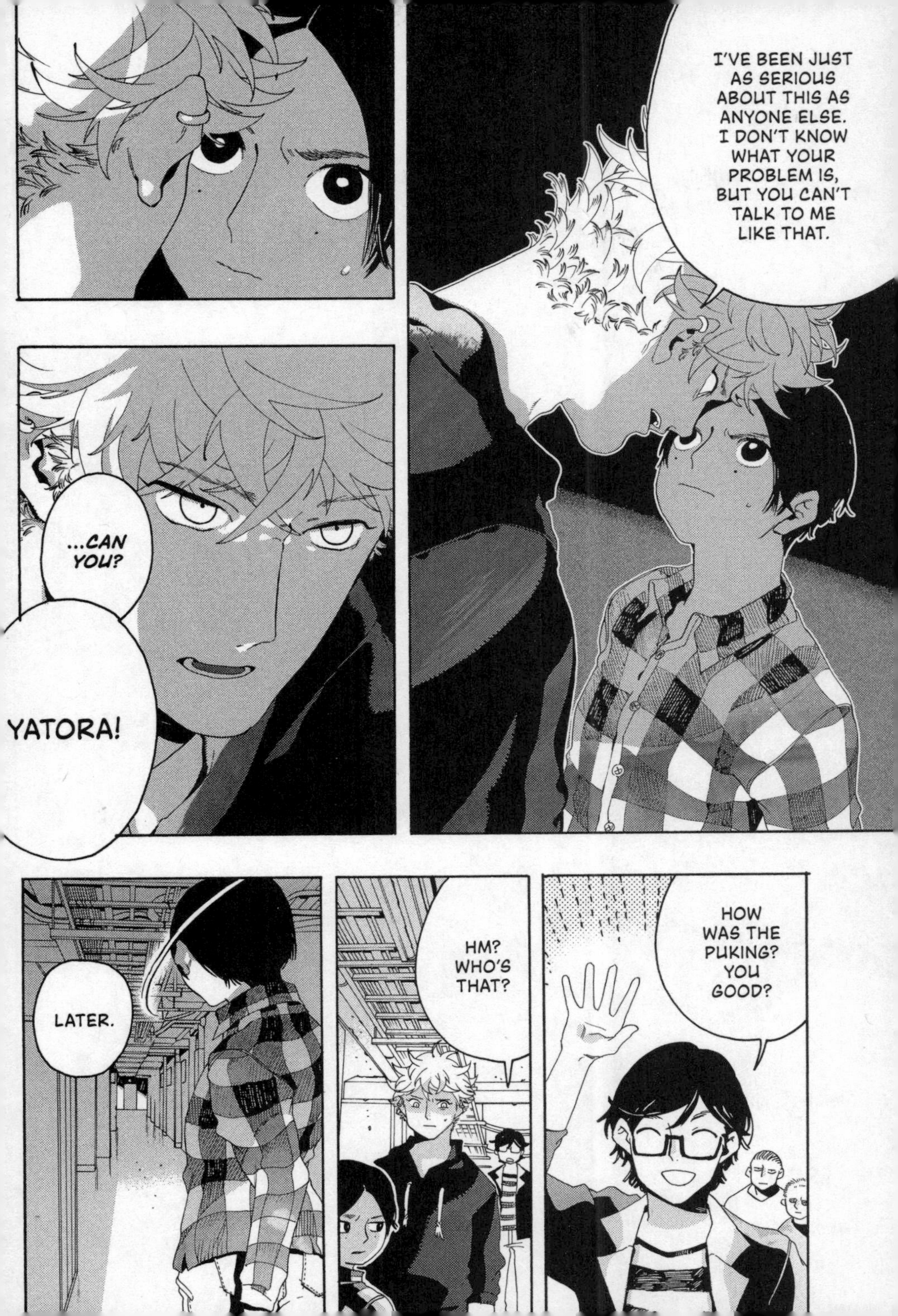
I'VE BEEN JUST AS SERIOUS ABOUT THIS AS ANYONE ELSE. I DON'T KNOW WHAT YOUR PROBLEM IS, BUT YOU CAN'T TALK TO ME LIKE THAT.
...CAN YOU?
YATORA!
HOW WAS THE PUKING? YOU GOOD?
HM? WHO'S THAT?
LATER.

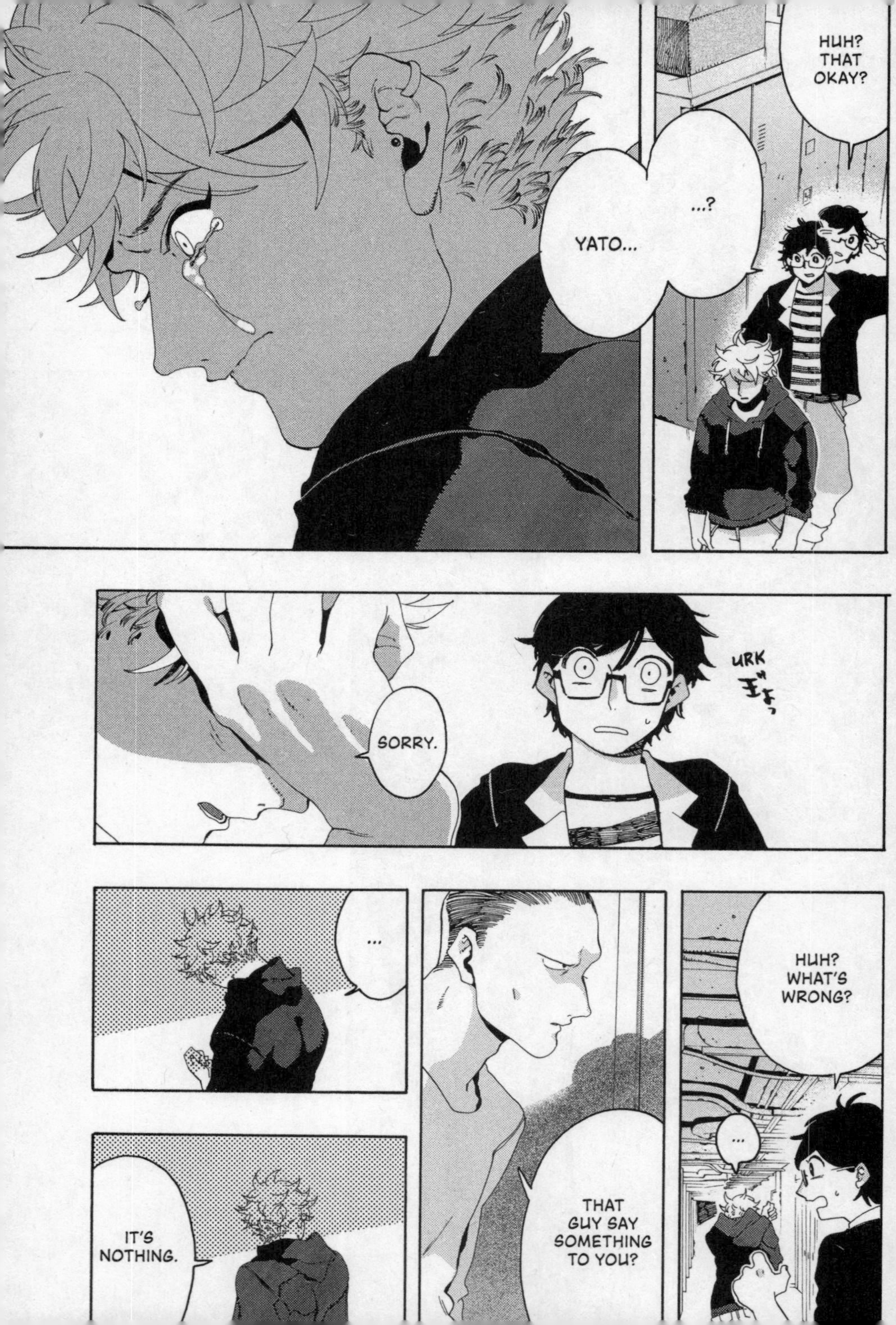
HUH? THAT OKAY?
...?
YATO...
URK
SORRY.
HUH? WHAT'S WRONG?
...
THAT GUY SAY SOMETHING TO YOU?
...
IT'S NOTHING.

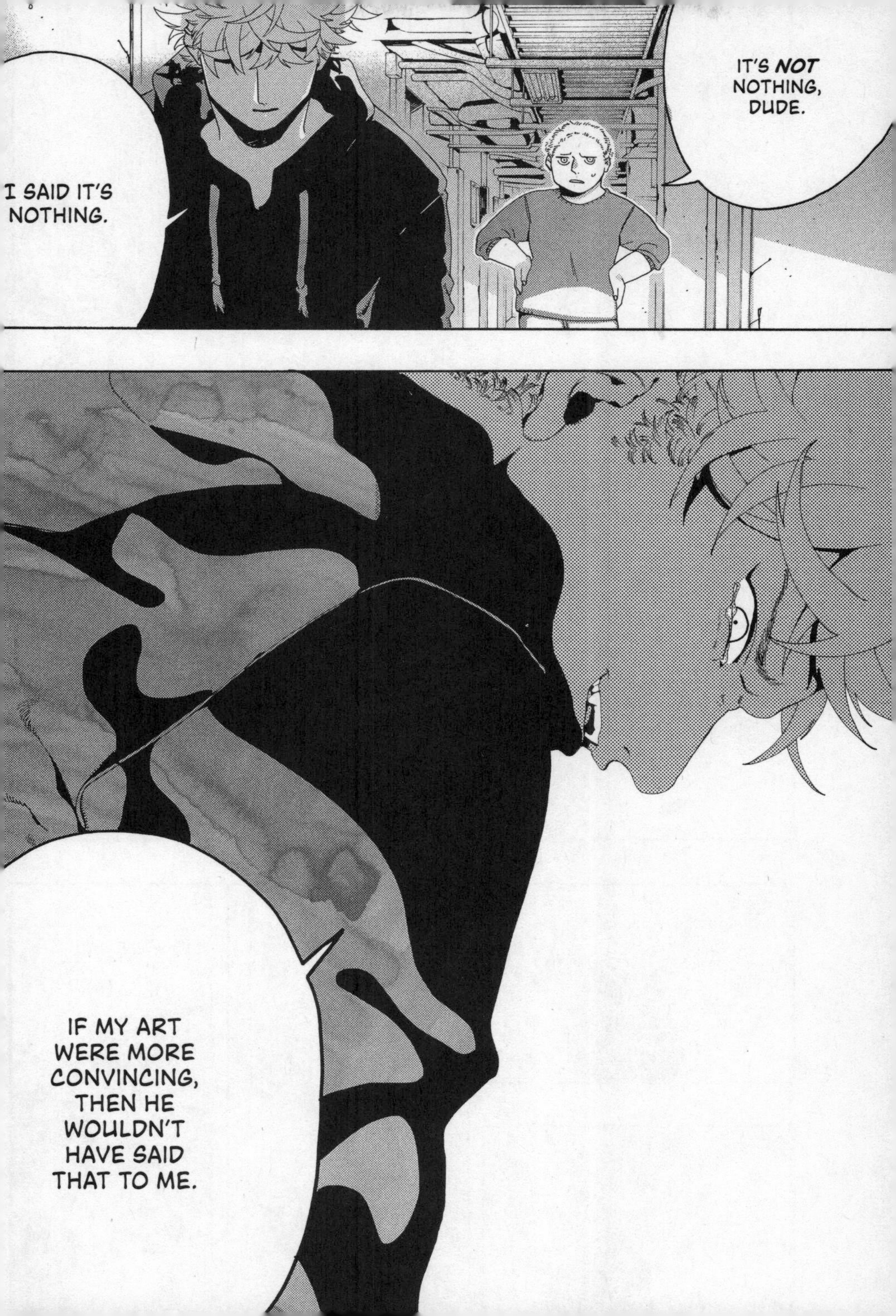
IT'S *NOT* NOTHING, DUDE.
I SAID IT'S NOTHING.
IF MY ART WERE MORE CONVINCING, THEN HE WOULDN'T HAVE SAID THAT TO ME.

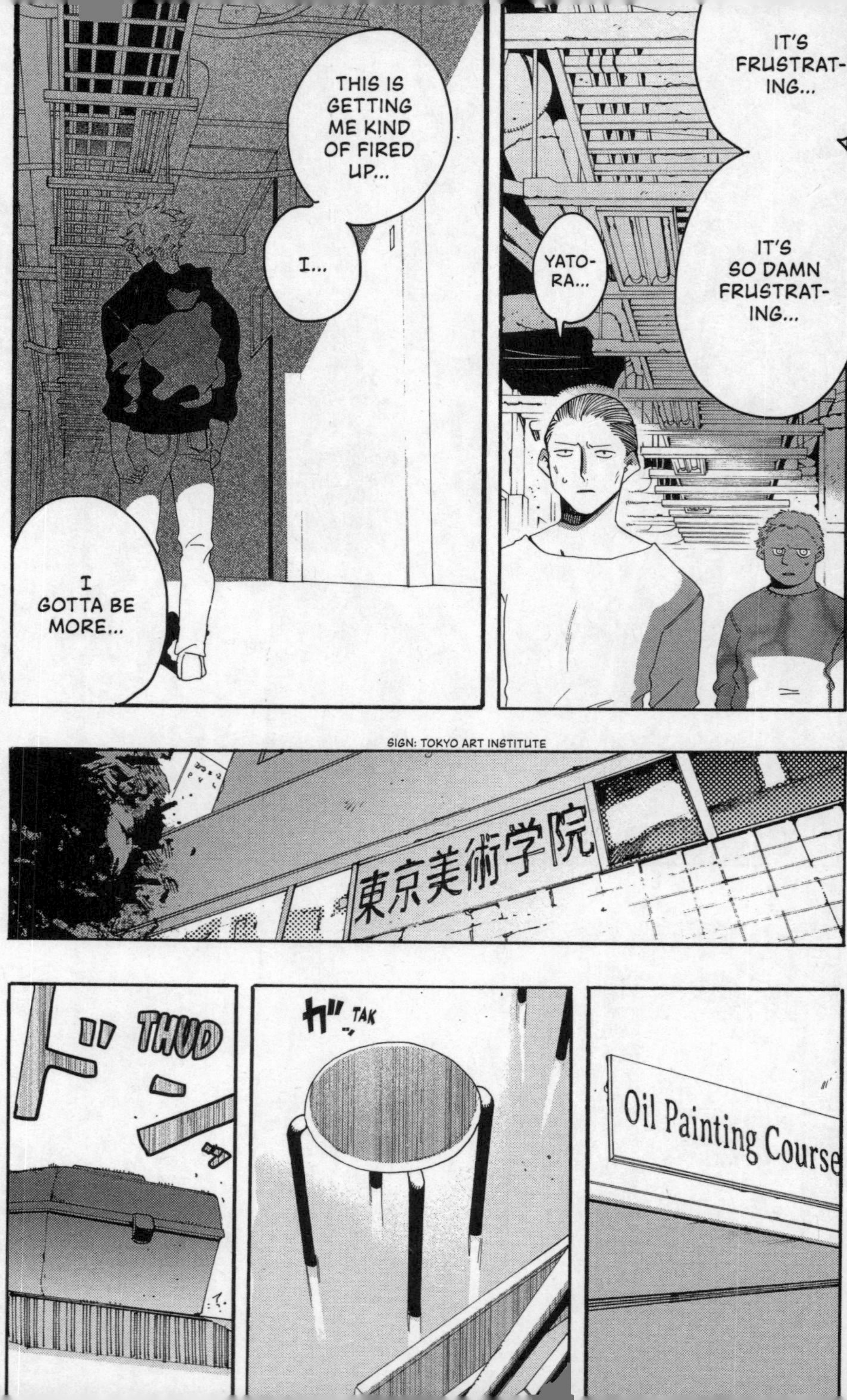
IT'S FRUSTRATING...
IT'S SO DAMN FRUSTRATING...
YATORA...
THIS IS GETTING ME KIND OF FIRED UP...
I...
I GOTTA BE MORE...
SIGN: TOKYO ART INSTITUTE
東京美術学院
Oil Painting Course
カッ TAK
ドン THUD

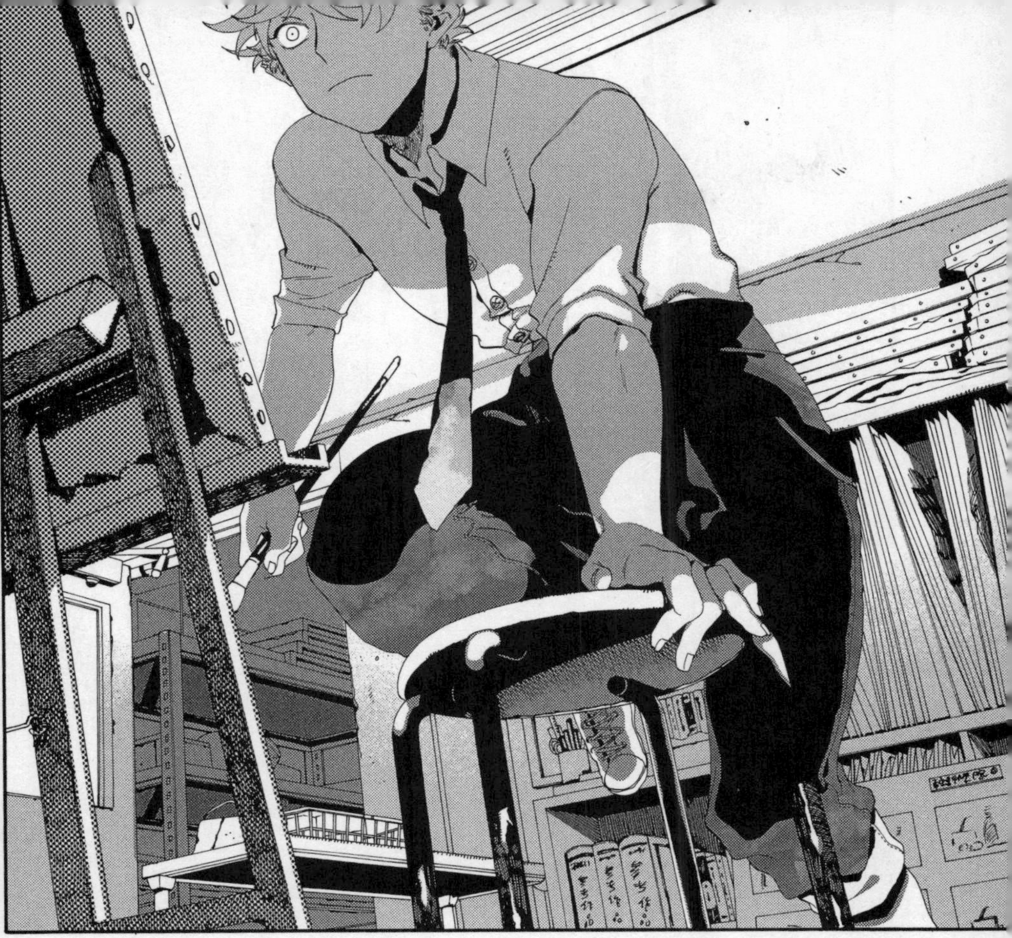

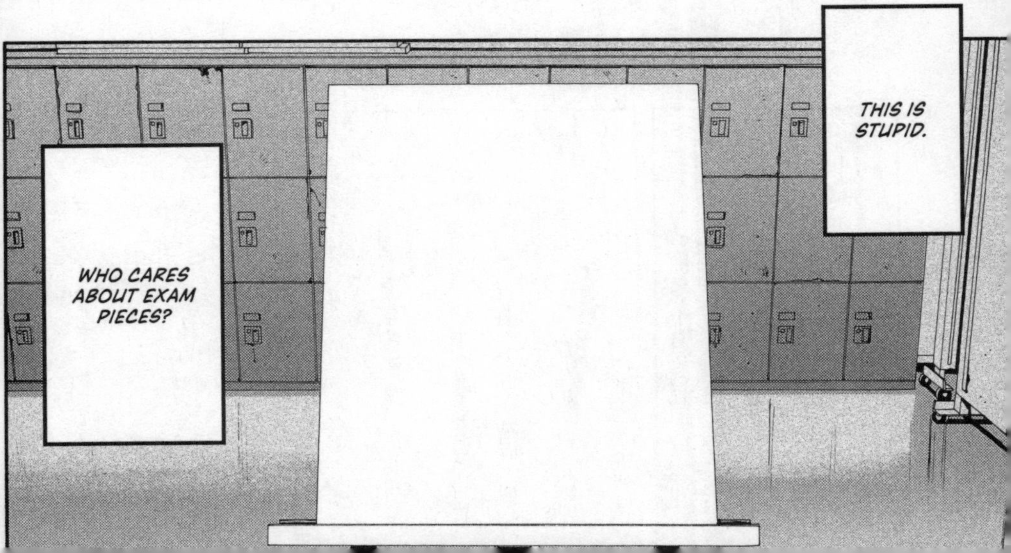
THIS IS STUPID.
WHO CARES ABOUT EXAM PIECES?

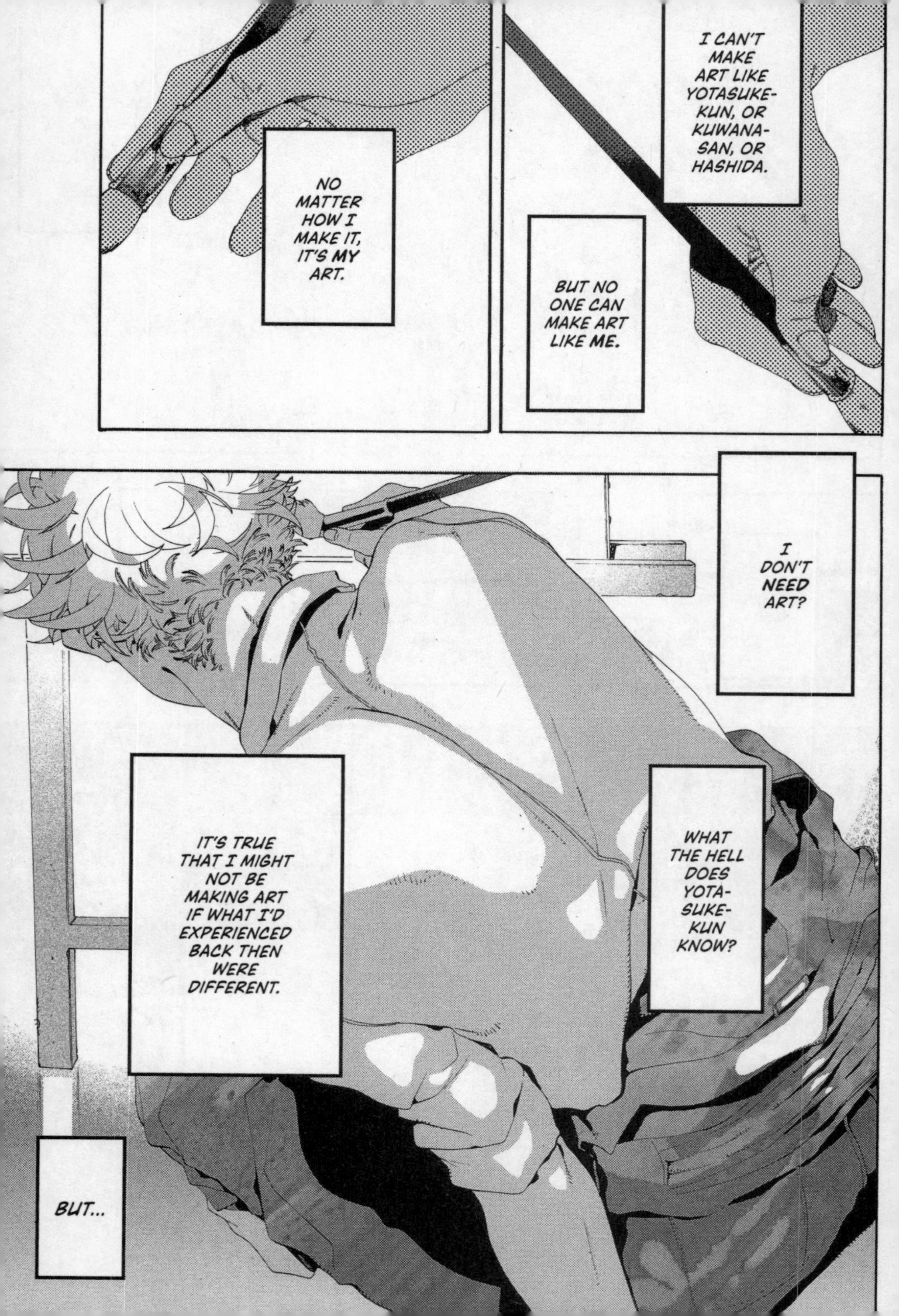
I CAN'T MAKE ART LIKE YOTASUKE-KUN, OR KUWANA-SAN, OR HASHIDA.
BUT NO ONE CAN MAKE ART LIKE ME.
NO MATTER HOW I MAKE IT, IT'S MY ART.
I DON'T NEED ART?
WHAT THE HELL DOES YOTA-SUKE-KUN KNOW?
IT'S TRUE THAT I MIGHT NOT BE MAKING ART IF WHAT I'D EXPERIENCED BACK THEN WERE DIFFERENT.
BUT...

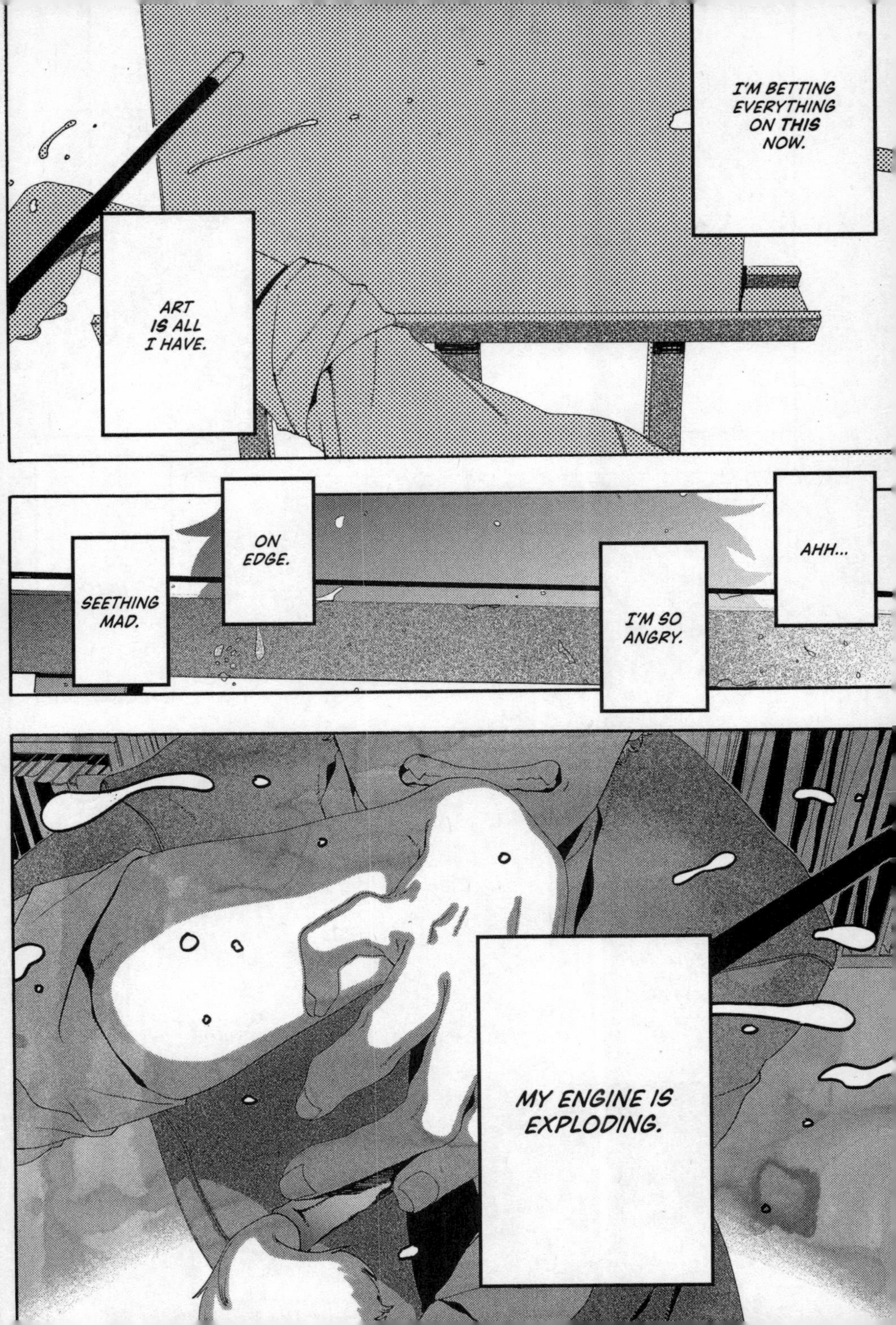
I'M BETTING EVERYTHING ON THIS NOW.
ART IS ALL I HAVE.
AHH...
I'M SO ANGRY.
ON EDGE.
SEETHING MAD.
MY ENGINE IS EXPLODING.

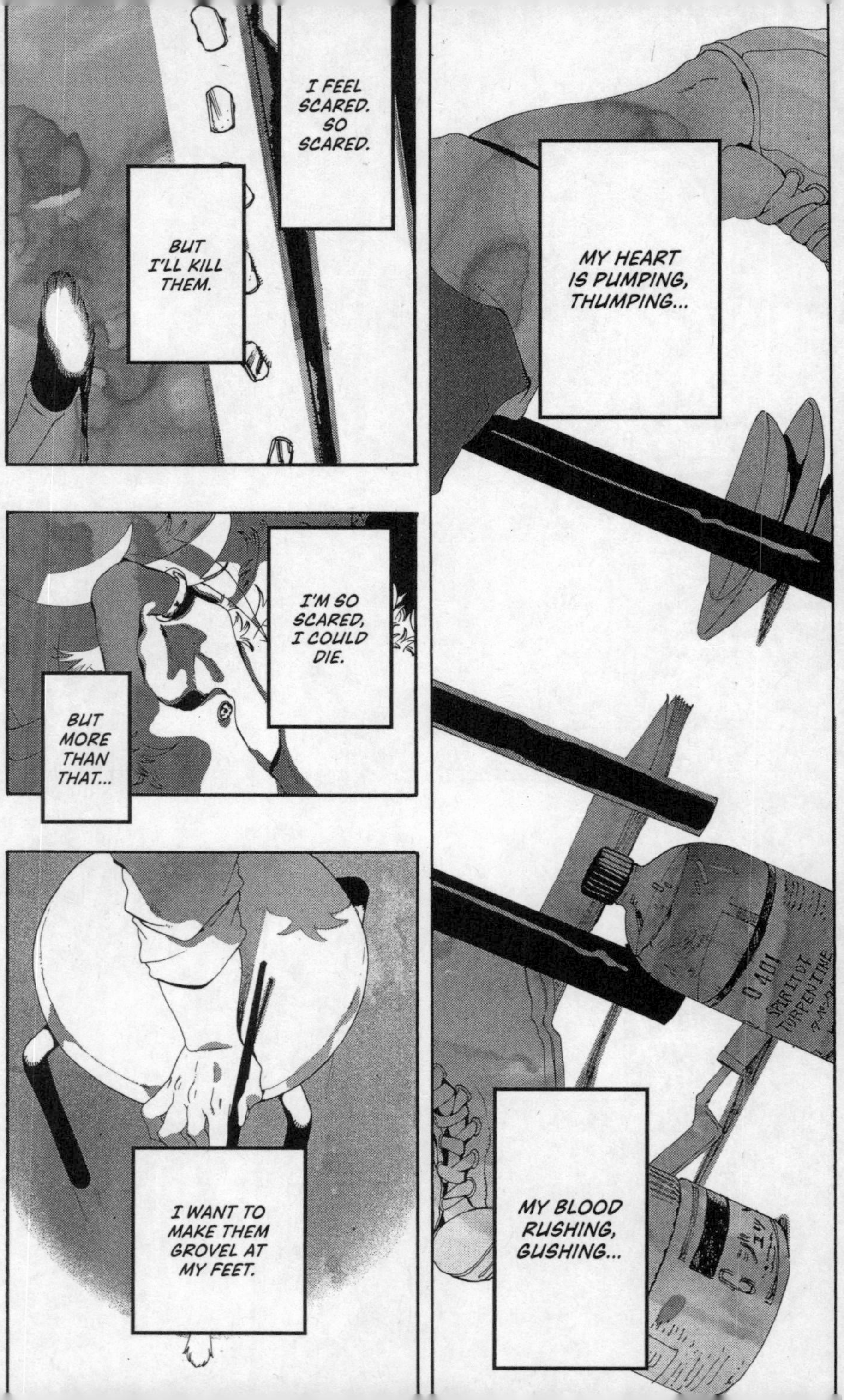
MY HEART IS PUMPING, THUMPING...
MY BLOOD RUSHING, GUSHING...
I FEEL SCARED. SO SCARED.
BUT I'LL KILL THEM.
I'M SO SCARED, I COULD DIE.
BUT MORE THAN THAT...
I WANT TO MAKE THEM GROVEL AT MY FEET.

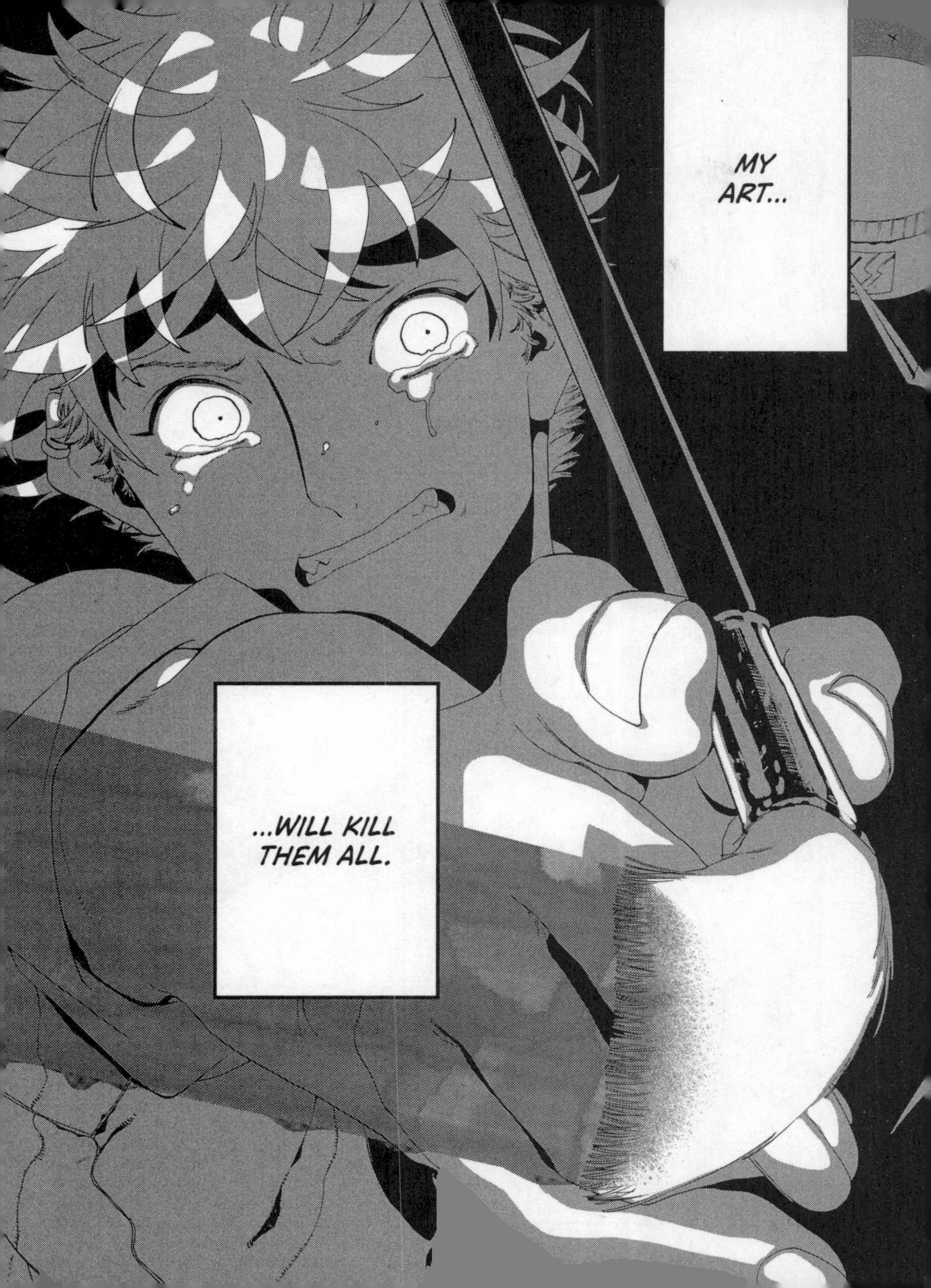
MY ART...
...WILL KILL THEM ALL.

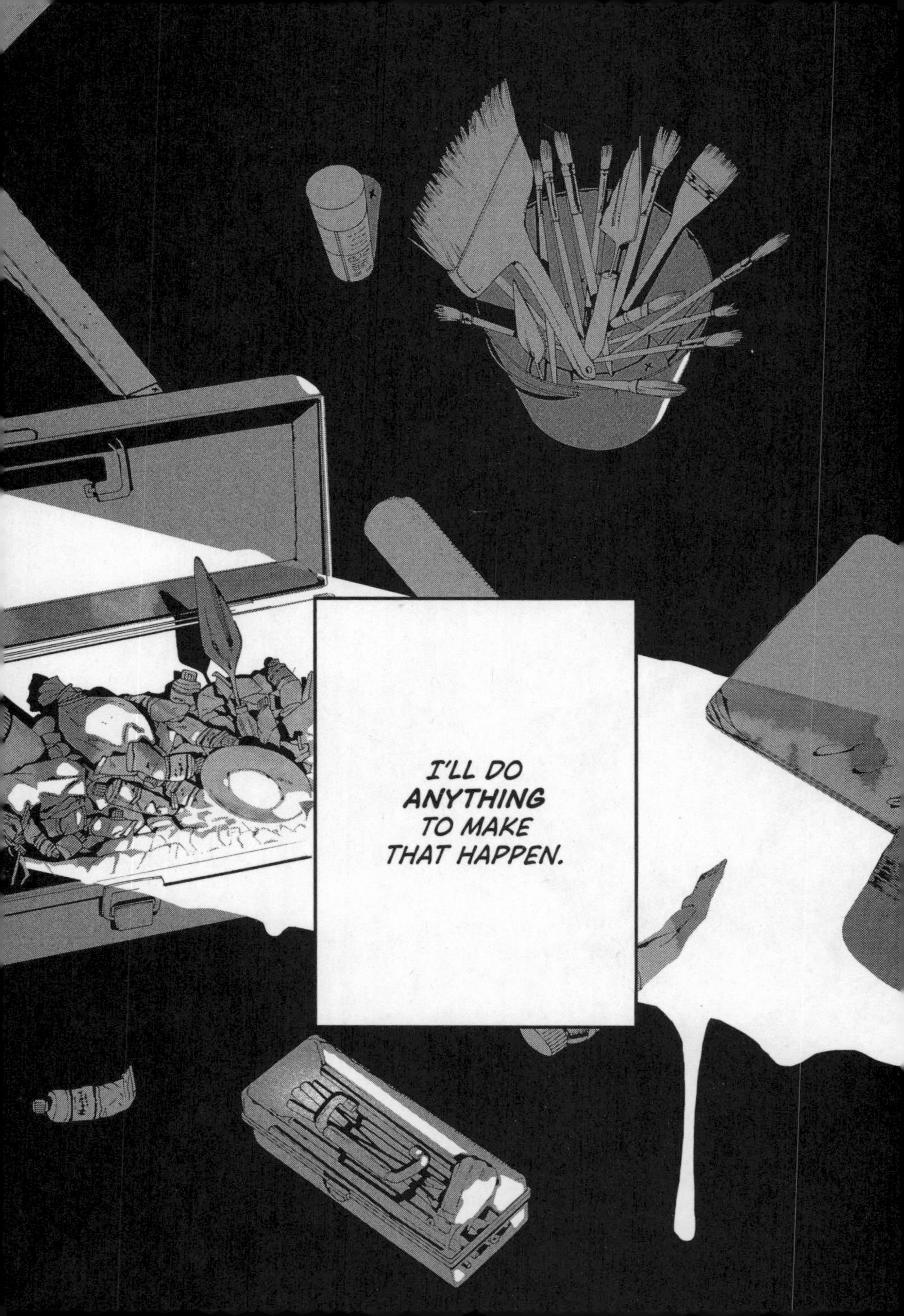
I'LL DO ANYTHING TO MAKE THAT HAPPEN.

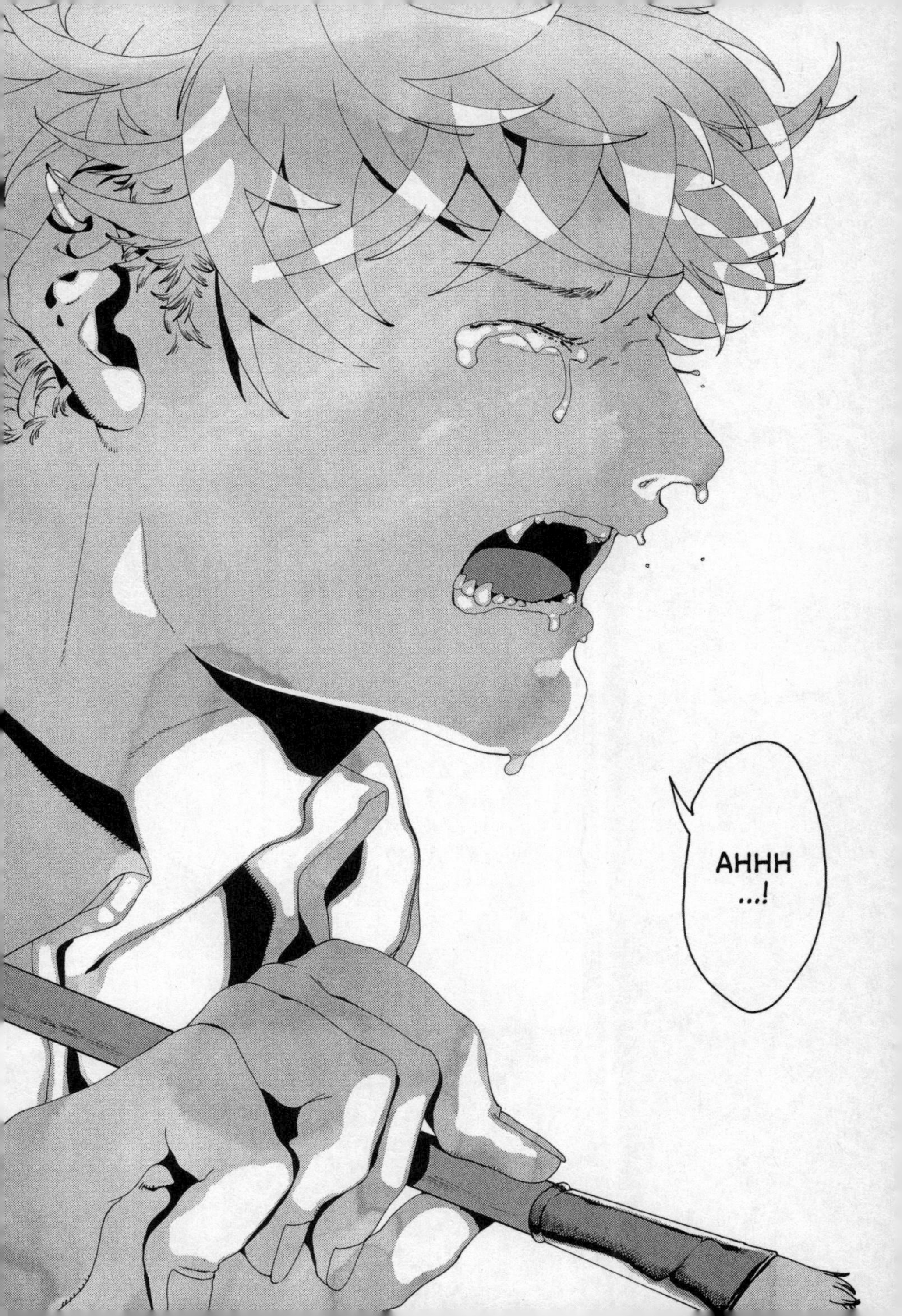
AHHH ...!

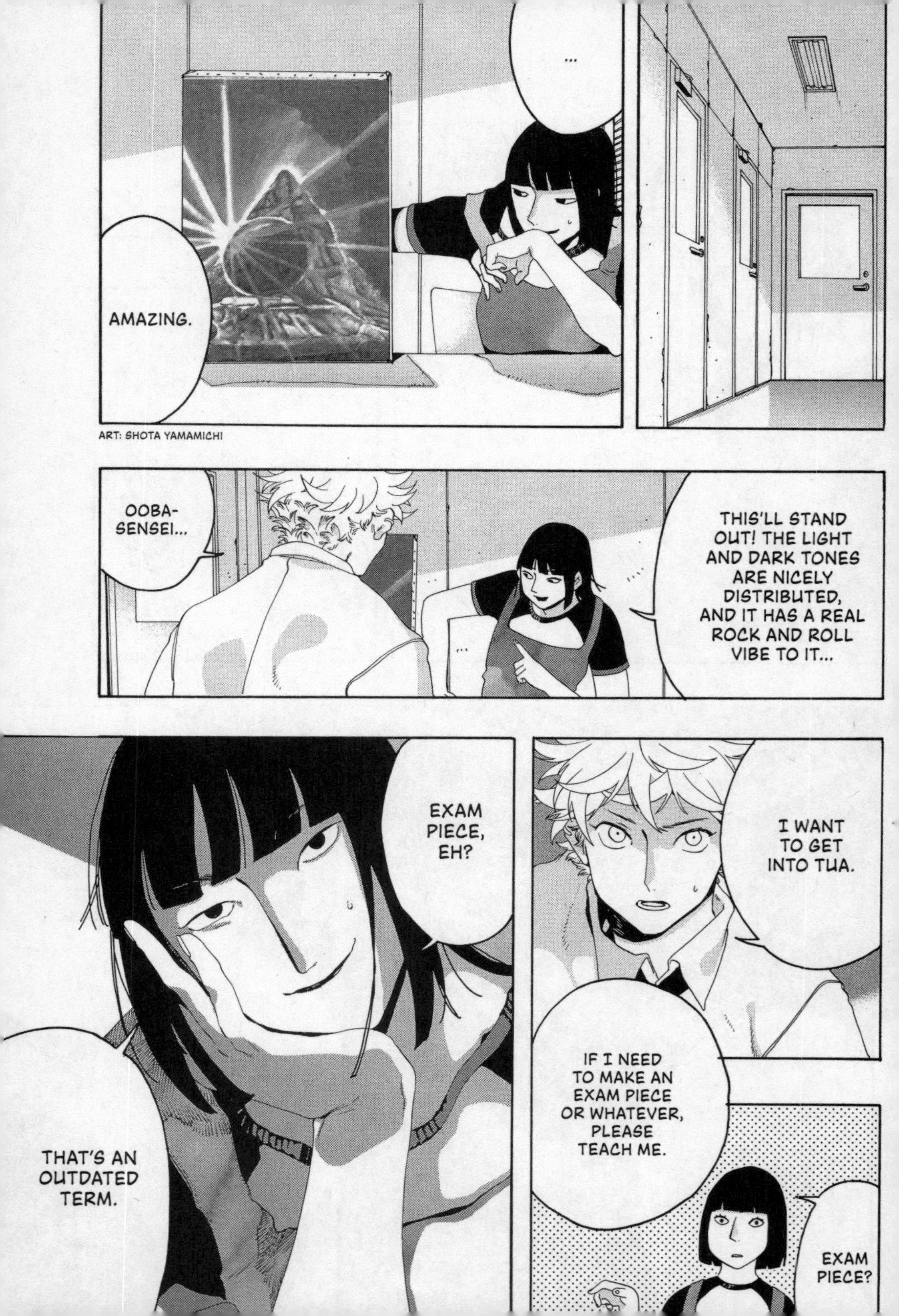
...
AMAZING.
ART: SHOTA YAMAMICHI
THIS'LL STAND OUT! THE LIGHT AND DARK TONES ARE NICELY DISTRIBUTED, AND IT HAS A REAL ROCK AND ROLL VIBE TO IT...
OOBA-SENSEI...
I WANT TO GET INTO TUA.
IF I NEED TO MAKE AN EXAM PIECE OR WHATEVER, PLEASE TEACH ME.
EXAM PIECE?
EXAM PIECE, EH?
THAT'S AN OUTDATED TERM.

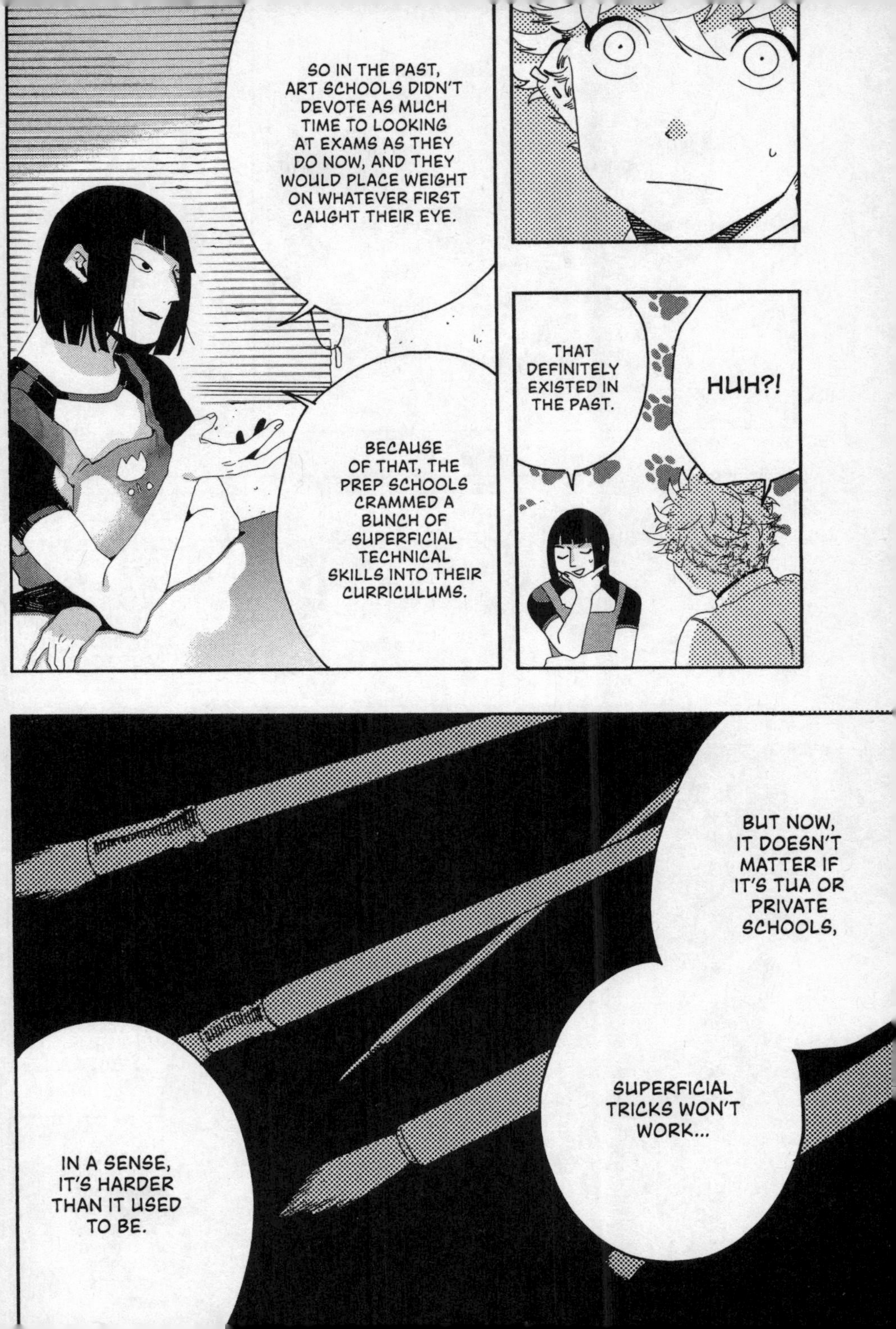
HUH?!
THAT DEFINITELY EXISTED IN THE PAST.
SO IN THE PAST, ART SCHOOLS DIDN'T DEVOTE AS MUCH TIME TO LOOKING AT EXAMS AS THEY DO NOW, AND THEY WOULD PLACE WEIGHT ON WHATEVER FIRST CAUGHT THEIR EYE.
BECAUSE OF THAT, THE PREP SCHOOLS CRAMMED A BUNCH OF SUPERFICIAL TECHNICAL SKILLS INTO THEIR CURRICULUMS.
BUT NOW, IT DOESN'T MATTER IF IT'S TUA OR PRIVATE SCHOOLS,
SUPERFICIAL TRICKS WON'T WORK...
IN A SENSE, IT'S HARDER THAN IT USED TO BE.

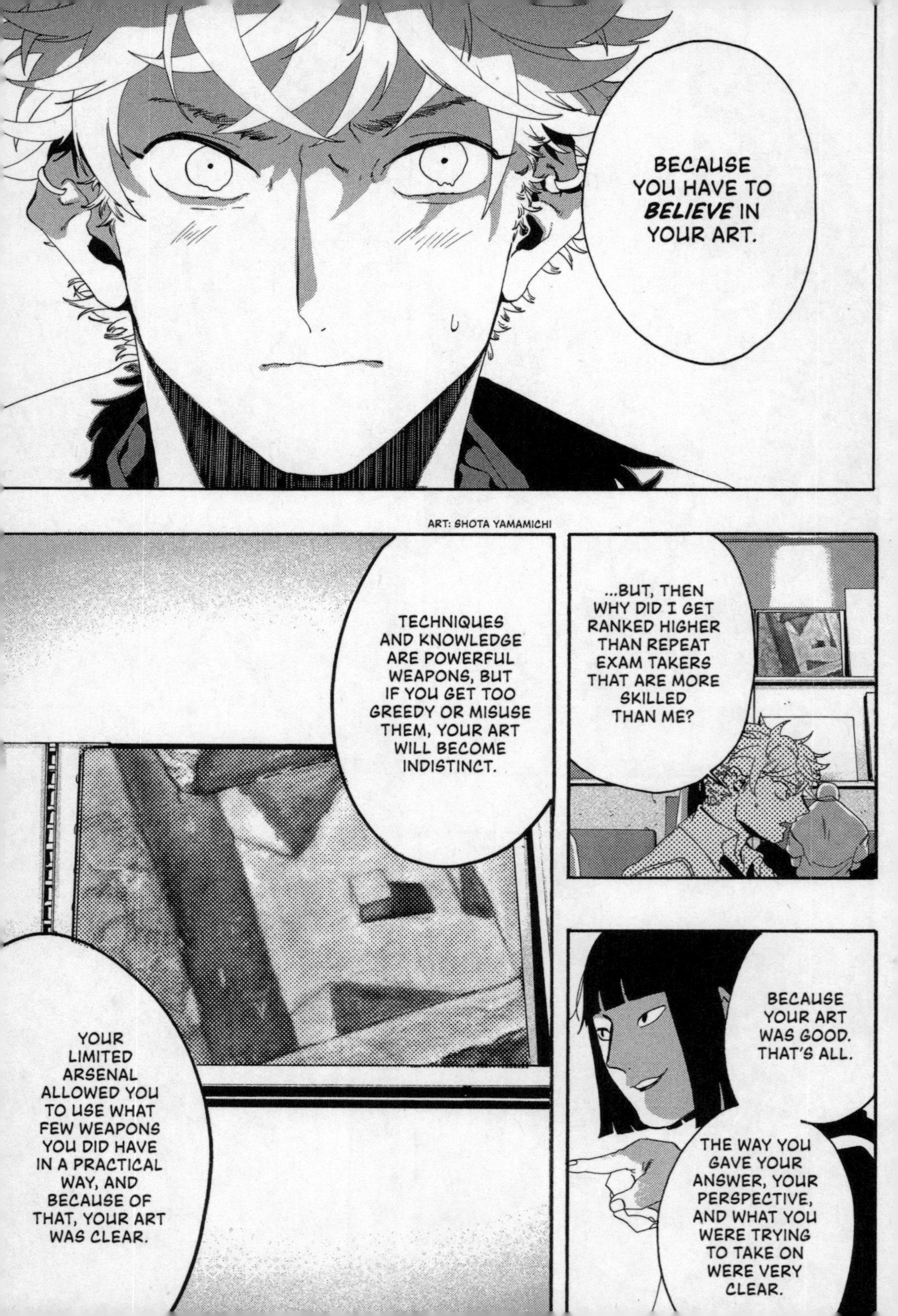
BECAUSE YOU HAVE TO ***BELIEVE*** IN YOUR ART.
ART: SHOTA YAMAMICHI
TECHNIQUES AND KNOWLEDGE ARE POWERFUL WEAPONS, BUT IF YOU GET TOO GREEDY OR MISUSE THEM, YOUR ART WILL BECOME INDISTINCT.
...BUT, THEN WHY DID I GET RANKED HIGHER THAN REPEAT EXAM TAKERS THAT ARE MORE SKILLED THAN ME?
BECAUSE YOUR ART WAS GOOD. THAT'S ALL.
THE WAY YOU GAVE YOUR ANSWER, YOUR PERSPECTIVE, AND WHAT YOU WERE TRYING TO TAKE ON WERE VERY CLEAR.
YOUR LIMITED ARSENAL ALLOWED YOU TO USE WHAT FEW WEAPONS YOU DID HAVE IN A PRACTICAL WAY, AND BECAUSE OF THAT, YOUR ART WAS CLEAR.

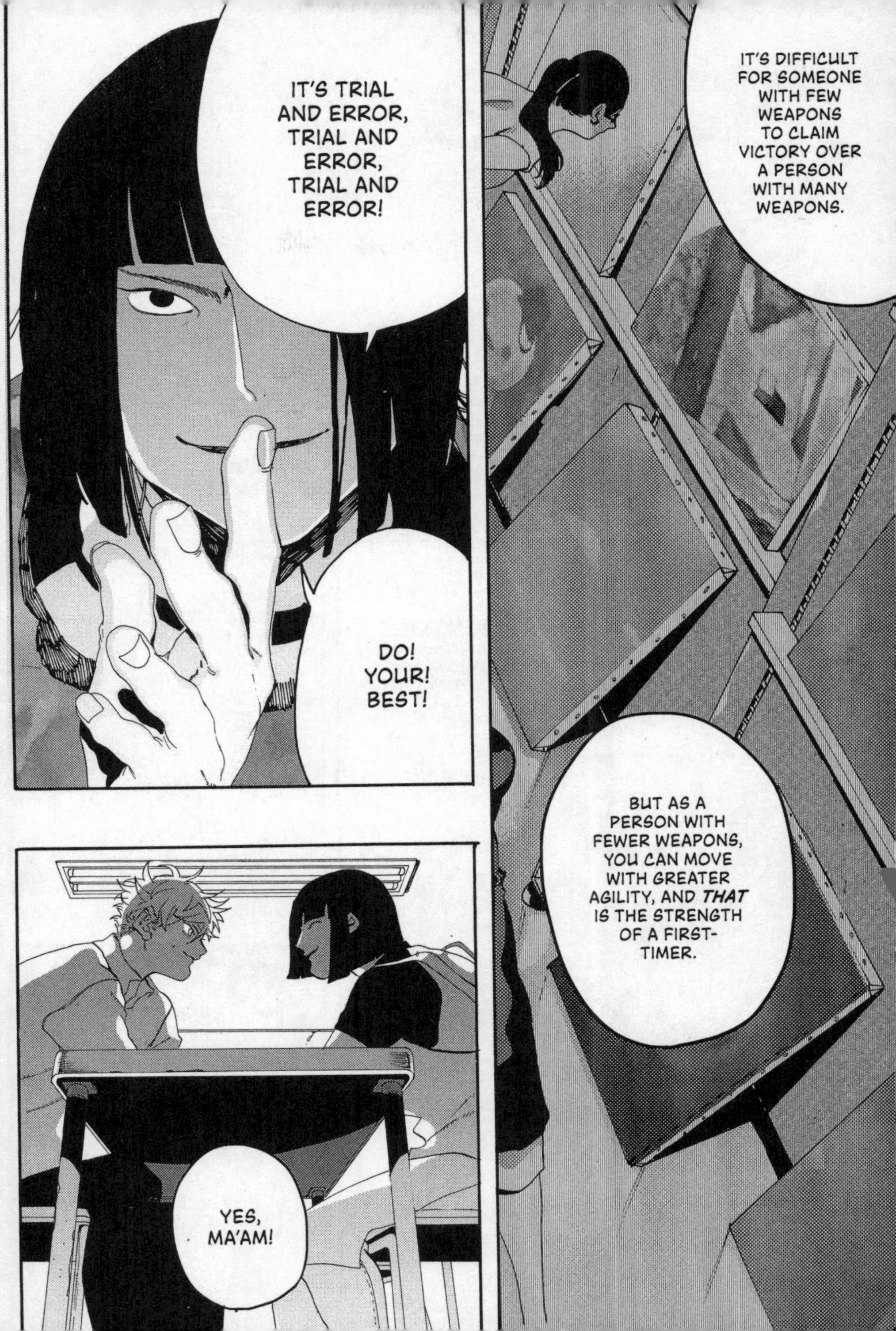
IT'S DIFFICULT FOR SOMEONE WITH FEW WEAPONS TO CLAIM VICTORY OVER A PERSON WITH MANY WEAPONS.
BUT AS A PERSON WITH FEWER WEAPONS, YOU CAN MOVE WITH GREATER AGILITY, AND *THAT* IS THE STRENGTH OF A FIRST-TIMER.
IT'S TRIAL AND ERROR, TRIAL AND ERROR, TRIAL AND ERROR!
DO! YOUR! BEST!
YES, MA'AM!

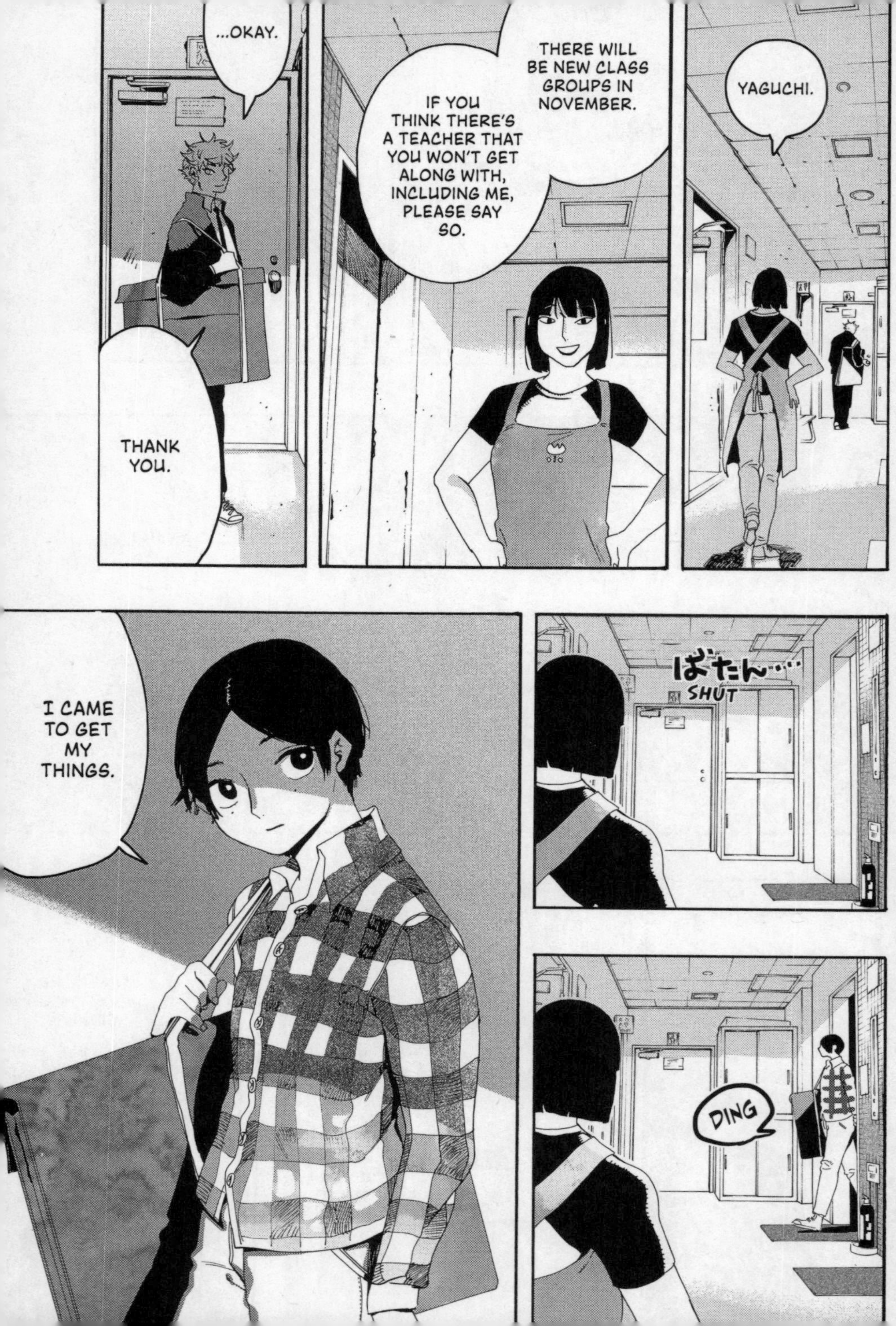
YAGUCHI.
THERE WILL BE NEW CLASS GROUPS IN NOVEMBER.
IF YOU THINK THERE'S A TEACHER THAT YOU WON'T GET ALONG WITH, INCLUDING ME, PLEASE SAY SO.
...OKAY.
THANK YOU.
ばたん…
SHUT
DING
I CAME TO GET MY THINGS.

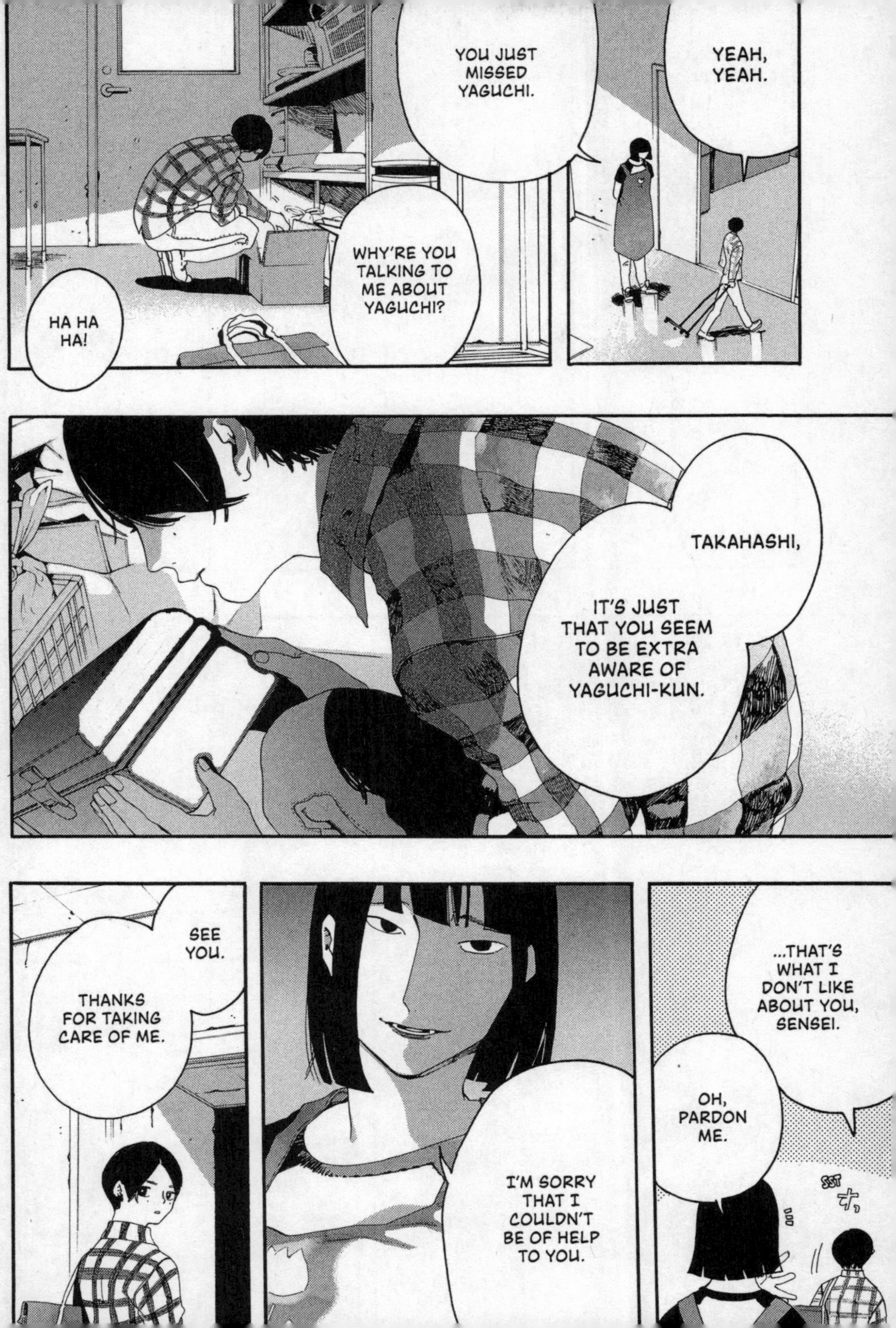
YEAH, YEAH.
YOU JUST MISSED YAGUCHI.
WHY'RE YOU TALKING TO ME ABOUT YAGUCHI?
HA HA HA!
TAKAHASHI,
IT'S JUST THAT YOU SEEM TO BE EXTRA AWARE OF YAGUCHI-KUN.
...THAT'S WHAT I DON'T LIKE ABOUT YOU, SENSEI.
OH, PARDON ME.
SST
I'M SORRY THAT I COULDN'T BE OF HELP TO YOU.
SEE YOU.
THANKS FOR TAKING CARE OF ME.

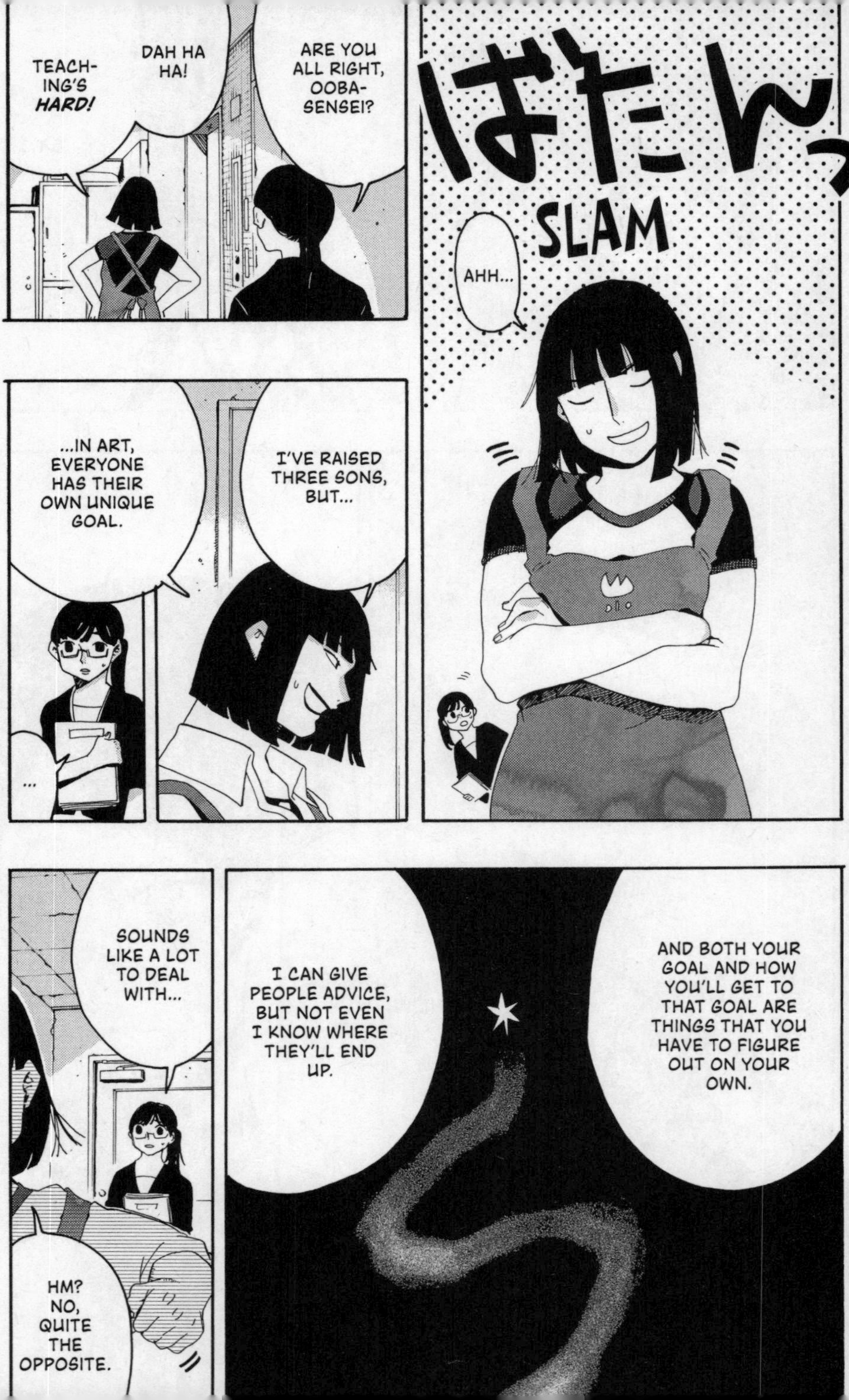
ばたんっ
SLAM
AHH...
ARE YOU ALL RIGHT, OOBA-SENSEI?
DAH HA HA!
TEACHING'S *HARD!*
I'VE RAISED THREE SONS, BUT...
...IN ART, EVERYONE HAS THEIR OWN UNIQUE GOAL.
...
AND BOTH YOUR GOAL AND HOW YOU'LL GET TO THAT GOAL ARE THINGS THAT YOU HAVE TO FIGURE OUT ON YOUR OWN.
I CAN GIVE PEOPLE ADVICE, BUT NOT EVEN I KNOW WHERE THEY'LL END UP.
SOUNDS LIKE A LOT TO DEAL WITH...
HM? NO, QUITE THE OPPOSITE.

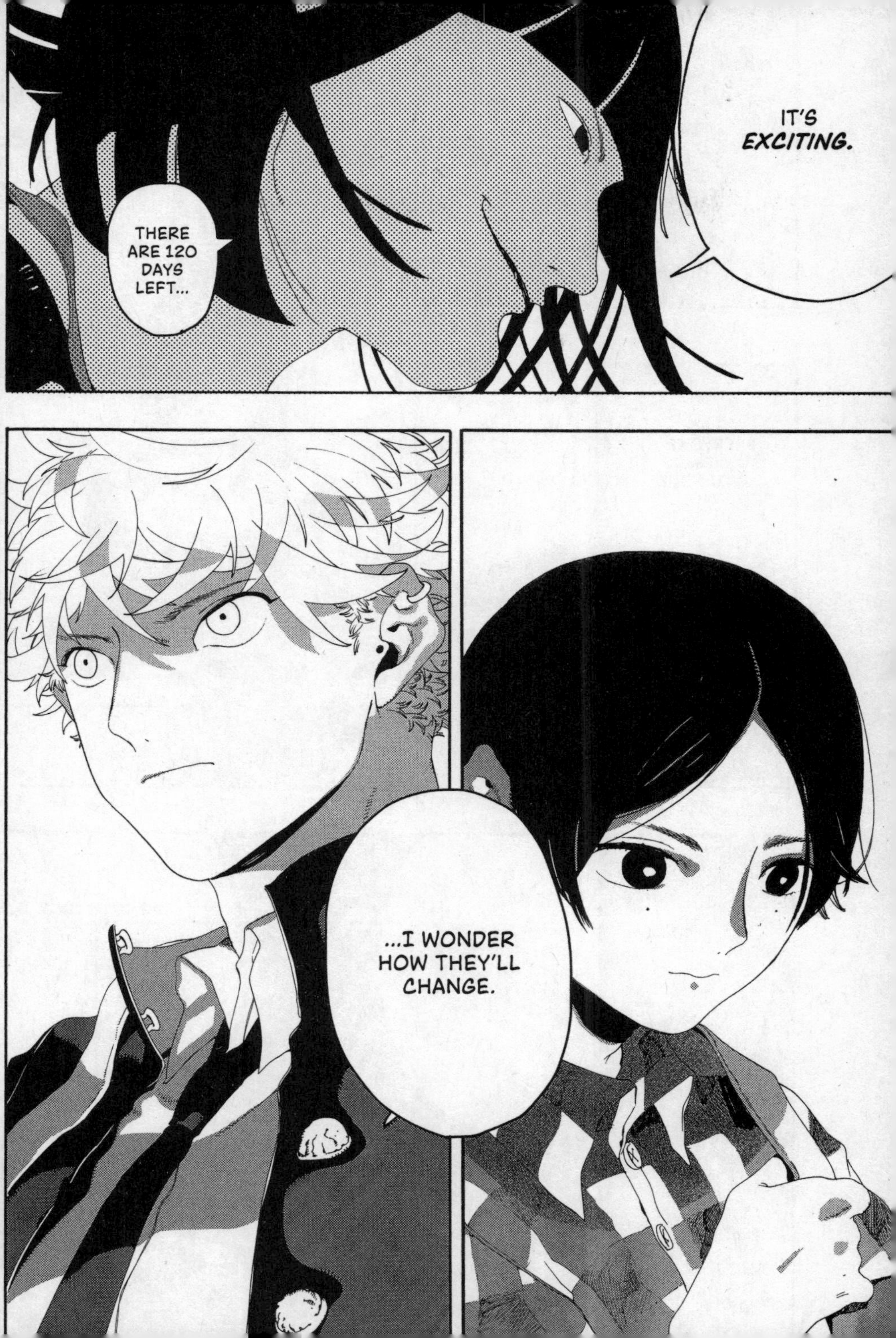
IT'S *EXCITING.*
THERE ARE 120 DAYS LEFT...
...I WONDER HOW THEY'LL CHANGE.

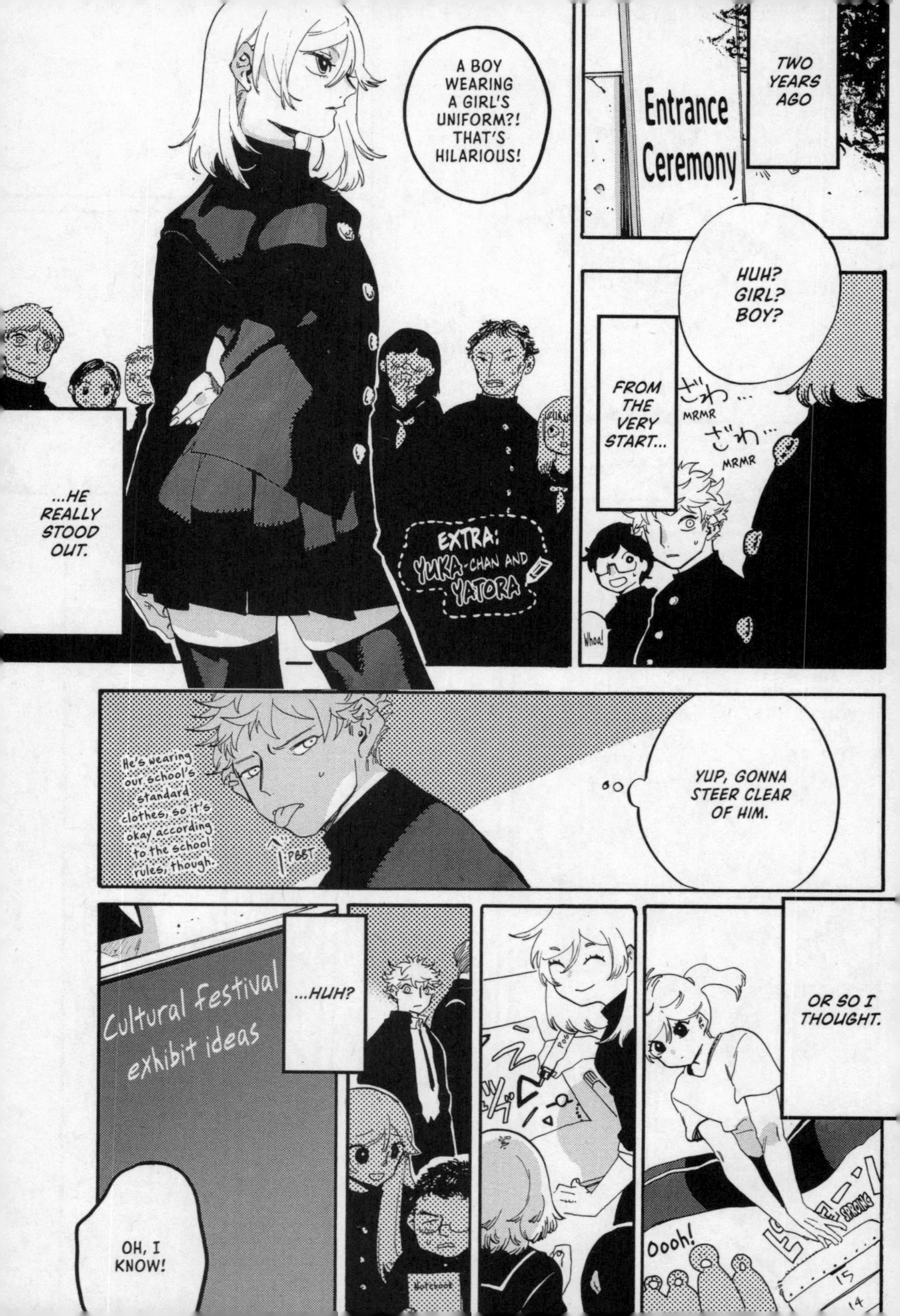
TWO YEARS AGO
Entrance Ceremony
HUH? GIRL? BOY?
FROM THE VERY START...
ざわ... MRMR
ざわ... MRMR
Whoa!
A BOY WEARING A GIRL'S UNIFORM?! THAT'S HILARIOUS!
...HE REALLY STOOD OUT.
EXTRA: YUKA-CHAN AND YATORA
YUP, GONNA STEER CLEAR OF HIM.
PBBT
He's wearing our school's standard clothes, so it's okay according to the school rules, though.
OR SO I THOUGHT.
Oooh!
...HUH?
Cultural festival exhibit ideas
OH, I KNOW!
Notebook

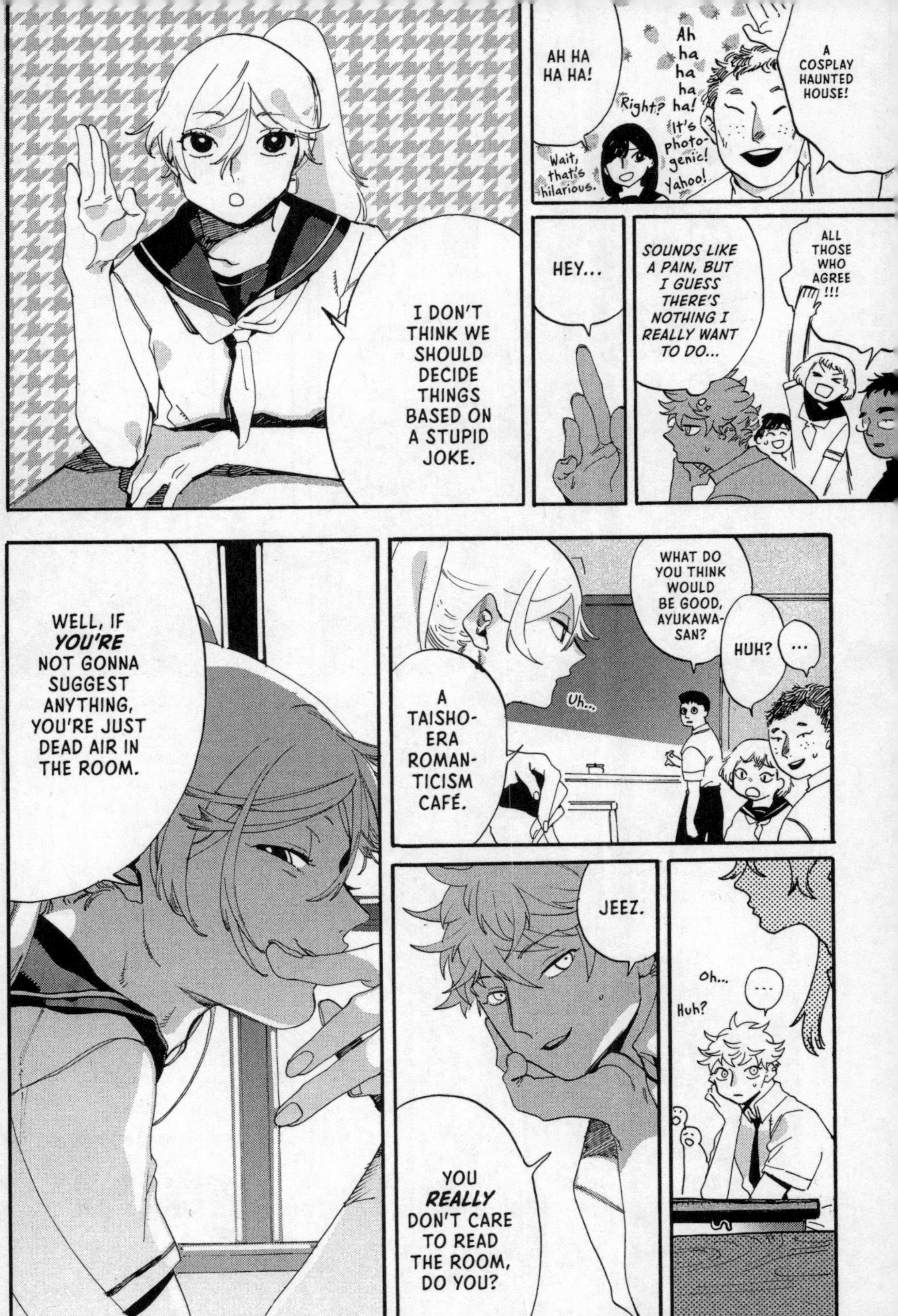
A COSPLAY HAUNTED HOUSE!
Ah ha ha ha ha!
It's photogenic! Yahoo!
AH HA HA HA!
Right?
Wait, that's hilarious.
ALL THOSE WHO AGREE!!!
SOUNDS LIKE A PAIN, BUT I GUESS THERE'S NOTHING I REALLY WANT TO DO...
HEY...
I DON'T THINK WE SHOULD DECIDE THINGS BASED ON A STUPID JOKE.
WHAT DO YOU THINK WOULD BE GOOD, AYUKAWA-SAN?
...
HUH?
Uh...
A TAISHO-ERA ROMANTICISM CAFÉ.
Oh...
...
Huh?
JEEZ.
YOU REALLY DON'T CARE TO READ THE ROOM, DO YOU?
WELL, IF YOU'RE NOT GONNA SUGGEST ANYTHING, YOU'RE JUST DEAD AIR IN THE ROOM.

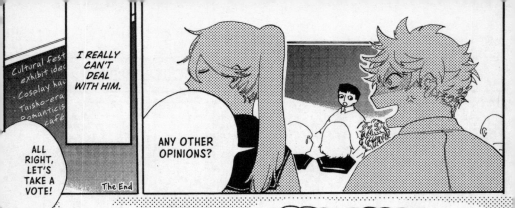

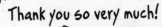

ANY OTHER OPINIONS?
I REALLY CAN'T DEAL WITH HIM.
The End
Cultural fest exhibit idea
· Cosplay ha
· Taisho-era Romanticis café
ALL RIGHT, LET'S TAKE A VOTE!

Blue Period was created with the support of many people!

Special Thanks

Thank you so very much!

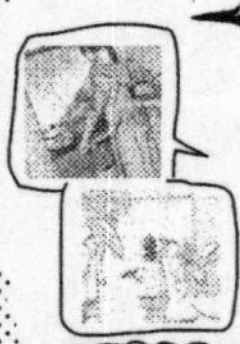

Daise Saito-san

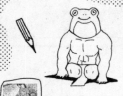

Thank you for continuing to create such wonderful art since Volume 1! We both have to be careful about playing too much Monster Hunter!

Manami Uetake-san

Thank you for letting me borrow your wonderful art! It's me Yamaguchi, who occasionally used photos of your works as reference. I'm really looking forward to your future activities!

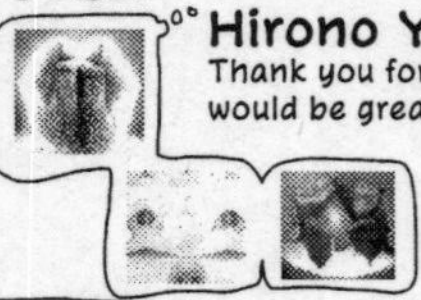

Hirono Yamazaki-san

Thank you for letting me use your work for Hashida's art, etc.! I love Yamazaki's art, so it would be great to have the opportunity to show his work in the future!

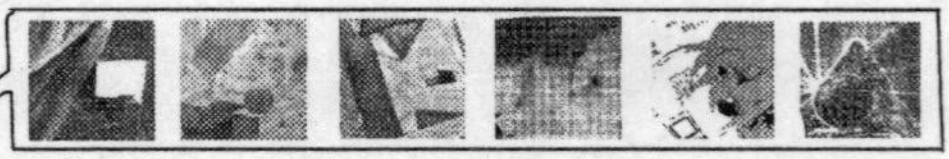

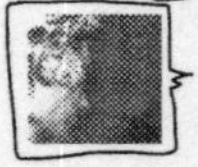

Shota Yamamichi-san

Thank you so much for all of your cooperation! Without Yamamichi-san, the scenario for this manga might have been vastly different. I leave Yatora's art in your hands!

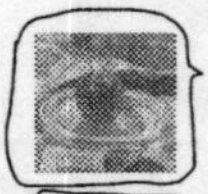

Tamana Moteki-san

Thank you for letting me use your pieces for the composition reference pieces! I love the cool and cute Tamana-chan and her works!

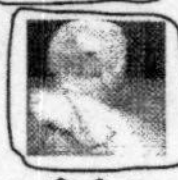

Moeko Natsui-san

I borrowed your art to use as Kawana-san's! Let's go drinking! I haven't drunk enough! Please!

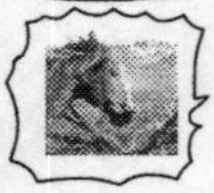

Mei Tanimoto-san

Sorry to use your work in a somewhat negative way... I've been having some good opportunities to use your seashell earrings!

Assistants: **Marimo Tomori-san, Maiko Saki-san, Nishi Aikawa-san, Asuma Sato-san**

Editors: **Kawamura-san, Furihata-san**

ABOUT SENSEI

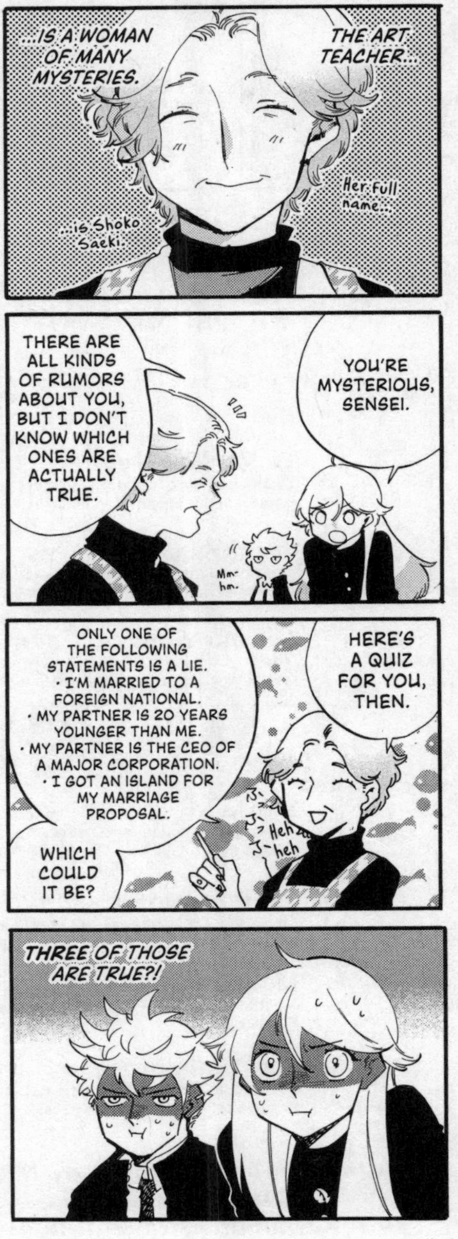
THE ART TEACHER...
...IS A WOMAN OF MANY MYSTERIES.
Her full name...
...is Shoko Saeki.
YOU'RE MYSTERIOUS, SENSEI.
THERE ARE ALL KINDS OF RUMORS ABOUT YOU, BUT I DON'T KNOW WHICH ONES ARE ACTUALLY TRUE.
Mm-hm.
HERE'S A QUIZ FOR YOU, THEN.
ONLY ONE OF THE FOLLOWING STATEMENTS IS A LIE.
· I'M MARRIED TO A FOREIGN NATIONAL.
· MY PARTNER IS 20 YEARS YOUNGER THAN ME.
· MY PARTNER IS THE CEO OF A MAJOR CORPORATION.
· I GOT AN ISLAND FOR MY MARRIAGE PROPOSAL.
Heh heh
WHICH COULD IT BE?
THREE OF THOSE ARE TRUE?!

ABOUT THE OTAKU OF THE ART CLUB

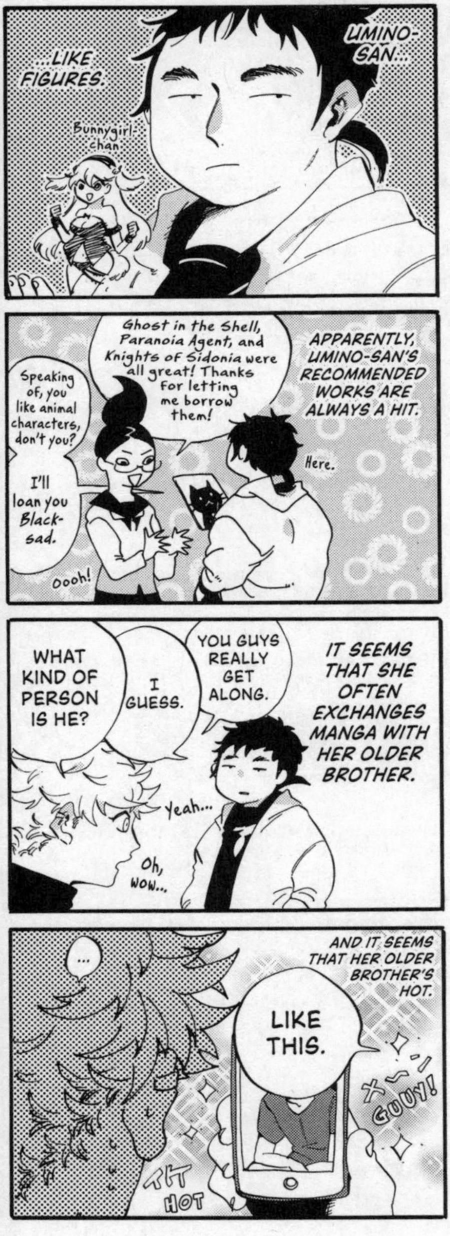
UMINO-SAN...
...LIKE FIGURES.
Bunnygirl-chan.
APPARENTLY, UMINO-SAN'S RECOMMENDED WORKS ARE ALWAYS A HIT.
Ghost in the Shell, Paranoia Agent, and Knights of Sidonia were all great! Thanks for letting me borrow them!
Speaking of, you like animal characters, don't you?
Here.
I'll loan you Blacksad.
Oooh!
IT SEEMS THAT SHE OFTEN EXCHANGES MANGA WITH HER OLDER BROTHER.
YOU GUYS REALLY GET ALONG.
I GUESS.
WHAT KIND OF PERSON IS HE?
Yeah...
Oh, wow...
AND IT SEEMS THAT HER OLDER BROTHER'S HOT.
LIKE THIS.
...
HOT

ABOUT PANDA GIRL

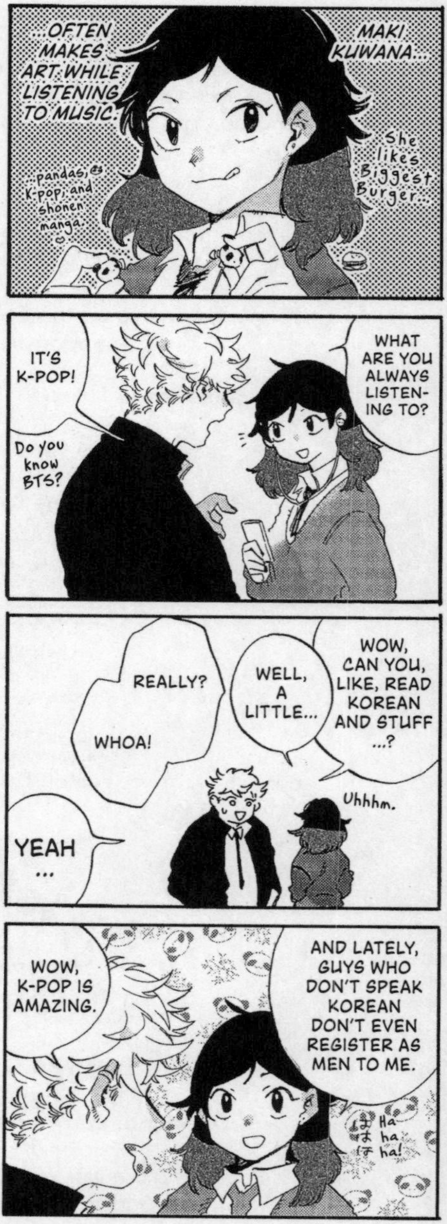
MAKI KUWANA...
...OFTEN MAKES ART WHILE LISTENING TO MUSIC.
She likes Biggest Burger...
...pandas, K-pop, and shonen manga.
WHAT ARE YOU ALWAYS LISTENING TO?
IT'S K-POP!
Do you know BTS?
WOW, CAN YOU, LIKE, READ KOREAN AND STUFF ...?
WELL, A LITTLE...
REALLY?
WHOA!
Uhhhm.
YEAH ...
AND LATELY, GUYS WHO DON'T SPEAK KOREAN DON'T EVEN REGISTER AS MEN TO ME.
Ha ha ha!
WOW, K-POP IS AMAZING.

ABOUT BOY GENIUS

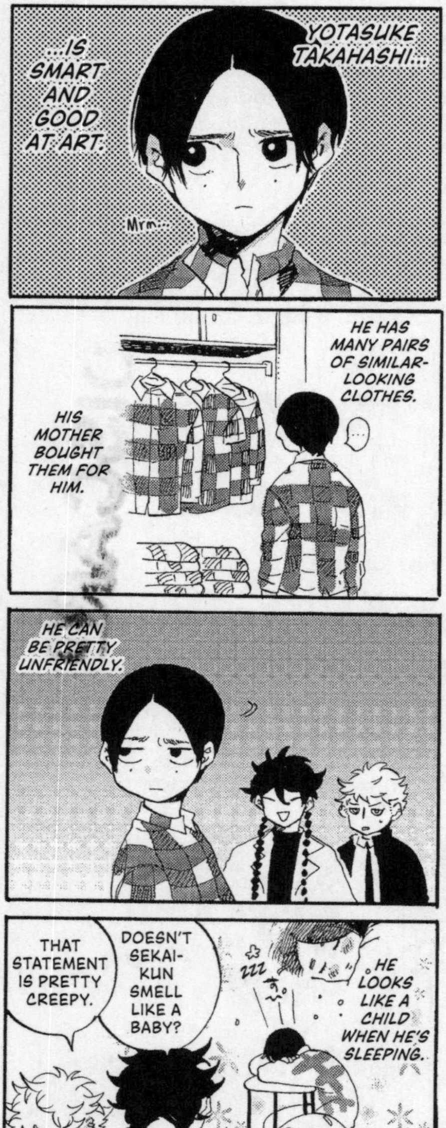
YOTASUKE TAKAHASHI...
...IS SMART AND GOOD AT ART.
Mrm...
HE HAS MANY PAIRS OF SIMILAR-LOOKING CLOTHES.
...
HIS MOTHER BOUGHT THEM FOR HIM.
HE CAN BE PRETTY UNFRIENDLY.
HE LOOKS LIKE A CHILD WHEN HE'S SLEEPING.
ZZZ
DOESN'T SEKAI-KUN SMELL LIKE A BABY?
THAT STATEMENT IS PRETTY CREEPY.

Blue Period 2 is a work of fiction. Names, characters, places, and incidents are the products of the author's imagination or are used fictitiously. Any resemblance to actual events, locales, or persons, living or dead, is entirely coincidental.

A Kodansha Comics Trade Paperback Original

Published in the United States by Kodansha Comics, an imprint of Kodansha USA Publishing, LLC, New York.

Publication rights for this English edition arranged through Kodansha Ltd., Tokyo.

First published in Japan in 2018 by Kodansha Ltd., Tokyo.

ISBN 978-1-64651-124-2

Original cover design by Yohei Okashita (Inazuma Onsen)

Printed in the United States of America.

www.kodansha.us

9 8 7 6 5 4 3
Translation: Ajani Oloye
Lettering: Lys Blakeslee
Editing: Haruko Hashimoto
Kodansha Comics edition cover design by Matthew Akuginow

Publisher: Kiichiro Sugawara

Director of publishing services: Ben Applegate
Associate director of operations: Stephen Pakula
Publishing services managing editor: Noelle Webster
Assistant production manager: Emi Lotto, Angela Zurlo